D1738865

40 YEARS OF EXCELLENCE

Alan Hummel
Foreword by Tom Sneva

Iconografix

Iconografix
PO Box 446
Hudson, Wisconsin 54016 USA

Library of Congress Control Number: 2007927568

ISBN-13: 978-1-58388-195-8
ISBN-10: 1-58388-195-6

07 08 09 10 11 12 6 5 4 3 2 1

Printed in China

Cover and book design by Dan Perry

BOOK PROPOSALS

Iconografix is a publishing company specializing in books for transportation enthusiasts. We publish in a number of different areas, including Automobiles, Auto Racing, Buses, Construction Equipment, Emergency Equipment, Farming Equipment, Railroads & Trucks. The Iconografix imprint is constantly growing and expanding into new subject areas.

Authors, editors, and knowledgeable enthusiasts in the field of transportation history are invited to contact the Editorial Department at Iconografix, Inc., PO Box 446, Hudson, WI 54016.

www.iconografixinc.com

DEDICATION

Tom Branoff Photography

In memory of Galen "Bud" Hummel,
who gave me my love for racing, and so much more.

ACKNOWLEDGMENTS

Half the fun of writing this book was in having the opportunity to work with so many other enthusiasts who share my passion for the sport of auto racing. I first need to thank Tom Sneva, one of my childhood heroes and one of Penske Racing's most colorful and talented drivers, who graciously agreed to write the foreword for this story. I also owe special thanks to Kirk White, owner of the infamous Ferrari 512M that the Penske team campaigned at Le Mans and other world endurance races in 1971. Kirk's recollections of a spontaneous young Roger Penske launching an impromptu Le Mans program were priceless.

I also want to acknowledge the people who contributed their photography—and many times the stories behind the pictures—which really brought this book to life. Many of these individuals have web sites marketing their racing work, and would be happy to sell copies of images that are included in this book. In no particular order, they include: Pat Smith and Mike Smith (TurboRacingPhotos.com), Tam McPartland (TamsOldRaceCarSite.net), Pack Rat Enterprises, Greenfield Gallery, Ron Nelson (PraireStreetArt.com), Mike Odell (SportsRacingLtd.com / Forget-Me-Not Race Pix), George Standaar, HighBankSlope Classic Race Photos, Larry Arnt, Bill Daniels (Bill Daniels Sports Collectibles), Laini Peterson, Scott Curbow (freewheelingdaredevil.blogspot.com), Doug Haack (VintageRacingPhotos.net), Mike Levitt (LAT USA), Peter Burke, OnlyClassics.com, Paul Powell (UnfairAdvantageRacing.com), James T. Brandon, Jones Morris, Tom Branoff Photography, Bob Jordan, Michael Sesit, Kirk F. White and my father, Galen Hummel.

I owe a great debt of gratitude to *AutoWeek* for their decades of outstanding racing coverage. My personal collection of *AutoWeek* magazines, which dates back to the early 1970s, was an invaluable resource in developing this book. Other significant reference resources included *The Indianapolis Star* newspaper and the racing books: *Can-Am*, by Pete Lyons (MBI Publishing); *The Unfair Advantage*, by Mark Donohue with Paul Van Valkenburgh (Bentley Publishers); *Trans-Am—The Pony Car Wars 1966-1972*, by Dave Friedman (MBI Publishing); *Rusty Wallace—the Decision to Win*, by Bob Zeller with Rusty Wallace (David Bull Publishing); and *CART—The First 20 Years 1979-1998*, by Rick Shaffer (Hazleton Publishing).

Race statistics were compiled from a variety of sources, including race programs, newspaper and magazine articles, numerous books and the Internet. The most noteworthy web site resources included: Motorsport. com, OldRacingCars.com, NASCAR.com, GrandPrix. com, IndyCar.com, ChampCarWorldSeries.com, and PenskeRacing.com.

I've tried to make every reasonable effort to ensure that all the information presented in this book is accurate and complete. Thanks again to all who contributed toward making this project a reality.

CONTENTS

PREFACE

Sitting with my dad in the grandstands at Pocono International Raceway on July 3rd 1971, I never would have dreamed that 35 years later I'd be writing the story of the team that won the race that day. When Mark Donohue took the checkered flag in Roger Penske's Sunoco McLaren Special on that hot Pennsylvania afternoon, it marked the young team's first-ever Indy-Car victory and the beginning of an incomparable sports dynasty that would redefine American auto racing in the years to come.

The following Memorial Day, Donohue would give Penske Racing its first Indianapolis 500 title. Although I wasn't there to witness that momentous event, I've been at the Brickyard for all thirteen of the team's subsequent Indy wins. Over the past 35 years, I have followed Roger Penske and his all-star drivers as they triumphed in the Can-Am, Trans-Am, NASCAR, endurance racing, Formula-1 and, of course, Indy-Cars—always recognizing that I was witnessing something very special, something historic.

I first began to contemplate the idea of writing this book early in the 2000 season, as Penske Racing's Indy-Car program was emerging from the only true slump in the team's history. It always seemed odd to me that no one had ever written this story before, considering the dramatic impact that this one organization had made on an entire sport. What I would later discover is that there was a practical reason for this void—very simply, Roger Penske apparently wanted it that way. Over the years, he has been presented with a number of proposals for such a project, and has always declined to participate.

Creating this book without the collaboration of Roger Penske or the Penske Racing organization has presented its challenges. Although the framework of the story is built on my own first-hand knowledge of the events as they unfolded, piecing together the thousands of details required to make this a comprehensive and accurate account that properly reflected the magnitude and importance of this team's achievements was a painstaking, yet gratifying endeavor. Although I strived to present this story from an objective and unbiased perspective, I found that it was not always possible to entirely conceal my admiration and respect for the individuals involved and the extraordinary accomplishments they achieved. But then, maybe that's why I undertook this project in the first place.

Author (left) and a friend on the racetrack at Watkins Glen, July 1972.

FOREWORD

Thirty-one years ago, I was just getting starting in Indy-Car racing when I had the good fortune to be noticed and hired by Roger Penske. Although I didn't realize it at that time, and would not fully appreciate it until many years later, this was probably the single most significant development in my racing career.

By that point in time, Penske Racing had already won several racing championships and the 1972 Indianapolis 500. But after three years of struggling, they were having very little success putting together a serious challenge for the USAC Indy-Car title. Mark Donohue was already retired by then, and Roger Penske had just released Gary Bettenhausen at the end of the 1974 season after he was injured in a dirt car accident. Roger was looking for an aggressive younger driver with short-track oval racing experience, and luckily, I was in the right place at the right time.

Over the next four seasons, we had a remarkable run. Although I was involved in a very spectacular accident in my first Indy 500 with Roger, which put me in the hospital for two weeks with burns and broken vertebrae in my lower back, we came back to win my first Indy-Car race later that same year. We won back-to-back Indy poles in 1977 and 1978, recording the first official 200-mph lap at the Speedway. We finished second in both of those races and went on to win the USAC national championship both years. It was an exciting time to be racing Indy-Cars because the sport was evolving so rapidly in the late 1970s. And it was an ideal time to be with the Penske team, because they were right at the forefront of this change. We always had the latest and best equipment—and in hindsight, I think we also had the best overall team.

When I parted company with Penske Racing at the end of the 1978 season after we won the second championship, I was frustrated by all the little problems that prevented us from winning more races even though we typically had the quickest car. There were things that I thought the team could have been doing better. As I saw it, we were operating at maybe an 85% efficiency level and I wanted to be at 100. In the years that followed, as I drove for several other top Indy-Car teams, I realized just how exceptional the Penske operation really was.

I owe a great deal of the success that I enjoyed throughout my driving career to the things I learned and experiences gained during my years with Penske Racing. To be with one of the top teams and have the budget to do all the testing that we did was invaluable to my learning curve in the sport of Indy-Car racing. When I won the Indianapolis 500 in 1983 over Penske drivers Al Unser and Rick Mears, it was particularly gratifying because I knew that I'd beaten the best team in the business. That was true in 1983, and it is still true today.

This book tells the extraordinary story of Penske Racing's rise to the top of American auto racing, and the unparalleled impact the team has had on the sport over the past 40 years. It will be fascinating reading for any auto racing enthusiast, past or present.

—Tom Sneva,
1983 Indianapolis 500 Winner

Ron Nelson / Prairie Street Photos

CHAPTER 1
Two Captains
Birth of the Dynasty

"It is difficult to imagine how the relationship endured: Penske's towering ego vs. Donohue's monumental stubbornness and pride. However, they were both dedicated to a goal: success in racing." – Mike Knepper, Road & Track, 1974

Auto racing is altogether different today than it was 40 years ago; not just in the inevitable evolutionary sense, but philosophically and fundamentally different. In the early-1960s, even at its highest levels, racing was still predominantly an amateur, non-commercial endeavor. Certainly there was money involved, but it was insignificant by today's standards. Race teams were

not built around corporate sponsorships. When they existed at all, such arrangements typically consisted of a few automotive-product decals haphazardly applied to a racecar's fenders at the track. Mainstream corporate interest in auto racing as a marketing opportunity was limited, largely because of the dangerous and irresponsible image the sport portrayed.

The danger was real. The mortality rate of contemporary Indy-car and Formula I drivers was alarming. A review of the starting grid from any 1960's-era Indianapolis 500 or FI event will typically reveal a handful of competitors, sometimes more, who ultimately perished in auto-racing accidents. Between 1967 and 1975, thirteen Formula-1 drivers died on the racetrack – a sobering statistic by today's relatively safe standards. Corporate CEOs had little interest in associating their products and company names with such a reckless and too-often tragic sport.

Yet despite the lack of monetary support and the considerable personal risks involved, auto racing not only survived, but actually flourished in the 1960s. Organization at the time was limited, with much of the control in the hands of local racetrack owners and promoters. Rulebooks were thin, almost incidental in many classes. Innovation, not in today's professional engineering sense, but the gut-feeling, seat-of-the-pants brand, created racing grids filled with a variety of unique and interesting, if not always successful, racecar designs. Auto racing, by a combination of luck and the shear excitement of the product, was a sport on the verge of a major breakthrough. What it needed was a visionary leader who could bring organization, structure and the basic elements of good business management to the table, someone who could help take this sport to the next level.

It was into that environment, in 1966, that Penske Racing was born. In the 40 years since its inception, this team, more than any other, has influenced the development, growth and direction of auto racing as both a sport and a business, not only in the United States, but around the world. With victories in sports cars, Indy cars, NASCAR, and even Formula I, the Penske Racing Team has produced and showcased many of racing's superstar drivers over the last two generations. Mark Donohue, Gary Bettenhausen, George Follmer, Bobby Allison, Tom Sneva, Mario Andretti, Rick Mears, Al and Bobby Unser, Al Unser Jr., Emerson Fittipaldi, Paul Tracy, Rusty Wallace, Ryan Newman, Helio Castroneves, Gil de Ferran and Sam Hornish Jr., have all piloted Penske Racing entries to victory over these past four decades.

As with any exceptional organization, a great deal of this team's sustained success is attributable to the talented and dedicated personnel who have been involved over the years, both on and off the track. This includes drivers, team managers, mechanics, engineers, pit crews and many others. Penske Racing has had countless gifted and capable people in these roles throughout its history. But the one constant, the founder and leader of this team from its inception, Roger Penske, has clearly been the heart and the soul of the operation from the very beginning. Even today, with a multi-billion-dollar business empire to oversee, hardly a weekend goes by that he can't be found behind the pit wall, calling the shots for his drivers on the racetrack.

Roger S. Penske was born in a suburb of Cleveland, Ohio in 1937. By the time he graduated from Lehigh University in 1959 with a degree in Industrial Engineering, he had already begun a short, but illustrious race driving career. He recorded his first victory driving a Porsche at Lime Rock, Connecticut in 1959 and won his first championship, the Sports Car Club of America (SCCA) Class D competition, in 1961. His early successes earned him *Sports Illustrated's* "Driver of the Year" honor. In 1962, Penske scored victories in the Grand Prix of Puerto Rico and the Riverside Grand Prix in California, major sports car races of that time, and was named "Driver of the Year" by both the *Los Angeles Times* and the *New York Times*. Penske's driving résumé also included two Formula 1 races, the 1961 and 1962 U.S. Grand Prix events held at Watkins Glen, New York. Driving independent entries, he finished 8th and 9th in these two world championship events.

In the early 1960s, Roger Penske was widely regarded as one of the future superstars of U.S. and even international auto racing. He had raced and won against

Roger Penske in his #6 Porsche RS60 practices a little NASCAR-style bump drafting on the #25 Maserati of Gaston Audrey at Elkhart Lake in 1960. Notice the total lack of safety barriers along the racecourse. *Greenfield Gallery*

In October 1961, Roger Penske raced his Dupont-sponsored "Telar Special" Cooper Monaco sports car and a Cooper Formula Jr. at Laguna Seca. *Tam McPartland*

Tam McPartland

Roger Penske's driving credits include two Formula-1 starts—the 1961 and 1962 U.S. Grand Prix events at Watkins Glen. He finished 8th and 9th in these world championship races driving independent entries. *Ron Nelson / Prairie Street Photos*

During his own brief driving career, Roger Penske established himself as a pioneer in the sport. His unique and controversial single-seat "Zerex Special" sports car won races and landed him advertising endorsements from companies like DuPont and Champion Spark Plugs at a time when corporate sponsorship in this type of racing was virtually nonexistent.

Roger Penske, running second in this pack, races his "Zerex Special" at Elkhart Lake in 1963. In response to competitors' complaints, the SCCA had implemented rules that forced Penske to modify the "Special" into a more legitimate two-seat sports car. *Mike Odell / Forget-Me-Not-Race Pix / SportsRacingLtd.com*

many of the prominent drivers of the time, including Jim Hall, Dan Gurney, Lloyd Ruby, Roger Ward, Walt Hansgen and Bruce McLaren. He had also competed against a then-unknown amateur named Mark Donohue, who would later become a critical link in the early success of a new Penske Racing team.

Penske's short driving career was colorful and sometimes controversial. In 1962, he rebuilt a wrecked Formula I Cooper-Climax into an SCCA sports car. He replaced the 1.5-liter FI engine with a 2.7-liter powerplant, draped aluminum fenders over the wheels and bolted in a pair of headlights. To satisfy the technicality that a sports car, by definition, must have two seats, he added a tiny and completely non-functional passenger seat to the left of the driver. This seat was actually outside the cockpit framing, hidden beneath a removable hatch in the bodywork. His competitors objected loudly to this liberal interpretation of the rules, but the SCCA could find nothing in its inadequate rulebook to disallow the entry. Penske went on to win several races in his "Zerex Special" before the SCCA re-wrote the rules to effectively ban the design. The new regulations that resulted were the basis for what later became FIA Group 7 specifications, the rules that governed the United States Road Racing Championship (USRRC) from 1963 - 1968 and the Canadian-American Challenge Cup (Can-Am) from 1966 - 1974.

Roger Penske (left with cup) raced as a teammate to Jim Hall (center-right) in 1964. For most of the next four decades, these two competitors would face off against each other as team owners in Can-Am, Trans-Am and Indy cars. *Larry Arnt*

When the SCCA's rule changes made Penske's original Zerex Special design illegal, he modified it into a more legitimate two-seat sports car for the 1963 season. He later sold the car to a competitor named Bruce McLaren. McLaren rebuilt the Special with a big block Oldsmobile engine and reintroduced it, bearing his own name, in the USRRC series. This car was one of the first purpose-built rear-engine racing sports cars ever created. Its successors would go on to dominate the new Can-Am series from 1967 through 1971.

Roger Penske's innovative design—many called it a "cheater car" at the time—was foretelling of what would become a Penske Racing hallmark. Several years later, the auto racing press would coin a phrase for Penske's incomparable ability to engineer the very most out of a rulebook—they called it "the Unfair Advantage." To this day, racing fans, the news media and even the team's rivals continue use this expression to acknowledge that elusive Penske Racing edge.

Also noteworthy about Penske's Zerex Special entry

was the fact that it carried sponsorship from Dupont's "Zerex" antifreeze. This kind of formal corporate financial support was unheard of at the time, particularly in sports car racing. In a May 1962 *Road & Track* interview, Penske recounted how he went to the DuPont company and pitched the novel idea to use their antifreeze product exclusively in his racecar in return for their financial support of his racing program. Interviewer Jerry McNamara noted, "Penske entered into his contract with DuPont after only his third year of racing, and actually only after his first year of note. It says much for Penske's ability as a salesman." McNamara ended his article with this bold prophecy: "Penske is one of the youngest and most promising of the elite corps of American drivers. In a period when most of the top U.S. drivers are in their thirties and forties, his age, ability, and uncommon business sense may, in a few years, see him fall heir to the racing crown of the U.S."

The DuPont arrangement was just the beginning. In the years to come, Roger Penske would repeatedly attract major corporations to fund his team's programs. Names such as Sunoco, Sears, First National City Bank, Norton Industries, Gould, American Motors, Miller Brewing, Pennzoil, Mobil, Alltel and Marlboro would adorn the immaculately painted sheet metal and fiberglass of future Penske Racing entries. While some of these companies are the traditional automotive-product suppliers that might logically be expected to have an interest in the sport, others such as First National City, demonstrated Penske's pioneering ability to sell motor racing as a mainstream promotional vehicle outside the auto industry.

Despite his impressive successes on the racetrack, Roger Penske was torn between continuing the promising driving career and the pursuit of his entrepreneurial business interests. In 1963, he was named sales manager of a Chevrolet dealership in Philadelphia. The following year, he would buy a stake in that dealership, and in 1965, at just 28 years of age, he would own it outright. Because of pressure from his business associates, insurance companies and investors, who felt that driving racecars was too risky for a person in his key position, Roger Penske suddenly and dispassionately announced

Roger Penske's business empire originated with this Philadelphia Chevrolet dealership, which the young entrepreneur purchased in the mid-1960s. When forced to choose between his successful driving career and the increasing demands of his growing enterprise, Penske retired his helmet for a business suit.

United States Road Racing Championship (USRRC) and the new Can-Am series. To finance this venture, he secured sponsorship from the Sun Oil Company (Sunoco), in a deal that was conceived during the sale of a Corvette from his Chevrolet dealership to a Sun Company executive. In the course of closing the car sale, Penske mentioned that he was searching for sponsorship for his new race team. The resulting arrangement with Sunoco was to become a critical factor in the early success of the new Penske Racing enterprise.

With the car, sponsorship, race shop and team coming together, all that was missing was a driver. Roger Penske obviously understood the vital importance of finding the right person for this key role. He clearly wanted someone who could not only handle the on-track driving duties, but also had the technical skills to develop and set up a racecar. In the spring of 1966, Penske attended the funeral of a friend and former competitor, Walt Hansgen, who had been killed in a testing

his retirement as a race driver at the end of the 1964 season so that he could devote full attention to his business endeavors. In a 2004 *USA Today* interview, Penske recalled: "They told me if you want to be a dealer there's that opportunity, but you can't go racing ….I just made the decision that the business opportunity looked to be one I wanted to pursue, and I did the right thing because I've been able to hire people that were better drivers than me." Fortunately, however, that was not the end, but only the beginning of the real 'Penske Racing' story.

Barely a year after his retirement as a driver, Roger Penske was back in the auto racing business, this time as owner of the newly established Penske Racing Team. In 1966, he bought a Lola T70 sports car, and set up operations in a little garage behind a watchmaker's shop in Newtown Square, Pennsylvania, to go racing in the

Mark Donohue had very little in common with Roger Penske other than an intense commitment to succeed in auto racing. They were not social friends, but for the task at hand, Donohue's technical engineering skills perfectly complemented Penske's business savvy and talents. During their nine-year partnership, these two men would revolutionize the accepted approach to success in racing.

accident at Le Mans. There, he ran into Mark Dono-hue, who was a friend and teammate of Hansgen. In his 1974 autobiography, *The Unfair Advantage*, Donohue recalled this meeting: " … when [Roger Penske] saw me at the funeral, he came over and said, 'Hello, Mark. How are you?' That kind of surprised me at the time, but I've since learned that he prides himself on never forgetting anyone. He told me he was feeling around for a driver for his new Lola, and had tentatively considered Dick Thompson. Then he asked me if I would be interested in trying it out on a race-to-race basis, for fifty dollars a day."

When hired by Penske in 1966, Donohue already had three SCCA amateur championships to his credit and had spent a year with the factory Ford Le Mans program. However, racing was still very much a part-time "hobby" while he held down an engineering job to pay the bills and support a young family. After being with Penske for a little more than a year, Donohue would make the important decision to give up his day job and go racing full-time. This would begin what was arguably the most perfect partnership of team owner and race driver in the history of motorsports.

Donohue, born March 18, 1937, was the same age as Penske. Also like his new boss, he was college-educated, with a degree in mechanical engineering from Brown University. However, it was not these common-alties, but rather their different, yet complementary skills and talents, that made this such a perfect relationship. Penske was the shrewd business manager. He did the wheeling and dealing, and worked with the sponsors and the news media. He lived by the credo: "Effort equals results." His commanding, no-nonsense business style earned him the nickname: "the Captain."

Conversely, Donohue focused on the technical end of the racing business, using his mechanical engineering training and skills to get the most out of the equipment. Today, all major teams employ race engineers to lead the design, development and set-up of their racecars. In 1966, this was extremely rare. Donohue's ability to play that engineering role from the driver's seat gave Penske Racing a double advantage—truly an unfair advantage. In his book, *Can-Am*, auto racing journalist

Pete Lyons elaborated on the unique talents and abilities that Donohue brought to the table: "Some drivers are clever with machinery; Donohue was not only brilliant, he took formal training and then built vast and varied experience. Some have an innate knack at the wheel; he strove to understand the engineering dynamics behind performance, and relentlessly honed his skills in extracting it. Where others prepared their cars well, he was obsessive about preparation. Some racers had dedication: Donohue was driven. And he never stopped thinking, thinking, thinking."

Donohue's personality was quite different than Penske's. He didn't like being in the spotlight, and would later seem uncomfortable with the fame and attention that his racing successes would bring. He was often described as being shy, introspective, and soft-spoken—uncommon traits for a racecar driver, especially in that era. The auto racing press gave him an unusual, but strangely fitting nickname. They called him "Captain Nice."

David Hobbs, who would drive for Penske Racing in 1971, put Mark Donohue's unique character into perspective, saying: "I suppose the first thing that hit me was that, for a guy that was a multiple Trans-Am champion by that time, he was, I suppose 'humble' would be the word. … He would do everything in the shop. He'd spend all his time working on the car and then at the end of the day sweeping up the trash and taking it out to the dumpster."

Over the next nine years, Roger Penske and Mark Donohue would prove to be an odd but brutally effective team, bringing to auto racing something that had never been witnessed before. *Road & Track* author Mike Knepper would, years later, reflect on the magic of this unlikely partnership, writing: "Penske and Donohue became individual legends within the framework of the team. Their racing operation revolved around two principles, neither of which was new to the sport but which had never been combined so effectively before. From Penske came an unending stream of solid sponsorships and a philosophy of professionalism that meant military-like organization with pit stops refined to an art and team members dedicated to perfecting any job they were assigned. Donohue offered meticulous car preparation, innovative engineering, development and testing results bordering on the miraculous, and of course his skill behind the wheel."

It was the perfect partnership. Roger Penske couldn't possibly have found another driver who possessed the combination of engineering skills, driving talent and selfless dedication that Mark Donohue brought to the team. Signing Donohue to be his first driver was unquestionably the single most important decision that Penske has ever made relative to his auto racing empire. "Mark obviously was a key to Penske Racing's early successes," he would say many years later. "He was a great friend of mine, and he committed his life to auto racing."

In the summer of 1966, 'The Captain,' Roger Penske, and 'Captain Nice,' Mark Donohue set out to challenge some of the world's best teams and drivers in the United States Road Racing Championship. They would conquer this formidable challenge with a ruthless efficiency that quickly became their trademark, then move on to something bigger and do it all over again. Some forty years later, it would be easy to say that the record book speaks for itself; but that would be an inexcusably simplistic understatement. The races and championships won, the careers defined, and the endless records broken, tell only a fraction of the Penske Racing story. The true measure of this team's achievement is not so tangible or easily quantified. The real legacy of this unique organization is that it has, over these past 40 years, altogether redefined the sport of auto racing.

Taken at the 1971 24-Hours-of-Le Mans, this photo of "The Captain" and "Captain Nice" was symbolic of the young Roger Penske-Mark Donohue partnership—the sky was the limit.

Mike Smith

CHAPTER 2
United States Road Racing Championship and CanAm (1966 – 1969)

"Mark and his team, Penske Racing, were in at the beginning of the Canadian-American Challenge Cup series in 1966, and some say they brought it to an end in 1974. That's not strictly accurate, but anyway it's less an indictment than a compliment in the fiercely competitive motorsports arena."
—Pete Lyons, *Can-Am*

Up until the late 1950s, sports car racing in the United States was generally an amateur concern, sanctioned loosely by the Sports Car Club of America (SCCA) from its inception in1948. Although money undeniably changed hands, race winners claimed trophies rather than monetary rewards. This began to change in 1958 when the United States Auto Club (USAC), the organization that sanctioned the Indianapolis 500 and other professional open-wheel racing, recognized that there was a business opportunity for professional sports car racing in the U.S. USAC staged the U.S. Grand Prix for Sports Cars in October of 1958, with a noteworthy purse of $14,500, enough to attract a diverse array of American and European drivers, teams and equipment.

Following this and other similar USAC-sanctioned events, the SCCA grew concerned about losing its hold on U.S. sports car racing, and recognized the need to create its own professional road racing series. The subsequent races were not initially organized into a formal championship series, but were governed by a common, albeit inadequate, SCCA rulebook. It was in this early series that Roger Penske raced his controversial Zerex Special.

By 1963, the SCCA had formalized this series into what it called the United States Road Racing Championship (USRRC). The rulebook deficiencies had been addressed with the adoption of a more detailed package that was endorsed by the FIA, auto racing's international governing body. This new series, which debuted in 1963 and continued through 1968, would be the first serious challenge for the newborn Penske Racing team in 1966.

1966

Roger Penske had purchased a new Lola T70 chassis, and was assembling his organization when he offered Mark Donohue the driving role on a trial basis. Donohue immediately stepped in and worked with chief mechanic Karl Kainhofer to get the Lola prepared. The 1966 USRRC season was already half over when Penske Racing entered its first event in St. Jovite, Quebec. The weekend turned out to be totally forgettable, as Roger Penske and his new driver quickly discovered just how unprepared they were against a strong field that included international Formula-1 drivers such as Bruce McLaren, Chris Amon, and John Surtees. Donohue struggled with engine trouble, bad handling, and a first-lap off-track excursion before eventually retiring the Penske Racing Sunoco Lola with an overheating problem. The second outing wasn't much more success-

The Lola T70 is generally considered to be the car that launched Penske Racing. Mark Donohue later remembered it as having one of the most beautiful racecar shapes he'd ever seen. After early teething problems, Donohue and Penske Racing would take this car to several USRRC and Can-Am victories and the 1967 United States Road Racing Championship. *Jones Morris*

ful, ending with another DNF due to a blown engine.

It looked like the third time might be the charm, as Donohue qualified 3rd on the U.S. Grand Prix circuit at Watkins Glen, New York. He went on to lead a good part of the race before calamity struck. Flying blindly over the crest of a hill, Donohue's Lola suddenly encountered two cars that had been involved in an incident and were stopped broadside on the racetrack directly in his path. With little reaction time and even fewer options, Donohue plowed right through one of the cars, causing his Lola to explode in flames. After being momentarily trapped in the blazing racecar, he was extremely fortunate to escape with no broken bones, although there were some pretty nasty burns. That was the end of the first Penske Racing Lola.

Fortunately, Roger Penske was not a quitter. Five weeks after the Watkins Glen accident, he had his driver back in a brand new Lola for the USRRC event in Kent, Washington. With a little help from attrition among the top-runners, Donohue and the Penske team unexpectedly found themselves celebrating a hard-earned first victory—and maybe not a minute too soon, as sponsor

Sunoco was apparently already having second thoughts about their investment.

Capitalizing on the popularity and success of the USRRC series, the SCCA entered into a partnership with the Canadian Automobile Sports Club in 1966 to launch an "international" sports car racing series designed to draw participants from both the USRRC and the Formula-1 Grand Prix circuit. The new Canadian-American Challenge Cup (Can-Am) was a big-dollar, professional championship. In its inaugural year, Can-Am race purses typically equaled or exceeded those of most Formula-1 events. This was the hook that drew many European stars across the ocean to compete in sports cars against America's best. Mark Donohue later acknowledged that this was the real prize that Roger Penske was chasing.

Following their USRRC victory at Kent, Penske and Donohue set out to prepare for the first Can-Am race, which was scheduled for St. Jovite in September. They took the Lola to Riverside, California, to do some testing, only to experience another expensive setback. Going into a turn at over 100 mph, an improperly installed brake hose failed, sending Donohue helplessly through a wall of hay bales and then a chain-link fence. Fortunately, he walked away unhurt this time, but the car was totaled—again!

Now working on their third Lola T-70 chassis, Penske Racing arrived for the St. Jovite Can-Am event and qualified a respectable 7th in the 34-car field. Unfortunately, Donohue didn't even make it through a lap in the race, and finished dead last. The winner of this very first Can-Am contest was former Formula-1 World Driving Champion, John Surtees.

A week later, the Can-Am crowd reassembled in Bridgehampton, New York, for round-2 of the condensed championship series. The Penske team fared much better there, with Donohue qualifying 6th and finishing 5th behind winner Dan Gurney, Chris Amon, Bruce McLaren, and Phil Hill, all accomplished F1 drivers.

The third event of the new championship was held at Mosport, Canada, the following week. For the young Penske Racing team, this turned out to be nothing less than a Cinderella story. Starting in 6th position, Donohue managed to avoid a first-corner pile-up that took out several of the top contenders. He then proceeded to out-run or out-last the rest of the field to take his first Can-Am victory and the points lead after the third race of the series. Considering the level of completion they were facing, this was a phenomenal achievement for Roger Penske's rookie team.

Donohue went on to post fourth place finishes at Laguna Seca and Riverside, and a third in the finale at Las Vegas. Although he later remembered his first-year Can-Am season as being less than spectacular, the Mosport win and overall consistency left Donohue in second place in the final points standings behind only John Surtees. Competitors who finished behind him read like a "who's who" list of the most accomplished race drivers of the era, including: Bruce McLaren, Phil Hill, Jim Hall, Chris Amon, Dan Gurney, Graham Hill, and Peter Revson.

In retrospect, especially by today's standards, it was an extraordinary first year for the Penske-Donohue partnership. For an upstart team to go head-to-head with the very best drivers and teams in the world would be unthinkable in today's competitive environment. But that's exactly what Penske Racing did in its debut season. Amazingly, despite this early success, Donohue did some serious soul-searching during the off-season and decided that he just couldn't continue the demanding pace. Although he had been racing against, and often beating, the very top drivers in the world, his employment with Penske Racing was still only a part-time arrangement, and he had to maintain a full-time engineering job to support his family. Unbelievably, racing was still just a hobby! So in the winter of 1967, Captain Nice drove to Philadelphia to thank Roger Penske for the great experience, and inform him that he had decided to retire from racing. Penske, who certainly recognized already that Donohue was an invaluable asset to his organization, not just as a driver, but maybe even more importantly as an engineer, quickly offered Mark a full-time salaried position to stay with the team. And that made it official—Donohue turned pro and the super-team was set.

By 1967, Donohue and the Penske team started to engineer improvements into the "customer" Lola chassis, replacing the rear spoiler with a larger wing and adding bigger wheels and tires. The Penske Lola dominated the United States Road Racing Championship, but had to settle for "best-of-the-rest" behind the McLarens in the Can-Am. *Mike Smith*

Larry Arnt

1967

With Mark Donohue now working full-time, Penske Racing's second season got off to an impressive start. Driving an improved Lola T-70, Donohue charged to a dominating six wins in the 7-race USRRC championship. Although competition was somewhat diminished this year because many of the Formula-1 stars chose to

George Follmer drove for Penske Racing on two occasions—in the 1967 USRRC and Can-Am championships and again in the 1972 Can-Am series. Follmer's career highlights included a 1965 USRRC title, Trans-Am championships in 1972 and 1976, the 1972 Can-Am title with Penske Racing, and a season of Formula-1 with the UOP Shadow team in 1973.

wait for the more lucrative late-season Can-Am series, Donohue still had to contend with some very talented challengers that included Peter Revson, George Follmer and Sam Posey. But in an interview with *Road & Track* magazine, he later acknowledged that the Can-Am was the real prize, lamenting: "The USRRC was fine, but it was like playing tennis with your wife."

Indeed, the Can-Am was the grand prix in 1967. After its unqualified success the previous year, and offering a 40% increase in the already-generous prize money, there were new teams, new cars and new drivers galore for the second season. Roger Penske bought another Lola T-70 and hired George Follmer to drive as a teammate to Donohue. Follmer was already an accomplished road racer, with a USRRC title to his credit, as well as experience in the previous year's Can-Am series.

Although Donohue had finished second in Can-Am points the previous year, and the whole Penske Racing

effort was unquestionably much stronger for 1967, it was immediately obvious on the first race weekend at Elkhart Lake that someone had raised the bar for this new season. Bruce McLaren, who built and campaigned his own cars for the USRRC and Can-Am series, had finished third, one point behind Donohue in the 1966 Can-Am championship. McLaren already had a successful Formula-1 driving career, but his love for sports car racing led him to design and build a series of race cars that would virtually own the Can-Am series for many years to come. McLaren's first design was actually the reincarnated Zerex Special that he had purchased from Roger Penske.

The best that the two Penske Lolas could produce in the 1967 Can-Am championship was a pair of second-place finishes by Donohue—one in the first event at Elkhart and the other in the season finale at Las Vegas. Bruce McLaren and his teammate, fellow New Zealander Denny Hulme, won five of the six races, with McLaren taking the championship and Hulme finishing close behind. Donohue was fourth in the final points and Follmer sixth. While this was surely not the result that Roger Penske had anticipated, when considered in conjunction with Donohue's USRRC title and a runner-up finish in the new Trans-Am championship series, it was certainly a very respectable sophomore year for the Captain's team.

Penske Racing ran a year-old McLaren M6A in the 1968 USRRC and Can-Am championships. Mark Donohue is seen here at Riverside where he won the USRRC event in April and finished second to Bruce McLaren in the October Can-Am race. *Mike Smith*

1968

By the end of the 1967 season, it was clear to Roger Penske and Mark Donohue that the Lola T-70 chassis was no match for the McLaren, so they arranged a deal with Bruce McLaren to buy one of his used M6As after the final race of the year. Penske and Donohue reasoned that they would simply take this obviously superior racecar, add an unfair advantage or two, and be able to compete with whatever new design the McLaren team rolled out for 1968. Donohue later articulated the flaw that they would soon discover in that logic: "[Team McLaren] had spent a season with that design, and they knew all its weaknesses—or at least what they didn't like about it. They would simply go back and change the drawings a little bit and update what they had."

Once again, Penske had Donohue entered in both the USRRC and the Can-Am championships. The season got off to a poor start with engine problems at the first USRRC event in Mexico City, where the Penske McLaren didn't even take the green flag. Things improved dramatically after that, however, and Donohue went on to win the title again, in what would turn out to be the last year of the USRRC. With the overwhelming success and popularity of the Can-Am series, the USRRC had really outlived its usefulness, and the SCCA dropped it from the schedule at the conclusion of the 1968 season. During the groundbreaking 6-year run of the United States Road Racing Championship, Mark Donohue was the only two-time champion, and winner of the most races overall, with a total of 12 victories.

For the 1968 Can-Am campaign, after not seeing any significant advantage from running a two-car team the previous year, Penske reverted to a one-car program with Donohue as the lone driver. In the late 1960s, the science of aerodynamics was just beginning to be understood and applied in racecar design. The Can-Am was one of the first series to exploit large wings to produce down-force that helped racecars stick to the road through fast turns. The big "unfair advantage" that Donohue and the Penske Racing team had developed on the McLaren prior to the season was an adjustable rear wing. The idea was that the driver would be able to lower the wing angle on long straights, thus reducing aerodynamic drag and

The Sunoco-blue 1968 McLaren M6A, covered with miles of gold pin striping, was undeniably the sharpest-looking car on the track. Mark Donohue won five USRRC races and his second consecutive title in that series, but managed only one victory and a disappointing third place in the Can-Am championship. Donohue is seen here racing the Lola T160 of Chuck Parsons. *Mike Odell / Forget-Me-Not-Race Pix / SportsRacingLtd.com*

Jones Morris

increasing top-end speed. The first time Donohue tried this was in a pre-season test session at Bridgehampton. In his book, he described the exhilarating experience: "I was going to trim it out on the straightaway, and that car would take off like a rocket. So about halfway down the pit straight, going well over 170 mph, I released that beauty—and I damn near lost it! On the straightaway! It happened so suddenly that it was like being hit with a brick. Naturally I backed off immediately and kept it in a straight line, but that scared me so bad that I could never bring myself to use it again….Our one Unfair Advantage for the Can-Am was history, seconds after we tried it the first time."

At Elkhart Lake, for the first race of the Can-Am series, it was immediately obvious that Team McLaren had done its homework in the off-season. The new McLaren M8A was clearly faster than the year-old M6As, and everything else on the track for that matter. Donohue qualified 4th behind both of the McLaren team cars and Jim Hall's Chaparral. Despite an early-race spin, he managed to hang on for a third place finish behind Denny Hulme and Bruce McLaren.

At Bridgehampton two weeks later, both of the Team McLaren cars suffered engine failure and Donohue went on to claim his only Can-Am win of the season. But despite being hopelessly outclassed by Team McLaren, the Penske-Donohue effort was consistently the best-of-the-rest for the remainder of the year. With third, second and eighth-place finishes in the next three events, Donohue found himself going into the final race of the 1968 season tied for second place with Bruce McLaren, just 3 points behind leader Denny Hulme. With some luck, he still had a realistic shot at winning the championship. Unfortunately, that luck didn't come, as the Penske McLaren sat dead on the grid when the field took the green flag—a very frustrating end to an otherwise respectable, if not spectacular, Can-Am campaign.

1969

Even after coming up short three years in a row, Roger Penske was still intent on winning a Can-Am title. Having tried and failed with an off-the-shelf Lola and the second-hand McLaren, Penske realized that he would need a "factory" effort to challenge Team McLaren. With that in mind, in 1969 he entered into an arrangement with Lola to purchase a total of four new racecars: a T163 lightweight Can-Am car, two Indy cars, and a T-70 coupe that he would run in several World Endurance events. This comprehensive commitment was intended to elicit an extraordinary effort from the Lola factory, giving Penske special privileges and support not available to "regular" customers.

1969 turned out to be an incredibly busy year for Penske Racing. They ran the Lola coupe at Daytona and Sebring, and were planning for a run in the 24 Hours of Le Mans before the racecar was stolen from the parking lot of a motel while on its way home from Sebring. This was also the year of Penske's first assault on the Indy 500. And on top of that, there was an intensely competitive Trans-Am title to defend.

With all these "distractions," Penske and Donohue were not prepared for the start of the Can-Am season. In 1969, the series opened much earlier in the year and was expanded from 6 to 11 events because of the demise of the USRRC. The Penske team did not even enter a race until Mid-Ohio, already the fifth event on the schedule. It was a very un-Penske-like effort, with the car not really properly developed or ready to race even by the time they arrived in Ohio. Yet despite the poor preparations, Donohue managed to qualify third on the grid. Unfortunately, he lasted only 9 laps in the race before an axle snapped and ended the day.

After that disappointment, Roger Penske assessed the situation, and wisely decided that there was no point in continuing with the Can-Am effort that year. They were too far behind and the Team McLaren program was stronger than ever. As much as the Captain really wanted that Can-Am title, it was obvious that it would take a much more focused approach than his team would be able to devote that year. So at that point, he simply decided to cut his losses and call it quits. For 1969, there were plenty of other irons in the fire. As for the Can-Am, Penske and Donohue would return 3 years later—with a vengeance!

The Sunoco-Penske Lola T163 made it off the trailer only one time before the program was abandoned. Mark Donohue qualified third fastest but retired after just 8 laps in the car's lone appearance, the Mid-Ohio Can-Am event in August 1969. Penske Racing would not return to the Can-Am series after that until 1972. *Mike Odell / Forget-Me-Not-Race Pix / SportsRacingLtd.com*

Mike Smith

CHAPTER 3
Trans Am (1967 – 1971)

"We won 18 out of the 25 Trans-Am races run in 1968 and 1969. That was a pretty good record....My goal was to have the best team and the best cars in the series. If we couldn't have achieved that, I would have gotten out."
— Roger Penske (Trans-Am, The Pony Car Wars)

In 1966, the same year that the Can-Am was born, the Sports Car Club of America launched another new professional road racing series called the Trans-American Sedan Championship. More than 40 years later, the "Trans-Am" stands as one of the longest continuous-running professional racing series in the world. Although today's Trans-Am races still provide competitive and exciting racing among talented and colorful drivers, the first seven years of the championship, commonly known as the "Pony-Car" era, were indisputably the glory days of the series.

The Trans-Am was conceived as a manufacturer's championship, designed to showcase American "sports cars" such as the Dodge Dart, Plymouth Barracuda, and the new Ford Mustang, competing for factory bragging rights on road courses around the United States. The inaugural event, run at Sebring Raceway in March of 1966, was won by future Formula-1 champion Jochen Rindt. Other competitors during the first year included big name drivers such as A.J. Foyt, Richard Petty, and Formula-1 star Jacky Ickx. By the second year of the series, the Trans-Am really found its niche and established itself as one of the foremost championships in American auto racing. Boasting starting grids packed with factory-supported Mustangs, Mercury Cougars, and the new Chevrolet Camaros, this new series was the place to be in 1967.

1967
During the winter of 1966-67, Roger Penske decided to add a Trans-Am effort to his young racing program. Not surprisingly, given his business relationship with Chevrolet, Penske chose the new Chevy Camaro for this challenge. He bought a new street stock Z/28 and had Mark Donohue transform it into a racecar in

When Roger Penske decided in January of 1967 that he wanted to enter a car in the Daytona 24-Hours race a month later, he asked Mark Donohue to put together a Chevy Camaro to run in the T/A class. After Daytona and Sebring, he decided to run the car in the full Trans-Am series. Penske Racing would go on to win two Trans-Am titles for Chevrolet in the next three years. *Jones Morris*

a little over a month. Not without a litany of problems, Donohue and crew got the car together and "ready" for the first race of the season at Daytona in February. The strongest competition in 1967 came from Bud Moore's factory-backed Mercury Cougar team, with drivers Parnelli Jones, Dan Gurney, and Ed Leslie; and Caroll Shelby's factory Ford Mustang team, with drivers Jerry Titus, Dick Thompson, and Ronnie Bucknum.

Almost surprisingly, the Penske Camaro qualified 4th on the grid in its Daytona debut and Donohue was able to lead the race for several laps before the car was sidelined with a fuel starvation problem. Even while running, however, the under-developed Camaro was brutally difficult to drive, with terrible handling and almost non-existent brakes.

The second Trans Am race of the 1967 season was on the airport runways at Sebring, Florida. With little time to sort out the handling and braking problems that plagued the car at Daytona, the Penske team took their Camaro to Sebring with basically the same setup and got predictably poor results. Donohue crashed in practice and then qualified well down in the field. In the early stages of the race he struggled to keep the leaders in sight. Thanks to attrition however, he ultimately managed to move up to finish in second place behind Jerry Titus, but nobody was impressed.

Round 3 of the Trans-Am championship was at Green Valley, Texas. Based on their experiences at Daytona and Sebring, Donohue and the team experimented with some changes to the springs before going to Texas. Unfortunately, handling continued to be a big problem and the brakes were still so bad that Dono-

In the team's first Trans-Am race, Mark Donohue started the Sunoco Penske Camaro 4th on the grid at Daytona, behind the Bud Moore Mercury Cougars of Parnelli Jones and Dan Gurney, and Carroll Shelby's Ford Mustang driven by Jerry Titus. *From the Collection of Pack Rat Enterprises*

hue later recalled he would have to drive for several laps at a time using no brakes at all, allowing them to cool down enough so there would be something there when he would attempt to execute a pass or defend against being overtaken. The combination of handling and braking troubles made for an exhausting 4-hour race. Donohue manhandled the Sunoco Camaro home for a hard-earned 4th place finish behind Dan Gurney, Parnelli Jones, and Dick Thompson. It was another embarrassingly uncompetitive showing for the upstart Penske team—a team that was, at the very same time, totally dominating the United States Road Racing Championship.

Donohue and the Chevrolet engineers continued working to diagnose the braking and handling problems with limited success. Mark did manage to drive the Camaro to a second place finish at Lime Rock. Then George Follmer, who was called in by Penske to cover while Donohue was at Le Mans finishing up his responsibilities with the Ford GT team, scored a third-place finish at Mid-Ohio. Despite the fact that the car was still far from right, the Penske entry was the highest placed Camaro in four straight races. That string was broken in the next event, when a snapped rear axle sent Donohue into the wall at Loudon New Hampshire, tearing up the Camaro's chassis badly and putting him out of the race.

After that discouraging experience, the Penske team and the Chevrolet engineers did more work with different spring rates, and finally achieved a major breakthrough, finding a balance that drastically improved the drivability of the Camaro. At the same time, Donohue also took advantage of the rulebook's allowance for a safety roll cage to add a chassis-stiffening structural frame inside the cockpit. This, along with the addition of a rear anti-roll bar, finally got the Camaro handling like a competitive racecar. With these improvements, Penske Racing headed for the next event in Marlboro, Maryland, where Donohue put the Sunoco Camaro on the pole and won the race, claiming the team's first Trans-Am victory. The winner's purse was a laughable $1,250. Prize money in the Trans-Am series increased gradually over the next four years, with the winner taking home $4,000 for the 1971 races—still not very impressive money, even for the era.

Two weeks after the Marlboro win, Donohue had problems and struggled to a disappointing 8th place finish in Colorado, although he was again the highest placed Chevrolet. For the next race in Modesto, California, Penske Racing entered a brand-new lighter-weight Camaro. Unfortunately, in the last-minute rush to get the new car ready, they installed the wrong differential, with gear ratios that weren't right for the Modesto circuit. Donohue persevered to a disappointing third place finish. After Modesto, the next Trans-Am event was at Riverside. Roger Penske had Donohue running a Can-Am race that weekend, so he brought in Bob Johnson to pilot the Camaro. Johnson drove to a respectable third place result behind NASCAR star David Pearson and Ed Leslie, both in Mercury Cougars.

By this point, the Camaro was finally running pretty well. At Las Vegas, Donohue scored the second win of the Trans-Am season for Penske Racing and Chevrolet. A week later, in the season finale at Kent Washington, he took the pole and a second-straight victory. With that, Mark Donohue had won three Trans-Am races in Penske Racing's debut season. After the shaky start, this was good enough for the young team to finish second in the championship standings. While that certainly did not compare to winning the title, Donohue got some satisfaction out of beating the big-bucks factory teams by the end of the season. "There is a kind of perverse pleasure," he said, "in loading the winning car on a trailer behind a beat-up rental truck, while the factory team is winching their "also-rans" into their exotic tractor-trailer rig." Of course, Penske Racing wouldn't be traveling in "beat-up rental trucks" much longer.

1968

After the strong finish in 1967, Penske Racing returned with every intention of conquering the Trans-Am in its second attempt. Once again, the season started with races in Daytona and Sebring, Florida. In 1968 however, the Trans-Am races actually ran concurrently with the World Endurance Championship events there.

Roger Penske had Mark Donohue paired with Bob Johnson for the 24 Hours of Daytona. Donohue had the fastest qualifying time in the Trans-Am field, and

Roger Penske waits to congratulate Mark Donohue after one of his record 10 Trans-Am victories in 1968. In five seasons of Trans-Am competition, Donohue scored a total of 29 race wins, a record that would stand for 33 years. *Larry Arnt*

Mark Donohue in the #6 Sunoco Penske Camaro races Jerry Titus in the Shelby team Ford Mustang at Riverside in 1968. Titus was one of the top competitors in the early years of the Trans-Am, but would become the series' first fatality two years later in an accident at Elkhart Lake. *Jones Morris*

the Penske Camaro led the TA class for most of the first 13 hours before a cracked cylinder head necessitated a two-hour pit stop. Donohue and Johnson recovered to finish second in class behind Jerry Titus and Ron Bucknum in a Mustang. This got Roger Penske nervous, however. With so many Mustangs entered, he decided it would be wise to run a second team Camaro to help level the playing field. For Sebring, he had Donohue paired with Craig Fisher in the 1968 Camaro and Bob Johnson co-driving with Joe Welch in an updated version of the 1967 car.

One of the areas where the Penske team had lost ground to the Mustangs at Daytona was in pit stops for brake pad changes. Between the Daytona and Sebring races, the Chevrolet engineers worked with Donohue to develop a vacuum system that would retract the hydraulic brake caliper pistons so that new pads could be installed quickly. Donohue later recalled that Roger Penske was initially skeptical about the idea. When they got to Sebring for the race, Penske saw the system operate for the first time. Donohue remembered: "We jacked the car up in the garage with the engine running to create a vacuum. By the time the wheels were off the pistons had retracted, and the mechanics whipped the old pads out and the new ones in—just like popping bread into a toaster." The Captain changed his mind quickly after that demonstration. He knew an unfair advantage when he saw it. In the 12-hour race, brake pads would have to be changed three times. With the vacuum system, the Penske team could fuel the car, change four tires, and install new brake pads in about a minute and forty seconds. It took the Mustang teams four minutes to complete the same tasks. The Penske Camaros gained a lap over the competition every time they did the brake service.

This advantage, coupled with strong reliability and excellent driving, led to a 1-2 finish for the Penske Camaros in the Trans-Am class, with Donohue/Fisher third overall and Johnson/Welch fourth overall in the 12-hour endurance race. In his 2001 book, *Trans-Am, the Pony Car Wars (1966-1972)*, racing historian Dave Friedman noted: "The outstanding performance of the Trans-Am cars at Sebring in 1968 (three of the top five overall were Trans-Am cars), led to no official Trans-Am race at Daytona or Sebring the following year. It certainly may have been that the powers to be were afraid that a Trans-Am sedan just might win one of those races overall and make fools out of all of the FIA entries."

The next Trans-Am race after Sebring was at War Bonnet Raceway in Oklahoma. Mark Donohue battled with Parnelli Jones in the early stages before Jones lost two laps with a problem in the pits. Donohue then cruised to his second straight victory, this time over his Can-Am teammate George Follmer, who was driving the new AMC Javelin. The next two races were at Lime Rock and Mid-Ohio. Donohue won both convincingly for his third and fourth consecutive victories.

Roger Penske ran two Camaros in the 1969 Trans-Am series. Mark Donohue drove one while Ron Bucknam and Ed Leslie shared driving duties in the other. By this point, Donohue and the Chevrolet engineers really had the Camaro perfected, but competition from the Ford teams was intense. An early season scoring dispute between Roger Penske and Bud Moore's Mustang team set the tone for a season of cutthroat racing. *Mike Smith*

Beginning with the race at Bridgehampton, Penske recruited Sam Posey to drive the second Camaro as an "insurance policy." Donohue and Posey finished first and third respectively at Bridgehampton, Meadowdale, and St. Jovite. Donohue ran by himself in the next race at Bryar, extending his winning streak to an unbelievable eight straight races. Fading brakes then cost him the win at Watkins Glen, where he finished third behind winner Jerry Titus in a Mustang and Sam Posey in the other Penske Racing Camaro. Posey had led the race for a while after Donohue began to experience problems, but he couldn't hold off Titus. This apparently disappointed Roger Penske so much that it was the last time Posey would ever drive for the team.

Mark Donohue won the next race at Castle Rock, Colorado. He finished the season with a DNF at Riverside and then another win in the final event at Kent, Washington. For the year, he won a remarkable 10 out of 13 races, including that record string of eight in a row. And, most importantly, Penske Racing gave Chevrolet its first Trans-Am championship, absolutely humiliating the previously dominant factory Ford effort.

Mark Donohue later shared that it was during this season, with the help of the General Motors engineers, that he gained invaluable knowledge and experience in the application and analysis of instrumentation data, the effective use of skidpad testing and development, and a lot of practical information about vehicle dynamics and driving techniques. These were techniques and methods that he would later apply to all the Penske Racing cars that he would develop throughout his career. "A million monkeys, working on a race car for a million years, will eventually put together a car that can beat anyone," said Donohue in his book. But it was his ability, based on the rare combination of engineering background and practical experience, which allowed Donohue to logically and efficiently combine the volumes of technical data with hands-on driving input, to optimize the performance of almost any racecar.

1968 was a banner year for the young Penske Racing Team. Donohue not only won, but thoroughly dominated both the United States Road Racing Championship and the Trans-Am Championship, in addition to making a strong challenge to the untouchable McLaren team in the Can-Am series; all this while getting their feet wet on the USAC Indy-car circuit. In only its third year of existence, this young Penske Racing team was making its mark, and a lot of people were noticing.

1969

Penske Racing's dominating performance in the 1968 championship provoked a new level of intensity and ruthless determination from the competition for the new season. In *Trans-Am, The Pony Car Wars 1966-1972*, Dave Friedman wrote: "The 1969 Trans-Am season had all of the qualities found in one of Hollywood's epic western movies. There were good guys, bad guys, angry words, an uncaring sheriff, treachery, cheating, suspense, and several good shootouts. In the end, the crowd favorite mounted his white horse, scooped up the girl, and rode off into the sunset."

For 1969, Penske Racing would run two Camaros to defend Chevrolet's title. Mark Donohue would again be the number-1 driver, with Ron Bucknum piloting the second team car. In the first race, run on the

The lower portion of Penske Racing's infamous 20-ft tall refueling rig can be seen behind Mark Donohue's Camaro in the Michigan pits during this first race of the 1969 Trans-Am season. Also seen behind pit wall is the still-modest team transporter—obviously before the days of PENSKE TRUCK LEASING. *High Bank Slope Classic Race Photos*

road course at Michigan International Speedway, the Penske team unveiled what was probably their most famous "unfair advantage." Exploiting a loophole in the rulebook that did not set any restriction on the mounting height of the pit refueling tank, Donohue worked with the Sunoco engineers to design and build a fuel rig that stood 20-feet above the ground, using the force of gravity to pressure gasoline into the car for faster pit stops. As with most other Penske Racing unfair advantages, the competitors gathered around, scratched their heads, complained to Roger and then to the officials. But at the end of the day, they knew they'd been beat—once again, Penske Racing had built a better mousetrap. Unfortunately, after only the third race of the season, the SCCA issued an addendum to the rulebook arbitrarily limiting the height of the refueling tank to 12 feet. It was an unfortunate misapplication of authority, changing rules in mid-season specifically to negate a legitimate advantage that the Penske team had spent considerable time and money to develop. Donohue and Penske protested, but in the end, had no choice but to accept the decision.

In the Michigan race, rain was a major factor. Things started out tragically as Mustang driver Horst Kwech slid off the wet track into a spectator area, killing one person and injuring 12 others. When the race continued, there were numerous pit stops for tire changes because of changing weather conditions. While Mark Donohue was always considered to be an excellent driver in wet conditions, his Goodyear rain tires didn't seem to have nearly as much grip as the Firestones that were used by the Ford teams. At the end of the race, the SCCA officials mistakenly declared Donohue the winner, although Penske's own scoring records showed him second to Parnelli Jones' Mustang. The ensuing protest meeting got ugly. While Roger Penske listened quietly, someone from Jones' team began making derogatory comments about him, saying something to the effect that he was just a spoiled rich kid trying to get away with cheating. Mark Donohue said that he'd never seen Roger Penske so mad. "I don't care what else we do this year," the Captain said afterward. "It is my firm intention to beat those guys, no matter what it takes." And with that, this first race would set the tone for the rest of the 1969 season. From then on, it was going to be personal—and it was going to be ruthless!

The second race of the Trans-Am season conflicted with Donohue's Indianapolis 500 debut, so Penske called on Bob Johnson to run the team Camaro at Lime Rock. Johnson drove to a respectable third place finish in a race won by Sam Posey, himself subbing for Peter Revson who was also moonlighting at Indy. The Chevrolet people were not happy about Donohue missing this race, feeling that they had an agreement, if not a contract with Penske, to have his number-one driver at the wheel. This incident marked the beginning of a rift between Roger Penske and Chevrolet that eventually led to Penske Racing's switch from Camaros to AMC Javelins for the 1970 season.

Round three of the 1969 Trans-Am season was at Mid-Ohio, and Penske Racing was back in the winner's circle—but it was Bucknum, not Donohue who took the honors this time. Donohue's Camaro had led most of the race but was sidelined by a bad wheel bearing, and Bucknum managed to hold off Parnelli Jones for the win.

The next couple of races turned out to be a test of wills between Roger Penske and the increasingly unreasonable SCCA rule enforcers. Donohue had installed some ducts that vented air from the engine compartment back through the doors and into the rear wheel wells. This removed heat from the engine area and also served as cooling for the rear brakes. Also added to the Penske Camaros were vinyl tops. There was apparently no performance advantage, and contrary to some speculation, it was not a Chevrolet marketing gimmick—it just saved on the cost of repainting the cars. At the Bridgehampton race, the chief steward ruled both of these modifications illegal, even though there was absolutely no basis in the regulations for that decision. Donohue appealed and managed to persuade the full board of stewards to reverse the ruling. He then went out and put his Camaro on the pole. Unfortunately, he had to start the race at the rear of the field in the backup car after loosing an engine in the morning warm-up session. In one of the most inspired performances of his career, Donohue charged from his 31st starting position to 12th place on the first lap. He passed 19 cars, two-thirds of the entire field, in a single lap—on a road course! By the 15th time around, he was running third, and eventually finished in second place, running on 7 cylinders with a broken pushrod.

Next on the schedule was Donnybrook, Minnesota, and another confrontation with the SCCA officials. In an agreement reached after the Bridgehampton event, Penske had already conceded to remove the vinyl tops and the air ducts, but not until they got the cars back to the Pennsylvania shop after the Donnybrook race. When the race officials insisted that the cars could not run unless the modifications were un-done immediately, Penske was prepared to withdraw from the event. After a day-long showdown, during which time Roger Penske sat in a hotel room waiting patiently while his cars stayed loaded on the trailer, the SCCA finally agreed to a compromise. The Penske team would tape off the air ducts immediately and remove the vinyl top before the next race. To further complicate matters for the Donnybrook weekend, Ron Bucknum broke his wrist in an auto accident on the way to the track, so Penske had to recruit Ed Leslie at the last minute to take over driving duties in the second Camaro.

In the race, Donohue and Leslie battled against four factory-backed Mustangs. Five laps from the end, Donohue had a 20-second lead over Parnelli Jones when he lost another rod in the Chevy engine and the car stopped. Jones went on to take the win with Ed Leslie in second place.

Up until this point in the season, it had been pretty frustrating for defending series champion, Mark Donohue; but things improved dramatically at Bryar. Donohue and Leslie finished one-two after outrunning or outlasting all the Mustangs. Then in St. Jovite, the Penske team introduced their second fast-refueling innovation of the season. Using an elaborate system of gear-operated valves, they were able to dump 22 gallons of gasoline into the car in 3.5 seconds. Donohue later recalled that "the few seconds we saved didn't mean all that much over a two-hour race, but it demoralized everyone else and provided us with a lot of publicity." Roger Penske couldn't have asked for anything more.

In the St. Jovite race, Donohue and Leslie trailed the Bud Moore Mustangs until Follmer blew an engine and triggered an 8-car pile-up that also took out teammate Parnelli Jones. After that, Donohue and Leslie cruised to an uncontested 1-2 finish. "The Penske Camaros were fantastic and they were probably the best all-around cars in the series in 1969," Ed Leslie said years later. "Bud Moore's Mustangs, with Parnelli and Follmer driving, were probably the fastest cars out there, but they had serious tire problems and they were driven very hard….Our engines were built by Traco, and they were very strong and extremely reliable. I don't think anyone except Roger, Don Gates, or Chuck Cantwell really knew what was done to our cars. All I can say is that after we took the points lead at St. Jovite, there was no looking back."

From that point on, it was all Penske Racing for the rest of the season. Donohue won round 8 at Watkins Glen, while Leslie dropped out with an engine problem. Next, at Laguna Seca, they finished 1-2, Donohue taking his fourth straight victory. In Kent, Washington, Mark had problems, but Ron Bucknum, who was back in the second Penske Camaro by that point, was there to take his second win of the season, the team's sixth.

Donohue came back to win the final two events, at Sears Point and Riverside, although the latter turned out to be a rather ugly affair. Ever since the disputed season opener, there had obviously been tension between Donohue and Parnelli Jones. "You had to be there," said fellow competitor, Sam Posey, "to feel the electricity between Parnelli and Mark. It was truly the good guy versus the bad guy, or you could say it was Mr. Clean against the sprint car driver. In reality, Parnelli is a hell of a guy and there was much to be admired about what he brought to the table. On the other hand, Mark could be very devious and very tough."

By the final race of the season, the feud had reached its boiling point, and Jones apparently decided it was time to take off the gloves. As Donohue pulled out of the pits after a routine fuel stop, Jones came up behind him and intentionally rammed into the back of the Penske Camaro. Ironically, Donohue's car escaped relatively unscathed while Jones' Mustang sustained considerable front-end damage. A few laps later, Donohue came up behind Jones, who was still on the racetrack but running well off the leader's pace. As the Penske Camaro closed in to overtake, Jones slammed on his brakes, resulting in another major impact between the two rivals. This time Donohue spun off the track, yet still managed to recover and go on to win the race—which surely infuriated Mr. Jones.

Years later, Parnelli Jones reflected on his tense relationship with Donohue, saying: "I think that Follmer, Gurney, and I made better drivers out of Mark, Revson, and the rest of those guys because we pushed them so hard. Donohue got better and better as a driver during the 1969 and 1970 season, and it was all because he was being pushed to his absolute limit every week. Mark worked harder and harder, and he had to if he was going to beat us."

After Mark Donohue's dominating performance the previous year, the 1969 season got off to a shaky start. But in the end, the good guy in the white hat came through and gave Chevrolet its second consecutive Trans-Am title, and almost everyone—except Parnelli Jones—was thrilled.

Switching from the Camaro to AMC's Javelin in 1970 proved to be a bigger challenge than expected. Donohue struggled through much of the year before correcting a serious engine problem. By that point, Roger Penske's pre-season prediction of 7 wins was long forgotten. A strong finish to the year, however, may have facilitated the decision by GM, Ford and Chrysler to abandon the Trans-Am at year end, realizing that the Penske AMC program would only be stronger for '71. *Mike Odell / Forget-Me-Not-Race Pix / SportsRacingLtd.com*

1970

Heading into only its fifth season of competition, the Trans-Am series enjoyed an elite status in American auto racing. Although its following could not realistically be compared to modern-day NASCAR statistics, relative to its peers at the time, this series boasted the best teams, drivers, and factory support in the sport. American Motors vice president William McNealy said: "In 1970, the Trans-Am is where it's going to happen. There is going to be a hand-to-hand struggle among the behemoths of Detroit and we want to be right in the middle of it. That's the primary reason that we approached Roger Penske to take over our program. Roger and his team are proven winners and they will ensure that we have the most competitive program possible."

Even as Roger Penske was winning a second con-

Donohue puts his mark on the Javelin.

Starting now you can buy a Javelin with a spoiler designed by Mark Donohue.

You couldn't before this, but an exciting development has changed everything.

Mark Donohue and Roger Penske, the most successful driver-manager team in road racing, recently signed a three year contract with American Motors.

Together they've won two straight Trans-Am championships. They'll go for a third with the Javelin.

One of the modifications in their Trans-Am Javelin is a spoiler designed by Donohue.

This means that according to Trans-Am rules, the spoiler has to be homologated.

In other words we must incorporate the spoiler into 2,500 Javelins that the public can buy.

And that's just what we've done. But the Donohue designed spoiler isn't the only extra these Javelin SST's will have.

Dual exhausts, power front discs, E70 x 14 white lettered wide profile tires, 14 x 6 wheels, handling package, and a Ram-Air induction system with an AMX hood are also part of the deal.

And you can choose between a 360 or a 390 CID engine. Console shift automatic or 4-speed with a Hurst shifter.

We expect that a lot of the competition are going to see the rear end of Mark Donohue's Javelin this season.

American Motors Javelin

In this 1970 advertisement, American Motors spotlighted the "Mark Donohue Edition" Javelin. AMC built 2,500 of these special Javelins, adding a rear spoiler that Donohue designed to make the car competitive in the Trans-Am series. A likeness of Donohue's signature appeared on the spoiler.

secutive Trans-Am title for Chevrolet in 1969, relations between the two parties were becoming increasingly strained. Compared to the financial support provided by Ford for the Mustang and Cougar teams, Chevrolet contributed relatively little to the Penske Racing Camaro program. To the businessman Penske, who understood the marketing value these championships provided the automaker, this was an unreasonable situation, especially when there were other car companies out there ready to offer the two-time defending series champions substantial financial incentives to make a change.

American Motors had first entered its new Javelin in the 1968 Trans-Am championship, with an in-house racing team headed by Ron Kaplan and a strong driver lineup that included veterans Peter Revson and George Follmer. Although they went winless in their debut season, the AMC Javelin team managed six second-place finishes and two thirds, finishing a close third in the championship behind Penske's Camaros and the Ford Mustang team. It was a fairly respectable start considering the level of competition. In 1969, AMC continued a two-car effort with drivers John Martin and Ron Grable, but the results were much less impressive. At that point, American Motors management decided to turn the Javelin program over to a team that it believed could guarantee success. They approached Roger Penske with an offer that the Captain couldn't refuse. In return for AMC's vote-of-confidence, Penske made a bold and highly publicized promise to win at least seven races in the first season. Considering that the Javelin had not seen the winner's circle in two years of trying, this was a startling commitment—and nobody was more surprised than Mark Donohue, who would be charged with making it happen. Donohue had already seen what they had inherited from the Kaplan Racing program, and he knew that he'd basically be starting from scratch. He knew it would be a daunting task to win any races that first year, let alone seven.

As a first step, Roger Penske hired engineer Don Cox away from the Chevrolet Racing organization. Cox had worked closely with the team during the Camaro program, and both Penske and Donohue had a high regard for his talents. Donohue and Cox started with a stripped Javelin chassis from the factory and methodically assembled a first-class racecar, applying the knowledge and experience gained from their three years of racing Camaros. Still, there were problems, some anticipated and some unforeseen.

First, there were the aerodynamic challenges. Trans-Am rules allowed very few deviations from the stock showroom vehicle. Although the Javelin had fairly "clean" body lines, the lack of a rear spoiler was going to seriously hamper the car's high-speed handling performance. To address this shortcoming, Mark Donohue

Roger Penske hired Peter Revson as his number-2 driver for the 1970 Trans-Am in an effort to better compete with the multi-car Ford teams. Revson and Donohue were fierce rivals throughout most of their driving careers, competing in Trans-Am, Can-Am and Indy-Cars. After Donohue's 1973 retirement, Penske signed Revson to drive for the team again, but he was fatally injured in a Formula-1 practice accident before that came to fruition. *Ron Nelson / Prairie Street Photos*

by the Camaro's 307 Chevrolet. To make matters worse, it took nearly half of the first season to diagnose and resolve an oil starvation problem that ultimately resulted in the destruction of twenty-three engines. Donohue suspected that the engines were failing because of a loss of oil pressure, but without the sophisticated data telemetry that is used extensively on modern-day racecars, the only way to finally identify this problem was to put an observer in the "back seat" of the Javelin while Donohue muscled the car around the racetrack under simulated race conditions. This experiment revealed that the oil pressure was momentarily dropping to zero under extreme combinations of braking or accelerating and turning. With this knowledge, Donohue was able to make changes to the oil sump configuration that finally corrected the problem. But by the time that all happened, it was really too late to salvage the Javelin's first season.

Roger Penske hired Peter Revson as Donohue's teammate for the 1970 Trans-Am campaign. Revson and Donohue had raced against each other throughout their amateur and professional careers, and there was more than a friendly rivalry between them. Revson came from a very privileged background and was heir to the Revlon Cosmetics fortune. He had dropped out of two Ivy League schools before finally devoting his full attention to racing. His personality was the polar opposite of Donohue's. With his flashy, playboy image, he would go on to be the perfect poster boy for Formula-1 a few years later.

Revson was undeniably a dedicated and talented driver, though he didn't possess the engineering and car development skills of Donohue. But that wasn't really an issue because he was clearly hired to be the number-two driver, a backup to ensure that AMC still collected points in case Donohue's car failed. Of course, there is always the possibility too that Roger Penske was applying some psychology to bring out the best in Donohue's driving, knowing that he wouldn't want to be upstaged by his old rival.

Before the start of the Trans-Am season, Penske Racing entered the Javelin in the 24 Hours of Daytona as a final testing and development exercise. Although there

went to Detroit and convinced the American Motors executives and engineers to make a special production run of 2500 cars equipped with the required spoiler. This was the minimum number of vehicles that needed to be produced by an automaker in order for the modification to be considered "stock." These special Javelins were sold as "Mark Donohue" editions, with Donohue's autograph on the back of the spoiler.

In addition to the aerodynamic challenges, there were also major engine issues. AMC's 290 cubic inch small-block V-8 motor was only good for about 375 horsepower, compared to the 475 hp that was produced was no official "Trans-Am" class this year, there were a number of Trans-Am teams participating. It was encouraging that the Donohue/Revson Javelin was the fastest of the "TA" cars in qualifying and the first quarter of the race. But then the motor blew, beginning the long frustrating saga of engine failures.

For the season-opening Trans-Am event at Laguna Seca, Donohue and Revson destroyed three engines just in practice. In the race, Mark managed to hang on for a distant second-place finish behind a gloating Parnelli Jones, while Revson had brake problems and ended his day parked in the hay bales. Donohue later recalled feeling totally exasperated after that race, knowing that they had put a monumental effort into developing the new Javelin, and now it was apparent that it was nothing more than a mediocre racecar.

The second race of the season was at Lime Rock. Revson blew an engine coming into the pits and spun in his own oil, ending his day early. Donohue ran in second place for most of the race and took the lead briefly when Parnelli Jones made a mistake and went off course. But then on the 72nd lap, Donohue's engine self-destructed again, and Jones recovered to win the race. It was after this disastrous weekend that Donohue finally pinpointed the oil starvation problem. With some initial modifications made to address the problem, the Penske Javelins finished second and third in the next race at Bryar. This time it was the Mustang of George Follmer taking first-place honors after Jones had the hood fly off his car, putting him out of the show early.

Mark Donohue ran the lone Penske Javelin in the next two races, as Revson was attending to his Team McLaren Can-Am responsibilities. At Mid-Ohio, Donohue ran a distant third to Mustang teammates Jones and Follmer, all but guaranteeing the manufacturer's championship to Ford at this early point in the season. After four races, Roger Penske had still not been able to put a Javelin in the winner's circle, and with only 7 races remaining, his prediction of seven victories was looking highly improbable.

Finally, at Bridgehampton, New York, in the fifth race of the year, things started to come around—and probably not a moment too soon. In a race that was run mostly under wet conditions, Donohue won by more than two laps over second-place George Follmer and third-place Parnelli Jones, giving American Motors their long-awaited first Trans-Am victory. "We've been trying very hard this year and now we are almost to where we want to be," said Donohue after the win. "We've got all of the right ingredients, but it's just a case of getting all of the details sorted out. The Mustangs, with Parnelli and George driving, are very competitive and it's going to be a very tough rest of the season." Had Donohue not won that race, AMC was apparently ready to withdraw its support for the program, leaving Penske to go it alone for the remainder of the season.

The next race, at Donnybrooke, Minnesota, was another setback. Donohue lost an engine in practice and took over Revson's car for the race. Then only 14 laps into the main event, the engine in the second Javelin blew. Just when they thought that the motor problems were resolved, here appeared a new and different gremlin. As it turned out, these latest failures were actually the indirect result of changes made to correct the oil starvation issue. The ultimate fix for that problem was to install a secondary oil sump pump. What Donohue and Don Cox eventually realized was that the extra load put on the camshaft gears by this secondary pump was destroying these gears, allowing the ignition timing to change considerably over time. Under race conditions, this was enough to burn up the engine. Armed with that understanding, they were able to modify the camshaft gears to eliminate the problem. Finally, the AMC Javelin engine problems were resolved, but it was far too late to salvage the 1970 season.

The next race, at Road America in Elkhart Lake, Wisconsin, was marred by Jerry Titus' fatal practice crash. Titus had been one of the early Trans-Am contenders, and although he had been less successful over the previous couple seasons, he was still a crowd favorite. It was the first driver fatality in the Trans-Am's five-year history.

In the race, Roger Penske introduced a new pit stop strategy that is frequently employed in modern-day racing of all types. With the Javelin still handicapped by at least a 50-horsepower deficit, Penske decided to pit

In 1970, the Trans Am series reached its peak. Factory money was so abundant that they could barely fit all the cars on the racetrack. The two Penske Javelins are seen here starting in the 3rd and 4th rows at Elkhart Lake, but Mark Donohue would go on to win because of Roger Penske's out-of-sequence pit stop strategy. *Ron Nelson / Prairie Street Photos*

Donohue out of sequence with the rest of the leaders. That would separate him from the leader traffic, allowing him to run considerably faster by himself. Donohue explained, "I was running in second place early in the race, when suddenly I went piling into the pits at 100 mph, the hood was thrown open, oil added, a can of fuel, and I was back out again—way down in the standings. Everyone else forgot about me at that point; they thought I was having trouble and was out of the picture. Meanwhile, I got down to business….I ran as hard as I could for the rest of the race. I never saw anybody or passed anybody—and at the end of the race I was ahead of everybody. People were standing around scratching their heads, saying, 'What the hell happened? Where did he come from?' Parnelli was saying, 'How could he win the race? I never even saw him.'"

Two weeks later, in St. Jovite, Canada, Penske utilized the same pit stop strategy and got the same result, with Donohue winning over the Mustangs of Follmer and Jones. It was the second consecutive victory for the AMC Javelin—things were really looking up. All the major reliability problems had finally been resolved, and although horsepower was still an issue, it seemed that Penske Racing was back on even ground with the Ford teams.

Round 9 of the 1970 series at Watkins Glen produced a surprise winner, as Vic Elford in one of Jim Hall's Chaparral Camaros took the honors. It was the second of only two victories for the 1969 title-winning manufacturer. Donohue finished second at the Glen, ahead of Follmer, Jones, and then Revson in the other Penske Javelin. In Round 10 at Kent, Washington, Donohue was runner-up to Parnelli Jones, with Revson back in 7th spot. The season ended at Riverside, California, with Donohue coming up short to both of the Fords, taking a third place finish.

In what has generally been considered the greatest Trans-Am season ever, Bud Moore's Mustangs, with drivers Parnelli Jones and George Follmer, took the championship with 72 points, while the Penske AMC Javelins of Mark Donohue and Peter Revson finished second with 59 points. Jones edged Donohue by a single point in the driver's standings. The list of also-rans included names like Jim Hall, Dan Gurney, Swede Savage, Vic Elford, Milt Minter, Ed Leslie and Sam Posey driving factory-backed Chevrolet Camaros, Plymouth Barracudas, Dodge Challengers, and Pontiac Firebirds. According to long-time ABC auto racing commentator and editor of *National Speed Sport News*, Chris Economaki, "The [1970] Trans-Am series was intensely com-

Mark Donohue started on the pole at Elkhart Lake next to the #68 ARA Javelin of Peter Revson. The 1971 Trans-Am championship was a virtual cakewalk for Donohue and the Penske AMC team. Unfortunately, the loss of factory support from Ford, GM and Chrysler markedly diminished the significance of the victory, leading Roger Penske to drop his Trans-Am program at season's end after claiming his third title in five years. *Mike Odell / Forget-Me-Not-Race Pix / SportsRacingLtd.com*

petitive because the manufacturers spent a fortune to make it so. The cars were magnificently prepared, the engines were powerful, the drivers were the cream of the crop, and the pit crews worked with military precision. These factors gave Trans-Am racing a spectator appeal that was second to none. The factories didn't compete to run second, because they were competing for the world championship of Detroit."

This extraordinary Trans-Am season also hosted the retirement performances for two of auto racing's greatest American drivers. Jim Hall stepped down after the Road America race, almost certainly influenced by the

death of Jerry Titus in that event. Gentleman Dan Gurney cut his retirement cake after taking 5th place with his Plymouth Barracuda in the Riverside season finale. After winning in Formula-1, Indy-cars, Can-Am, stock cars and endurance racing, Gurney's decision to conclude his celebrated career with a Trans-Am event reflected the stature of this series at that point in history.

1971

Like a shooting star, the Trans-Am's brilliance faded quickly after the 1970 season. Having reclaimed the manufacturer's title after two years of humiliation at the hands of the Penske/Donohue Camaros, Ford assessed the situation and concluded, probably correctly, that they had nothing left to gain by continuing. They had beaten Penske and Donohue in a moment of weakness, and they knew that the updated Penske Javelins would be much stronger for 1971. Chevrolet also withdrew its support from the Camaro campaign. In 1970, they had entrusted their program to Jim Hall, one of the most respected drivers and designer/innovators of the era. The result was a single win and third place in the extremely competitive manufacturer's standings. Chrysler pulled out too, dropping support for the unsuccessful Barracuda and Challenger efforts. That left only American Motors with factory money in the pot, still determined to claim a Trans-Am title for whatever publicity and marketing value it could offer. There would still be a healthy field full of Mustangs, Camaros, and Firebirds, but they would all be independents, operating on a fraction of the financial support that was available a year earlier. It was truly as shame, not just because it signaled the imminent demise of a great racing series, but also because it denied Penske Racing the opportunity to win an "undisputed" Trans-Am title with the AMC Javelin.

With such a strong hand going into the season, Roger Penske saw no need to run a two-car program, so Mark Donohue ran the lone Penske Racing Javelin in 1971. As it turned out, the Captain got his seven victories, although a year later than he originally predicted. In the season opener at Lime Rock, it looked like Donohue's primary competition would still come from Bud Moore's Mustangs, driven by Parnelli Jones and Peter Gregg. Other challengers would include the new Roy Woods AMC Javelin team, with drivers Peter Revson and Tony Adamowicz, the Boss 302 Mustangs of Jerry Thompson and Tony DeLorenzo, and a shockingly competitive 1964 Pontiac Tempest driven by Bob Tullius. Jones got bumped off the track early in the rainy race and, as it turned out, that would be the end of his Trans-Am career. Donohue went on to win easily over Tony DeLorenzo, but only after Tullius lost an engine in his feisty 7-year-old Tempest.

In round two at Bryar, Donohue suffered his only DNF of the season when the Javelin's carburetor floats stuck open while he was leading the race. George Follmer, back in the Bud Moore seat vacated by Parnelli Jones, was there to pick up the win. Next, at Mid-Ohio, the Penske Javelin faltered again, this time with brake problems. Donohue managed to hang on for a second-place finish to Follmer, but only after a frightening pit incident in which he misjudged the braking problem and plowed into his boss, carrying Roger Penske 15 feet on the hood of the car before getting stopped. Fortunately, the Captain was unhurt.

The remainder of the 1971 season was pretty much a Donohue steamroller, as Mark piloted the Penske Javelin to six consecutive wins and gave American Motors their long-awaited Trans-Am championship. At this point, the record book would show that Penske Racing had won three series titles in five years. They had claimed a total of 31 wins in 58 races. Twenty-nine of those victories were scored by Mark Donohue, a record that would not be equaled for 33 years until Paul Gentalozzi logged his 29th Trans-Am win in 2004.

In many ways, the Trans-Am series and Penske Racing helped to define each other. Although Penske and Donohue had won races and even United States Road Racing championships before their Trans-Am success, it was in this series that they established themselves as a dominant force, maybe the dominant force in American road racing. The Trans-Am benefited from the relationship as well. Roger Penske's professional, business-savvy approach to racing helped to establish the young championship as a high-quality marketing product, a product that the major U.S. automakers were eager to support with big factory dollars—for a while, anyway.

When Roger Penske assessed the situation after the 1971 season, he saw no reason to continue in the Trans-Am. Not only had they been there and done that—exceptionally well, in fact—but it was evident that the series had already seen its best years. And so, although the names "Penske Racing" and "Trans-Am" had become almost synonymous, the Captain decided that the time was right to move on to other challenges. The Trans-Am years, however, will always hold a very special place in Penske Racing history.

Michael Sesit

CHAPTER 4
World Endurance Championship (1966 – 1973)

"They've come to see one thing, the blue Ferrari from America, the Penske car, the one that's always so shiny. They've crowded in so close that their shoe toes are mirrored in its polished-aluminum sills."
— Patrick Bedard, *Car & Driver*, 1971

From 1953 through 1992 the FIA, which is the organization that sanctions Formula-1, also presented the World Sportscar Championship. Over the years, the title of this series changed many times, as did its regulations. In the late 1960s and early 1970s, under the monikers "World Endurance Championship" and "World Championship for Makes," the series saw some of its most famous and powerful racing machines, including the Ford GT40 and Mk IV, the Lola T70 Mk III, the Ferrari 330 and 512, the Porsche 907s and 908s, and the legendary long-tail Porsche 917 coupe. During this era, the championship consisted of about 10 races per year, including the 24-Hours-of-Le Mans, the 24-Hours-of-Daytona, the 12-Hours-of-Sebring, and the Watkins Glen Six Hours, in addition to events at some of Europe's most famous racetracks. Although never campaigning in the full series, from 1966 through 1973 Penske Racing participated several times in some of the biggest and most demanding of these world championship races.

1966

Even before Mark Donohue was recruited to drive the USRRC/Can-Am Lola, Roger Penske's first venture as a race team owner came in February of 1966 when he entered a Sunoco-sponsored Corvette Stingray in the 24-Hours of Daytona. Drivers Dick Guldstrand, Ben Moore, and George Wintersteen posted a very respectable 12th-place overall finish, taking first in the GT 3-liter class. Penske entered the Stingray again in the 12 Hours of Sebring the following month, with Moore and Winter-

In his first venture as a team owner, Roger Penske entered this Corvette Stingray in the 1966 24-Hours-Of Daytona and the 12-Hours-of-Sebring endurance races. Drivers Dick Guldstrand, Ben Moore, and George Wintersteen won the GT 3-liter class at Daytona; Moore and Wintersteen co-drove to another class victory at Sebring. *Larry Arnt*

The Penske Racing Corvette is seen here going through tech inspection at Sebring, which was conducted in the parking lot of the Piggly Wiggly grocery store. *Larry Arnt*

steen finishing 9th overall and first in class again. Interestingly, Mark Donohue finished second overall in this event, co-driving a factory Ford Mark II with Walt Hansgen in what turned out to be Hansgen's last race before his fatal practice crash at Le Mans. This, of course, was the unfortunate event that precipitated an impromptu meeting between Roger Penske and Donohue, which resulted in Mark being hired to drive the new Lola.

1967

According to Mark Donohue, Penske Racing's legendary Trans-Am dynasty actually evolved out of Roger's desire to have an entry in the 1967 Daytona 24 Hours and Sebring 12 Hours endurance races. The Group-7 Lola that they were campaigning in the Can-Am and USRRC series was not legal in world endurance events, so Penske had Donohue build a Camaro that they could run in the new "TA" (Trans-Am) class for these two races. Then they would run the same car in the popular new Trans-Am series.

Donohue quickly discovered that turning a stock street automobile into a racecar was a little different than buying a purpose-built racing machine, like the USRRC/Can-Am Lola, and "tuning" it for optimum performance. With little time for preparation and absolutely no development, the Penske team took their Camaro to Daytona in February for the Trans-Am and 24-Hour races. Donohue drove the car in the Trans-Am race, but he was still under contract with the Holman & Moody Ford GT team at that time, so the Penske Camaro was co-driven by George Wintersteen, Joe Welch, and Bobby Brown in the 24-hour event. The car ran 456 laps, about two-thirds of the distance covered by the winners, before being sidelined with mechanical problems. For Sebring, Penske entered a Chevrolet Corvette in the GT class, with Wintersteen and Welch driving again, and chalking up another DNF. Overall, 1967 was certainly not a memorable assault on the World Sportscar Championship by this young American team.

After suffering engine problems at Daytona, which relegated Donohue and co-driver Bob Johnson to second-in-class behind the Shelby Mustang team, Roger Penske decided to enter a second car at Sebring for insurance. With the mechanical issues resolved, the Penske Camaros finished first and second in class and a remarkable third and fourth overall in the Sebring 12-hour race. *Mike Odell / Forget-Me-Not-Race Pix / SportsRacingLtd.com*

1968

For 1968, with a lot more experience behind them, the Penske Racing team returned to run their new Trans-Am Camaro in the 24-Hours-of-Daytona and the 12-Hours-of-Sebring. By now, Donohue was no longer moonlighting with the Ford team, so he was able to devote his full attention to the Penske effort. Bob Johnson would co-drive with Donohue at Daytona and Craig Fisher at Sebring. The Camaro was much better developed than the previous year, and Donohue and the team had more time prior to the start of the season to get everything right. They even had the "luxury" of running a 24-hour test at Daytona prior to the race to make sure the car was ready. The only serious problem that was encountered in this test was a cracked cylinder head. And not surprisingly, the same problem plagued the team during the race itself. Donohue was the fastest qualifier in the Trans-Am class, and led for 13 hours before the head failed. With the time lost in the pits, the Penske Camaro finished a disappointing second in class, 12th overall. This was particularly painful as the Shelby Racing Mustang of Jerry Titus and Ron Bucknum won the TA class with an impressive 4th place overall finish.

Disappointed by the poor showing at Daytona, Roger Penske was apparently determined not to get beat again at Sebring. To be safe, Penske Racing entered two Camaros for this 12-hour race. Donohue and Fisher would drive one, while Joe Welch and Bob Johnson would pilot the second, which was actually an updated version of the 1967 car. This was the race in which the Penske team introduced its vacuum-assisted brake disc changing system. With this unfair advantage and an excellent overall team effort, Donohue and Fisher took first in class, third overall behind two prototype Porsche 907s, while the Welch/Johnson Camaro was second in class, fourth overall. Clearly, this was the result Roger Penske was looking for.

1969

For 1969, Roger Penske moved up to the top-tier Prototype class in World Endurance competition. As part of the four-car deal that he had arranged with the Lola factory, Penske Racing got a Group 5 Lola T70 Mk

III coupe, a car designed to challenge the top prototype endurance entries of the era.

Donohue later recalled that the team had about three weeks from the time they took delivery of the new car until they had to pack up and head for Daytona. In that short period of time, they had to fit one of their proven small-block Camaro engines, build an exhaust system, determine proper spring rates and take care of a lot of other details. Fortunately, they had an opportunity to test at Daytona before the race, and Donohue was very pleased with how quickly they were able to get the Lola dialed in. Driving duties for Daytona were shared between Donohue and Charlie Parsons, which is particularly interesting when considering that four-driver teams are the norm in modern-era endurance races.

Donohue qualified the Sunoco-Penske Lola second fastest behind the Porsche 908 of Vic Elford. He ran in the lead pack with several factory Porsches for the first hour, but then started experiencing fuel starvation problems followed by a failure of the exhaust header system. After an hour and a half in the pits to re-weld the headers, the Penske Lola returned to competition hopelessly behind the leaders. But then the Porsche cars started having their own problems, and Donohue and Parsons starting picking their way back through the field. Later in the race, the Porsches also began experiencing a series of terminal camshaft failures. In the end, all five of the factory 908s dropped out with engine problems, leaving a surprised but elated Penske Racing team with a 26-lap lead over another Lola T70, taking the overall victory in the 24-Hours-of-Daytona.

Re-energized after the Daytona success, the Penske team corrected the known problems with the Lola and headed for Sebring with high expectations. Donohue was teamed with Ron Bucknum for this historic 12-hour race on the old airport runways in Sebring, Florida. The Sunoco-Penske Lola again qualified second, this time behind a new factory Ferrari 312P that was entered for Mario Andretti and Chris Amon. But the good news was that Donohue was much faster than the Porsche 908s that had been the main competition at Daytona.

In the race, Donohue moved into the lead early and the Penske Racing Lola looked like the class of the field. Unfortunately, it didn't last long. About a third of the way through the 12-hour event, the rear suspension broke and that was the end. It was a disappointing result, but with the win at Daytona and a dominating showing at Sebring before the mechanical failure, Penske Racing was still looking like a strong contender early in the 1969 World Endurance Championship.

The next outing for the Lola was to be the 24 Hours of Le Mans, the only race in the world that rivals the Indianapolis 500 in terms of history and tradition. Donohue had competed there before with the Ford GT team, but this was to be a first for Penske Racing. Unfortunately, it didn't happen—at least not that year. On the way back from the Sebring race, the Penske Racing trailer, with the Daytona-winning racecar aboard, was stolen from the parking lot of a Daytona Beach hotel. All the work that went into the Lola and all the big plans that were taking shape went right out the window. There was no time to start from scratch to build a new racecar, not with all the other programs that were underway that year. So that was the strange and anticlimactic ending to the Penske Racing World Endurance challenge for 1969.

1971

Roger Penske evidently had a personal fascination with endurance racing, because despite less-than-spectacular results and some unbelievably bad luck, it seemed that he kept coming back, even though it was never really a core part of the Penske Racing program. After skipping the 1970 season, the Captain's team returned for 1971 with a privately entered Ferrari 512, competing again in the top-level prototype class. It was a somewhat unusual arrangement, with the car being provided by Kirk F. White, a Philadelphia-area businessman who used this high-profile relationship to promote his exotic car dealership. The two men were just social acquaintances in 1970 when Penske dropped by White's office unexpectedly early one morning with an idea to field a Ferrari in the World Sports Car Championship series. After a brief discussion, Kirk White drafted a two-paragraph proposal and the deal that would result in Penske Racing's lone appearance in the 24 Hours of Le Mans was consumated by a handshake within four days.

The Ferrari that Kirk White provided was actually a used car that had been raced in the 1970 Can-Am series with little success. Despite the fact that it was not in particularly great condition when delivered to the Penske Racing shop, Donohue and the team managed to turn the car into a formidable competitor in a very short period of time. When they got it on a racetrack for its first serious testing just two weeks before the Daytona 24 Hours race, everyone was excited to see that they had a really fast racecar.

Roger Penske recruited Englishman David Hobbs to co-drive the Ferrari with Donohue. Hobbs, like Donohue, drove just about everything in his career—Can-Am, Trans-Am, Formula A, Formula-1, and Indy cars. He was a likeable and capable driver who just never seemed to find a permanent home with a top team. Hobbs is now retired from competitive driving and serves as a race analyst and commentator for the Speed Channel network. His vast and diverse racing experience, coupled with his entertaining British character, makes him the ideal candidate for this television role.

Mark Donohue called him "Matey." Englishman David Hobbs was hired by Roger Penske to co-pilot the Ferrari in the 1971 endurance races. Hobbs also drove for Penske at Indianapolis that year, running the team's year-old Ford-Lola while Donohue drove the new McLaren-Offy. *Ron Nelson / Prairie Street Photos*

In practice and qualifying for the Daytona race, the Penske Ferrari was overwhelmingly superior to the competition. In his 1974 autobiography, Donohue recalled playing mind games with the factory Porsches, letting them struggle to get close to his fast time, then going out and taking another 2 seconds a lap off his pace with apparent ease. After putting the Ferrari on the pole— just to add insult to injury—the Penske crew pulled out the 600-hp "practice" engine and installed a new 630-hp "race" motor.

In the race, the Penske Ferrari ran out front for most of the first 8 hours, with Donohue fighting off the challenge from Pedro Rodriguez in one of the factory Porsche 917s. Donohue and Rodriguez had developed an intense personal rivalry, a situation that was going to come to a head a month later at Sebring. Just after midnight, Vic Elford blew a tire on the Daytona banking and triggered a multi-car pile-up, collecting Donohue's Ferrari in the process. Donohue blamed himself for making a wrong split-second decision when he came upon the developing accident. "I had made a deliberate choice, and it turned out to be a serious mistake in judgment. We had put months into that car, and now I had turned it all into thousands of dollars worth of junk." Of course, when driving at speeds over 150 mph in the dark, it seems unreasonable to find fault with any emergency reflex decision, but Donohue expected perfection of himself and he felt that he'd let the team down.

Despite heavy damage, the Penske crew patched the Ferrari back together with parts from another car and "ten miles of racer's tape, fourteen broomstick handles, and anything else we could find lying around," according to Donohue. They went on to finish third in the race, only 14 laps behind the winning factory Porsche of Pedro Rodriguez and Jackie Oliver and another Ferrari 512 driven by Tony Adamowicz and former Penske driver Ron Bucknum. All things considered, it was not a bad outcome. But, of course, it really should have been a dominating victory.

In the month and a half between the Daytona and Sebring races, Donohue and the team made a number of improvements to the Ferrari. They installed a locked differential and fabricated a new, larger rear

The Penske-Kirk F. White Ferrari 512M, driven by Mark Donohue and David Hobbs in 1971, was a fast and beautiful racecar that never lived up to its potential. As the only Penske entry to ever race at Le Mans, it is undoubtedly the most famous of the team's endurance cars. Seen here at Watkins Glen in its final outing, the Ferrari was always a threat to win, but it was notoriously unreliable, and never delivered on that promise. *Mike Odell / Forget-Me-Not-Race Pix / SportsRacingLtd.com*

wing, changes that made the car even faster. The really unfortunate thing about the whole program was that the Ferrari factory seemed to have little interest in the success or failure of the Penske/White privateer entry. In fact, when it began to threaten the factory Ferrari 312s that were running in the same series, Roger Penske started finding it difficult to even get spare parts for the car. Before Sebring, Penske's engine builder was having trouble getting the Ferrari engine to seal properly when put back together after a routine rebuild. They called the Ferrari factory about the problem and were simply advised to torque it correctly and it would be fine—of course, it wasn't. On the dyno, the rebuilt motor would only produce 580 horsepower, compared to the 630 that it had run before. This left the team no choice but to race the practice engine at Sebring, a disappointing handicap.

To make matters worse, Mark Donohue twisted an ankle while loading up the Ferrari for the trip to Sebring. Then, he ended up personally driving the Pen-ske team transporter from the race shop in Pennsylvania to Sebring, Florida—a 24-hour straight-through trip—just before competing in the grueling 12-hour endurance contest. An hour outside of Sebring, the truck broke down and had to be towed the rest of the way to the track. When Donohue finally arrived at Sebring—late, exhausted and injured—Roger Penske was not happy about the situation. His lead driver was in no condition to get into a racecar until he got some rest and attention for his sprained ankle. Fortunately, David Hobbs did an excellent job getting the car set up; and even with the old practice motor, it qualified on the pole.

Prior to the start of the race, Roger Penske cautioned Mark Donohue not to mess with Pedro Rodriguez, concerned that their rivalry might have reached a point that it could be detrimental or even dangerous. From the start, the Penske-White Ferrari was clearly the fastest car on the track, but because it had to pit more frequently than the 3.0-liter factory Ferrari driven by Mario Andretti and Jacky Ickx, it was shaping up to be a close race. Donohue had dropped to third place behind the Andretti/Ickx Ferrari and the Porsche 917 of Pedro Rodriguez when he made a mistake, or at least an error in judgment. Trying to get around Rodriguez, he moved to the inside of the Porsche on a high-speed turn, but the fiery Mexican driver closed the door on him—not once, but three times, as Donohue later recalled. Both cars ended up in the pits with considerable damage. Roger Penske wasn't happy. Donohue later conceded that he should have just waited for a clear straightaway to make the pass. As it was, the Penske-White Ferrari lost a lot of time in the pits for repairs, and eventually finished in 6th place, 17 laps behind winners Vic Elford and Gérard Larrousse in another Porsche 917. For the second time in as many outings, the Ferrari had demonstrated awesome potential, but had to settle for "also ran" status because of an unfortunate racing incident.

After the Sebring fiasco, Roger Penske and Mark Donohue were both ready to be finished with the Ferrari project, but car owner Kirk White still wanted to go to Le Mans in June, which was part of the original arrangement. Of course, that was right in the middle of the racing season. Donohue was running both the McLaren Indy car and the Trans-Am Javelin, which didn't leave much preparation time for the troublesome Ferrari. As a result, the Le Mans challenge was, unfortunately, not up to the normal Penske Racing standards. Even so, the European fans seemed fascinated by this peculiar blue Ferrari from the United States, and the meticulous team that brought it to France.

Luckily, Donohue had run the 24-Hours-of-LeMans before, so he was familiar with some of the bureaucracy involved. When the technical inspectors wanted to be difficult, they could find fault with something as simple at the lettering font used for the numbers on the car. The Penske-White Ferrari was assigned the number "11." But the inspectors didn't like the serifs—to them the number looked like "77." So the Penske crew had to re-paint all the numbers on the car to appease the race stewards. Race officials also had a problem with Penske's Sunoco sponsorship. British Petroleum was the official gasoline supplier for the race, and there was a heated debate about allowing the Ferrari to run with Sunoco

logos. After dispensing with these and other senseless issues, the racing could finally begin.

Donohue was unable to qualify the Ferrari better than fourth on the grid, behind three "long-tail" Porsche 917s. Le Mans was like no other racetrack in the world—8.34 miles in total length with the unbelievable 3.5-mile long "Mulsanne Straight," making top-end speed the most important factor in this event. The long-tail Porsches were built specially for this one track—this single race—to minimize the effect of aerodynamic drag on the racecars at high speed. With this design, the Porsche 917s could approach 240 mph on the Mulsanne. The Penske Ferrari, even with a theoretical horsepower advantage, could "only" manage 212 mph top end, resulting in a dramatic handicap. To make matters even worse the new engine, which had just been rebuilt by the Ferrari factory this time, began to make a knocking noise in practice, forcing the Penske crew to resort to the old faithful backup motor again. So here they were, halfway around the globe, competing in the second most-famous race in the world, and they were forced to start this 24-hour endurance test with an old, tired, practice engine. Ironically, the new "knocking" engine was sold to another Ferrari 512 team and actually held together until the car was sidelined with suspension problems.

Surprisingly, Donohue and Hobbs managed to be competitive with the Porsches in the early stages of the race. The first pit stop, which occurred after just 16 laps, turned out to be a 'Keystone Cops' routine, although nobody was laughing at the time. Patrick Bedard reported in his *Car and Driver* account of the race, "Just as the [Penske] Ferrari starts to move the commissaire de stande from the N.A.R.T. pit next door, having apparently spotted some diabolical infraction, vaults himself in front of the car, spreading his arms like a second-base umpire about to pronounce Maury Wills out. Always with an eye toward shortening a pitstop, Penske muscles him out of the way in a very USAC manner. The flagman then joins the fray by cracking Penske across the back of the head with the shortened broom handle he has been assigned as a flagpole. In the confusion Donohue sneaks out." Maybe this explains

A tired and discouraged Mark Donohue (left) looks on as Roger Penske inspects the sick Ferrari in the pits at Le Mans. The Ferrari qualified fourth and was competitive early, but just four hours into the 24-hour race, the engine failed. *Michael Sesit*

why Roger Penske hasn't taken a team back to Le Mans since then.

About four hours into race, Donohue coasted into the pits with the Ferrari engine silent. The post-mortem revealed a clogged oil passage to the cam bearings, not at all surprising considering the sorry condition of the old practice motor before the race even began. Within an hour, the official Le Mans race bulletin reported: "À 20 H 16, la voiture 11 pilotée par DONOHUE abandonne: moteur bloqué." The race was over.

Le Mans wasn't a total loss, however. It was after this adventure that the Porsche factory contacted Roger Penske and asked if he'd like to talk about running their 917 in the Can-Am series. Having seen what the Penske operation was able to accomplish with the troublesome Ferrari, without benefit of factory support, the Porsche folks recognized the opportunity for a major breakthrough in their struggling Can-Am program. Penske and Donohue saw an opportunity too, to go back at Team McLaren with a formidable factory effort. In that sense, all the aggravation, frustration and disappoint-

ment of the Ferrari 512 project was certainly worth it.

Penske Racing ran the Ferrari in two more events that year. The final race of the World Endurance Championship was on the same weekend as the Can-Am event at Watkins Glen, New York. The Glen, which was the premiere road course in the United States at the time, and host to the U.S. Grand Prix, was located just five hours from Penske Racing's shop in Newton Square, Pennsylvania. Logistically, it would be an easy and relatively inexpensive race weekend. They decided to run the Ferrari in both the Six-Hours endurance race and the Can-Am event. Even though they knew that the 5.0-liter engine wouldn't be competitive with the 7-liter McLarens, it would give them a chance to scope out the Can-Am field in preparation for the 1972 assault. Also, Donohue reasoned, a fourth place finish in the lucrative Can-Am race would have had a better payout than a win in the Six-Hours event.

The World Endurance contest took place on Saturday. With David Hobbs co-driving again, the Penske Ferrari easily took the pole and ran away from the com-

The Porsche factory lured Roger Penske back into endurance racing in 1973, offering a "turnkey" factory-prepared Carrera for Mark Donohue and George Follmer to drive in the Daytona 24 Hours and the Watkins Glen 6 Hours races.

petition in the early stages of the race. On this much shorter racetrack, the Porsche 917 challengers didn't have the top-end speed advantage they'd enjoyed at Le Mans. For a while, it looked like the problematic Ferrari might finally redeem itself in this last outing—but it was just not meant to be. On the 54th lap, as Donohue came charging into a 90-degree downhill right-hand turn, the left steering arm pin snapped and the Ferrari went straight off the corner, coming to a rest in a sand trap—just one more disappointment.

Sunday's Can-Am race didn't go much better. Donohue managed to qualify a respectable sixth behind world champion Jackie Stewart in a Lola, the two McLarens, another big-block Chevy, and a special 7-liter Ferrari entered for Mario Andretti. In the race, Donohue complained, "I'd get stuck behind a backmarker with a big V-8, and I'd have to stay there until he crashed. They would blow me off on the straights, and I couldn't pass in the corners. Then the bloody engine failed again." And that was finally the end of the disappointing Ferrari 512M program.

1973

Like the Ferrari campaign, Penske Racing's 1973 return to endurance racing was a collaborative effort.

After an incredibly successful 1972 Can-Am program, the Porsche factory approached Penske and asked if he'd like to have Donohue and George Follmer run a new model Porsche 911 Carrera in the Daytona and Sebring races. Porsche was willing to provide the car and resources to do the development and other preparation. They were looking at this as a marketing opportunity to sell the new Carrera to other racing teams. Porsche was also providing an identical car for Brumos-Porsche dealer/racer Peter Gregg to co-drive with Hurley Haywood, another loyal Porsche campaigner. This arrangement, intentional or not, would pit the two teams against each other and provide some spirited competition in the production class for these races.

1973 was the year that Penske Racing did everything—Indy cars, Can-Am, F-5000, NASCAR, and now—just for fun—a few endurance races. Fortunately, most of the development and testing was easily coordinated with the preparation work already underway for the 1973 Porsche Can-Am car. Also, Porsche was doing a lot of things that would have normally been left to Donohue and the crew, which made the whole exercise almost manageable.

For the Daytona race, tire-supplier Goodyear asked Donohue to consider running on their new radial tires—a 'marketing opportunity.' This was the time when radial tires were just being introduced to the public for street use. Donohue tested both the radials and regular bias-ply racing tires, and found the radials to be slower by about 1.5 seconds per lap. Despite this unfair disadvantage, Donohue reasoned that they had enough other tricks to keep the Penske Porsche ahead of the Gregg/Haywood entry, and that's about the best they could really hope for—there was no way they were going to be able to compete with the prototypes for the overall win anyway.

In the early stages of the race, Donohue was discouraged as all the prototype racers and Peter Gregg in the other Carrera just pulled away from him. The Penske crew made up ground on pit stops, but because of the radial tires, their car was at a slight disadvantage to the Brumos Porsche on the racetrack. By midnight, however, an interesting thing had happened. All of the faster

For the Watkins Glen 6-hour race, Porsche added a huge rear wing, a 3-liter motor and larger wheels and tires to their Carrera, making it necessary to run the car in the prototype class. Donohue and Follmer beat the sister car of Peter Gregg and Hurley Haywood, but couldn't compete with the "real" prototypes. *Mike Odell / Forget-Me-Not-Race Pix / SportsRacingLtd.com*

prototypes had already dropped out and the two rival Porsche Carreras were running 1-2 overall in the race—a very unexpected development. Donohue and Penske reworked pit strategy on the fly to get an advantage over the Brumos team, and eventually led the race for about six hours. But then, with only six hours remaining, Geoge Follmer coasted into the pits in a cloud of oily smoke. The supposedly "bulletproof" Porsche engine had let go. Gregg and Haywood went on to win in the other Carrera, so at least the Porsche factory was happy, but there should have been another Daytona 24 Hours trophy on Roger Penske's mantle.

The original plan was to run at Sebring next, but as it turned out, because that race was not included in the World Championship in 1973, Porsche decided they were not interested. Later in the season, however, the Porsche factory did come back and asked to have

Donohue and Follmer run a new "prototype" Carrera in the Watkins Glen Six-Hour race. This time, the car held together but unfortunately, so did most of the real prototype racecars. The Penske Carrera finished in 6th place behind a Matra-Simca, two Ferraris and two Mirages. There was some satisfaction, however, as they were one spot ahead of Gregg and Haywood in the sister Porsche.

With the 1969 Daytona 24 Hours victory being the only real bright spot in five seasons of endurance racing, Roger Penske apparently decided to table these extra-curricular activities for the time being. It wouldn't be until 2005 that a Penske Racing entry would test these waters again, and then under much different circumstances. Maybe its time finally for the Captain to think about taking another shot at Le Mans. The guy with the broomstick is probably gone by now.

Mike Odell / Forget-Me-Not-Race Pix / SportsRacingLtd.com

CHAPTER 5
USAC Indy-Cars
(1968 – 1978)

"When all the winged racers of Indy had finished the fast-est 500 miles ever, right there in the winner's circle sat the mild-mannered, much-beset—and deserving—Mark Donohue."
—Robert F. Jones, *Sports Illustrated*, June 5, 1972

Today, with the phenomenal popularity of NASCAR and the devastating Indy-car civil war between the IRL and CART/ChampCar, there is no clear consensus on which American racing series crowns an overall "U.S. National Champion." But in the late 1960s, there was no question that the pinnacle of U.S. racing was the Indy-car championship, which at that time was sanctioned by the United States Auto Club (USAC). Anchored by the Indianapolis 500, the oldest auto race in the world, and supported by a collection of short-track paved oval sprints at state fairgrounds and other tradition-rich venues, the USAC National Championship was indisputably the ultimate American racing crown. It was only logical, therefore, that the quickly maturing Penske Racing team would soon find its way into this series.

It was in 1967, only the second year of the team's existence, that Mark Donohue was offered an opportunity to drive for legendary chief mechanic George Bignotti in a rare USAC road race at Riverside, California. Just as today's NASCAR teams bring in "hired guns" with road racing backgrounds to hedge their bets on the unfamiliar road courses, Bignotti tried to recruit Donohue to get an unfair advantage over the "left-turn-only" USAC guys.

Donohue was interested, but Roger Penske wasn't willing to jeopardize the investment he had in his young driver. He didn't want Donohue driving an unfamiliar car that potentially wasn't prepared to his own high safety standards. He probably also didn't want to take the chance that Donohue might be lured off to another team. But rather than simply rejecting the idea, Penske agreed to buy a car and do some Indy-car racing under the Penske team banner.

1968

1967 was an extremely busy time for the young Penske Racing team—competing in the USRRC, Can-Am and Trans-Am championships—so the Indy car program didn't actually come together until the following year. 1968 wasn't really any less hectic, but Penske purchased a new Eagle chassis from Dan Gurney and, in what Donohue later described as "a typical last-minute operation," they put the car together with a gasoline-powered Chevrolet engine and entered the USAC race at Mosport, Canada, another road course where Donohue's experience figured to be an advantage. Despite the total lack of experience in this type of racing, and the non-existent development effort, Donohue managed a fifth place finish in this first outing behind USAC veterans Dan Gurney, Mario Andretti, Ron Bucknum, and Al Unser.

From an objective point of view, Mosport was an impressive debut in the highest level of professional auto racing in the United States. But of course, Penske and Donohue were hardly satisfied with a 5th place finish. Before the next race—the Riverside road course—they installed a new methanol-powered engine, and completed some fundamental development and testing in

"I think the people at Indy thought we were the college guys with the crew haircuts and the polished wheels. We used to clean our garage out every night, and that was something people didn't understand. I think at that point we started to bring the sport to a higher level." — Roger Penske. Photo by Greenfield Gallery

an attempt to cure handling problems that had plagued Donohue at Mosport. In what looked like another Penske Racing Cinderella story, Donohue found himself pressing Dan Gurney for the lead early in the race until a front upright broke, sending him off the track and ending the day. The result in the record book wasn't very impressive, but the Penske team had quickly proved that they could run with the big boys.

1969

Feeling pretty confident after their second Indy-Car experience, Penske and Donohue reasoned that they should be able to run competitively with the USAC teams in the biggest race of all, the Indianapolis 500. The original plan was to continue with the Eagle-Chevrolet program, but after a disappointing test session at Indy before the start of the 1969 season, Roger Penske aborted that plan in favor of a more conventional Offenhauser-powered Lola. The Lola T-152 was a new 4-wheel drive design that would be available that year to defending Indy 500 champion Bobby Unser and Penske Racing only. Because of a late delivery from the Lola factory, Unser worked with Donohue and the Penske team on the initial testing and setup of the new chassis. Donohue later acknowledged that during this process, Bobby Unser was invaluable in helping him through the steep learning curve of high-speed, open-wheel oval racing.

Mark Donohue ultimately qualified the Sunoco Lola-Offy fourth on the 1969 Indy 500 starting grid, another inspiring rookie performance. He dropped back at the start and spent the early part of the race getting comfortable with running wheel-to-wheel at 160 mph. Then he began to methodically pick his way back up through the field until he was finally running second to eventual winner Mario Andretti. Midway through the race, the Offy engine began mis-firing, and Donohue had to make a lengthy unscheduled pit stop to change the magneto, costing him eight laps and any chance of winning the race. But the impressive qualifying effort followed by his strong showing in the race earned him the coveted 'Indy 500 Rookie of the Year' award.

Following the Indy 500, Penske Racing did not make another USAC appearance until the fall Riverside event. For that race, they used a shorter two-wheel-drive Lola T-150, powered again by the Chevy engine. Although Donohue qualified second and led the race a one point, an engine failure brought the weekend to a disappointing early ending.

1970

For the 1970 season, Penske and Donohue ran the Lola-Chevy in two more USAC road races, with a best showing of second place. For the USAC oval tracks, Penske made a deal with Ford to use their 8-cylinder motor, which was the hot ticket in USAC at that time. Donohue had the Lola factory fabricate a two-wheel drive version of the previous year's T-152 to be fitted with the Ford V8 engine. Working with new engine builders for the Ford motors, it took longer than anticipated to sort out the new package. The Penske team

skipped the season opener at Phoenix, and made their first appearance with the Lola-Ford at Indy.

Donohue was fast at the beginning of May, but wasn't able to add much more speed as the month progressed. By qualifying day, others had caught up and he managed 'only' a fifth place starting position—certainly nothing to be ashamed of for the sophomore team, but compared to the previous year, it was a step backward. Donohue drove a clean and steady race, the team executed its pit stops with trademark efficiency, and Mark brought the Penske Lola-Ford home to a very respectable second place finish behind veteran Al Unser. Realistically, this was an exceptional result for the second-year team. But as Mark Donohue would often say, "Racing is only fun when you're winning."

After Indy, Penske Racing entered only one other USAC oval race that year, the Ontario 500 on Labor Day weekend. That turned out to be an altogether forgettable experience, as Donohue struggled with overheating and setup problems, qualified poorly, and finally dropped out of the race after only 7 laps with a blown engine. Real progress rarely comes without some setbacks.

1971

For the 1971 USAC season, Roger Penske went to his old Can-Am rival and bought their radical new McLaren M16 chassis. Team McLaren was never willing to sell their new Can-Am cars to other teams, but they were in an entirely different competitive environment in USAC, and realized that they could benefit from such an arrangement. The McLaren M16 was the first Indy car designed and engineered from the ground up to maximize aerodynamic efficiency. It had huge front and rear integral wings, side-mounted radiators, and an overall wedge-shape that looked fast just sitting still. Donohue was excited about the design the first time he saw it during a visit to the McLaren factory in the fall of 1970. At that time, Penske hadn't decided yet if they were going to focus on a return to the Can-Am or go for a full USAC Indy car campaign in 1971. The potential of the new McLaren convinced Donohue to lobby Penske for the Indy option.

The Indianapolis 500 was the third race of the

Mark Donohue qualified the stubby looking Sunoco Lola-Ford fifth for the 1970 Indy 500 and finished a very respectable second. Penske Racing ran this car only one other time this year—in the inaugural Ontario 500—where Donohue lasted only seven laps before blowing the engine.

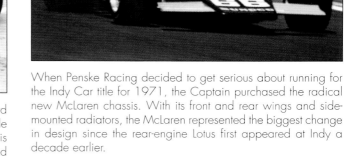

When Penske Racing decided to get serious about running for the Indy Car title for 1971, the Captain purchased the radical new McLaren chassis. With its front and rear wings and side-mounted radiators, the McLaren represented the biggest change in design since the rear-engine Lotus first appeared at Indy a decade earlier.

USAC season, but it was not uncommon in those days for teams to run their year-old equipment in the first two events and save the new car to debut in the big race. So while Donohue was testing the McLaren, he raced the old Lola-Ford at Phoenix and Trenton in the spring. Phoenix was a mediocre learning experience for the team, qualifying mid-pack and finishing an uninspiring sixth. Trenton was worse, chalking up a DNF as a result of transmission failure. Donohue never did particularly well at Trenton, which is ironic because the news media always made such a big deal about his road racing experience being an unfair advantage on the "tricky" backstretch dogleg. Captain Nice probably laughed to himself at that suggestion.

By the time May arrived, Penske Racing had done a considerable amount of testing and development work with the new McLaren. The first public display of the car's potential came when Donohue turned a lap at 172 mph during tire testing at Indy in March. That got everyone's attention and competitors starting questioning the legality of all the aerodynamic appendages on the new McLaren. But the USAC officials deemed the car to be within the rules, and Penske Racing had what was probably its greatest unfair advantage ever. Mark

Donohue was never one to gloat, but he seemed to get a particular satisfaction out of this well-deserved advantage. In his book, he wrote: "…when we came back [to Indy] in May, we set off a bombshell. We unloaded and ran 178 mph almost the first time out. We had raised a few eyebrows at 172, but a jump of six miles per hour was inconceivable…. All of a sudden the 1969 'Rookie of the Year' was the focal point. I was like Superman, because no one else had done anything like that before. It was really an enviable position to be in….We went to our garage and sat around wondering what to do next. We were in a state of shock. About that time Al Unser came over….Al said, 'Look, we've been competitors for a long time, and you have your way of doing things and I have mine, but when you can come here and run six miles per hour faster than anyone else – I gotta shake your hand.'

"But the nicest compliment came the next day at Lime Rock. I had to fly there for a Trans-Am race, and word of my new record hadn't gotten there yet….So Vel [Miletich] came over and asked how fast I had gone at Indy. I tried not to shout and scream. I just said, '177.8.' Vel is a great big guy, but he looked like I'd hit him with a bulldozer. He reeled around a little bit, then

Mark Donohue's Penske Racing Sunoco McLaren-Offy was the dominant car at Indy in 1971. A disappointing qualifying run left him second to Team McLaren driver Peter Revson on the starting grid. In the race, Donohue led the field by a full mile before his gearbox failed. *Greenfield Gallery*

Peter Revson and Mark Donohue were rivals throughout their racing careers. When Donohue was awarded "Rookie-of-the-year" honors at Indy in 1969 for his 7th place finish, Revson—who finished two positions higher—felt that he'd been snubbed. Two years later, driving one of the McLaren "team" cars, "Peter Perfect" benefited from setup information provided by Penske Racing to steal the Indy pole from a disbelieving Donohue.

came back and said, 'Of course, you're kidding.' I said, 'No I'm not.' He reeled around some more, then turned and headed for Parnelli [Jones] as fast as a guy that size can move. I could see them talking, and Parnelli just sat there gritting his teeth and shaking his head."

For the entire month of May, Donohue was in a class by himself. Even the McLaren Team cars of Peter Revson and Denny Hulme were not close. Mark eventually practiced as fast as 181 mph, and it was a foregone conclusion that the Penske McLaren had a lock on the pole position. In the morning practice on qualifying day, Donohue noticed a slight oversteer in the car on the hot racetrack, but because they were so far ahead of everyone else, he was afraid to make any adjustments for fear of making the situation worse. His four-lap qualifying average was a record-breaking, yet still disappointing 177.080 mph. But that would still be enough to take the pole—or so everyone thought. As Mark was doing the "pole-winner" interview, Peter Revson made his qualifying run in one of the Team McLaren cars and did a completely unexpected 178.690 mph, stealing the pole honors from Donohue and the stunned Penske team. Mark Donohue was devastated; but realistically, he knew he still had the upper hand.

In the race two weeks later, Donohue jumped into the lead at the start, and easily pulled away from the field in the early stages. Just as it looked earlier in the month that the pole was a sure thing, it now appeared that the Penske Sunoco McLaren was going to run away with the 1971 Indianapolis 500. But fate would intervene again. On lap 66, with a one-mile lead on the field, the McLaren's gearbox came apart in the third turn and Donohue coasted to a stop on the infield grass in turn 4. It was a very frustrating end to the awesomely dominating month-long performance.

Roger Penske had also entered the year-old Lola-Ford in this race with Englishman David Hobbs, who had been co-driving Penske's Ferrari in World Endurance races, at the wheel. Hobbs was a 31-year-old rookie driving in his first oval track race. Like most Europeans, his background was all road racing, making him a curious choice for this one-time driving assignment. But Hobbs qualified respectably at 169.570 mph to take the 16th

Mark Donohue gave Penske Racing its first Indy Car win with a dominating performance in the inaugural Pocono 500. After qualifying on the pole, Donohue led 126 of 200 laps, driving the McLaren that had been totaled a month earlier in a freak accident at Indianapolis.

Donohue lost the pole to Bobby Unser at Michigan, but in the race the Penske McLaren was untouchable, leading 75 of 100 laps to score a second-consecutive victory for the Penske Racing team.

starting spot on the grid and he was running a very good race until his luck ran out. Forty laps after Donohue's retirement, while running in 12th position, Hobbs' gearbox also failed; but unfortunately, as he slowed suddenly, he was hit hard from behind by another car. Luckily, Hobbs was not injured in the incident, but the Lola was a write-off. So now, both of the Penske team cars were out of the race, and Roger Penske's problems were not over yet. Coming out of turn 4 on lap 159, driver Mike Mosely lost control of his Eagle, hit the outside wall hard, and then careened across the track squarely into Donohue's disabled McLaren, exploding both cars into flames. In a very short period of time, Penske lost not only the biggest race in the world—which everyone had all but conceded to him before the start—but he also lost both of his painfully expensive racecars and a once-in-a-lifetime unfair advantage. Without a doubt, it was a long trip back to Pennsylvania after that Memorial Day weekend.

When Mark Donohue lost the Indy pole to Peter Revson's Team McLaren, he was doubly upset because he knew that Revson's sudden burst of speed came as a result of setup information that he had reluctantly shared with the McLaren team at Roger Penske's insistence. Penske recognized the value of fostering a long-term relationship with Team McLaren, and this included some reciprocal sharing of data for the mutual benefit of both teams. The wisdom of that arrangement became apparent when Penske and Donohue needed McLaren's help to rebuild their destroyed racecar in time for the inaugural Pocono 500, which was scheduled just five weeks after the Indy demolition derby.

The Pocono race was a big deal for the Penske team because it was so close to Sunoco's headquarters in Philadelphia, and Sun went all-out promoting this inaugural event at the brand new 2.5-mile tri-oval racing facility in the Pocono mountain resort. Penske obviously wanted to make a good showing here for his sponsor. Donohue claimed the pole with a speed of 172.393 mph in the rebuilt McLaren and dominated the 500-mile rac, leading 126 of 200 laps. The only apparent challenge came nine laps from the finish when Joe Leonard, the eventual USAC national champion in 1971, snuck past the Penske McLaren in traffic. Donohue followed Leonard for three laps, patiently waiting for the right opportunity, and then decisively reclaimed the lead for good six laps from the end to take the victory. It was a gratifying and hard-earned first Indy-car triumph for the Penske team. Nobody could have realized at that time that this victory was the beginning of an incomparable racing dynasty that continues strong more than 35 years later.

After Pocono, the reinvigorated Penske team went to the next USAC race at the high-banked two-mile Michigan speedway. Although they failed to win the pole this time, Donohue again demonstrated the Penske McLaren's superiority in the race as he ran away for what appeared to be an effortless second straight victory. At that point, it was beginning to look like everyone not driving a blue and yellow McLaren was going to be fighting for second place for the remainder of the 1971 USAC championship season.

But as it turned out, various gremlins conspired to keep the Penske-Donohue super-car out of victory lane for the final three races. At Ontario, Donohue made a rare driving error and backed the car hard into the concrete during a practice session several days before the race. Fortunately, he wasn't seriously hurt, but the car ended up in multiple twisted pieces. The team did a tremendous job putting everything back together in time for the race, and Mark went out and shattered the qualifying record with a one-lap speed over 186 mph. Then there was an uncharacteristic pit communication error that resulted in Donohue running out of fuel while leading in the race. He ultimately dropped out with a burnt valve, presumably caused by running the motor lean when it ran out of fuel earlier.

After Ontario, Trenton was a disappointment again, this time with fuel injector problems preventing the car from performing up to par. And then, in the season finale at Phoenix, Donohue dropped out with overheating troubles. Interestingly, Donohue later acknowledged in his book that he never really mastered the skill of outside passing, a technique that is peculiar to short-track oval racing. This was an area where the drivers with dirt-track backgrounds excelled over those, like Donohue, who came up through the road racing ranks. It is unfortunate that Mark Donohue wasn't around in the 1980s when Indy-car racing, then running under CART sanctioning, became predominantly a road-rac-

Roger Penske hired Gary Bettenhausen to team with Mark Donohue in 1972. Bettenhausen was a second-generation Indy Car driver with four Indy 500 starts on his resume. His oval track background was a logical compliment to Donohue's road racing talents.

ing series. Donohue's combined driving and development talents would have been an overwhelming advantage.

1972

Going into 1972, the Penske team had a couple of major new projects in the works in addition to their USAC Indy-Car program. After a two-year absence, Penske Racing was back in the Can-Am series, campaigning a factory-backed turbo-charged Porsche 917, an endeavor that demanded a monumental amount of development effort by Mark Donohue. Also new for the team this year was a NASCAR program built around the ill-suited American Motors Matador, which would prove to be another substantial drain on the team's finite resources.

Mark Donohue qualified his Penske Racing McLaren on the front row at Indy in 1972. Bobby Unser's Eagle won the pole and Peter Revson's Team McLaren took the second starting spot. This was a particularly notable accomplishment considering that Donohue had blown a total of seven Offenhauser engines in the two weeks prior to qualifications. *Only Classics*

For the 1972 Indy-car season, Roger Penske bought two new McLaren M16Bs for Donohue and new team-mate Gary Bettenhausen, determined to make a full assault on both the Indy 500 and the USAC national championship. Bettenhausen, the son of Indy legend Tony Bettenhausen, was a likeable and popular veteran of four Indy 500s. Unlike Donohue, he had an oval-racing background, with a lot of dirt track sprint-car experience before his Indy career. With Bettenhausen, Penske got the short-track oval skills and knowledge that Donohue lacked.

The M16B McLaren was an evolution of the 1971 M16, the biggest change being a higher and even larger rear wing, which resulted in another significant jump in speed. Unfortunately, the McLarens were not the only cars in 1972 that were taking advantage of this newly discovered aerodynamic magic. Dan Gurney's completely redesigned Eagle chassis would prove to be a formidable challenger. Penske entered both of his new cars in the Phoenix and Trenton spring races with mixed results. Donohue and Bettenhausen qualified 7th

Roger Penske went to Indianapolis in 1969 with a three-year plan to win the "500." It actually took four attempts, but Mark Donohue delivered on that plan in 1972 with an unlikely victory. After struggling all month to find speed and engine reliability, Donohue came through with Penske Racing's first Indy 500 title.

and 8th respectively at Phoenix, and Mark led 24 laps before loosing a wheel and retiring at the halfway point. Bettenhausen went on to finish a respectable 4th in his Penske Racing debut. At Trenton, Donohue's traditional bad luck continued, with a broken turbocharger taking him out of competition only 10 laps into the race, but Bettenhausen upheld the team honor leading a race-high 85 laps and going on to take the victory in only his second outing with Penske Racing.

At Indy, it quickly became apparent that the Gurney Eagle was going to be the chassis to beat in 1972. Donohue struggled all month, burning up a total of seven engines before qualifying day, his dominating advantage of the previous year just a haunting memory now. On pole day, which had thankfully been delayed because of weather, armed with a new Offy engine that Roger Penske bought from a competitor just a day earlier for $35,000, Donohue managed a very respectable 191.4 mph run to qualify on the outside of the first row. Gary Bettenhausen, who'd had a relatively uneventful month by comparison, qualified a solid fifth. But the real story this May was Bobby Unser in the Dan Gurney Eagle, who qualified on the pole at 195.9 mph, an advantage comparable to that which Donohue had enjoyed the year before.

Only Classics

Because of all the engine problems Donohue experienced in pre-qualifying practice, he elected to race with a smaller turbocharger than most of his competition, including teammate Bettenhausen. The smaller blower put Donohue at a 50-hp disadvantage on the long Indy straightaways. As the race unfolded, that looked like a really a bad decision, as Bettenhausen, Bobby Unser, Mike Mosley and Peter Revson just ran away from the underpowered #66 Penske McLaren in the early going. But then an interesting thing happened. Just as Donohue's incredible advantage had slipped away the year before, one by one, all of the faster cars began to experience problems. First Revson dropped out with a bad gearbox. Then Bobby Unser's dominant Eagle was sidelined by a simple distributor rotor failure. Not long after that, Mike Mosely lost a wheel and ended his race with a hard impact into the turn 4 wall for the second time in as many years. That left Gary Bettenhausen in the #7 Sunoco Penske McLaren with a comfortable lead over Jerry Grant in the second Gurney Eagle team car. At that point, Donohue was running a safe, but seemingly uncompetitive third.

Bettenhausen led a race-high total of 138 laps and it was looking like Roger Penske had his first Indy 500 title in hand with his new driver. But then on lap 173, with Bettenhausen holding a comfortable 7-second advantage over Jerry Grant, the yellow flag came out because of debris on the track, and the field slowed to 80 mph behind the pace car. During the caution period, Bettenhausen's McLaren developed an ignition problem, possibly as simple as fouled spark plugs caused by running at the reduced speed. When the green flag flew on lap 177, Grant blew past Bettenhausen's sick McLaren to take the lead. Suddenly it appeared that the Captain was going to come up just short again after yet another dominating performance at Indy.

Bettenhausen's departure moved Donohue up to second place, but at that juncture, it seemed unlikely that he would be able to challenge for the lead. Donohue later recalled Penske coming on the radio and screaming, "you gotta catch Jerry," which seemed like a pretty unreasonable request under the circumstances. But Donohue later said that for the first time all month, he suddenly felt really enthused. He started driving more aggressive lines and taking bigger chances getting around slower traffic. In the process, he not only caught up to Grant's Eagle, but he recorded the fastest lap of the race, a dramatic and unexpected turn of events! It looked as if the race was headed for an exciting finish as Donohue began to challenge Grant for the lead. But as it played out, Grant's purple "Mystery Eagle" had to make an unplanned pitstop for a tire problem and suddenly, just 12 laps from the finish, Donohue found himself in the lead by a whole lap. It was an unbelievable development. After struggling desperately for the entire month of May, Mark Donohue cruised to an easy victory, setting a record for the fastest 500 miles ever run, and an Indy race record that stood for 12 years. Roger Penske got his first Indianapolis 500 win after all.

The Indy-car community was surprisingly enthusiastic about the Donohue's victory. Even after four years at the speedway, the college boys of Penske Racing were still viewed by the hardcore Indy fraternity as outsiders. Yet the consensus among fans and the auto racing press was that this was a hard-earned and well-deserved victory. Some of this sentiment may have been rooted in leftover sympathy for the disheartening loss a year earlier. Also apparent was a unique empathy for this very atypical racecar driver that they called 'Captain Nice.' "Fate tends to be unkind to racing drivers more often that not, and sometimes it kills them," wrote Robert Jones in his *Sports Illustrated* account of the 1972 race, "but Donohue's victory somehow rekindled a feeling that is rapidly eroding in this strange century, a feeling that perhaps the deserving can indeed be rewarded."

"Gee," said one Donohue fan after the race, "Charlie Brown finally won a ball game." Donohue was characteristically modest about the achievement. "The guys on the crew worked the hardest," he said, "they deserve this. I'm just the guy who pushes the pedal and turns the wheel." Of course, nobody really believed that.

When Mark Donohue published his autobiography in 1975, some fans expressed disappointment that it focused too much on the technical aspects of his driving career and didn't offer enough insight into the personal side of this unique individual. In describing his feelings after winning the 1972 "500," Mark offered a rare glimpse at the personal side of Captain Nice, writing: "...by far the most memorable part of winning was taking the victory lap in the Oldsmobile convertible pace car. A long time had passed since the finish of the race, and the stands were still packed with screaming, cheering spectators. They all looked so happy, like they really meant it. It's impossible to describe the feeling I was having. Roger and Karl were there in the car with me. We had started out together back in 1966, never anticipating that six years later the three of us would still be together as winners at Indianapolis."

As Paul Newman said in the movie, *Winning:* "After Indy, everybody goes to Milwaukee." The 'Milwaukee Mile' at the Wisconsin State Fairgrounds is one of the oldest and most tradition-rich racetracks in the country, and was customarily the first Indy-car event following the "500." Donohue and Bettenhausen qualified 4th and 5th and they both ran strong races, finishing second and third respectively to Bobby Unser's Eagle. Although inevitably a letdown after the big Indy win, this result left the two Penske team drivers well positioned in the

Gary Bettenhausen won two races in three years driving for Penske, but he is probably best remembered for dropping out of the 1972 Indy 500 after dominating for most of the day. Gary's career with Penske Racing ended after a serious sprint car accident in 1974 sidelined him for the season and left his arm permanently incapacitated.

Mark Donohue qualified his Eagle-Offy on the outside of Row 1 for the 1973 Indy 500, the lone bright spot for the Eagle program. It was during the long month of May, as Donohue struggled to sort out the new chassis, that he began to seriously contemplate retirement. The car failed to finish a single race all season.

early stages of the 1972 USAC national driving championship.

Then, in mid-July, a near-tragic twist of fate derailed Penske's promising championship run. In a violent testing accident with the Porsche Can-Am car at Road Atlanta, Donohue was fortunate to escape with his life, but sustained a serious knee injury that would require surgery and more than 3 months of rehabilitation. That left Gary Bettenhausen alone to carry the Penske colors for most of the remainder of the 1972 USAC season.

At Michigan in mid-July, Bettenhausen qualified his Sunoco McLaren 3rd and appeared ready for a strong race. On only the third lap, however, Gary's younger brother Merle, driving in his very first Indy-car race, was involved in a serious two-car accident. Trying to climb out of his burning racecar while it was still moving, young Bettenhausen's arm got caught between the car and the guardrail and was severed above the elbow. Shaken and obviously concerned about his brother, Gary Bettenhausen withdrew from the race after only 6 laps and finished 24th. Merle survived the accident and

did recover, although his arm could not be saved.

Next on the 1972 schedule was the Pocono 500, the race Donohue had won a year earlier. Bettenhausen qualified a solid 5th and led 40 laps of the 200-lap event before retiring with ignition problems near the midway point of the race. There was no celebration for the Pennsylvania hometeam this year.

The rest of the 1972 Indy-car season became a game of musical chairs for the Penske team. Inexplicably, despite now being the number-1 driver for arguably the premiere U.S. racing team of the day, Bettenhausen could never kick his addiction to dirt-track racing. While Donohue was still out recovering from his knee injury, Bettenhausen was hurt in a sprint car accident and was sidelined for the remainder of the season. For a team that had managed to avoid serious driver injuries through its first six years, 1972 was turning out to be a sobering reminder of the serious nature of the auto racing business.

For the August 13th Milwaukee 200, Penske worked out a one-race arrangement to borrow Gordon Johncock from Team McLaren and put him into Bettenhausen's #7 Sunoco Penske McLaren. Johncock qualified 7th, but lasted only 10 laps before retiring with transmission problems. For the next race, the Ontario 500, Penske signed Mike Hiss, a 30-year old California native who had earned 'Rookie-of-the-Year' honors at Indy earlier in the season. Hiss qualified a mediocre 20th, but drove a smart and consistent race to finish in second place behind veteran Roger McCluskey. Penske would remember Hiss' performance a couple years later when he needed a substitute driver again.

Mark Donohue returned to the Sunoco McLaren cockpit for the fall Trenton race, a full month earlier than the original rehabilitation schedule projected. With his injured leg still too weak to support itself against the high cornering g-forces, Mark struggled through qualifying and the early part of the race. Eventually, he found a way to wedge his left foot behind the clutch pedal to keep it out of the way, and he made an inspired late-race charge to lead 15 laps and eventually finish second to pole-sitter Bobby Unser. Ironically, this was Donohue's best-ever finish at Trenton.

Bobby Allison would enjoy moderate success a couple years later with the Penske AMC Matador program, but his first experience with the team came in 1973 when Roger Penske tapped him to drive a third car in the Indianapolis 500. Bobby would drive in a handful of Indy car races for the team over the next few years with little success.

Greenfield Gallery

In the final USAC race of the once-so-promising 1972 season, Donohue claimed his first and only short-track pole position, which was a very gratifying personal accomplishment and a much-needed morale boost for the team. In the race, he was running a strong third when the Offy's turbocharger blew. Mark lamented, "an anticlimactic end to our great Indianapolis-winning combination."

1973

For 1973, Penske Racing had a lot of irons in the fire. They were defending a Can-Am championship with a significantly updated Porsche 917 that needed considerably more development effort than originally anticipated; they were running a frustrating NASCAR campaign with the underpowered and aerodynamically-inferior AMC Matador; there was a new AMC

Lola program for the SCCA Formula-5000 series; and finally, there was that Indianapolis 500 title to defend. For a modern-day racing fan who has hasn't followed the sport for long, it must be inconceivable to think that all of these programs were run out of the same race shop, with the same personnel and, most amazingly, the same driver. In its early years, Penske Racing was legendary for it's versatility, but this may have been the season they just tried to do too much.

Roger Penske made the executive decision to limit Donohue's USAC driving schedule in 1973 to only the three 500-mile races on the big speedways, relying on a recuperated Gary Bettenhausen to carry the team colors for the full Indy-car championship schedule. The team was again planning to run new McLarens, but after disappointing results in March tire testing at Indy, Donohue convinced Penske to hedge their bet by purchasing a Dan Gurney "customer" Eagle to run as a third entry in the Indy 500. Donohue took the new Eagle and Penske signed NASCAR star Bobby Allison to pilot the extra McLaren for the Indy race only.

The season got off to a good start, with Bettenhausen qualifying second on the grid at the high-banked, very fast two-mile oval at College Station, Texas, then leading a couple laps in the race, and finishing second behind Al Unser. The next event was at Trenton, where USAC ran a "twin-150" format that year. Bettenhausen qualified 9th and finished 6th in the first heat, but dropped out before the halfway mark of the second race with engine problems.

May proved to be another interesting experience for the team at Indy. Donohue struggled all month trying to sort out the "superior" Eagle chassis, while Bettenhausen and Allison made steady progress preparing their more familiar McLarens. But once again, on pole day, Donohue posted his best time of the month just when it really counted. He claimed the outside front-row starting spot again with a 4-lap average speed of 197.412 mph. Bettenhausen qualified 5th at 195.6 mph and Allison 12th at 192.3. Johnny Rutherford won pole in the Team McLaren car at 198.4 mph with Bobby Unser in the middle front row at 198.2 in the Gurney Eagle.

The 1973 Indianapolis 500 was arguably the most tragic racing event in modern history. The carnage started when veteran driver Art Pollard was killed in a one-car practice accident on the first day of qualifying. On Memorial Day two weeks later, the weather was wet and there was a lengthy rain delay before the race finally got underway. Immediately at the start, there was a spectacular accident on the front straight as the field passed under the green flag. Over a dozen cars were involved. Rookie Salt Walther inexplicably veered sharply into the outside wall and flipped upside down, rupturing the fuel tank in his McLaren. His car then pin-wheeled down the front straightaway, spewing burning methanol fuel in all directions, including into the crowd. Thirteen spectators were burned, two critically. Walther was trapped for some time, still upside down in his flaming racecar, his legs protruding grotesquely from the front end of the battered tub as other drivers stopped and ran to his aid, trying in vain to upright the flaming wreckage before the track rescue crews arrived. Miraculously, Salt Walther did survive and, after many months of rehabilitation for severe burns and other injuries, he courageously returned to compete again.

Luckily, all three of the Penske cars were ahead of the melee and escaped unscathed. But by the time all the wreckage was cleared from the racetrack, the skies had opened up again, and the race was postponed until the next day. Still, the rain continued, resulting in a total washout on Tuesday. It was not until Wednesday, after even more weather delays, that the ill-fated event finally got started in the early afternoon.

As the race began, Bobby Allison's engine expired on only the second lap—exit one Penske Racing entry. Bobby Unser and Donohue passed Rutherford's McLaren and steadily pulled away from the field, setting up what looked to be a great fight between the two Eagles as Mark battled to defend his title. Then on lap 58, 4th place qualifier Swede Savage, driving in his second Indy 500, lost control of his STP Patrick Racing Eagle in the 4th turn. Rather than spinning backward into the outside wall, Savage tried to power his way out of the spin, causing his car to dart down the track almost head-on into the inside concrete wall. The impact exploded the fuel tank and ripped the car into two pieces, both of which rebounded back into the middle of the racetrack, blocking all traffic. The race was red-flagged while rescue crews struggled to extinguish the inferno and extricate a critically injured Savage from what was left of his shattered and charred racecar. During the rescue effort, a member of Savage's STP crew was hit by an emergency vehicle that was racing through pit lane toward the accident scene. The crewman was thrown through the air and killed instantly. Swede Savage, 27 years old, survived for 32 days before succumbing to his injuries.

After the race was finally restarted, Donohue and Bettenhausen ran with the leaders until lap 92, when Donohue's Offenhauser engine expired, ending his day and his title defense. Gary Bettenhausen ended up 5th, the only one of Penske's three entries to finish what turned out to be a rain-shorted race that was eventually won by a tired and somber Gordon Johncock.

For the Penske team and the entire auto racing community, May of 1973 was a month to forget. When it was all said and done, there were three people dead and three critically injured, in addition to a handful of hospitalized spectators with lesser injuries resulting from the first aborted start. Responding to public outcries, some demanding a complete ban of auto racing in the United States, the Indianapolis Motor Speedway and the

USAC sanctioning organization implemented a number of drastic safety improvements aimed at significantly reducing risks to the drivers, crews, and spectators. The results were commendable. In the 33 years since that fateful race, there have been three drivers and one spectator killed in racing or testing accidents at Indianapolis Motor Speedway. Although it may seem somewhat callous to characterize "only four deaths" as a success story, in contrast to the 63 drivers and other participants that had perished in the speedway's prior 62 years, the statistical improvement is undeniably profound.

By its very nature, there will always be some element of danger involved in auto racing. Although the expectation is that every reasonable effort will be made to continually enhance the safety of the sport, the participants recognize and accept the inherent risks of their chosen profession. For them, maybe selfishly, the potential rewards simply outweigh those risks. Often, it's hard for people outside the sport to understand that, especially when tragedy does occur. But, examining the way racing families have responded to their personal tragedies in the past sheds some light on a drivers' rationale. Over the years, the Unsers, Bettenhausens, Pettys, Earnhardts and others have lost brothers, sons, husbands and fathers to racing accidents, and yet they continue in the sport. The common sentiment expressed by families in the wake of these tragedies is this: "We are comforted in knowing that he was doing what he loved to do." Several years ago, there was a young driver attempting to raise sponsorship money for an Indy 500 entry. Unable to attract funding from major corporations, he sold spaces on his racecar where individuals could have their names displayed. He received a check with a note that said: "I know my son Peter would have appreciated this." It came from the mother of 1972 Indy pole-sitter Peter Revson, years after her son was killed in a Formula-One racing accident.

The remainder of the 1973 USAC season was unremarkable for Penske Racing. Mark Donohue ran the ill-tempered Eagle in only two more events, the Pocono 500 and the Ontario 500. At Pocono, he struggled just to get the car into the field, qualifying a very disappointing 23rd. In the race, he was more competitive and even moved to the lead at one point, but then the engine quit again. Ontario was an even more discouraging experience, with a poor qualifying effort and an uncompetitive showing in the race before yet another engine failure ended his day prematurely.

Bettenhausen's season was just marginally better. At Milwaukee, he qualified and finished third, keeping him in contention for the championship. But then at Pocono, he started 11th and crashed in the third turn on lap 37, finishing a dismal 27th. Next up was the Michigan 200 in mid-July, which turned out to be another altogether forgettable weekend. Bettenhausen started 16th on a grid of 26 cars and lasted only 35 laps before parking his stalled McLaren on the backstretch. The August Milwaukee race ended much the same way. After qualifying 7th and moving to the lead in the early stages, the Sunoco McLaren was sidelined by a loss of oil pressure.

After three straight DNF's, the 1973 Indy car season was becoming a demoralizing struggle for the Penske team. Things looked a little brighter when Gary Bettenhausen qualified third and finished second in the 100-mile qualifying race a week ahead of the Ontario 500. But in the main event, he lasted less than half the race before the McLaren's Offenhauser engine quit again, leaving him with a 19th place finish. Coupled with Donohue's 29th place result, it was another disheartening weekend for the team, with two more DNFs in the record book.

Next on the schedule was a second stop at Michigan International Speedway for the mid-September twin 125-mile events. In the first heat, Bettenhausen led a race-high 25 laps and finished second to Billy Vukovich, his best showing in some time. In the second heat, however, he had a less-impressive 8th place result. A week later, back in Trenton for the fall event, he suffered yet another DNF, crashing on lap 27.

Sometimes it will seem that a driver has an unexplainable combination of luck and skill on a particular racetrack. For Gary Bettenhausen, in the otherwise undistinguished 1973 season, that track was College Station, Texas. Earlier in the year, he had driven to a strong second place finish there. In the fall event, he

Mark Donohue, standing behind the frustrating Eagle-Offy at Pocono in 1973, had a very difficult Indy car season. Mark had convinced Roger Penske to buy the Eagle chassis, believing that it was superior to the McLaren. But he never quite managed to get it set up correctly and did not finish a single race in the car. *Galen Hummel*

charged from his 14th starting position to record the Penske team's only 1973 USAC victory. Although far too late to salvage the season, it was nonetheless a sorely needed morale boost for the team, and possibly a last-minute career-saver for the beleaguered Gary B.

The USAC season ended back in Phoenix with the traditional fall 150-miler. Coming off his Texas win, Bettenhausen qualified the Sunoco Penske McLaren 4th on the grid and ran a competitive race before spinning 30 laps from the end, concluding the disappointing 1973 campaign with a 6th place finish.

By the end of the 1973 season, team leader Mark Donohue was feeling overwhelmed and frustrated by the disappointing results in Indy-cars, an unsuccessful F5000 program and the exasperating NASCAR effort. Roger Penske was asking him to do too many things, and the understandable result was that he wasn't doing any of them particularly well, at least not by the typical high Penske-Donohue standards. The only highlight of the season was a superb Can-Am Porsche program, but that couldn't compensate for Donohue's grow-

ing frustration with the overall situation. During the long month of May, while struggling to sort out the uncooperative new Eagle at Indy, Mark first began to contemplate the possibility of retirement. As the difficult year wore on, this idea became more and more enticing, until in the end, it seemed like the only logical choice. And so, at the conclusion of the 1973 season, Mark Donohue announced his retirement from driving. He was immediately appointed to the position that he had held unofficially for the previous seven years, "President" of Penske Racing.

1974

For 1974, Penske Racing entered into uncharted territory, for the first time operating without the benefit of engineer/driver Mark Donohue in the cockpit. In theory, Donohue would be able to function even more effectively as team manager and engineer from the sidelines, unencumbered by the demands of being on the front line as a driver. The reality proved to be something altogether different.

Penske Racing's overall program was scaled back somewhat this year, including "only" the NASCAR Matador effort in addition to the continuing USAC Indy-car campaign. Early in the season, they would also begin development of a Penske-built Formula-1 car. Gary Bettenhausen was retained as the team's primary Indy-car driver for the full 1974 USAC campaign. At the end of the '73 season, Roger Penske announced that he had hired Peter Revson to pilot a second entry for the Indy 500; but that plan never materialized as Revson was killed in South Africa while practicing for a Formula-1 race in March of 1974. Penske then turned to 1972 Indy 'Rookie-of-the-Year' Mike Hiss to fill his second seat. Hiss, a 32-year-old California native, had subbed for the injured Gary Bettenhausen in the Ontario 500 at the end of the 1972 season, giving the Penske team a solid second place finish. Since then, he had been handicapped driving for under-funded teams with second-class equipment, but Roger Penske apparently thought that he saw potential in this third-year driver.

Penske Racing abandoned the unsuccessful Eagle experiment and returned in 1974 with a new pair of

McLaren Offys. After the 1973 oil crisis, long-time sponsor Sunoco scaled back its support for the new season, in part because of the unfavorable image of an oil company encouraging the "wasteful" use of fuel during a national energy crisis. It didn't matter that the Indy-cars ran on methanol, a non-petroleum-based alcohol; it just wasn't politically correct. Sunoco did sponsor Bettenhausen's car for the '74 season, showcasing a new oil product called "Score," which was later renamed 'CAM2.' For the second car, Penske arranged a limited sponsorship package with Norton Industries, a worldwide manufacturer of abrasive products, ceramics, sealants, and industrial safety equipment. The "Norton Spirit" would go on to be a familiar Penske Racing entry into the 1980s.

The 1974 USAC season began in Ontario, California, with a pair of 100-mile qualifying heats followed a week later by the 500-mile race. Bettenhausen started second in his qualifying race and led 6 laps before dropping out with a loose wing flap and finishing 11th. In the main event, he had a disappointing 20th place finish. Next, in the spring Phoenix race, he qualified 8th and dropped out at the halfway mark, finishing 14th. Things continued to deteriorate at Trenton, where he crashed in practice and did not even qualify for the race. This string of problems did not bode well for the Indianapolis 500, which was the next event on the schedule.

Indy marked the first appearance of Mike Hiss in the Norton Spirit. Hiss promptly upstaged his senior teammate with a 3rd place front-row qualifying run of 187.490 mph, while Bettenhausen was only able to manage 11th place on the grid with a speed of 184.492 mph. The pole went to three-time '500' winner A.J. Foyt at 191.832 mph, nearly 7 mph below Johnny Rutherford's 1973 record, the result of safety improvements implemented after the previous year's accident-filled spectacle.

For the second year in a row, Penske Racing suffered a second-lap retirement in the race, as Bettenhausen's Offenhauser engine expired with a broken valve. Hiss' day was only marginally less disappointing, as two lengthy pit stops to diagnose and correct an electrical problem left the Norton Spirit many laps behind the leaders. Although still running at the end of the race, Hiss finished in 14th place, 42 laps short of winner Johnny Rutherford.

Two weeks later in Milwaukee, Bettenhausen qualified the Penske McLaren fifth on the grid and finished second, even with a late-race spin. This was the Penske team's first, and as it would turn out only, respectable result for the 1974 USAC season. In the next event, the Pocono 500, Bettenhausen qualified 11th and retired after only 9 laps with a broken piston. That, unexpectedly, proved to be his last race for the Penske team. Shortly afterward, while driving a dirt-track race in Syracuse, New York, Bettenhausen crashed and sustained serious permanent nerve damage to his left arm, putting him out for the rest of the season. Although he would continue to race for many years with his incapacitated arm literally taped to the steering wheel, Roger Penske had apparently had enough of Bettenhausen's penchant for getting himself injured driving in these "unnecessary" dirt-track races, and his contract with Penske Racing was not renewed.

Penske turned to Mike Hiss to take over driving duties for the next race, the July Michigan 200. He needed to have an entry in this race because he now owned the Michigan racetrack, an acquisition he'd made a year earlier. The track, which previously struggled to sell its 26,000 seats, had run into financial difficulties and Penske shrewdly bought it for the bargain price of $2.5M in bankruptcy court. The Penske Corporation quickly turned Michigan into a beautiful, clean, first-class racing facility, with 106,000 steeply banked stadium seats that provided outstanding viewing for the spectators and served as a model for modern-day super-speedway designs. Penske maintained ownership of the track until he sold it in 1998, along with his Nazareth and California facilities, for the tidy sum of $610M.

Hiss qualified at Michigan well down in 17th position, but drove a steady and uneventful race to finish 7th. By this time, however, Roger Penske seemed to be losing interest in this very disappointing season, skipping the August Milwaukee event altogether to focus his attention on a single-race encore performance with the Can Am Porsche at Mid-Ohio. Penske Racing returned

Needing a replacement for the injured Gary Bettenhausen, Roger Penske hired a young charger named Tom Sneva. Tom was an ex-schoolteacher raised on the dirt tracks in the Pacific northwest. In a four-year career with Penske Racing, he would win three races, the team's first two Indy 500 poles and its first two Indy car championships.

with Mike Hiss in the cockpit of the Norton Spirit for the September Michigan 250. Hiss logged another mediocre qualifying run followed by a steady, but uninspired 4th place finish. That was apparently enough for Penske to conclude that it wasn't worth wasting any more time or money on the USAC circuit for 1974. With his much-anticipated Formula-1 effort now getting underway, the Captain chose to skip the remaining two events on the Indy car calendar and regroup for the 1975 season. It was by far Penske Racing's worst showing in its 10-year history.

1975

Penske Racing returned in 1975 with a clean slate and a renewed commitment to the USAC Indy Car championship. Gary Bettenhausen was replaced by Tom Sneva, another driver with a dirt-track background. Sneva came from a racing family in Spokane, Washington. His father raced sprint cars. His older brother was killed driving one and his younger brother, Jerry, would go on to race Indy cars alongside Tom a couple years down the road. Tom Sneva was a former teacher and high school principal who had driven his

In his Penske Racing Indy 500 debut, Tom Sneva qualified his Norton Spirit McLaren in fourth place and was running a strong race until he was involved in a frightening accident. He came back and won the first Indy car race of his career at Michigan Speedway later that summer. *Bill Daniels*

Bobby Allison drove the second Penske entry at Indy and three other races in 1975. Long-time sponsor Sunoco had scaled back its support after the 1973 oil crisis, choosing to promote its new CAM2 oil product rather than Sunoco gasoline. *Bill Daniels*

first USAC race at Trenton, New Jersey, in 1971. He ran the entire 1974 season for the second-tier Grant King Racing team, more often than not finishing better than the Penske drivers. Sneva's consistency and his ability to get results out of second-class equipment impressed Penske enough to make this relative newcomer his number-one driver. Despite the dismal outcome of the 1974 season, Roger Penske managed to secure a full-year sponsorship package with Norton Industries for Sneva's McLaren.

After a year's absence, Penske brought NASCAR driver Bobby Allison back to pilot a second McLaren for Indianapolis and three of the other bigger races. Allison never really enjoyed driving the open-wheel Indy cars, which he considered much more dangerous than the 3500-lb enclosed stockers he normally raced. Future Penske NASCAR star Rusty Wallace once echoed the sentiments of many stock car drivers regarding open wheel racing when he was quoted saying: "I wouldn't get out of an electric chair to climb into one of those things!" But when the Captain called, Allison answered. The second Penske entry was sponsored by Sunoco's CAM-2 motor oil.

The season opened again in Ontario, California, with twin 100-mile qualifying races followed a week later by the Ontario 500. In the first heat race, Tom Sneva qualified the Norton Spirit 3rd but lost several laps with a faulty fuel vent cap, ultimately finishing in 9th position. In the second 100-mile heat, Bobby Allison qualified the CAM-2 Penske McLaren 8th and cruised to an uneventful 6th place finish, his best-ever Indy-car finish. In the 500-mile race, Allison experienced another one of those all-too-familiar second-lap retirements, this one the result of a broken valve. Sneva ran a strong and steady race, moving up from his 14th position on the starting grid to a respectable sixth-place finish.

Next on the schedule was the 150-mile spring event at Phoenix, where Tom Sneva qualified a promising 4th and finished 7th after recovering from a spin two-thirds of the way through the race. Following that, it was the Trenton 200, where Sneva found himself starting on the pole by the luck of the draw, as high winds had prevented qualifying runs the previous day. The new Penske driver managed to hold the lead through the first 20 laps, but later faded to another 6th place finish.

Going into the Indy 500, Roger Penske had more reason for optimism than he had a year earlier. Tom Sneva qualified 4th fastest behind pole-sitter A.J. Foyt, 1973 race winner Gordon Johncock and 1974 winner Johnny Rutherford. Allison was a little more conservative, putting Penske's CAM-2 entry 13th on the grid.

Bobby Allison had one of his better Indy car drives, actually being credited with leading the 24th lap during the first pit stop shuffle. But shortly after the halfway point, a gearbox failure took him out, leaving his Penske CAM-2 Special with a 25th place finish. Sneva pitted early for a tire problem and then fought his way back up to fifth position before being involved in a spectacular crash, one that most witnesses agreed should not have been survivable. While attempting to pass the lapped car of Canadian rookie Eldon Rasmussen on lap 121, Sneva's right rear tire touched Rasmussen's left front, catapulting the Norton Spirit into the air and over Rasmussen's racecar. Upside down and backwards, Sneva's McLaren slammed into the turn-2 concrete wall. The car disintegrated, shearing the engine and rear suspension from the driver's cockpit. Having just pitted for fuel, Sneva was carrying nearly 40 gallons of highly flammable methanol. Although there was a frightening flash fire as the fuel and oil lines were severed, the fuel cell's rubber bladder, a safety improvement mandated after the 1973 tragedies, remained intact. "Had the fuel cell ruptured," said Roger Penske afterwards, "the resulting fire could have been fatal." After the initial impact, the remains of the cockpit rebounded back onto the track and did two more somersaults before coming to a stop right side up. Track safety workers arrived on the scene quickly, dousing Sneva with fire extinguishers as he scrambled out of the flaming wreckage. All of this took place directly in front of the VIP luxury suites where Tom's wife was watching the race with many of the other drivers' families. Eldon Rasmussen, who had the front-row seat as this incident unfolded, was so shaken that he stopped and got out of his car the next time around to see if Sneva had survived. Bobby Unser, the eventual race winner, was directly behind the crash as it developed.

While he was passing the lapped car of Eldon Rasmussen midway through the race, wheels touched and Tom Sneva's car flipped into the air and rammed the concrete wall, erupting into flames. Tom was extremely fortunate to escape with relatively minor injuries.

"I didn't know who was driving the car that broke up," he said at the victory banquet the following day, "but I thought he was a goner. When I came around again and saw Tom walking away, I couldn't believe it."

Author Dan Gerber was taking pictures when the crash developed 40 feet away. "For an instant," Gerber wrote, "I'm certain I'm witnessing a man's death, and that it will also be my own. I turn…and see the reflection of the flames in the glass door, feel the heat sweep across my back. I turn back just in time to see the disembodied engine tumble by in a ball of flames. Debris fills the air like a flight of sand grouse. The Nikon takes over, zipping off exposures like a digital computer, one last somersault before the car comes to a rest, right side up and on fire. It really doesn't resemble a car anymore, just a tub of burning metal, not 30 feet away, a driver's helmet protruding from the flames. I'm certain Sneva is dead. It's the most brutal, spectacular and horrifying crash I've ever seen—and I've seen a dozen that were fatal. Then I see something that, for a moment, I'm certain is an illusion. Sneva moves."

Tom Sneva was extremely fortunate to escape with "only" second and third-degree burns and two broken vertebrae in his lower back. "There was never a question about wanting to drive again," he later recalled. "The question was, would I be able to drive on the ragged edge. Everybody draws the line between being in and out of control, but some do it with a crayon and others with a sharp pencil. I wasn't sure if I could find that fine line again. It was a difficult experience. At first, I treated the accelerator gingerly."

Sneva's injuries would keep him out of the Milwaukee USAC race the following week. With Allison committed to the NASCAR schedule, Penske Racing had to pass on Milwaukee altogether. Sneva was back in a new Norton Spirit for the Pocono 500 on June 29, just five weeks after his Indy crash. Allison was also entered at Pocono in the second Penske McLaren. That Tom Sneva was able to force himself into a racecar at all, so soon after his horrifying accident, was a tribute to the courage and determination of Roger Penske's young driver. He qualified the Norton Spirit 12th on the grid, one spot behind teammate Allison. In the race, which was won by A.J. Foyt, both Penske cars were relatively uncompetitive and suffered early mechanical problems, finishing in 27th and 29th positions.

Three weeks later, the USAC circuit was at Penske's high-banked 2-mile oval in Brooklyn, Michigan. Both Sneva and Allison were entered again for this 200-mile event. With three more weeks of recuperation under his belt, Sneva was looking a lot more racy than he had at Pocono. He qualified the Norton Spirit 6th on the grid, led 11 of the race's 100 laps, ultimately finishing a strong second to A.J. Foyt. Meanwhile, Bobby Allison started 15th in the CAM-2 Penske McLaren and dropped out after 37 laps with a blown engine. As it turned out, this would mark the conclusion of Allison's undistinguished Indy-car career. In six starts that spanned three seasons, he had finished only one race, the Ontario 100-mile qualifier earlier that year where he came home sixth. Bobby wasn't having any fun, and mechanical failures aside, he never was very competitive in the open-wheel cars. He continued to drive for Penske's NASCAR program through the end of the 1976 season—he and the boss apparently finally agreed that was where he belonged.

Next on the schedule after Michigan was the August Milwaukee 200. Penske Racing had just one car entered in this event. Tom Sneva only managed to qualify 8th fastest, but ran another strong and smart race to finish third. It was apparent to almost everyone at this point that Penske Racing and Tom Sneva were on the verge of becoming a strong force on the USAC circuit.

But everything changed after that day. Only hours before Sneva had driven to his third place Milwaukee finish, Mark Donohue, who had ended his brief retirement to drive for Penske Racing's new Formula-1 program, crashed while practicing for the Austrian Grand Prix. Although his injuries were not initially thought to be serious, hours after the accident he lapsed into a coma as a result of an undetected blood clot on the brain. The original prognosis after brain surgery was hopeful, but two days later, the guy everyone called 'Captain Nice' was gone forever. Penske Racing would go on, but it could never be the same.

It's hard to imagine the emotions of Roger Penske and the rest of the team at this time. They were still a relatively small, close-knit group of friends—many of them had been together through a 10-year-long fairytale full of unimaginable success stories. Had Roger Penske said he was through with racing for the rest of the season, or even that he was done with the sport forever, it wouldn't have been a big surprise to the auto rac-

Mario Andretti drove for Penske Racing on a part-time basis from 1976 through 1980, scoring two victories. When Roger Penske hired the 1969 Indy winner to partner with Tom Sneva, it was a clear indication of the Captain's commitment to return to the Indy's victory lane.

Bill Daniels

65

ing community. But he didn't do that. Probably because they knew what Mark Donohue would have wanted, Roger and the team continued. It was a fitting tribute, back at Penske's Brooklyn, Michigan, racetrack just four weeks later, as Tom Sneva charged through the field to his first-ever Indy-car victory. He started in 7th spot, a full 10 mph off the pace of pole-sitter A.J. Foyt who had qualified at 201.1 mph. "Sneva won the race because he charged when he had to charge and drove conservatively when caution and fuel preservation were mandatory," wrote Jim McQueen in his *AutoWeek* report. "For a guy who spent one frightful day in May on the top of his head, it was a pleasant Saturday drive to the top of the USAC world. For the Penske team, which had seen its fortunes hit rock bottom this year, it was…a much-needed win at a critical time." It was also the first win for sponsor Norton Industries and the first USAC race victory for the Penske team since Gary Bettenhausen took the checkered flag at Texas nearly two years earlier. Finally there was something to celebrate again!

At the New Jersey State Fairgrounds in Trenton a week later, Tom Sneva qualified 5th and ran strongly until blowing a tire and exiting halfway through the race. Then, in the season finale at Phoenix, a racetrack that he would go on to dominate later in his career, Sneva turned in another inspired performance, leading eight laps and ending up second to the driver who was winning almost everything that year, A.J. Foyt.

1976

For 1976, Roger Penske continued with McLaren equipment and Tom Sneva as his number-one USAC driver, sponsored again by Norton Industries. For the Indy and Pocono 500-mile races Penske Racing would enter a CAM-2 sponsored McLaren driven by one of the most experienced and respected drivers of the era, 1969 Indy-winner Mario Andretti. This was a dramatic departure from Penske's prior strategy of hiring young, up-and-coming drivers such at Bettenhausen, Hiss, and Sneva. And it was a clear signal that the Captain was determined to score another Indianapolis 500 win. In Sneva, he had a reliable and talented young charger who had already proven he could find his way to the win-

Mario Andretti was the fastest qualifier at Indy in 1976, but he posted his 189.404 mph speed on the second weekend of qualifying and had to start in the 7th row. Mario ran as high as 6th in the race before finishing in the 8th position. *Greenfield Gallery*

Tom Sneva, seen here in the bicentennial Norton Spirit at Indianapolis, went winless in 1976, prompting Roger Penske to replace him late in the season with Mario Andretti. Mario fared no better in the car for the final two races. *Bill Daniels*

ner's circle. With Andretti, he was paying for a wealth of experience and name recognition, resulting in the strongest lineup he'd fielded at Indy since 1973.

The Ontario race was moved back to its "traditional" Labor Day weekend date this year, and the season opened in mid-March with the 150-miler in Phoenix. In a race that made history as Arlene Hiss, Mike's estranged wife, became the first woman ever to start a USAC Indy-car event, Tom Sneva qualified 8th and dropped out at the halfway mark with a blown tire—an inauspicious beginning to the new season.

The next time out, at Trenton in early May, Sneva and the Penske team fared much better. After qualifying a solid 4th, Sneva led 9 laps en route to a third place finish behind Johnny Rutherford and Gordon Johncock. As it turned out, this would be the front row for the Indy 500 four weeks later. Rutherford would take the Indy pole with a 4-lap average of 188.957 mph, followed by Johncock at 188.531 and then Sneva in the Penske Racing Norton Spirit at 186.355 mph. Mario Andretti was in Belgium for a Formula-1 race on the first weekend of qualifying. When he made his run a week later in the Penske CAM2 Motor Oil Special, he posted a time of 189.404 mph, faster than Rutherford's pole speed; but because it was not recorded on the first day of qualifications, Andretti had to start back in the 7th row in 19th position. After the qualifying run, Andretti said: "This is the best championship car I've ever driven," a profound statement from the former winner.

In the race that was shortened to only 102 of the scheduled 200 laps because of rain, both Penske cars were fast, but suffered problems that cost them time early. Sneva lost a lap when a coil spring from Roger McCluskey's 8th lap crash cracked his windshield and dented his helmet. He fought back to a sixth place finish, but the shortened race distance prevented him from getting back up front to challenge the leaders. Still, it was much better than the disastrous ending a year earlier. Andretti charged from his 19th starting position to sixth place before mechanical problems slowed him to an 8th place finish. The race was won by pole-sitter Johnny Rutherford, followed by A.J. Foyt and Gordon Johncock. It was the first time in their 8-year Indy history that Penske Racing had finished the Indianapolis 500 with two cars in the top ten. Certainly, that didn't beat a win, but it was much better than recent results and very encouraging for the rest of the season.

Milwaukee was a letdown for the team, with Sneva qualifying 8th and running out of fuel to finish 13th. Next on the schedule was the Pocono 500, where Mario Andretti again paired up with Sneva for a two-car Penske Racing assault. Starting positions were determined by draw because of rain. Andretti drew the front-row, number three starting spot, while Sneva got stuck back in 13th. Mario led 45 of the 200 laps, second only to eventual race winner Al Unser, and went on to finish 5th in the CAM2 Special. Sneva had a less remarkable race, driving to a 7th place finish in the Norton Spirit.

Three weeks later, back at Penske's Brooklyn, Michigan, track where he had claimed his first career victory the previous year, Sneva turned in another solid, if unspectacular performance, qualifying 10th and finishing sixth in the 22-car field. Following that, there was a DNF at College Station, Texas, before another decent third place showing in the August Trenton 200 race. A week later, Sneva qualified third at Milwaukee, but his race ended after 127 of 200 laps with an engine failure.

Ontario dropped the twin-100 qualifier format this year and ran the 500-mile race on Labor Day weekend. Andretti had an F1 commitment, so Penske Racing entered only one car. Sneva put the Norton Spirit on the front row and moved to the lead for a couple of laps early in the race, but he ultimately dropped out with ignition problems and was credited with a 26th place finish. Two weeks later, back in Michigan, the team had another consistent, if unspectacular weekend, with Sneva qualifying 9th and finishing 5th.

Roger Penske was getting frustrated at this point, thinking that maybe his young driver was not getting the results that the equipment was capable of producing. After all, at Indianapolis, Mario Andretti had said that his car, which was identical to Sneva's, was the best championship car he'd ever driven. Now, with the season almost over, Penske still didn't have a single victory to show for it. With the championship already out of reach, the Captain decided to bench Sneva for the final

1977 was a breakthrough year for Tom Sneva and the Penske Racing Indy car program. With a new Cosworth engine replacing the aging Offenhauser, Sneva started the season in this McLaren and ended in a brand new Penske-built PC5. He won two races and two poles en route to claiming Penske Racing's first Indy car championship.

two races of the 1976 season and put Mario Andretti into the Norton Spirit to see if he could do any better. It was a demoralizing vote of "no-confidence" for Tom Sneva, but Penske evidently felt that he had to try something.

In the Texas 200 on October 31st, Andretti qualified the Penske McLaren 4th on the grid and finished in 4th spot, a lap behind the leaders. The following week, in the season finale at Phoenix, Andretti turned in a similar performance, starting and finishing third. The apparent lesson learned was that the Penske McLarens were good racecars, but not necessarily the very fastest ones on the track, regardless of who was behind the wheel.

1977

Roger Penske was apparently convinced after the late-season Andretti experiment that Tom Sneva was, in fact, getting the full potential out of his racecar. For the first time in it's Indy-Car history, Penske Racing returned with the same driver lineup for the second year in a row.

Once again, Sneva would be piloting the Norton Spirit for the full championship campaign and Mario Andretti would be in the CAM2 Special for Indy and other select races as his Formula-1 schedule permitted. Penske again fielded a pair of new McLarens, but this year, power was provided by the new 8-cylinder turbocharged Cosworth engine rather than the venerable Offenhauser that had been used by the team since 1971. The arrival of Cosworth Engineering in the USAC series marked the first true engine-related technology advancement in years.

For 1977, Penske Racing focused almost all its effort on the USAC Indy car series. After four years of floundering around in NASCAR with relatively little success, Roger Penske wisely decided, as he had in the early Can-Am days, to come back again later when he could do it right. Although the team opened the season intending to run a full NASCAR schedule, by mid-year the Captain sold the team and said goodbye to the stock car series. Also dropped from the 1977 program was the short-lived and tragic Formula-1 effort, even after it finally began to show promise late in the 1976 season.

Although this new focused approach would prove to be a good business plan, it was, at the time, a disappointment for longtime Penske Racing fans that had grown accustomed to the trademark versatility of this team. A half dozen years earlier, it was possible to compete for championships in two professional series and wins in a couple other series all at the same time. That kind of aggressive diversity no longer seemed feasible. Partly because of the higher standards of professionalism that the Penske team itself had brought to the table, and partly because of the loss of Mark Donohue's unique engineer-developer-driver contribution, it no longer seemed realistic for one team to excel in more than one major league racing series at a time. Even when Penske would return to NASCAR many years later, it would be done with a totally separate team, operating out of a different shop, with dedicated personnel, and of course, different drivers. In a sense, 1977 was the beginning of a new era for the Penske team.

The 1977 USAC season started in Ontario with a 200-mile event on March 6th. Sneva was quick right out of the box in the new Norton Spirit McLaren-Cosworth, qualifying second to Johnny Rutherford for this opening race. Unfortunately, the new motor burned a piston on the 64th of 80 laps, leaving the team with a disappointing 14th place finish. Three weeks later, it was a similar story at Phoenix, where Sneva started third behind Rutherford and Gordon Johncock and led a couple of laps before a broken oil cooler relegated him to a 16th place DNF. After two outings, it looked like the new Penske McLaren-Cosworth combination had the speed, but maybe not the reliability.

Things improved significantly a week later in College Station, Texas. Bad weather again dictated a lottery-style starting grid, with Sneva pulling the 8th spot. This time, the new Cosworth engine held together and performed flawlessly, carrying Tom Sneva and the Norton Spirit to an impressive and satisfying win over veterans Al Unser, Wally Dallenbach, and Johnny Rutherford.

For the Trenton 200 on April 30th, the last race before Indy, Penske entered cars for both Sneva and Mario Andretti. Once again, the Penske team cars showed their speed, qualifying second and third behind Johnny Rutherford, who had won every pole position of the season up to that point. Andretti jumped into the lead at the start and stayed there for the first 29 laps of the race. But eight laps later he was out with a blown engine. Sneva lasted longer, but ended his race in the same manner, keeping engine reliability high on Roger Penske's list of 'things-to-worry-about' going into the month of May.

This year's Indianapolis 500, even more than usual, was two races in one. The race for the pole, which in those days attracted a crowd of 250,000 spectators, was unusually significant this time. Four years earlier, in qualifying for the accident-filled 1973 race, Johnny Rutherford had run over 199 mph. Safety-related rule changes following the '73 event dropped top speeds by 10 mph. But technology and a repaved Indianapolis Motor Speedway track put the magic 200 mph mark within reach for 1977. In March tire testing, Gordon Johncock had reportedly run over 200 according to somebody's stopwatch. Then, on the Wednesday before qualifying, late in the afternoon when the track temperature began to cool, Mario Andretti took the CAM2

In 1977, Tom Sneva won Penske Racing's first Indy 500 pole, becoming the first driver to ever officially top the 200 mph barrier at the Speedway. Years later, Roger Penske commented on Sneva's driving: "[he] was a tremendous qualifier. Every time I saw him come off of Turn 4 I thought he would never get the thing turned. He drove it right on the edge." *Only Classics*

In pre-qualifying practice for the 1977 Indy 500, Mario Andretti drove Penske Racing's CAM2 McLaren to the first 200 mph lap ever recorded on the Speedway's timing and scoring system, though it was still considered "unofficial." On pole day, Andretti's qualifying run was a very disappointing 193.325 mph. *Greenfield Gallery*

Penske McLaren out for a final "practice" run and became the first driver ever to record a 200+ mph lap on the speedway's electronic timing system. Although still not "official," because only qualifying and race laps are recorded for official statistics, Penske Racing could now lay claim to being first team over the 200 mph speed barrier. The next day, A.J. Foyt would turn in his own 200+ mph performance, setting the stage for an exciting battle on pole day. Two drivers who were conspicuously absent from the 200 mph club were Johnny Rutherford, who had won all four poles of the young season, and Tom Sneva who was driving a Penske McLaren identical to Andretti's. Sneva was very close. He ran 199.9 mph on Friday afternoon, and looked like he had a 200+ going on the following lap before spinning and ending his day.

On Saturday, A. J. Foyt was the first to make a qualifying attempt. His 193.465 mph average was a huge disappointment to the large crowd gathered to witness the first official 200 mph lap. After his run, USAC officials found a problem with Foyt's turbocharger pop-off valve, a USAC-mandated control device, and decided to let the Texan have another free run. But that didn't make much of a difference, as Foyt could only improve his speed to 194.5. Al Unser made a run of 195.95, which ultimately put him on the outside of the front row, but nowhere near the magic number. Tom Sneva was the next legitimate contender to take the green flag, and then the official records started falling. With a best lap of 200.535 mph and a 4-lap average of 198.884, Tom Sneva went into the record books as the first driver to break the 200 mph mark at the hallowed Indianapolis Motor Speedway. His average speed, also a track record, would easily hold up for the pole position, giving Roger Penske another long-coveted prize. When Andretti qualified later, he found that his setup was wrong for the weather conditions, and managed only a disappointing 193.353 mph. That left Johnny Rutherford as the only serious potential challenger to Sneva's records and pole position. After running three laps at an average above 197 mph, Team McLaren made the risky decision to wave off Rutherford's initial run, which would have been good enough for the number-two starting spot, in

favor of waiting for cooler conditions later in the day, still hoping to go for the pole. "You got to gamble," said Roger Penske after Rutherford's aborted run, "that's the only way you get anywhere in this game." For Rutherford and Team McLaren, however, this one turned out to be a bad gamble. When he rolled out of the pits less than 45 minutes before the end of the qualifying session, Rutherford's McLaren stalled on the backstretch, and he never got a chance to get back on the track before time ran out. He ended up doing a 197.325 mph run the next day, but rather than starting next to Sneva on the front row, he found himself buried back in 17th position on the grid.

The 1977 race will always be most remembered for A.J. Foyt's record 4th Indy 500 victory. Two other drivers have accomplished the same feat since then, but at the time, it seemed like an untouchable achievement. Tom Sneva may have robbed Foyt of that record win, were it not for two costly unscheduled pit stops; one because he had flat-spotted his tires on an earlier stop, and the other because of a fueling system malfunction. Even with these handicaps, Sneva brought the Norton Spirit Penske McLaren home in second place, just 28 seconds behind the winner. Mario Andretti had a much less successful day, dropping out of the race after only 47 laps with a broken exhaust header. For Penske Racing, it was certainly the best overall Indy 500 since Mark Donohue's victory five years early. And it was a clear signal that this team was going to be a serious contender for the USAC national championship.

Two weeks later, in Milwaukee, Sneva repeated his second-place performance, this time following Johnny Rutherford to the checkered flag and racking up another 240 important championship points. At the end of June, the USAC caravan was back in Pennsylvania for the Pocono 500. This event, practically in the backyard of Penske Racing's Reading, Pennsylvania, headquarters, had surely become a source of irritation for Roger Penske. Since winning the track's inaugural race in 1971, at the same time recording the team's first-ever Indy-car victory, Penske's entries had experienced nothing but frustration here. Except for Andretti and Sneva's modest 5th and 7th place results in the 1976 event, no

Penske entry had even made it to the end of a Pocono 500 since Mark Donohue's 1971 win.

The Penske Racing McLarens qualified third (Andretti) and fourth (Sneva) on the Pocono grid behind Indy-winner A.J. Foyt and Johnny Rutherford's Team McLaren. But in the race, which was billed by *Sports Illustrated* as the year's best, the Penske cars were the class of the field. Although Foyt, Rutherford, Al Unser and the Patrick Racing Wildcats of Gordon Johncock and Wally Dallenbach all diced with Sneva and Andretti during the long afternoon, at the end of the day it was Tom Sneva in first, Mario Andretti in second, and everybody else at least a lap behind. Roger Penske had another first-time achievement—a one-two Indy car sweep, and it happened at the very same hometown track where he scored his first USAC win five years earlier. The *AutoWeek* race report said: "Tom Sneva has completed his apprenticeship and has become a journeyman racer. His win in the Schaefer 500 was proof to everybody, especially his boss, racing impresario Roger Penske. Sneva did the job the hardest way possible: he just drove everybody into the ground. And—this is important—he did it his way." Tom Sneva

Tom Sneva debuted Penske Racing's first in-house Indy car design, the Penske PC5, at Michigan in 1977. This car was a virtual clone of the McLaren and Sneva put it on the pole in its first outing with a speed of 200.278 mph.

and Penske Racing came away from Pocono with one more first—a commanding lead in the points battle for the USAC National Championship. "We're going for the USAC Citicorp Championship," said Penske. "We've never won it and I think we can this year." As *AutoWeek* noted, "Now that's certainly a vote of confidence for the driver that Penske benched last year for a third of the season."

A week after Pocono, the championship trail went to the road course in Mosport, Canada, for the first time in many years. Despite being a reluctant road-racer, Sneva qualified the Norton Spirit 6th and finished 3rd behind A.J Foyt and Gary Bettenhausen, who had his best showing since parting company with Penske Racing three years earlier. It was a fortunate result for Sneva, considering that his day included an off-course excursion that cost him over two laps in the pits. But many of the other normal front-runners also had problems, and Tom was able to persevere his way to a decent finish.

After Mosport, it was on to Penske's track in Michigan for the July 200-mile race. This race marked the debut of the first Penske-built Indy-car chassis, the PC-5. With the demise of the Formula-1 program at the end of the 1976 season, Penske had no other use for his racecar design and fabrication shop in England, so he put the personnel and facilities to work building Indy cars. The PC-5 was basically a clone of the 1977 McLaren, and it was fast right out of the box. Sneva made another strong qualifying effort at Michigan, taking the pole at a record speed of 200.278 mph in the car's very first appearance. In the race, however, he managed to lead only one lap and had to settle for a fourth place finish.

July ended in College Station, Texas, where Sneva again ran the new Penske PC-5 / Cosworth. He qualified 6th and advanced one position for a 5th place finish, enough to keep him out front in the championship points battle. The next race on the schedule was the August 21st Milwaukee 200, which turned out to be the first really disappointing showing for Sneva and the Penske team since before Indy. Back in the McLaren, Sneva managed only a 10th-place qualifying run, and he dropped out of the race with a broken exhaust header just past the halfway point, being credited with an 18th-place finish.

For the Labor Day weekend Ontario 500, Penske Racing was back to a two-car effort, with Mario Andretti behind the wheel of the CAM2 McLaren while Sneva piloted the Norton Spirit Penske PC-5 chassis. Andretti was the second fastest qualifier at 194.900 mph behind Johnny Rutherford's 195.111 mph pole speed. Al Unser was third on the grid and Sneva fourth at 193.736 mph. Andretti jumped into the lead at the drop of the green flag and stayed out front for the first 12 laps. Both Penske cars ran with the leaders all day, Andretti putting up the most challenge until a pit stop miscue cost him 42 seconds and effectively ended his bid for the win. In a race that saw only 11 of the 33 starters still running at the end, Al Unser took the win over A.J. Foyt, with Tom Sneva third and Mario Andretti fourth. With two races still remaining in the season, Tom Sneva had clinched Penske Racing's first USAC national championship. To make it even sweeter for the Captain, he did it driving a Penske-built chassis.

Two weeks later, back in Michigan for the fall 150-miler, Penske Racing entered PC-5s for both Sneva and Andretti. Newcomer Danny Ongais earned the pole in his Parnelli-Cosworth, but the Penske cars took second and third on the grid. In the race, Andretti lasted only 21 laps before his clutch gave out. Sneva had a strong day until running out of fuel six laps from the end and finishing 10th.

For the final event of the 1977 season, Tom and Mario were back in McLaren-Cosworths for the one-mile Phoenix oval. This time it was Sneva's turn to exit early after putting the Norton Spirit hard into the fourth turn wall—certainly not the way he wanted to end his championship season! Andretti ran a solid race and went on to finish fourth, a lap behind winner Gordon Johncock. It would have been much nicer to finish the season with a victory, but the important thing was that Penske Racing had finally won the national championship. Nobody could have dreamed then how many more would follow.

At the USAC awards banquet, in addition to the USAC National Champion Citicorp Cup, Tom Sneva

Defending USAC National Champion Tom Sneva wore the #1 on his Norton Spirit Penske PC6 in 1978. The PC6 carried Tom and Penske Racing to their second-consecutive USAC Indy car title and second Indy 500 pole.

was presented the Olsonite Triple Crown Award for the best overall performance in the year's three 500-mile races, and the STP Most Improved Championship Driver Award. Penske Racing chief mechanic, Jim McGee, was also honored as the Loctite Championship Mechanic of the Year. It seemed like a long time since the team's last championship, Mark Donohue's Can-Am title in 1973. Roger Penske's decision to focus the full resources of his team on the USAC National title seemed justified now, as did his faith in the school-teacher from Spokane.

1978

1978 would turn out to be a pivotal year for Penske Racing and the entire Indy-Car championship organization, but that was not evident as the season opened in Phoenix on March 18th. Tom Sneva was back in an all-new Penske-designed and built PC-6 Norton Spirit, this year proudly sporting the number "1," identifying him as the defending national champion.

Roger Penske used the team's 1977 success to attract electronics manufacturer Gould Industries as a new full-season sponsor for a second team car. Again,

Mario Andretti would be at the wheel of the second entry when his Formula-1 schedule allowed. For the other races, Penske added a surprise newcomer named Rick Mears to the team roster. The 26-year-old former off-road racer had driven his first USAC championship race in 1976 where he turned in an impressive 8th place performance. He followed that with equally respectable 9th place finishes in both the Texas and Phoenix races that year. Mears ran the majority of the 1977 season for the under-funded Theodore Racing team, earning several top-10 finishes, including a 5th in the Milwaukee race. Penske obviously saw the potential in this young driver, both on and off the track.

In his book, *CART—The First 20 Years*, Rick Shaffer reflected on the origins of the Penske-Mears relationship, saying, "Penske was looking for a promising young driver, much like the pleasant young man who had taken his team to the heights in its formative years—Mark Donohue. Like Donohue, Mears had a boyish look and an ever-present smile. Like Donohue, he also had exceptional talent." Despite some initial skepticism, it would quickly become obvious that Roger Penske had a real find in his young new driver.

With Mario Andretti's Formula-1 schedule preventing him from running the full USAC series, Roger Penske hired sophomore Rick Mears to drive the second team car as needed. Mears quickly proved to be an excellent choice, winning three races for Penske in his part-time debut season with the team.

For the 1978 Phoenix opener, Tom Sneva was in the new Penske PC-6 Norton Spirit while Rick Mears drove the older PC-5 Gould Charge. Sneva started third and was running strong in the early laps until he had a tire blow on the backstretch, sending him into a wild spin and ending his day. Mears was impressive in his Penske Racing debut. Starting 7th, he drove a steady and smart race to a 5th place finish.

In qualifying for the Ontario 200 a week later, Sneva took the pole and set a new track record at 202.384 mph. Mario Andretti was in the Gould Charge for this race, and took the second spot on the grid beside his Penske Racing teammate. At the start of the race, Sneva missed a shift and fell back several positions, but he quickly worked his way back up to the front of the pack. Then, while leading comfortably, the defending series champion was black-flagged by race officials for passing the pace car in a controversial incident that ended up costing him over 30 seconds in the pits, and ultimately, the race. At the end of the day, he was in second place, only 7 seconds behind winner Danny Ongais. Mario Andretti had another tough day. From his number-two starting position, he jumped into the lead when Sneva faltered at the green flag, and led for the first 19 laps. But shortly after giving up the top spot to Ongais, the Cosworth engine in Andretti's Gould Charge expired, ending his day in 15th position.

Next on the schedule was the April 15th 200-mile race at College Station, Texas. Andretti qualified the Gould Charge second fastest and Sneva put the Norton Spirit fourth on the grid. Mario led 23 of the first 42 laps, but then faded to a fifth place finish. Sneva never led, but he pushed winner Danny Ongais to the end, the only other car on the lead lap even though he ran out of fuel and coasted across the finish line. After his last-place finish in the season opener, this second place result moved the defending USAC champion up to second position in the points battle.

At Trenton a week later, Tom Sneva claimed his second pole of the young season, setting another track record at 172.249 mph on the tight dog-legged 1 1/2-mile state fairground track. Andretti, at the wheel of the other Penske, qualified third fastest. Sneva led the

first 14 laps of the race before he started to experience handling problems. After making several extra pit stops to get the balance back, he wrestled the Norton Spirit home in third place. Mario Andretti suffered yet another engine failure, dropping out after 92 laps for a 13th place finish.

For the 1978 Indianapolis 500, Penske Racing fielded a 3-car team with Tom Sneva in the Norton Spirit, Mario Andretti in the Gould Charge and young Rick Mears in the CAM2 Motor Oil Special. All three cars were new Penske PC-6 chassis with Cosworth engines. Sneva made history again, breaking his own one and four-lap qualifying records to take his second straight Indy 500 pole with an average speed of 202.156 mph. The first weekend of qualifying had been completely rained out, so the full field had to be determined on May 20th and 21st. With Andretti racing in Europe, Penske called in Mike Hiss to qualify the Gould Charge. Hiss' 194.6 mph average would have been good for a third row starting position, but under USAC qualifying rules, the driver change required Andretti to start 33rd and last on race day. Danny Ongais, who would be one of the strongest challengers all season, took the number-two starting spot at 200.122 mph. The real surprise in qualifying, however, came when Penske's rookie driver, Rick Mears, clocked a four-lap average speed of 200.078 mph to take the outside spot of the all-200-mph front row. Roger Penske had plenty of reason for optimism going into this year's "500."

When the green flag fell, Sneva dropped in behind Ongais and ran in the number-two position for most of the first half of the race, trying to conserve fuel. When Ongais dropped out with engine problems, Al Unser moved to the front with Sneva close behind. Mario Andretti charged from his 33rd starting spot up to 9th position before a bad ignition coil resulted in a 7-minute pit stop that left him 15 laps behind the leaders. He went on to a 12th place finish. Meanwhile, Rick Mears had a strong run going until loosing an engine just past the halfway mark, ending up in 23rd position. Despite this setback, he would still share 'Rookie-of-the-Year' honors because of the outstanding qualifying effort. Mears' exit left Tom Sneva as the lone challenger for the

Penske Racing entered cars in the 1978 Indy 500 for Tom Sneva, Mario Andretti and Rick Mears. When rain washed out the first weekend of qualifications, Roger Penske called in Mike Hiss to get Andretti's car into the field while he was in Europe for a Formula-1 race. *Bill Daniels*

Penske team. After the first two pit stops, it was obvious that the Norton Spirit wasn't getting near the 1.8 miles-per-gallon fuel economy needed to make it to the end of the day. In order to assure that he could go the full 500 miles, Sneva had to cut his turbocharger boost from 70 to 65 inches for the second half of the race, leaving him unable to run with the leader on the straights. Sneva said later, "We were working the corners better than anybody else, just super in the corners, but I didn't

know if we'd ever get to the finish because we had to worry about our fuel. It was real close to running out at the end, maybe less than a gallon." Roger Penske made no excuses, "We got beat, that's all I can say. Tom did a great job for us. Unser was just quicker."

Despite the obvious disappointment of not winning the race when he clearly had the faster car, the second-place finish did move Sneva back into the lead for the USAC championship. Also, Roger Penske had a chance to assess the potential of his newest driving talent, Rick Mears; and certainly he had to be delighted with what he saw. The second Indy 500 crown for Penske Racing surely wasn't far away.

After Indy, the USAC bandwagon took a detour to Mosport, Canada, before the traditional stop in Milwaukee. With Andretti back in Europe chasing the Formula-1 championship, Rick Mears was in the Gould Charge along with Tom Sneva in the Norton Spirit. On the twisty road course, the two Penskes qualified 7th and 8th, with Mears edging his senior teammate. Danny Ongais dominated the race, leading 66 of the 76 laps to take the win. Rick Mears led 7 of the remaining 10 laps and came home a strong second. Tom Sneva ran a consistent race and finished a respectable fourth, hanging on to the points lead.

Sneva's fuel mileage problems returned at Milwaukee a week later, as he was one of four cars that failed to make the finish after running out of methanol. Danny Ongais, who had earned the nickname "the Flyin' Hawaiian," took the pole again, with Sneva second and Rick Mears third on the grid. They ran in that order through most of the first two thirds of the race until Ongais cooked his engine, and then Sneva took over with Mears and Al Unser right behind. On lap 128, while in the lead, Sneva's Penske ran out of fuel and his day was over. Al Unser inherited the top spot at that point and stayed out front until seven laps from the finish, when his tank ran dry too. That left Penske's rookie sensation, Rick Mears, with his first career Indycar win, Penske Racing's first victory of the season, and Tom Sneva still leading in championship points.

For the Pocono 500 in late-June, Roger Penske put Mario Andretti back in the cockpit of the Gould Charge despite Mears' impressive performance at Milwaukee. Tom Sneva qualified second behind Ongais, with Andretti starting 6th. In the race, Sneva was again forced to run conservatively to save fuel. He ran near the front all day, leading just 10 laps and finishing third behind Al Unser and Johnny Rutherford. Andretti also ran with the leaders in the early stages of the race until being sidelined with a broken gearbox on lap 73.

Two weeks later at Michigan, Tom Sneva bounced

back to take the pole at 211.392 mph, almost 6 mph faster than second-place qualifier Johnny Rutherford. Rick Mears put the Gould Charge third on the grid. At the drop of the green flag, Sneva jumped into the lead over Rutherford and stayed there for the first 28 laps. Mears had a problem right at the start, dropping a valve in the Cosworth engine and ending his day on the very first lap. Sneva ran with leaders Danny Ongais and Johnny Rutherford for the remainder of the afternoon, until being black-flagged for a loose wheel nut and losing a lap to the field. He ultimately unlapped himself and finished second to Rutherford after Ongais ran out of fuel four laps from the finish. Although these top-5 finishes were keeping Sneva at the front of the points chase, not getting to victory lane was becoming a source of frustration for both Sneva and the boss, Roger Penske.

In late July, the USAC series returned to the Atlanta Motor Speedway for the first time since 1966. Tom Sneva showed everyone how much things had changed in those 12 years as he took the pole at 202.475 mph, some 33 mph faster than Mario Andretti's previous track record there. Danny Ongais was second on the grid with Rick Mears starting third. In the race, Sneva led the first 10 laps before being passed by the Flyin' Hawaiian. On the very next lap, however, Ongais blew his engine and Sneva returned to the front for another two circuits until being forced to pit with a flat tire, giving up the lead to teammate Rick Mears. Mears went on to lead a race-high 68 laps, being challenged only by Johnny Rutherford, on the way to his second Indycar win. Sneva never recovered from the unscheduled stop and eventually finished in 8th position, three laps behind the leaders.

Tom Sneva gave Penske Racing another pole position two weeks later in the Texas 200. Teammate Mears qualified third behind veteran A.J. Foyt. At the start of the race, Sneva fell in behind Foyt, but came back to take the lead for laps 12 through 30. A lap later, Rick Mears moved to the front and stayed there for the next 18 circuits before experiencing suspension problems. In a race that became a battle of attrition, with only six of the 21 starters reaching the checkered flag, Tom Sneva struggled to a 5th place finish after pitting to change a bad shock absorber and being penalized with another black-flag for a pit infraction. Mears was credited for 9th even though he completed only 63 of the 100 laps. Texan A.J. Foyt pleased the hometown crowd, taking his first win of the season.

Back in Milwaukee for the August 200-mile race, Tom Sneva and Rick Mears qualified their Penskes second and fourth respectively behind pole-sitter Danny Ongais. Mears managed to lead 9 laps and hold on for a second-place finish, but the race was dominated by the Flyin' Hawaiian. For a change, Ongais didn't break the car and he led 179 of the 200 laps. Sneva lost a lot of time with problems in the pits and finished a disappointing 15th. He was still leading in the championship points battle, but two-time Indy 500 winner Al Unser was now closing fast.

Next on the schedule was the Labor Day weekend Ontario 500, on the track that was theoretically identical to Indianapolis. The top four qualifiers were Sneva, Rutherford, Ongais, and Mears, the same four who started out front at Indy, although not in exactly the same order. Tom Sneva held the lead for the first seven laps of the race, which were run under caution because of a 3-car accident at the green flag. He ran second and third behind Ongais and Rutherford until lap 18 when a broken suspension ended his day. It was another attrition race, with only six of 31 starters making it to the end. Al Unser won by 5 laps over Pancho Carter, with Rick Mears being credited for 9th place even though he dropped out with a blown engine after 150 laps. With the DNF, Sneva fell to second place behind Unser in the championship battle.

At Michigan in mid-September, Mario Andretti was back in the Gould Charge for the first time since being crowned the 1978 Formula-1 World Driving Champion, the ultimate prize in auto racing. He remains the only American to win the title in nearly half a century. It was a tragically bitter-sweet victory, however, as his Lotus teammate and close friend, Ronnie Peterson, died of injuries sustained in a 10-car pileup at the start of the Italian Grand Prix, the race in which Andretti clinched the title.

In the Michigan race, Andretti qualified a solid fourth but didn't even make a lap before his engine went sour. Sneva fared better, qualifying second to Johnny Rutherford and, after struggling with wing problems through the early stages of the race, ending up second behind the hard-charging Danny Ongais.

At Trenton a week later, Andretti was in the Gould Charge again. He qualified third fastest with Sneva fourth behind pole-sitter A.J. Foyt and Danny Ongais. Foyt led the first 13 laps of the race before dropping out with a burned piston. Andretti and Sneva battled with Ongais for the lead throughout much of the afternoon before Danny crashed on the 75th lap. Sneva then fell back to fourth place behind Mario, an unusually competitive Johnny Parsons, and Al Unser. Two laps from the end of the race, Sneva turned up the boost and passed Unser to take third place. It was Mario Andretti's first Indy-car win since 1973 and his first victory in three seasons with Penske Racing.

The USAC teams then packed up and headed to England for two road course races at Silverstone and Brands Hatch. Rick Mears and Tom Sneva qualified the Penske team cars 4th and 9th respectively at Silverstone, with Danny Ongais taking another pole. Weather conditions were cool, overcast and rainy for the weekend. The race had to be stopped on two occasions for major downpours. In between, there were numerous spins and off-course excursions, including one by Tom Sneva on the pace lap, as the oval-track drivers attempted to come to grips with the unfamiliar, damp road course. It must have been an amusing site for the British road racing fans. A.J. Foyt went on to win the event, with Rick Mears and Tom Sneva following in second and third-place respectively. Coupled with Al Unser's DNF, this moved Penske Racing's defending champion back into the points lead.

At Brands Hatch the following weekend, however, Al Unser signaled his intention to continue the championship challenge, taking the pole position ahead of Rick Mears, with Tom Sneva starting in 5th place. Fortunately for Sneva, Unser lost his clutch at the very start and finished dead last. Danny Ongais controlled most of the race before breaking his gearbox on the 83rd of

100 laps. Rick Mears, who had pursued Ongais all day then moved into the lead for the remainder of the race to take his third career win, Penske Racing's fourth of the season. Tom Sneva followed in second, the only other car on the lead lap, padding his championship lead over Al Unser with only one race left in the season.

Going into the season finale at Phoenix, Sneva held a 264-point advantage over Al Unser in the championship battle, with 300 points to be awarded in this final event. Andretti was back in the other Penske car, while three-time winner Rick Mears was left without a ride—probably not one of the Captain's smartest decisions. Sneva started second and was running a competitive race until he experienced turbocharger problems at the 90-lap mark. He lost 17 laps in the pits getting the problem resolved, but with the championship on the line, he returned to the race to make sure he collected every possible point. Johnny Rutherford won the event, while Mario Andretti brought the Gould Charge home to an uncompetitive 7th place finish. Sneva ended up 16th, collecting only 8 points, but with Al Unser's 5th place result, that was just enough to give Tom and the Penske Racing team a second consecutive national title.

This championship would be more significant than most, as it would turn out to be the last time that the undisputed national champion would be determined under USAC sanctioning. As the 1978 season was playing out, a behind-the-scenes power struggle was developing that would result in a civil war among the Indy-car principals. The upcoming 1979 season would bring uncertainty, lawsuits, and many, many changes. But for the time being, Tom Sneva enjoyed his second title, the last legitimate USAC National Champion.

The end of this year would bring changes in Penske Racing's Indy-car program too. As Tom Sneva marched through his championship season without scoring a single race victory, friction between the Captain and his number-one driver began to resurface. Winner's circles provide photo opportunities, the kind that sponsors pay hundreds of thousands of dollars to attain. The championship was an important goal, but Roger Penske obviously wanted to see his drivers on the podium, in front of the cameras, and Sneva didn't deliver that in 1978. Sneva faulted the team for not operating at maximum efficiency, a charge that he would later retract after having the opportunity to compare Penske Racing to several other top organizations. But the unfortunate result was that, after a 4-year partnership that produced two national championships, two Indianapolis 500 poles, and some of the most memorable records in motorsport, Tom Sneva and Roger Penske would go their separate ways at the end of the 1978 season.

Tom Sneva would be an anomaly among ex-Penske Racing drivers, as he would go on to achieve greater career successes after leaving the team than while driving for the Captain. A year after departing, Sneva would narrowly miss winning a record third straight Indy pole, being knocked out of the top spot in the final minutes of qualifying by none other than his Penske Racing successor, Rick Mears. The year after that, driving a 5-year-old McLaren, Sneva would charge from 33rd starting position to lead the "500," eventually settling for a third bridesmaid finish. Finally in 1983, "the Gas Man," as he was then called, would find his way to the Indy 500 winner's circle at the expense of Penske Racing team drivers Al Unser and Rick Mears, who finished second and third behind him. In 1984, Sneva would take his third Indy 500 pole, becoming the first driver to break the 210 mph barrier at the Speedway, and he would battle all day with eventual winner Rick Mears before being sidelined with a broken CV joint late in the race. That year, he would also fight to the very last race of the season, falling just short of taking a third national championship. In the six years after leaving Penske Racing, Tom Sneva won a total of 10 races, compared to three victories during his Penske Racing tenure. After the 1984 season, he was handicapped with less-than-competitive equipment and failed to add to his win total. He ran his last Indy 500 in 1992 and then announced his retirement. In 2004, Tom Sneva was awarded one of the highest honors in the sport, induction into the Indianapolis Motor Speedway Hall of Fame. Also inducted in that 2004 ceremony, posthumously, was a guy named Mark Donohue.

Mike Odell / Forget-Me-Not-Race Pix / SportsRacingLtd.com

CHAPTER 6
Formula A /F5000
(1969-1973)

"I figured it would be easy. We would select the right springs and anti-roll bars, tweak the motor and the wings, go to the races, unload the car from the trailer, and win all the money—and then walk off into the sunset."
—Mark Donohue, *The Unfair Advantage*

Formula 5000, originally known as Formula A, was an SCCA-sanctioned series for open-wheel "formula-style" racecars with production-based 5.0 Liter engines. The series was run on road courses throughout North America from the late 1960s through the mid-70s. It was basically a poor-man's Formula-1 championship. Over the years, the series attracted some of the best U.S. road racing drivers, as well as a sprinkling of young European talent. Unfortunately, it never managed to establish a sustainable fan base and financial backing that the Can-Am series enjoyed in its heyday. After the Can-Am folded at the end of the 1974 season, the SCCA tried to convert its fans to F-5000, but there was just something about the lack of fenders that kept the customers away. Finally, in 1977, with the series spiraling toward a certain death, the SCCA created specs for "body kits" to turn the single-seat F-5000 machines into something that resembled the old Group-7 cars—and they even changed the name of the series to "Can-Am." Surprisingly, this superficial reincarnation of the popular old sports car championship actually did increase interest for a while, but that interest ultimately fizzled out and the series folded after the 1986 season as many of the strongest competitors moved up to CART Indy-cars, which had by then become predominately a road-racing series.

Penske Racing dabbled in the Formula-A/5000 series on two occasions. In both cases, their primary motive was to pick up some quick, easy wins. In both cases, they experienced unforeseen problems, frustration, and much more disappointment than gratification.

1969

At the end of the 1969 season Carl Haas, who was Lola's North American distributor, approached Roger Penske about having Mark Donohue drive a new Lola T190 in the Sebring Formula-A race. This was a fairly big event because it took place after all the other major series had finished for the season, so a lot of international drivers participated. Lola was trying to showcase their new design, using this race as a marketing tool to sell cars for the upcoming season.

Using the same basic Chevy 302 engine that powered the Trans-Am Camaros, Donohue and the crew threw the new Lola together quickly and headed for Sebring. Fortunately, despite the lack of any real development or preparation, the car was fast right off the trailer. Even though unfamiliar with this form of racing, Donohue managed to qualify the car third on the grid behind Mario Andretti and Swede Savage. The event consisted of two 100-mile heat races. Donohue was running second in the first heat when his fuel filter clogged and choked the engine. At that point, they realized that the filter they had installed was undersized, but it was too late to do anything about it. For the second heat, Donohue started with a new filter element and moved to the lead before being taken out by the same problem. It was a disappointing experience, even though they were very competitive while running. Donohue's winnings for his 17th place finish totaled a whopping $225!

1970

The 1969 Sebring race was intended to be a one-time deal. But by the latter part of the following season, with the first year Trans-Am Javelin program going poorly, Roger Penske was getting nervous about generating some wins to keep his sponsors happy. Looking back at the apparent ease with which they were competitive in their initial Formula-A venture, Penske and Donohue decided to put together a last-minute program to run the remaining three races of the 1970 Formula-A season. Penske worked out another deal with the Lola factory to get a new car to "test-drive" in these three races. The new car had a longer wheelbase than the one they had run the previous year, and Donohue realized immediately when he got it on the track at Mosport that there was a major handling problem. With no time to troubleshoot, he somehow managed to qualify second to David Hobbs, but he was not optimistic about his chances for the race. Fortunately, the event was run in the rain, which typically proves to be a great equalizer. Despite going off-course and hitting a guardrail in the very first turn, Donohue recovered and came back to win by almost a lap over Hobbs. Roger Penske got his much needed "win," but Donohue knew it was by luck—there was still a big problem with the car that needed to be corrected before they would really be competitive.

Before the next race at Mid-Ohio, Donohue had Goodyear make some new tires that he thought would help the car handle better. Penske Racing arrived at the track several days ahead of the race weekend to do some much-needed testing. Unfortunately, it was immediately obvious that the problem wasn't the tires. Trying desperately to cut his lap times with the still-unruly Lola, Donohue had another accident; tearing up the car badly enough that they had to rush it back to the shop in Philadelphia for repairs. The Penske team trailer pulled back into Mid-Ohio track on Sunday morning, just hours before the race was to begin. Having missed qualifying, Donohue had to start from the back of the field. Despite the continuing handling problem, however, he managed to work his way up to a respectable third place finish behind winner George Follmer and runner-up John Cannon.

Before the final event at Sebring, Donohue worked with the Lola factory on the persistent handling problem. Based on his feedback, Lola quickly assembled a new chassis with a more rigid front suspension. Donohue qualified the new car on the pole at Sebring and ran away to an easy victory—finally!

With that success under their belts, Roger Penske decided to run the Lola in one more event. At the end of the 1970 season, the Ontario Motor Speedway staged a challenge race called the Questor Grand Prix, pitting the American Formula-A cars and drivers against Europe's Formula-1 stars. Representing the F-1 contingent were names such as Jackie Stewart, Denny Hulme, and Mario Andretti (driving a Ferrari). Notable Formula-A challengers included Donohue, Peter Revson, George Follmer, Swede Savage, Sam Posey, A.J. Foyt and Al and Bobby Unser.

Donohue didn't qualify very well because he was shuttling back-and-forth between Ontario and Phoenix, where he had a USAC race that same weekend. The Questor race was set up as a two-heat event. In the first heat, Donohue moved the Penske Lola up through the field until he was running a strong third, then he apparently ran out of gas and dropped to a disappointing 9th-place finish. With a little extra fuel in the tanks at the start of the second heat, Donohue charged from his 9th-place starting position to third, behind Andretti and Stewart. Then his engine sputtered and died again. It turned out that he hadn't run out of gas after all.

The AMC-Lola, seen here at Elkhart Lake, was a good plan that never lived up to its potential. Penske and Donohue thought it would be easy to drop their proven Javelin motor into a standard Lola chassis and then just go out and win a bunch of races. Various problems and a lack of development time resulted in a humiliating winless season. *Mike Odell / Forget-Me-Not-Race Pix / SportsRacingLtd.com*

What had happened was that the fuel vent had clogged, preventing proper flow out of the tank. Mario Andretti went on to win the race, but it was a victory for the Formula-1 side, with the highest-placed Formula-A entry finishing an embarrassing 7th.

Even though their little end-of-season Formula-A project ultimately netted two wins in just four outings, it was anything but "quick and easy." There was a lot more time, effort and cost involved than originally anticipated. Hopefully Roger Penske got a lot of promotional value out of those two wins because, monetarily, this little venture was anything but a success.

1973

Two seasons passed before Penske Racing returned to F5000. 1973 was a very busy year for the Penske Racing Team. In retrospect, the decision to go back into F5000 that season was probably an uncharacteristic error in judgment by the Captain. Like the 1970 campaign, some of the impetus was the perceived opportunity for "quick and easy" wins. But this time, there were two other "legitimate" reasons for the exercise. First, American Motors was getting a little anxious to see some results. After winning the 1971 Trans-Am championship with the Javelin, the Penske Racing-

AMC partnership shifted its attention to the NAS-CAR stock car circuit, running the American Motors Matador in the Winston Cup super-speedway events. Successes had been few and far between, and victories non-existent. Dropping a Javelin motor into a competitive F5000 chassis seemed an easy way to chalk up some wins to keep AMC happy. The other factor was that longtime sponsor Sunoco was interested in the series because, unlike the open-wheel Indy-cars, Formula-5000 ran on real gasoline rather than methanol, therefore providing a better marketing opportunity for their gasoline products.

Initially, it seemed that the team would be much better prepared for this F5000 assault than they had been in their previous two experiences. Although there were several chassis options available for the series, Penske again chose to go with the latest Lola model, the T330. After a little extra effort fitting the AMC motor into the car designed specifically for a standard Chevy package, Donohue and crew took the car out to Riverside, California, to do the initial testing and development. Once again, as with the 1970 Lola, he found that the T330's handling was terrible. To make matters worse, he also found that there was a throttle response problem, which made the car very difficult to drive. It was not a very encouraging first impression, but fortunately there was still plenty of time to sort out the problems before the season started. Then a bizarre thing happened. While two Penske team mechanics were working on the car in a garage at the Riverside track, a spark ignited some gasoline, which then set fire to racing tires that were stored nearby in the garage, and very quickly the whole place, racecar included, went up in flames. Fortunately, nobody was injured, but the new Lola was a total loss.

After this enormous setback, Roger Penske looked at all the programs his team was juggling and wisely decided to give up on the F5000 effort—but unfortunately, that was not to be the end of the matter. As the NASCAR season progressed and it became obvious that American Motors wasn't going to be spending much time in Victory Lane with the hapless Matador, Roger Penske reluctantly agreed to resurrect the AMC-Lola F5000 effort, jumping in after the season was already

three races old. In May, starting from scratch, Penske committed to field an AMC-Lola entry by the June 3rd Mid-Ohio event. If ever there was a serious point of disagreement between Mark Donohue and Roger Penske, this was it. Donohue scrambled, trying to throw together a reasonably competitive racecar, while at the same time juggling the Can-Am Porsche effort, the NASCAR Matador program, and an Indy 500 title defense. It was an impossible task.

Competition in the 1973 F5000 series was formidable. South African Jody Scheckter, a future Formula-1 World Champion who was also competing against Penske Racing in the Can-Am series that year, would ultimately go on to be the 1973 F5000 champion. Another notable contender was veteran road racer Brian Redman, who was driving the "factory" Lola for a team co-owned by driver/designer Jim Hall and Lola distributor Carl Haas. Certainly, this meant that Redman would enjoy special support and certain benefits from the Lola factory not available to "regular customers." But with Penske Racing's talent and resources, that should not have been an insurmountable challenge.

Donohue and the team had little success in their first attempt at correcting the handling and throttle response problems that were still plaguing the AMC-Lola. In the car's first outing at Mid-Ohio, Donohue recalled that he was a full four seconds a lap off the leader's pace. Still, he somehow managed to manhandle the misbehaving Lola to a third place finish behind Scheckter and Redman.

In the second outing, two weeks later at Watkins Glen, New York, Donohue struggled to a disappointing fourth place result. He later articulated his frustration with the AMC-Lola program, saying: "We had no more time to test, so we just kept going from race to race, getting nowhere." This was not what people had come to expect of the invincible Penske Racing team.

The next time out, at Elkhart Lake, produced another dismal result. But two things happened there that would be significant. First, at a point in his career when he was feeling overwhelmed and depressingly ineffective, Donohue had an immensely gratifying epiphany. He wrote in the epilogue of his book: "Per-

In the second outing with the AMC-Lola, Donohue started fourth on the grid at Watkins Glen next to Brett Lunger and labored on to a 4th place finish. In his autobiography, Donohue reflected on the disappointing AMC-Lola program, "We had no more time to test so we just kept going from race to race, getting nowhere." *Galen Hummel*

Mike Odell / Forget-Me-Not-Race Pix / SportsRacingLtd.com

haps I first realized what the public and I meant to each other when we took our Lola-AMC to Elkhart Lake. We were looking terrible, and yet, when we unloaded the car, there was a bigger crowd around us than anyone else at the track. I went out and qualified twelfth, and the crowd became even bigger. If I had been fastest, it would have been natural, but we seemed to have a following that didn't care if we were twelfth. I ran sixth in the race, until I lost the water and melted a piston. The car stopped at turn four, and the spectators there were so enthusiastic they offered me beers, asked me for my autograph, and wanted to know when we were going into Formula One. Why did they care so much about a guy who didn't even finish the race? Maybe there is something more important than just winning races."

It's not surprising that this unassuming champion that they called "Captain Nice" would have been blind to the fact that he had become a genuine hero to his many loyal fans; not simply because of his obvious talent and successes on the racetrack, but perhaps even

more importantly, because of the exemplary character he displayed in achieving those successes.

On the technical side, Donohue also had a revelation at Elkhart Lake, finally recognizing that undersized front tires were the root cause of the exasperating handling problems with the Lola. With larger tires fitted on the car, he made his best showing of the season with a second-place result at Road Atlanta. After one more setback, finishing a relatively uncompetitive sixth at Pocono, the Penske Racing AMC-Lola was finally pretty well sorted out for the season-ending race at Seattle. Donohue said the car finally felt "comfortable" to drive, and he came home a strong second to Brian Redman. With one more race, the Penske AMC-Lola would likely have been the dominant car in the series. But there were no more races—the season was over. After all the cost and aggravation, the AMC-Lola project ended without ever seeing the winner's circle. And this frustrating outcome would be just one of several disappointments that supported Mark Donohue's ultimate decision to retire from driving at the end of the 1973 season.

Mike Smith

CHAPTER 7
Can Am Turbo-Porsche 917 (1972 –1973)

"Perhaps this is what brings in the crowds—the desire to say, "I saw Mark Donohue drive that invincible Porsche. I was there and saw it and knew that it was the best combination of man and machine that ever appeared on the racetrack."
—Pete Lyons, *Can-Am*

When Penske Racing withdrew from the Can Am series in 1969, clearly there was business left unfinished. Roger Penske has never competed to finish second, but in 1969 it was apparent that second was the best any team could hope to achieve against the dominating McLaren effort. Faced with that reality, Penske made the difficult decision to cut his losses, to come back to fight another day—a day when he knew could win.

In the 3 years that followed, the Can Am series changed very little. Although there were occasional challenges by different teams and drivers, most notably world champion Jackie Stewart's Lola in 1971, the bright orange Gulf McLarens continued to win almost effort-

lessly. At one point they amassed a remarkable 19-race winning streak. Despite the tragic loss of team founder Bruce McLaren in a 1970 pre-season practice accident, the team continued with veterans Denny Hulme and Dan Gurney. When Gurney departed, Peter Revson was recruited to fill the number-two slot. Through all of this, Team McLaren never missed a beat, rarely lost a race, and handily won five consecutive Can Am titles.

While things had remained pretty much status quo in the Can Am series, the story was quite different at Penske Racing. Roger Penske's team had transformed quickly from a bunch of college-boy rookies into an established, professional force in U.S. auto racing. After winning three Trans-Am championships, the 24 Hours of Daytona, plus several Formula-A and Indy-Car races, Penske Racing was becoming recognized as a new standard of excellence in the sport. By 1972, the Captain was ready for the right opportunity to go back and take care of that business he'd left unfinished in the Can Am. And because of the winning reputation that his young team had earned, that opportunity came knocking on his door.

While campaigning the Ferrari 512 at Le Mans and other world endurance racing events in 1971, Penske's performance earned him the attention of the powerhouse Porsche factory racing team. In the late 1960s and early '70s, Porsche had committed its formidable technical and financial resources to successfully dominating world sports-car endurance racing. These prototype 5-liter sports coupes were similar in appearance to Can Am cars, but were heavier and less powerful than their more fragile, open-cockpit Group-7 counterparts.

Porsche's first appearance in a Can Am event came at Watkins Glen in the summer of 1969. The Glen scheduled its Can Am race on the same weekend as the 6-hour World Endurance event, hoping to entice some of the endurance teams that were already there to stick around to mix it up with the Can Am regulars. Under the very open Can Am rules, the endurance cars were legal, although hopelessly under-powered against the 7-liter Can Am machines. But Porsche took the challenge and entered a factory-supported 908, which was driven by Jo Siffert to a respectable 6th place finish. Through the remainder of 1969, 1970 and 1971, factory and private Porsche entries continued to compete periodically in the Can Am series. Although never capable of running with the purpose-built Can Am cars, their strong reliability and various circumstances led to several respectable finishes, including a first Porsche victory at Road Atlanta in 1970.

But Porsche, like Roger Penske, was not satisfied watching their cars run for show. Winning sold automobiles, and if their cars were going to compete on the world stage in the highly competitive and visible Can Am championship, Porsche was determined that they were going to be there to challenge for victory. With that mutual commitment to success, in November of 1971, Porsche and Penske Racing announced what was to become one of the most dominating partnerships in auto racing history. Teaming the technical and financial resources of the Porsche factory with Mark Donohue's driving, engineering and development skills, resulted in a crushing assault on the long-standing status quo in Can Am racing.

In a decision that surely contributed to the failure of his marriage the following year, Mark Donohue virtually moved to Germany and immersed himself in the development of the Porsche 917/10K. Unlike the big block Chevy engines that had dominated Can Am for so many years, the new 917 was to be powered by a 5-liter, 12-cylinder turbocharged motor. Turbocharging was nothing new in auto racing; it had been employed successfully for years in Indy-style oval racing. The challenge in applying it to road racing was to overcome the phenomenon known as "turbo-lag."

Technically, turbocharging works by using a turbine to force pressurized air into the engine, thus producing more horsepower. Unlike super-charging, which employs an electric motor to drive the turbine, turbo charging utilizes the exhaust gas flow. Under acceleration, this results in a classic 'chicken or egg' dilemma. At low RPMs, there is relatively little exhaust gas flow to drive the turbine, resulting in a limited boost in horsepower. As engine speed increases, exhaust flow increases, resulting in more turbo assist and more horsepower. So the problem to overcome was how to get power out of the "little" 5-liter engine under acceleration at low RPMs.

Donohue and the Porsche engineers struggled with this dilemma until the 11th hour before a breakthrough in fuel metering calibration was finally achieved, unlocking the mystery. Porsche was so concerned about not getting the turbo motor right that they concurrently developed a 7.2-liter, normally aspirated 16-cylinder engine as a fallback. But that powerplant was never needed, as the 5-liter turbo proved to be nearly invincible. On the dynamometer, it produced 1000 horsepower. On the racetrack it was rated at a mere 900-hp, enough to carry the striking white and red L&M-sponsored Penske Porsche 917/10K from zero to 60 mph in 2.1 seconds and 0-100 mph in 3.9.

In the first race of the 1972 season at Mosport, Canada, Donohue easily qualified the new Porsche on the pole. Early in the race, he pitted with a problem that turned out to be a sticking turbocharger valve. By the time the trouble was diagnosed and corrected, the Penske Porsche rejoined the race three laps behind the

Roger Penske and Mark Donohue had waited three years for the right opportunity to go back and challenge Team McLaren in the Can Am series. When Porsche offered them a factory-supported effort, the decision was easy. Donohue and the Porsche engineers collaborated to create the most technically sophisticated racecar ever seen, resulting in a crushing assault on the long-standing status quo in Can Am racing. *Mike Smith*

leaders. In what was clearly a sign of things to come, Donohue charged back through the field, regaining two of the lost laps and eventually finishing second to Denny Hulme in the lead Team McLaren car. It was not exactly the start that Penske wanted, but the prophetic headlines would read: "McLaren Wins the Battle, but may lose the war."

The second Can Am event of the season was at Road Atlanta. The Penske team headed south a week prior to the race to do some testing at the hilly, picturesque road course outside of Atlanta. Roger Penske later said that the Road Atlanta track was notoriously hard on brakes, so they made a decision to add new cooling ducts to the rear bodywork of the Porsche to channel more air to the brake calipers. Whether it was this impromptu design change or just an improperly fastened body panel as Donohue later claimed, the result was catastrophic. As Donohue flew down the back straight at 150 mph, the rear bodywork of the car literally ripped off of the chassis. The sudden loss of down-force produced by the huge rear wing caused the car to launch into the air, cart-wheeling end over end several times before coming to a hard stop against an unforgiving dirt embankment. Looking at the mangled remains of the racecar, it is almost inconceivable that Donohue was able to escape with his life. At first it appeared that he had suffered no more than a badly bruised knee. Unfortunately, after a couple days of intense pain and unsuccessful physical therapy, it became apparent that the damage was much more serious, and in fact, would require surgery and an estimated four months of rehabilitation—a devastating blow to the man who had just devoted nearly a year of his life to creating the ultimate racing machine. Donohue would now have to sit on the sidelines and watch another driver enjoy the fruits of his labor. He later said it was "like seeing another man in bed with your wife."

Penske turned to George Follmer, the talented but cantankerous 38-year-old veteran who had driven as Donohue's teammate in the 1967 Can Am season, and most recently had won the Trans Am driving championship. Yet despite his impressive credentials, there was still some question about whether Follmer would be able to handle the technical complexity of the turbo Porsche. One insider was overheard worrying: "This is a car that needs an engineer to drive it, and Mark is an engineer. Like it or not, George isn't."

Given this new uncertainty, Team McLaren still had reason to be hopeful about the 1972 season, and by outward appearances, drivers Denny Hulme and Peter Revson were still exceedingly confident, as *Sports Illustrated's* Robert F. Jones reflected on the conversation between the McLaren boys over dinner the night before qualifying: "'When should we take that extra second off our lap time?' asked Revvy. 'In the morning? Or should we wait until the last minute of qualifying?' Hulme rolled a mouthful of Cold Duck over his tongue and stared away through the terpentine pines at the cemetery across the valley….'I dunno,' said Denny finally. 'We can do it whenever we choose. Let's see how we feel in the morning.'"

But Hulme and Revson were noticeably less cocky the next day. With almost no practice time, and driving the most technically sophisticated racecar that had ever been built, George Follmer managed to qualify the hastily-assembled backup Porsche second on the grid, between the two orange cars. The race proved to be anti-climactic, as both McLarens retired early with mechanical problems, leaving Follmer to cruise to an unchallenged victory. In the record book, a win is a win; but two races into the season, the super Penske Porsche still couldn't claim an outright victory over the goliath McLarens.

Round 3 took the Can Am show to Watkins Glen, where the Penske Porsche, with George Follmer still at the wheel, stumbled again. Nobody at Penske Racing was ever willing or able to offer a definitive explanation, but the Porsche just didn't have it that weekend. Follmer was unable to qualify better than third, behind the twin McLarens. He fell in behind the orange cars at the start, and steadily lost ground to Hulme and Revson lap after lap. About half way through the race, as the two McLarens shot off the last turn onto the pit straight, there was a momentary roar from the crowd in the main grandstands. There, right behind the two leading orange blurs, was a white car! Had Follmer suddenly found and corrected a problem? Certainly, both McLarens couldn't have slowed that much at the same time. But as the cars raced toward the start-finish line, it became apparent that it was not Follmer's Porsche on Revson's tail, but rather a lapped back-marker. The Porsche followed along many seconds later and eventually straggled to a humiliating fifth-place finish. It was another disappointment for Penske Racing and one more celebration for Denny Hulme, Peter Revson, and the seemingly untouchable Team McLaren. But this McLaren victory would be different than all that came before. Although nobody could have believed it on that sunny July afternoon in upstate New York, after 5 years of unrelenting domination, this would turn out to be the very last Can Am battle that Team McLaren would ever win.

The tide turned for good two weeks later at Mid-Ohio. With Mark Donohue in the pits on crutches helping his former teammate sort out the complex and tempremental Porsche, Follmer put the Penske "Panzer" on pole. In the early stages of the race, he pulled away from his competition by as much as 2 seconds a lap. Both McLarens eventually struggled with mechanical problems, but that didn't really matter. It was obvious from the start that they had nothing for the Penske Porsche that day. Although Follmer spun twice in what turned out to be a wet race, he never lost the lead, and went on to finish comfortably ahead of a determined Jackie Oliver in a UOP Shadow/Chevy. Hulme finished several laps down in fourth place, while Revson DNF'd in the other McLaren.

George Follmer and the Penske Porsche won again two weeks later at Elkhart Lake, Wisconsin, in a race that proved interesting only because rain during qualifying caused Follmer to start deep back in the pack, in the 13th position. After a lap, he was in 10th. He moved up to 4th after 4 laps, and by the 11th round, he was on the tail of Denny Hulme's leading McLaren. Then—undoubtedly over-tuned and over-driven in a desperate effort to keep up with the superior Porsche—Hulme's McLaren expired, leaving Follmer to cruise off for his second consecutive victory.

If the McLaren folks were feeling pretty shaken after Elkhart Lake, they must have been numb when they saw the entry list for the next race at Donnybrooke,

Minnesota. There would be not one, but two Penske Porsches on the grid. And Follmer's teammate would be none other than the engineer himself, Mark Donohue, back at the wheel after only 10 weeks. Pete Lyons described Donohue's heroic return, writing: "Driving a brand-new car —though it was wearing the number '6' Follmer had been using—Mark started practicing on Thursday. That ended with a fuel leak. On Friday he had severe over-steer. On Saturday the balance was better, but it still wasn't as good as Follmer's. This puzzled Donohue the engineer. 'The two cars are set up perfectly identically and perfect should be perfect, but mine just isn't handling.' That afternoon, he took the pole."

In the race, the Porsches led into the first turn, but at the end of lap one, it was Donohue followed by Hulme, then Follmer and Revson, all tightly packed together. The four put on a great show until Hulme's McLaren expired first, followed by Revson's several laps later. That left the two Penske cars to entertain the crowd, swapping the lead several times until Donohue's rear tire exploded late in the race, sending him into a wild spin that was frighteningly reminiscent of the Atlanta wreck. Donohue said: "There I was, going sideways through a turn at 190 mph with the rear end flopping around. I thought, 'Oh shit! Here we go again!'" Fortunately, he walked away this time uninjured, although the same could not be said for the car.

It appeared then that Follmer would cruise home to an uncontested third consecutive victory, but fate would intervene one more time in this strange event, as the #7 Penske Porsche coasted to a stop on the very last lap, its fuel tank dry! That left the independent McLaren of flamboyant Frenchmen Francois Cevert to take the honors, his first and only Can Am triumph.

The next time out, in Edmonton, Canada, the Penske Porsches swept the front row in qualifying, with Follmer on the pole. This would be the race in which Mark Donohue finally scored his long-overdue and much-deserved first victory in the "turbo-Panzer" supercar that he created, while Follmer finished third. Then at Laguna Seca, it was Donohue on pole with Follmer beside him. Donohue was firmly in control of the race when he slowed at the end to let his teammate pass, thus

The familiar orange Gulf McLarens, shown here pacing the field ahead of Jackie Stewart's Lola in 1971, won two of the first three battles in the 1972 Can Am season. But it was apparent from the beginning that the Penske Porsche was destined to win the war despite some serious early setbacks. *Mike Smith*

assuring the driver's championship for Penske Racing. The dramatic 1972 Can Am season came to a close at Riverside, California. George Follmer put the #7 Penske Porsche on the pole, but there would not be another one-two Penske sweep of the front row this weekend. Denny Hulme, using a special 9-liter qualifying motor in his McLaren, bumped Donohue to third spot on the starting grid. George Follmer won the race over Peter Revson's McLaren, with Donohue dropping to third when, this time, he ran out of gas on the final lap.

Porsche, of course, won the manufacturer's title and Follmer won the driver's championship in a landslide with 130 points over second place Hulme with 65. Donohue was fourth, only 3 points back with 62. Had he finished 1st or 2nd at Riverside, it would have been a 1-2 Penske Porsche driver's championship. Regardless, it was an impressive season to say the least, and Roger Penske finally had his prestigious and long-awaited Can Am title.

At the end of the 1972 season, with 5 constructors and 5 driver championship trophies on the mantle, and what appeared to be an insurmountable challenge ahead, Team McLaren decided to call it quits, walking away from the series that it had virtually defined from the beginning. Officially, McLaren claimed that they wanted to concentrate on their Formula-1 and Indy car

programs; but the reality was that they knew nobody was going to be able to complete with the Porsche-Penske-Donohue partnership. McLaren surely anticipated what everyone else was to find out the following spring—we hadn't seen nothin' yet!

Mark Donohue missed half of the 1972 season because of a serious injury sustained testing the Porsche at Road Atlanta. Roger Penske recruited George Follmer to step in and carry the Porsche to the championship. Donohue, seen here at Riverside, was back in a second car for the final three races of the season. *Mike Smith*

Like all Penske racecars, the 1973 Porsche 917-30K was an immaculately prepared, beautifully painted piece of artwork, although the enormous rear wing gave the car a somewhat bulky, awkward look. Functionally, however, the design was so perfect that Mark Donohue called it a monument to his career. *Mike Smith*

1973

The 1973 Porsche 917/30K was a significant evolution of the '72 car. In appearance, it looked longer, heavier, and maybe even a little awkward compared to the beautiful clean lines of the 917/10K. Most noticeable was the enormous rear wing structure that made the car appear strangely bulky. The Porsche factory had contracted an aeronautical engineering firm to modify the body design in an attempt to get more top-end speed by reducing aerodynamic drag. The initial changes resulted in no appreciable improvements over the '72 body style. But based on his experience with the Ferrari 512 at Le Mans, Donohue convinced the Porsche engineers to adapt the 'long-tail' body design that had been so successful on the Porsche coupes there. The result was a dramatic increase in top-end straightaway speed from 212 to 240 mph!

In the engine compartment, the 5-liter motor was beefed up to a 5.4-liter twin-turbo 12-cylinder design that produced 1100 horsepower on the track and an unbelievable 1500 hp on the dyno. For 1973, the L&M sponsorship was gone, replaced with the familiar blue and gold Sunoco color scheme that had adorned so many other successful Penske racecars in the past.

From the grandstands, it looked like the Porsche's second season was a cakewalk for Donohue and the Penske team. But, at least in the early part of the year, that was not the case at all. Even though there was no Team McLaren to contend with, the '72 Porsche 917/10s were back, one of them in the hands of the very motivated defending Can Am champion George Follmer, who was now driving for Bobby Rinsler. Future F1 World Champion Jody Scheckter, a talented and exciting young charger, was at the wheel of another well-funded 917/10 effort.

The chassis design changes on the 917/30, which ultimately proved to be a great advantage, were initially problematic, and Donohue was still trying to get the aerodynamics properly balanced going into the first race weekend at Mosport. Although he took the pole, the beginning of the race turned into an interesting battle between the new Penske Porsche and the 917/10 of Jody Scheckter. The two exchanged the lead twice in the first couple of laps and were putting on

Mark Donohue is seen here sitting in the cockpit of the awesome Turbo-Porsche Panzer that he created. He is looking tired and probably thinking about his imminent retirement announcement. *Bob Jordan*

By the time the Can Am teams arrived in Riverside for the season finale, Mark Donohue and the Penske Porsche had beaten their challengers into submission. The competitive imbalance was so bad that the SCCA felt compelled to legislate changes for 1974 that would effectively ban the use of turbo-charged engines. Although the Can-Am series would continue for several years, this is considered the end of its glory days—an era when there were virtually no restrictions on engine size, design, or horsepower capabilities. *Mike Smith*

a crowd-pleasing show in the early stages of the race. But then, coming over the crest of a hill at more than 200 mph, the two leaders suddenly came upon a much slower back-marker in their path. Donohue, who was in front at the time, barely clipped the slower car, but it was enough to send the blue Porsche sliding off the track and through the grass. The car ultimately struck a 3-ft dirt embankment and punted sharply into the air. Although Donohue managed to limp it back to the pits for crude repairs, the aerodynamics of the car were destroyed and he lumbered on to finish 7 laps down—it was like déjà vu all over again!

Donohue's bad luck continued at Atlanta, where a fuel leak in the cockpit caused him to make an unscheduled stop, resulting in a second place finish to George Follmer. But things went dramatically better from that point forward, and the Penske Porsche was rarely challenged for the remainder of the season. At Mid-Ohio in mid August, Follmer got the jump on Donohue

at the start and led for the majority of the race, with the Penske Porsche right on his tail. Five laps from the end, Donohue cranked up the in-cockpit turbo-boost adjustment at the beginning of the long back straight, adding 450 hp to the rear wheels, and leaving Follmer in the dust.

There was also some excitement at Laguna Seca in mid-October, when the normally invincible Porsche had a rare engine failure in the race-morning qualifying heat. The Penske Racing crew, apparently with the boss himself getting his hands and his Gucci loafers dirty, executed a complete engine change in less than three hours to get Donohue into the main event. As Roger Penske has often said, 'effort equals results,' and the result of this considerable effort was totally predictable. Donohue started 16th in the 24-car field. He passed 12 cars in the first three laps, and the rest was academic. *AutoWeek* wrote: "Donohue obliged Scheckter, Redman, Elford, Oliver and Follmer by failing to finish the

As Mark Donohue cruised around Riverside Raceway virtually unchallenged in the final event of the 1973 Can-Am season, he knew that he was about to make an announcement that would change his life. From the winner's podium, Captain Nice informed the racing world that he had just completed his final season as a driver. *Mike Smith*

Road & Track magazine wrote: "His total domination of the season was a testament to his extraordinary skill as an engineer, car developer and driver. He won the last six races, setting new qualifying times each time out. Everything that had gone before—Indy, Trans-Am—all of it, was simply preparation for this final season. That beautiful, gaudy, immaculate, invincible Porsche was the ultimate effort of Donohue the engineer-developer and the 1973 Can-Am the consummation of a great driving career. We may well have been privileged…to witness the ultimate man-machine combination in the history of the sport…He was great. Almost perfect…."

In a desperate attempt to restore competition in the Can Am series, the SCCA imposed fuel mileage requirements for the 1974 season, in effect banning the use of gas-guzzling turbo-chargers. Although probably unavoidable and maybe appropriate under the circumstances, it was truly a pity, because the world never got to see the third generation 917 that was already under development in Germany. Porsche had built, and Mark Donohue had already tested, a 16 cylinder 6.5 liter turbo-charged engine that produced 2000 hp. Although the public never had the opportunity to see this engineering marvel on the racetrack, the engine was later placed on display in Porsche's Stuttgart museum.

The Penske Porsche 917/30 would eventually run one more Can Am event, at Mid-Ohio in 1974. This was reportedly the track at which the car had demonstrated the best fuel mileage the previous year. Therefore, with a little de-tuning and short-shifting, it was hoped that the gas-guzzling turbo might just barely make the new fuel mileage requirements. Donohue was retired at that point, and George Follmer was driving for the UOP Shadow team, so Penske called on veteran Brian Redman to handle driving duties. Redman handily put the Porsche on pole ahead of the two black UOP Shadows of George Follmer and Jackie Oliver, and he easily won the preliminary heat race. In the main event, Redman battled fiercely with Follmer and Oliver for the first 18 laps before he made a slight mistake, getting the power down a little too early coming out of a turn and putting the Porsche sideways. He managed to keep the car on the track, but he lost a lot of ground and even-

qualifier at Monterey and still came from the back to win the race, the money and the championship. Is there no justice?"

After disappointing losses in the first two events, Mark Donohue went on to win the remaining 6 races of the 1973 season, the most consecutive Can-Am victories ever recorded by a driver—more than Bruce McLaren, more than Denny Hulme. By the season finale at Riverside, it was apparent that the rest of the field was utterly demoralized. The Donohue-Penske Porsche was so dominating, so overwhelming, that it appeared nobody even had the will to fight back anymore. Pete Lyons penned the story for *Auto Week*, beginning: "With the sun setting early over the chrome and plastic dustbowl which is Riverside, a certain sadness set in. There were all the old Can-Am cars, circulating about with Mark Donohue so far in the lead that nothing short of the San Andreas fault could keep him from winning."

When Mark Donohue climbed from the car after his victory lap at Riverside in October of 1973, he shocked the racing world by announcing his retirement. He called the invincible Porsche 917/30 "a monument to my career as an engineer and a driver." Very simply, there was nothing left to prove.

In the summer of 1974, the Can-Am organizers persuaded Roger Penske to run the Porsche at Mid-Ohio in an attempt to inject some much-needed excitement into the series. With the turbo motor supposedly detuned for improved fuel economy, Brian Redman drove the #66 car, seen here leading George Follmer's #1 UOP Shadow, to a second-place finish. *Mike Odell / Forget-Me-Not-Race Pix / SportsRacingLtd.com*

In the summer of 1975, Roger Penske pulled the 917-30 out of mothballs, slapped a coat of red CAM2 paint on it, and sent Mark Donohue out on the high-banked Talladega Super-Speedway to break the world closed-course speed record. In conditions that were far less than ideal, Donohue pushed the Porsche to an average lap speed of 221.160 mph, establishing a record that would stand for nearly 20 years.

tually overheated his tires trying to catch up with the leaders. He ultimately finished a disappointing second to Jackie Oliver's Shadow.

Roger Penske brought the Porsche 917/30 out of mothballs one more time in August of 1975. Modified for absolute minimal aerodynamic drag, with Mark Donohue back at the wheel, the car set a new world closed-course speed record with a lap speed over 221 mph at Talladega Speedway, a record that stood for nearly 20 years. Donohue was clocked at over 250 mph on the straightaway. The racing world was left to imagine what 16 cylinders and 2000 horsepower might have done!

When Mark Donohue announced his retirement following the 1973 Riverside Can-Am race, there was one footnote—he would compete in one last race, the final event of the inaugural International Race of Champions, which was scheduled for Daytona Speedway in February. This initial IROC championship was not like the made-for-TV, NASCAR-dominated show of the 21st century. This first event was a genuine international competition among the very best drivers in the world's top racing series. Two-time defending World Driving Champion Emerson Fittapaldi was there along with fellow Formula-1 star Peter Revson and former World Champion Denny Hulme. Jackie Stewart, a three-time World Champion had to withdraw at the last minute because of a stomach ulcer. Stewart was replaced by George Follmer, who was at that time also competing in Formula-1 with the UOP Shadow team. NASCAR was represented by 7-time National Champion, King Richard Petty; the Silver Fox of the super-speedways, David Pearson; and future Penske Racing NASCAR star Bobby Allison. From the USAC Indy-car circuit, there was the defending Indy 500 winner, Gordon Johncock; 3-time Indy winner and USAC National Driving Champion, A.J. Foyt; 1973 USAC National Champion, Roger McCluskey; former Indy winner and USAC National Champion, Bobby Unser; and of course, Mark Donohue. This first IROC was contested in identically prepared Porsche 911 Carreras.

Pete Lyons said in his November 1973 *AutoWeek* account of the first three races: "If history doesn't look

Roger Penske was one of the founding partners in the original International Race of Champions. Mark Donohue, seen here at Riverside, competed in the inaugural 1973 IROC series against other top drivers from Indy cars, NASCAR, Formula-1 and sports cars. Donohue won three of four events and was crowned the first IROC Champion. *Mike Smith*

With a Can-Am championship, an Indy 500 victory, three Trans-Am series titles, two United States Road Racing Championships, and now an IROC crown, Mark Donohue had enjoyed one of the most successful and colorful careers in the history of auto racing. By the end of the 1973 season, he had concluded that there was nothing important left to accomplish and announced his retirement.

back on the IROC as the finest idea ever, then the whole sport had better quit now and be done with it." To win even one of the four races against this competition would be the highlight of most racing careers. For any driver to win more than once would have been almost unthinkable at the outset; yet going to the Daytona finale, Mark Donohue was the proud owner of two victories in the first three races.

At Daytona, the drivers qualified for starting positions in the final race, all using the same racecar. Donohue took the pole by almost a full second over Peter Revson. At the start of the race, David Pearson and George Follmer drafted around Donohue's Porsche on the speedway section of the Daytona track, but that was temporary. By the third lap, Mark had taken the lead back. "The uncanny precision that has won him a Can-Am title and a reputation for calculating faultlessness,"

wrote Gordon Kirby in his *Auto Week* story, "was once again carrying Donohue to a strong lead." It was a lead he would not relinquish; as he charged on to score a remarkable third win in the four-race series. It was a fairytale ending to an unbelievable career; he was the irrefutable champion of champions, the best of the very best. Mark Donohue had realized every athlete's dream, retiring at the very top of his game. Three-time World Driving Champion Jackie Stewart conducted the winner's interview for ABC Sports, very eloquently stating the sentiments of the many thousands of fans who had followed Donohue's remarkable career. "Mark, this is a fabulous moment," he said. "You are really going out in style. The way you retired is truly a mark of class."

Vintage Racing Photos

CHAPTER 8
NASCAR (1972–1977)

"…[The AMC Matador] may have been fine for containing opera hats and egret feathers in its tall interior, but it stuck up too high to make sense at Daytona and Rockingham."
— *AutoWeek*, November 17, 1973

Following Penske Racing's 1971 Trans-Am championship with the previously-hopeless AMC Javelin, it was beginning to look to American Motors, and much of the auto racing world as well, that there was nothing that this Penske team couldn't do if they set their minds to it. So when the Captain decided that he didn't want to continue in the Trans-Am series beyond the '71 season, both he and American Motors were interested in finding another forum in which to continue their successful partnership. Although NASCAR in 1972 was nothing compared to phenomenon that it is today, there was still a significant level of factory and fan interest in the stock car series. The motto, "Win on Sunday, sell on Monday," was already a marketing reality. The three biggest U.S. automakers, Ford, GM and Chrysler, were already actively involved. Roger Penske and American Motors agreed that this should be their next conquest.

1972

NASCAR, in some ways, has changed more dramatically in the past 30 years than any other form of racing in the world; yet in other respects, it has scarcely evolved at all. Although some would disagree passionately, modern-day NASCAR is really a "spec-car" series. There are Chevrolets, Fords, Dodges and Pontiacs on the entry lists, but remove the painted-on headlights and other superficial identifying features from the bodywork, and they all look pretty much the same—and nothing at all like the showroom version of the automobiles that they pretend to represent. In the interest of competition, NASCAR has created a standard template into which all models must conform. If the real car doesn't fit, it simply gets reshaped until it does. If the end product is too fast or too slow, NASCAR merely dictates more or less spoiler or some other controlled modification until it is acceptably competitive. In the end, the cars are regulated to be as equal as possible for the sake of the show. This is not necessarily an indictment of NASCAR's philosophy or approach, merely a statement of today's reality.

In 1972, "stock car" more-or-less meant stock car, at least in terms of the body. There were allowances for spoilers and a few other minor modifications, but the starting point was the actual production automobile. If your car was a box, you raced a box. And unfortunately, in 1972 the AMC Matador that Penske Racing would campaign was exactly that—a big red, white and blue BOX ON WHEELS. In addition to its aerodynamic handicap, the Matador's small-block engine was at a huge horsepower disadvantage to the top Ford, Chrysler, and GM competition. These factors, in addition to their unfamiliarity with the "good-'ol-boy" world of NASCAR, resulted in a monumental challenge for the Penske Racing organization.

With a new Can-Am program and a full-scale Indy-car effort on the table for 1972, Penske wisely decided to contract out some of the initial work. He went to Holman & Moody, a team that had been involved in stock car racing since the beginning of time, and worked out an arrangement for them to build the first Matador. Then, to help navigate through the unfamiliar NAS-

The tall, box-shaped AMC Matador was ill suited for a NASCAR career, but after the unqualified success with the Javelin Trans-Am program, American Motors believed Penske Racing could make their new Rambler competitive on the stock car circuit.

CAR bureaucracy, he made a deal with another stock car team, Hucherson and Pagan, to subcontract the racing operations.

The agreement between Penske and AMC was to run the Matador at all the super-speedway events and the Riverside road course races only, which amounted to about 12 races during the season. Mark Donohue was going to be the primary driver, and he was, unfortunately, totally unfamiliar with this form of racing. His background was in sports cars and road racing. Although he had already enjoyed some success in open-wheel Indy cars on the bigger oval tracks, NASCAR was going to be a whole new ballgame.

Donohue's impression of the completed Matador when he first tested it at Charlotte Motor Speedway was that it was a "basket case." He saw many things that needed to be improved, yet the car was still reasonably fast right out of the box and everyone else was fairly pleased with the starting point. Before the season-opener, Donohue and Don Cox replaced the drum brakes with four-wheel discs, changed the suspension and reinforced the frame. The first race was Riverside, California, NASCAR's lone road race at that time. This was expected to be a big advantage for Penske Racing because of Donohue's background. In fact, he qualified fourth on the grid in his NASCAR debut and even led the race in the early going before the Matador's rear axle came apart, ending

his day. All things considered, it was a pretty impressive start for the new Penske team in the unfamiliar and very competitive world of stock car racing.

At Daytona, however, it was a very different story. It was here that the Matador's aerodynamic and horsepower handicaps became glaringly obvious. Donohue had Traco build a 366 c.i.d. version of AMC's small-block motor that they'd used so successfully in the Trans-Am Javelin. But, even with NASCAR's carburetor restrictor plates, this left the Penske Matador at a tremendous disadvantage to the 427 c.i.d. engines used by the competition. Donohue started 7th his 125-mile qualifier race and finished a respectable fifth. In the Daytona 500 itself, however, he started 10th and slowly went backwards until the engine finally quit. He later recalled that he was running laps at 171 mph while the leaders were at 185 mph. "I just held my foot to the floor all the way around the track for as long as it lasted," he said. "The driver meant nothing. You could put a robot in there to do the steering." Unfortunately, the Daytona experience was indicative of the challenge ahead. The Matador was going to need a lot of work before it would ever be competitive on the NASCAR super-speedways.

The next race for the Penske team was at Ontario, California. Donohue qualified seventh but again was painfully uncompetitive. He was running toward the

Mark Donohue in the #16 AMC Matador is seen here ahead of Charlie Glotzbach's Dodge at Daytona. Donohue later recalled his first superspeedway experience in the uncompetitive Matador: "I just held my foot to the floor all the way around the track for as long as it lasted. The driver meant nothing. You could put a robot in there to do the steering."

back of the field when he got hit from behind under braking in turn one. He hit the wall hard enough to do serious damage to the car and leave himself stunned and very sore, but otherwise not injured.

Before their next race, which was at Atlanta Motor Speedway, the Penske team had a new and supposedly improved Matador. Because of his inexperience, however, Donohue had the car set up at the start of the race to be oversteering so badly that he actually lost control and spun it down the front straightaway. After recovering from that embarrassment, the Matador started to lose water and overheat. Donohue had to pit several times to add water, and he eventually finished 15th. "It would have saved us a lot of embarrassment had it just blown up," he said later. The race was humiliating for Mark Donohue and the team, as they were quickly becoming the laughing stock of NASCAR—the big-shot, high-tech SCCA and Indy-car champions were getting trounced by the good 'ol boys. It was becoming a totally demoralizing experience.

With Donohue commited to the Indianapolis 500 for Memorial Day weekend, Roger Penske recruited NASCAR journeyman Dave Marcis to drive the Mata-

dor in the World 600 at Charlotte. As it would turn out, because of Donohue's Can-Am practice crash in July, Marcis would be in the Matador's driver's seat for most of the remaining races in the 1972 season.

Marcis qualified 8th for the World 600, but retired early with suspension failure for a 31st place finish. Donny Allison, Bobby's brother, was at the wheel for the June Riverside race. Again, the Matador was reasonably competitive on the road course. Allison qualified sixth and appeared to have the field covered before a spin relegated him to a third place finish. As it turned out, that would be the team's best result for the 1972 season.

Marcis was back in the car for the remaining seven races of the season. In late July he ran in the USAC-sanctioned Pennsylvania 500 at Pocono Speedway, where he managed a 4th place finish, his best of the year. Then, back on the NASCAR circuit, he scored a 9th place finish at Michigan and a 7th at Darlington before a string of three DNF's at Dover, Martinsville and Charlotte. He closed out the season with another 7th place result at Rockingham.

For the year, the Matador started 13 races and finished only six. There were three engine failures, two rear end problems, a crash, and a suspension failure. Even when running, with the exception of the Riverside road course, the Matador was rarely very competitive. And by the end of the disappointing season, there weren't any easy answers.

1973

In 1973, the NASCAR season opened again on the road course at Riverside. Mark Donohue was back at the wheel of the Penske AMC Matador for the first time since early in 1972. With his road racing experience and the Matador's superior brakes, this appeared to be the best opportunity of the whole season for the struggling program to shine. Donohue was disappointed when he could qualify no better than fourth, but he knew that if the car would hold together, the four-wheel disc brakes would pay off later in the race. For the first time in the year-long ordeal of frustration and disappointment, everything finally went according to plan. Donohue ran with the leaders through the first half of the 500-mile marathon and then, as everyone's brakes began to fade, he pulled away to an easy victory. By winning in only his fifth Winston Cup start, Mark Donohue set a modern-era NASCAR record that stood for over 28 years until Kevin Harvik, replacing the late Dale Earnhart in 2001, found the winner's circle in just his third attempt. And although everyone recognized that Riverside was not the typical stock car race, Penske Racing and the AMC Matador could no longer be denied some measure of respect and credibility because of this accomplishment. It was clearly a highlight in what was going to be a roller coaster year for Mark Donohue and the entire Penske Racing team.

Dave Marcis was back in the Matador for the Daytona 500, where another rear end failure left him with a 27th place DNF. During the off-season the team had decided, in a desperate attempt to find horsepower for the super-speedways, to bore out the small-block AMC motor to a full 427 c.i.d. This engine was not actually used in the car until after the Daytona 500 race. When it was put into service, beginning with the Carolina 500 at Rockingham in March, the reliability results were disastrous. Marcis qualified a season-best sixth place,

but dropped out early with engine failure. Mark Donohue took the wheel for the Atlanta 500 on April 1, but the result was the same: DNF – Engine Failure. Marcis recorded two more engine failure DNF's at Martinsville and Charlotte before the over-stressed little AMC motor finally held together for a mediocre 8th place finish at Dover in June. A crash took Marcis out of the Texas Alamo 500 and then there were more engine problems at Bristol and Charlotte before a season-ending 5th place result at Rockingham. In eleven races, there were eight DNF's, six of which were engine failure. It was a dismal season, with the exception of Donohue's Riverside win. Certainly Roger Penske wouldn't let this bleeding go on much longer.

1974

The cover page of the November 17, 1973 *AutoWeek* magazine contained three headlines and a picture. The first headline read: "DONOHUE QUITS RACING!" The second was: "THE RACE OF THE DECADE— IROC: Even Better Than Expected." (Mark Donohue had won two of the first three races in this Penske-created international all-star series). And the final headline warned: "Penske Matador—Look out NASCAR—it's here!" This headline was followed by a picture of the boldly redesigned 1974 American Motors Matador, beautifully decked out in its familiar red, white, and blue paint scheme, and looking very, very racy.

A brief article on page two, titled: "Roger the Matador," introduced the object of the cover page declaration. "The message is pretty clear," it said. "Roger Penske, who has not had anywhere near the success in Grand National racing that he has had in everything else from Indianapolis to matched swan contests, has decided to do something about it." Refering to the changes in the Matador's design, the writer observed: "What looks to be another Penske Panzer is about to burst on the world."

AutoWeek's reference to Penske Racing's all-conquering turbo-Porsche Panzers that dominated the 1972 and 1973 Can-Am series reflected the perceived potential of the new Matador. Gone were the Rambler-inspired boxy lines of the original model. This

MARK DONOHUE'S PENSKE PREPARED 1974 AMC MATADOR

new bullfighter was smooth and low; it looked, in racing dress at least, at lot like the Javelin's big brother. If AMC's redesign was not influenced by the desire to be more competitive in racing, then the outcome was a remarkably fortuitous coincidence.

After the disastrous experiment with the 427 engine, the team reverted to a better-developed version of the 366 motor for 1974. NASCAR had, in fact, legislated out the big-block engines beginning with the March Atlanta race anyway, so the Matador would now be on even ground with the competition for the first time.

Roger Penske played musical chairs with drivers before finally hooking up with NASCAR star Bobby Allison at mid-season. To start the year, Penske put his Indy-car pilot, Gary Bettenhausen into the new Matador. In the season opener on the Riverside road course, Bettenhausen qualified fifth even though he was not a particularly strong road course driver. In the race, the Penske pit crew did an uncharacteristically sloppy job and Bettenhausen ended up finishing seventh, not what was expected on this track that had always brought out

the best in the AMC car.

Bettenhausen had a problem in his 125-mile qualifying race and was relegated to starting 33rd in the Daytona 500, which this year was shortened to 450 miles as a token concession to the national energy crisis. He hung on for an unspectacular 12th place finish, four laps behind winner Richard Petty; but it was the first time that Penske Racing had made it to the end of a Daytona 500. Things started to look up after that, however. The Atlanta 500 was the first race under the new small-block engine regulations, and Bettenhausen's second-place qualifying result reflected the Matador's new competitiveness. In the race, he managed only a 9th place finish, but the future looked brighter.

Dave Marcis was back in the Matador for the Rebel 450 in early April. In his lone Penske drive for the year, Marcis qualified fifth and finished sixth, leading the race for a total of 10 laps. Bettenhausen was in the driver's seat again for Talladega where he qualified second but was taken out of the race while leading because of a pit road accident. While the Matador was being serviced,

Bobby Allison had driven the Indy 500 for Penske Racing in 1973. When the Captain needed a proven NASCAR winner to rescue the struggling AMC Matador program in 1974, Bobby got the call.

Grant Adcox lost control of his car on the damp, oil-slick pit road and rammed into the back of Bettenhausen's parked car. Four Penske crew members were injured in the incident. Don Miller suffered the most serious injuries when he was pinned between the two cars on impact, crushing both of his legs. He would ultimately need to have the right leg amputated. What should have been a victory celebration quickly turned into a tragedy. Years later, however, Don Miller would end up playing a key role in Penske Racing's triumphant return to NAS-CAR after a 15-year hiatus from the series.

For the June Riverside race, Roger Penske put experienced road-racer George Follmer in the Matador, determined to get AMC back into victory lane. Follmer demonstrated the car's potential by securing Penske Racing's first NASCAR pole position; but in the race, he missed a shift and over-revved the engine, ending his day early. Bettenhausen was back in the car for one more event, the Motor State 400 at Michigan International Speedway in mid June. He turned in another steady but unremarkable performance, finishing fourth after qualifying sixth.

By this point, both Roger Penske and American

Motors certainly were frustrated that the all-new, highly acclaimed AMC Matador had not managed to produce anything better than a fourth-place finish. Penske made a bold move and hired established NASCAR star Bobby Allison to take over driving duties for the struggling pro-gram. Although it would still take nearly half a season to find success, this move finally put the Penske Matador program on the right course. Allison qualified second in his first race, the Firecracker 400 at Daytona. He led a good part of the event before dropping to a fifth place finish. After a DNF in the Dixie 500 at Atlanta, Allison had another strong showing in the August Talladega 500. A lengthy pit stop early in the race for a windshield replacement put him more than two laps down to the leaders, but he charged back to an impressive third place finish. Then there was a string of three DNF's at Michigan, Darlington, and Dover before he came back with a fifth place result at Charlotte in early October. Allison followed that with a fourth place at Rockingham two weeks later. Then, finally, in the last race of the 1974 season, he drove the Matador to its first oval-track victory in the Ontario 500. In a post-race inspection, NASCAR declared the engine tappets to be illegal and issued a stiff $9,100 fine to the Penske team, but the victory stood. Although the overall season certainly didn't live up to early expectations, it did set the stage for what would be Penske Racing's breakthrough year in 1975.

1975

1975 was Penske Racing's most ambitious and most successful NASCAR campaign to date. With Bobby Allison doing all the driving, the Matador was entered in 20 races, posting 4 wins, 3 seconds, and a total of eleven top-10 finishes. The new season picked up right where 1974 left off, with Allison taking the pole at Riverside and going on the a solid victory. In the 125-mile Daytona qualifying race, he dropped to the back of the field with a tire problem, then recovered to take another win. In the main event, the Matador developed an ignition problem, but Allison still managed to hang on for a second-place finish. It seemed apparent from the start that this was going to be a good season for the Penske-AMC program.

Bobby Allison and the Penske Matador competed in a number of USAC sanctioned events, normally racing with the number "12."

In NASCAR trim, the Penske Matador ran as the number "16."

In the Atlanta 500, Allison qualified second but was sidelined with an engine problem for the season's first DNF. He came back with win at Darlington and then a 4th place at Martinsville. At Talladega, in a race that was marred by the death of driver Tiny Lund, Allison dropped out with an engine problem after qualifying third. Back at Riverside for the June 400-miler, he put the Matador on the pole again and raced Richard Petty hard all day before settling for a close second. Engine problems put the Penske-AMC entry out of contention in the next four races before Allison rebounded with a fourth place at Michigan in August and then a solid win in the Labor Day Southern 500 at Darlington.

Bobby Allison ended the 1975 season with three DNF's in the last six races, but he also scored a third-place in the Old Dominion 500, a second-place at Rockingham, and a fifth-place in the season finale at Ontario. Despite his four wins and 11 top-10 finishes, Penske's popular driver from Hueytown, Alabama, placed only 24th in the overall Winston Cup championship for 1975. NASCAR's points system, which remains largely unchanged today, rewards participation and consistency above wins and top finishes. The only way to challenge for the title is to run the full schedule, and that's exactly what Roger Penske resolved to do for 1976.

1976

Surprisingly, after the relatively successful 1975 season, American Motors chose not to renew its partnership with Penske Racing. There were several factors involved, including AMC's struggling financial situation. Also, at this time in history just after the 1973 energy crisis, all automakers were feeling pressured to move away from their high-performance gas-guzzling car designs in favor of new 'econo-box' models. The American Motors Javelin had already been sacrificed, being replaced by the pathetic new Hornet and the infamous Gremlin—it was a dark time for the automobile enthusiast!

Despite AMC's departure, Roger Penske was not ready to give up on stock car racing after finally achieving some hard-earned success. Ironically, with the USAC program still struggling and no reason to expect any imminent success in Formula-1, the NASCAR campaign looked to be Penske Racing's best shot at a championship in 1976. To that end, the Captain made the commitment to run the full 30-race Winston Cup schedule.

For the season opener at Riverside, the Penske Matador appeared with its familiar red, white and blue stripes replaced by Sunoco's CAM2 motor oil colors. Allison again took the pole, but a blown engine in the

After American Motors withdrew its support of Penske's NASCAR program, the Captain switched to a Mercury Montego with Sunoco CAM2 sponsorship. Bobby Allison drove the full 1976 schedule for Penske Racing before leaving to form his own team the following year. Roger Penske, Dave Marcis and the crew pose here with the CAM2 Mercury at Daytona in 1977. *Vintage Racing Photos*

race relegated him to a 15th place finish. As it turned out, that would be the last outing for the Penske Racing AMC Matador. With no financial incentive to continue with the American Motors entry, Penske had decided to switch to the supposedly more competitive Mercury after the Riverside race. Of course, even if there was an inherent performance advantage with the Mercury, this move necessitated a complete new development effort, and that proved to be a costly handicap during the 1976 season. Roger Penske had evidently forgotten the lessons learned when he and Donohue switched from the Camaro to the Javelin in the Trans-Am series several years earlier. What was expected to be a fairly easy and superficial change turned out to be a major undertaking. In fact, history would, unfortunately, repeat itself

now with this move from AMC to Mercury.

Allison had an engine problem at Daytona in the first race with the Mercury and finished 25th. That was followed by an accident at Charlotte for a third-straight DNF, not a good start toward the championship. Things began to improve after that, however, with a third place finish after qualifying on the pole at Richmond and then a 5th in the Volunteer 500 before another engine failure at Atlanta.

Following Atlanta, Allison turned in a string of 12 consecutive finishes, 10 of which were in the top-ten. At that point, he was 4th in the championship standings and still very much a contender for the title, although he'd not won a single race. In the remaining 12 races of the season, Allison recorded another seven top-10

Penske Racing entered this CAM2 Chevrolet Monte Carlo in place of the Mercury for several races during the 1977 NASCAR season. This lack of manufacturer loyalty seems unthinkable in today's environment, but in the absence of factory support during the late 1970s, Roger Penske elected to put the best possible car on the track. *High Bank Slope Classic Race Photos*

Tom Sneva qualified this Penske Chevrolet at Michigan in 1977 but he crashed it after qualifying and did not compete in the race. Although he ran several NASCAR races for other teams, Sneva never did start one in a Penske car. *Greenfield Gallery*

results, but also five costly DNF's in the Penske CAM2 Mercury. For the year, he had a total of 19 top-10 finishes in 30 starts, but not a single win. He ended up fourth overall in the championship standings, behind Cale Yarborough, Richard Petty and Benny Parsons. At the end of the 1976 season, Bobby Allison decided to leave Penske Racing and run his own independent program for the following year. The car he chose to drive, not coincidentally, was the AMC Matador.

1977

Looking back over the previous two seasons, Roger Penske could clearly see the potential to win a championship in NASCAR. With his keen business sense, he probably also saw the great opportunity in this form of racing. So despite the departure of his chosen driver, Penske decided to regroup and take at least one more shot at the Winston Cup.

One thing that the team had learned in 1976 was that the Mercury was much better on the short tracks than on the super speedways. In the absence of factory support from any of the automakers, Penske elected to stick with the Mercury for the road course and short-track events, and run a Chevrolet on the super speed-

ways. Not many teams would be able to afford this type of arrangement, but Roger Penske was willing and able to spend money to make money.

For his driver, Penske returned to Dave Marcis, whom he had dropped a couple years earlier in favor of the more celebrated Bobby Allison. In the interim, Marcis had been at the top of his game, finishing second to Richard Petty in the 1975 championship standings and finishing sixth in the 1976 title chase with three wins. At the outset, it looked like Penske Racing might be ready to mount a formidable challenge in 1977. The season started off with a respectable fourth place result at Riverside, but that was followed by a poor showing in the Daytona 500. In the first 12 races, Marcis scored only six top-10 finishes, none higher than 4th place, and he was floundering back in 9th position in the championship standings. By this time, Roger Penske was quickly losing interest in the disjointed NASCAR effort, especially as his Indycar team was suddenly the class of the field on the USAC circuit. By mid-season, he began skipping races and before the year was over, the Captain sold the whole operation and got out of the NASCAR business completely. With the exception of a brief "experiment" in 1980, he would not return to the stock car circuit for 14 years.

George Standaar

CHAPTER 9
Formula-One
(1971, 1974 –1976)

"While Roger Penske prowled the pits during the French Grand Prix weekend at Dijon he left a worried wake of speculation behind him. Many of the Formula 1 team managers knew Penske only by reputation but that was enough for them to regard him as strong opposition even though he didn't have his team and car with him!"
—Eoin S. Young, *AutoWeek* & *Competition Press*, 1974

Roger Penske's first foray into Formula-1 was in 1961 when he entered himself in the United States Grand Prix at Watkins Glen. Driving an independent Cooper Climax, Penske qualified 16th and finished 8th in his first F1 outing. He returned to Watkins Glen in the fall of 1962 with a Lotus sponsored by Dupont Zerex antifreeze, qualifying 12th and finishing 9th. In the years that followed, Penske focused his driving efforts on the high-powered sports car circuit, precursor of the Can-Am, where he enjoyed his greatest racing successes. He ended his driving career in 1965, launched the Penske

Racing team in 1966, and did not find his way back to Formula-1 until 1971.

In that era, Formula 1 was far less restrictive and regulated then than it is today. There were no compulsory two-car teams with mandatory identical paint schemes and no restrictions on "guest" entries or "customer cars." In the fall of 1971, Roger Penske extended his relationship with Philadelphia businessman Kirk White, and entered a semi-works Team McLaren in the north American events at Mosport, Canada, and Watkins Glen, New York, the final two races on the 1971 Formula-1 calendar.

The Canadian event was a textbook Penske Racing success story. The prospect of a novice private entry arriving on the scene, unloading the trailer, and instantly being competitive in today's F1 world is absolutely absurd. It was only marginally more conceivable in 1971, but that's exactly how it happened. In a field of 28 cars, compared to today's grids of only 20 or 22 entries, Mark Donohue qualified the Penske-White Sunoco McLaren in 8th position, two spots ahead of Team McLaren lead driver Denny Hulme. In a race that was run mostly under wet conditions, Donohue charged through the field to a 3rd place podium finish, the only car on the lead lap with winner Jackie Stewart and runner-up Ronnie Peterson. To the auto racing world, this was an unbelievable accomplishment; for Penske Racing, it was "business as usual."

The U.S. Grand Prix at Watkins Glen was a logistical nightmare for the team. Donohue was committed to drive the USAC Indy-car race in Trenton, New Jersey, which had been rained out and rescheduled on the same day as the F1 event in upstate New York. So Penske recruited David Hobbs to drive the F1 McLaren. Weather along the east coast was marginal all weekend, raising the possibility that the USAC race could be postponed again and Donohue might drive at Watkins Glen after all, so he bounced back and forth between the two tracks trying to be prepared for either race. In the end, the Trenton race ran on schedule, and Hobbs drove the Penske entry at Watkins Glen, turning in a respectable 10th place performance.

This end-of-the-season fling was enough to convince

Penske Racing leased this McLaren M19A from the factory team to run in the final two races of the 1971 Formula-1 season. Mark Donohue drove the car to a podium finish at Mosport and David Hobbs finished 10th in the U.S. Grand Prix at Watkins Glen.

Roger Penske that Formula-1 was a challenge he wanted to pursue, but the timing was not right for a full assault at that point. By that time, he was already committed to the new Porsche Can-Am project for 1972, in addition to the ongoing USAC Indy-car program and a new venture into NASCAR with American Motors. This was clearly not the time to add something else to the already-overflowing plate. Instead, Penske put Formula-1 the backburner, and it did not resurface again until 1974.

1974

Until late in the 1973 season, Roger Penske's plan was to continue his wildly successful Can-Am campaign through 1974 and maybe longer. Porsche had already developed, and Mark Donohue had tested, a third generation turbo motor for the next year. Donohue's overwhelming dominance of the 1973 championship, however, had created a dilemma for the SCCA, the outcome of which was a back-door ban on turbo-charging in the Can-Am series beginning with the 1974 season. Basically, the turbo Porsche was just too good—too strong, too fast, and too expensive for anyone to compete with—so

the rules were rewritten to essentially make it illegal. This decision had not been finalized at the time of Mark Donohue's retirement announcement, but it was pretty clear that it was coming. In November of 1973, *AutoWeek* wrote: "In a sense, should the turbochargers be banned, it may be remembered that Mark Donohue was legislated from existence."

When the new Can-Am rules were published at the end of November, Roger Penske went to work quickly to revise his plans. He bought a racecar fabrication shop in Poole, England, and assembled a first-class team to build and develop a Penske Racing Formula-1 car. He hired Geoff Ferris, an experienced European racecar designer, to work with Mark Donohue and Don Cox on the design and construction of the new "Penske PC-1." He appointed Heinz Hofer, who had been a key player in the Indy-car and Can-Am programs, as team manager of the F1 project. And Karl Kainhofer, who had been with Roger Penske since his own driving days, would serve as chief mechanic. The car would be assembled in England, and then shipped to Penske's Reading Pennsylvania shops for testing and development under Donohue's direction. From the outset, this first Penske-built F1 car was intended to be very conventional in design. This would minimize potential reliability problems and afford Donohue and the team the best opportunity to navigate the sharp learning curve ahead.

With Donohue retired, Roger Penske's initial intention was to hire American Peter Revson to pilot the new car. Revson had driven for Penske Racing during the 1970 Trans-Am program and he already had two years of F1 experience with Team McLaren. Unfortunately, that plan ended tragically when Revson was killed during practice for the South African Grand Prix in February of 1974. So as the Penske PC-1 was being assembled in Poole England, Roger Penske began shopping for potential drivers.

Mark Donohue initially denied any consideration of changing his retirement plans, even though he'd always been interested in Formula-1. Penske talked to a number of candidates, primarily those who already had some F1 experience. When he attended the French Grand Prix in the summer of 1974 to meet with pros-

The Penske PC-1 frustrated Mark Donohue, the engineer. The relatively small F1 engine put a premium on chassis design and setup, and Donohue was never able to get the package properly sorted out.

pects, *AutoWeek* wrote, "You could almost feel the shivers run up and down pit lane as the meticulous Penske proceeded along." Speculation focused on German Jochen Mass, Englishman Brian Redman, and American George Follmer, all of whom met the criteria of having competed in Formula-1 already.

But by the time the completed PC-1 was delivered to Penske Racing's U.S. shops, Mark Donohue had, silently, begun to reassess his retirement status. Nearly a year out of the cockpit had changed his perspective on things. From outside of the car, operating as Penske Racing's president and team manager, he found a new appreciation for the driver's role. "I began to realize just how important the driver really is," he wrote in his autobiography. "Sometimes, I'd had the idea that I was just another donkey on the team. I would try my damnest to qualify on the pole, and everyone would take it for granted. That was what I was supposed to do. I got so used to it, I developed the idea that I was simply a mediocre driver with valuable engineer skills." From his management vantage point, he could see the obvious flaw in that logic. He could finally appreciate the immeasurable value he had brought to the team as a driver. And as the Penske F1 program grew closer to reality, he began to think—he could do that again.

Coming out of retirement was not an easy decision.

First, there was an element of embarrassment, coming back so soon after he'd received such a hero's send-off. Then, there was the concern that winning would probably not come quickly or easily in this new and highly competitive arena of Formula-1. And finally, there was the risk. In the mid 1970s, Formula-1 was often a deadly game. His long-time rival Peter Revson had died only months earlier. When he retired, Donohue had been applauded for having the self-discipline to walk away from his dangerous profession while still at the top of his game. Now he would put his life on the line again. Not everyone was happy about that.

Of course, Mark Donohue understood all of these issues. Certainly he had analyzed the pros and cons with the same methodical and calculating approach that had served him so well throughout his career. "After a year in the real world," he said, "I found out it wasn't for me. I'm a race-car driver. That's what I do best, and that's what I want to do more of." It was a fateful decision; but one that, to the educated observer, was entirely understandable, even inevitable.

Roger Penske's game-plan was to enter the final two races of the 1974 F1 season, the north American events at Mosport, Canada, and Watkins Glen, New York. Donohue's decision to drive the car was not announced until one week before the Mosport race.

With very limited track testing completed in the new PC-1, these races were to serve as final development in preparation for a full championship assault in 1975. Unlike the rest of the Formula-1 calendar, these two tracks were familiar to Penske and Donohue. In fact, they would be the only racetracks on the entire championship circuit where Penske Racing would have any baseline to start from.

Anyone expecting Donohue and the Penske team to show up for the Canadian Grand Prix and challenge for pole position would be bitterly disappointed. The PC-1's debut was unspectacular at best. In a starting field of 26 cars, Donohue could qualify no better than 24th. In the race, he struggled along to a 12th place finish, two laps behind the winner, Emerson Fittipaldi. To make matters worse, Penske Racing was not the only new American Formula-1 team to debut at Mosport. Donohue's old Trans-Am nemesis Parnelli Jones, now a team owner, introduced his new Parnelli chassis with driver Mario Andretti at the wheel. The Parnelli chassis was designed by Maurice Phillippe, whose prior credits included the infamous Lotus 72 that had won numerous F1 races over the previous four years. Jones and Andretti were surrounded by a team of experienced Formula-1 players, and their results reflected that fact immediately. Andretti qualified 16th and went on to a 7th place fin-

ish, just one position out of the championship points.

After the disheartening weekend in Canada, Penske Racing regrouped for the U.S. Grand Prix at Watkins Glen a week later. In Friday's practice, Donohue was a full two seconds off the leaders' times. When asked about the team's performance afterward, he said, "We're where we should be. I just don't have enough laps in the car to know what to do to make it work right. It's the same science as with any race car, but with the F1 car there just isn't the power I'm used to. With the Porsche Can-Am car, or even our Trans-Am cars, there was always enough power there to make up for minor faults in setting up the suspension. With an F1 car everything has to be perfect, not almost perfect....The changes it needs to go faster are so subtle you can't tell you're going any faster, but you are. If you made the right changes. My problem is discovering the right changes."

In Saturday's qualifying, Donohue cut three seconds off his time, but still found himself considerably slower than pole-sitter Carlos Reutemann, landing 14th on the starting grid. It was a big improvement over his 24th place starting position in Canada, but still a disappointment. At the same time, Mario Andretti, in the Parnelli entry, was actually challenging for the pole and eventually settled for an impressive third-place starting position. In the race, which was marred by the death of

Austrian driver Helmut Koinigg, the PC-1 lasted only about half the distance, dropping out on the 27th lap with suspension failure. Andretti experienced problems even earlier, requiring a push start on the grid, and retiring after just four laps.

1975

It was obvious after those first two races that the Penske Formula-1 program had a lot of work to do. Over the short off-season, minor refinements were incorporated into a new PC-1 chassis that debuted in the season opening Argentinean Grand Prix at Buenos Aires on January 12, 1975. Donohue still found himself hopelessly off the pace, qualifying 16th in the 23-car field. He drove an uneventful race to finish a respectable 7th, a lap behind winner Emerson Fittapaldi. This was not a terrible start, but it was quickly apparent that Penske Racing wasn't going to be a serious threat in its first full world championship season.

Two weeks later, for the Brazilian Grand Prix at Interlagos, Donohue put the struggling PC-1 15th on the starting grid and dropped out of the race after 22 laps with handling problems. In South Africa, he started 18th and finished 8th, a lap behind winner Jody Scheckter, his former Can-Am and F5000 challenger.

Next on the schedule were two non-championship races in England. Under the rules at that time, no country was permitted to host more than one championship event (although an exception would be made for the United States a year later). England, however, had a rich racing heritage and chose to host these events outside of the championship schedule. Typically, most of the regular F1 teams participated, even though no points were awarded. Donohue crashed out of the Brands Hatch event, but posted a respectable 6th place finish at Silverstone. Had this been an official race, this finish would have netted Donohue and the PC-1 their first championship point.

The European F1 season officially started with the Spanish Grand Prix on April 27. This event was filled with controversy from the beginning, as the Grand Prix Drivers Association refused to race because of safety concerns with the track. This virtually eliminated all

Mark Donohue buckles into the cockpit of the Penske PC1 during practice for the 1975 Dutch Grand Prix in Zandvoort, Holland. *George Standaar*

practice time, further aggravating Donohue's struggle to learn the new track and set the car up properly. With some of the concerns addressed and a threat of legal action by the promoters, all the drivers except Emerson Fittapaldi finally agreed to run. In qualifying, Donohue settled for 17th on the grid. On the fourth lap of the race, Jody Scheckter blew an engine and dropped oil on the track. Both Donohue and Australian Alan Jones spun in the oil and crashed.

The next event on the calendar was the world famous Grand Prix of Monaco through the city streets of Monte Carlo. After the uproar in Spain over track safety conditions, the organizers in Monaco implemented several safety measures aimed at averting a similar problem on this tight and inherently dangerous racecourse. Most significant of these changes was limiting the starting field to only 18 cars. With 26 cars entered, there seemed to be a very real possibility that the Penske would not make the field. After having crashed the PC-1/02 chassis two weeks earlier, Donohue was back in the "01" at Monaco, and he turned in a commendable qualifying performance to secure the 16th grid position. He then ran a reasonably good race on the very tight and tricky street circuit until an accident ended his day just 10 laps from the finish of the race.

Following another disappointing weekend in Zolder, Belgium, the first sign of any good news this season came at the Grand Prix of Sweden. Donohue had what was becoming a fairly typical qualifying session, landing 16th on the starting grid. But in the race, while never challenging for the lead, he did manage for the first time to stay on the lead lap and finished the race in 5th position, collecting his first two world championship points. Interestingly, it was also in this race that Mario Andretti and the highly touted Parnelli team finally scored their first championship points, finishing in fourth spot just ahead of Donohue's Penske. Andretti had shown moments of brilliance at times and had some very impressive qualifying runs, but because of reliability problems and other factors, had never been able to break into the top six until now. So it was a good day all around for the Americans in Sweden.

Two weeks later, in Zandvoort, Holland, for the Dutch Grand Prix, Donohue drove from his 18th starting position to an 8th place result; out of the points, but finishing was important at this stage. Then in France, he completed only six laps before being sidelined with a broken CV joint.

By this point in the season, both Roger Penske and Mark Donohue were struggling to understand why they were not improving faster. There were so many unknown factors—new car, new rules, new racetracks, and even a delicate question about Donohue's driving ability after his comeback. It was impossible to attack the problem with so many variables. But something had to be done. Roger Penske was certainly feeling pressure to produce results for his new sponsor, First National City Bank, so he made the bold and costly decision to purchase a "customer" March 751 as a test car.

The March chassis had been moderately successful during the 1975 season, and it was thought that this would give Donohue and the team a baseline from which to continue development of the Penske PC-1. When Mark Donohue first tested the car at Silverstone in early-July, it was immediately obvious where the problem lay. Within a handful of laps in the new March, Donohue was able to match his best-ever times in the Penske PC-1. "It seems a lot smoother," he commented. "And it gets the power down better." The difference was so striking that Roger Penske swallowed his pride, benched his namesake PC-1 chassis and let Donohue drive the March in the British Grand Prix race. Donohue matched his season-best qualifying effort and drove to a fine 5th place finish in the March's first appearance, equaling his best result in 15 starts with the Penske PC-1. The end of the Silverstone race was wild, with a sudden downpour causing almost all the front-runners, including Donohue, to spin off the track on the 56th lap. Fortunately, the race was red-flagged and finishing order was determined based on position at the end of the previous lap. Interestingly, Mario Andretti finished 12th, a lap behind Donohue, in his Parnelli.

After the high at Silverstone, Penske Racing went on to Nurburgring for the German Grand Prix with great expectations. The excitement didn't last long, however. Donohue's last-lap accident at Silverstone had done considerable damage to the March chassis, necessitating a major rebuild. Donohue spent most of the practice time just trying to learn the monstrous 14.2-mile high-speed circuit. Before the race, he commented about the setup of the March: "it's not right but I'm a little afraid to change anything at this stage." On the very first lap of the race, the left front tire exploded and Donohue had to nurse the car back to the pits for a replacement. With the new tire installed, he returned to the race and, before completing his second lap, the right front tire blew. At that point he wisely decided to call it a day.

And then they went to Austria. Driving the March chassis for the third time, Donohue had trouble getting the car sorted completely and had to settle for 20th spot on the starting grid. In the morning warm-up session on the day of the race, as he was making a final attempt to find a little more speed, Donohue's left front tire punctured going through a fast sweeping right-hand turn. The car skidded off the track, plowed through four rows of catch-fencing and flew over the steel guardrail before crashing through an advertising billboard. The racecar was severely damaged and Donohue was momentarily unconscious. But after he was removed from the wreckage and revived, he appeared to be otherwise unscathed. An examination by track medical personnel did not identify any significant injuries. Back in the garage immediately afterward, he seemed to be fine, walking around and talking to team manager Heinz Hofer about the accident. But he soon developed a severe headache and became disoriented. Fellow American Mario Andretti said that Donohue began having difficulty recognizing friends. At that point, he was rushed to the hospital in nearby Graz, Austria, where it was diagnosed that he had a blood clot on the brain. He immediately underwent an emergency three-hour brain surgery procedure to remove the clot.

An accident investigation later concluded that the fencing Donohue crashed through had apparently pried opened the visor on his full-face helmet, allowing a wooden fencepost to wedge into the opening of the helmet, twisting his head sharply to the left and backward. It was similar to the whiplash-type injuries that have largely been eliminated by the HANS Device in modern-day racing. Catch fencing, which was used extensively in that era, was a lightweight wire barrier installed at high-speed corners on the racetrack. It was designed to collapse as a racecar crashed through it, dissipating energy and slowing the car before it contacted a steel guardrail or other immoveable object. This was an improvement over steel guardrails alone, which could throw an out-of-control car back onto the track; or worse, shred it into pieces. It was a tragic irony that this "safety" feature was responsible for Donohue's injury. In the years that followed, these fences were gradually replaced by tire barriers or by large sand-filled runoff areas. Both of these alternatives have proven to be much better at preventing injury in high-speed accidents. Unfortunately, catch fences were state-of-the-art in 1975.

Initial reports following Donohue's brain surgery were fairly optimistic, suggesting that he was out of danger. But over the next two days there was very little additional information released by the hospital, and no good news at all. In fact, he never did regain consciousness after the operation, and died on Tuesday night, August 19, 1975. Mark Donohue was 38 years old. At his bedside were his father, his wife, and his close friend, Roger Penske.

Mark Neary Donohue,1937 – 1975.
"The only unfair advantage Mark Donohue ever had, was Mark Donohue."—An unknown fan.

Remembering 'Captain Nice'

In the autobiography he wrote during his brief retirement in 1974, Mark Donohue contemplated what legacy he might leave to the auto racing world. "I realize that retirement is inevitable," he wrote. "That eventually young spectators will have to ask, "Who was Mark Donohue? What kind of car did he drive?" All race drivers return to the obscurity they came from"

On August 9, 2004, thirty years after Donohue put these thoughts on paper, there was an article in *AutoWeek* introducing the new Chevy Corvette C6. The author began his story with some background information on the racetrack that Chevrolet had chosen to debut the C6 to the press. "Virginia International Raceway is a hidden gem," he wrote. "Located in Alton, Virginia, it opened for business in 1957. Over the years the legends ran there—Penske, Donohue, Foyt and Shelby..."

Just two weeks later, August 23, 2004, Mark Donohue's name appeared again in the pages of *AutoWeek*: "In Denver Paul Gentilozzi tied Mark Donohue's 33-year-old record of 29 Trans-Am wins....Gentilozzi reverently downplayed any comparison to Donohue, noting Donohue earned his 29 wins in 55 starts, compared to 196 starts for Gentilozzi."

These are weighty words, "legend" and "reverently." They aren't used to describe ordinary people and ordinary accomplishments. That America's foremost auto racing journal would find it appropriate to use such words to describe a race driver 29 years after his passing, leaves little doubt that Mark Donohue's concerns about fading into obscurity were unfounded. True, most of today's young fans will never have a fitting appreciation for the remarkable career that this unique man enjoyed. They probably can't really comprehend the idea of one driver having success in NASCAR, Indy-cars, sports cars and Formula-1. How could they fathom a single driver winning six national championships in just an 8-year professional career? And in this modern era, when top drivers fly to the racetrack to do their weekend's work and then fly home, how could today's new fans grasp the idea of a champion driver doing his own engineering, fabrication, development and testing. These extraordinary memories will, unfortunately, be reserved only for those who were privileged enough to be there and witness Mark Donohue's work first-hand. For those who were not, there is only the record book to document his unparalleled achievements. Some records that he established over 30 years ago are just now being challenged. Others, like his six consecutive Can-Am victories, his back-to-back United States Road Racing Championships, and his 12 USRRC wins will stand forever; this because his dominance was so overwhelming that it literally drove these series to extinction.

I was a teenager in the early 1970s when Mark Donohue was at the peak of his short, but spectacular career. Over the course of six years, my father and I spent many summer weekends traveling up and down the east coast witnessing this legend in the making. At Pocono International Raceway, on July 3rd, 1971 when Mark Donohue recorded Penske Racing's first-ever Indy-car win, we were there. We were at Watkins Glen later that same summer to watch him drive the AMC Javelin to victory on his way to dominating the 1971 Trans-Am championship. We saw him race that beautiful blue Ferrari there too. And the invincible, 1200 horsepower turbo Porsche, the "monument" to his career—we saw Donohue demoralize the competition with that car at Mid-Ohio and the Glen in the summer of 1973. On February 15th, 1974 we were at Daytona International Speedway. We saw Mark win his last race, the final event of the inaugural IROC series.

We watched him take an emotional victory lap as he set off on his brief retirement. And just seven months later, we were in Canada to witness his frustrating return, driving the new Penske Formula-1 car at Mosport. The last time I saw him was at the U.S. Grand Prix in October of 1974. He was struggling with the new car and trying to get himself back to 100 percent mentally and physically after his layoff from driving. He had a disappointing weekend and didn't finish the race, but nobody doubted for a second that he would be back. This was Mark Donohue.

1975 was a difficult year to be a fan. It was hard to read week after week about the DNF's and other poor finishes. As the season wore on and the results didn't improve significantly, it was distressing to hear about repeated spins and accidents as he was obviously pushing beyond his limits and those of the car in a desperate effort to find those last tenths of a second that would make him competitive again. When I first learned about his practice crash in Austria, the newspaper headline read "Donohue Out of Danger." But sadly, that wasn't true.

When he died two days later, it was a tragedy on many levels. Certainly for Donohue's parents who were his biggest fans, his two young sons, and his new wife, it was nothing less than devastating. It was a great loss, too, for the sport of auto racing. One of its brightest and most-respected personalities was gone forever. And it was a very real and personal tragedy for the thousands and thousands of fans that he had touched throughout his brilliant career. At St. Teresa's Catholic Church in Summit, New Jersey, we sat with more than a thousand people—family, friends, race drivers and other fans—as Mark Donohue was remembered as a graceful and dedicated man, a loving father and son who, contrary to his public image, wasn't above pulling a good practical joke when the opportunity presented itself. "Today, Mark has the [unfair] advantage over us," said Msgr. Harrold Murray in the funeral mass. "He has found the Lord while we're still trying."

Mark Donohue knew the risks. He made that clear when he came out of retirement. "If I get wiped out and they carry me away in a box," he said, "I wouldn't expect anybody to feel sorry for me." But at the end of the funeral mass, as Roger Penske and three others carried that box down the aisle, a lot of people found it very difficult to honor that request. A lot of people did feel sorry...very, very sorry.

Roger Penske hired Ireland's John Watson to drive for the team at Watkins Glen in 1975 and the full 1976 season. Watson's F1 career began in 1973, but he had enjoyed little success driving for uncompetitive teams. In less than a year, Watson would score his and Penske Racing's first Formula-1 victory.

Following Mark Donohue's funeral, Roger Penske was asked about his plans for continuing in racing following this unthinkable tragedy. "Mark was a complete realist in this regard," Penske answered. "He would want us to go on with our racing program, that I know."[11]

Six days later, Bobby Allison drove the Penske Racing AMC Matador to victory in the Southern 500. Two weeks after that, Tom Sneva scored his first win in Penske's McLaren, the team's first Indy-car victory in two years. Maybe this was just coincidence. Maybe it was fate. Or maybe it was the team's response to the personal philosophy Mark Donohue articulated after his agonizing 1972 injuries: "When it hurts and you want to cry, you just refuse. You clamp your mouth shut and you refuse." Clearly, difficult as it must have been, there was no better way to honor Mark's memory than to go on and do what he most loved to do—win races.

The team's Formula-1 program did take a brief hiatus, not returning until the season finale, the U.S. Grand Prix at Watkins Glen, New York. Penske hired Ireland's John Watson to take over driving responsibilities. Watson had been on the F1 circuit for the previous couple of years, driving for the Brabham and Surtees teams without a lot of success.

Even before Donohue's accident, work had started on a new Penske PC-3 chassis that incorporated many of the design features of the March. In fact, the PC-3 appeared to be nearly an exact clone of the March 751. The new car was supposed to be ready for the Watkins Glen race, but because of some last-minute problems, Watson ended up driving the old PC-1 in his first outing for Penske Racing.

Watson had an impressive qualifying run, putting the difficult PC-1 12th on the grid of 24 cars. In the race, which was won by newly-crowned 1975 World Champion Niki Lauda, Watson ended up in 9th position, two laps behind the leaders, a typical performance for the PC-1. During the course of the race, he pitted twice for no apparent reason other than a quick consultation with Penske and the crew. Almost certainly, he was asking, "what the hell is wrong with this car?" He was discovering what Donohue had to contend with throughout most of the season, and Watson knew from his previous experience with other Formula-1 cars that something was just not right.

After the race was over, a young fan approached Roger Penske in the pits and asked why Watson had made those extra two stops. The Captain politely but generically explained that this was the first time his new driver had raced the car and that he was still getting adjusted to everything. Roger Penske didn't realize that this particular fan was well aware of that fact, and the sad circumstances behind it. He certainly couldn't have known that this fan had been standing there with him in that Summit, New Jersey, church six weeks earlier, saying goodbye to the driver that should have been in the car that day. The young man wanted to tell him all that, but he didn't. He just asked for an autograph and said "thank you."

Remarkably, Penske Racing's design and fabrication shop produced three F1 chassis designs in less than two years. After opening the 1976 season with a moderately competitive PC3, rule changes prompted a mid-season move to this beautiful and successful PC4. *George Standaar*

1976

John Watson was retained by Roger Penske to drive the full Formula-1 season in 1976. The new PC-3 chassis was ready for the season-opener in Brazil, and initially it looked quite promising. With its new aerodynamic "skirts" the Penske PC-3 was one of the pioneers in the "ground-effects" revolution that significantly affected both Formula-1 and Indy-car designs from that time forward. Watson qualified a strong 8th on the grid, but lasted only two laps in the race, sidelined with an engine fire. It was then five weeks before the second round, held in Kyalami, South Africa. Watson had an outstanding qualifying effort here, putting the PC-3 third on the starting grid. The Penske driver battled with Mario Andretti's Parnelli throughout most of the race, ultimately finishing a respectable fifth with Andretti close behind.

The next world championship event was on a new street course through the city of Long Beach, California. With the unusually high level of American participa-

tion at the time (Penske, Parnelli, and Shadow chassis; Mario Andretti, George Follmer and Brett Lunger driving), the U.S. organizers and the F.I.A. negotiated an exception to the "one-race-per-country" policy. As with Monaco the previous year, concerns about safety on the tight and twisty street course limited the starting field, here to 20 cars. This time, however, there wasn't any doubt that the Penske entry would make the cut. John Watson qualified in the 9th position, but in the race, unfortunately, he encountered problems and posted a disappointing 12th place finish, 11 laps behind winner Clay Regazzoni.

At the Spanish Grand Prix, the F.I.A. introduced new aerodynamic regulations that limited the height of the air-intake boxes and reduced the size of the rear wings for the F1 cars. These changes dramatically upset the balance of the PC-3 design, and suddenly Watson found himself struggling at the back half of the field again. After qualifying 13th, he dropped out two-thirds

The last truly revolutionary Formula-1 chassis design was the 6-wheeled Tyrrell that raced against John Watson's Penskes in the 1976 championship season. The theory behind this design was that lower profile front tires would improve aerodynamics, but a second pair of wheels was necessary to maintain the same rubber contact area with the road surface. The design proved to be more interesting than successful. *George Standaar*

of the way through the race with an engine problem. Two weeks later, in Belgium, the story wasn't appreciably better. Watson qualified 17th and, only because of a high level of attrition, managed to finish 7th. This was a long way from the great potential seen in the first races of the season. Monaco was more of the same, qualifying 17th and finishing 10th, two laps off the pace.

With the PC-3 being clearly uncompetitive under the new regulations, the Penske team rushed to complete Geoff Ferris' PC-4 design. This new chassis bore absolutely no resemblance to its March-inspired predecessor. In appearance, it actually looked much more like the original PC-1, but that's where the similarity ended.

The PC-4 debuted at the Swedish Grand Prix in mid-June. But without much testing and developing time, Watson found himself qualifying well back in 17th position again. A sticking throttle caused him to

crash on the very first lap of the race. The race itself was interesting only because the radical new 6-wheel Tyrells of Jody Scheckter and Patrick Depailler managed to pull off a 1-2 finish.

In France three weeks later, John Watson and the Penske PC-4 looked like a different team. After qualifying decently in 8th position, Watson brought the PC-4 home to a third-place finish, the team's best result since Mark Donohue's podium in the 1971 Canadian Grand Prix. In a post-race inspection, Watson's Penske was disqualified for a slight rear wing infraction. Roger Penske, of course, appealed the decision and Watson was ultimately reinstated.

The British Grand Prix was another bureaucratic affair that eventually had to be settled in the appeals process. A first lap accident involving three cars, including British favorite James Hunt's McLaren, resulted in a red flag. Hunt's car was initially thought to be too badly damaged to continue, so Team McLaren started to bring out his backup car. That plan was immediately disallowed, after which Hunt's original car was quickly patched back together. With a considerable amount of confusion and debate, race officials decided to allow Hunt to restart the race, apparently fearing a riot from the British crowd if they ruled otherwise. Hunt went on to convincingly win the race, moving into contention for the world championship. John Watson had qualified the Penske PC-4 11th on the grid and ran a strong race, finishing fourth behind apparent winner James Hunt, defending world champion Niki Lauda, and the funny-looking six-wheel Tyrrell of Jody Scheckter. It wasn't until two months later, after a series of appeals were argued, that Hunt was ultimately disqualified and Lauda declared the winner. That moved Watson up to third position in the official race standings, but a little too late to enjoy the podium champagne.

In the German Grand Prix on August 1st, John Watson started 19th and finished 7th, but the race itself was a nightmare. The Nurburgring circuit had drawn safety protests from the Grand Prix Drivers Association, but the race went on anyway. In a rainy start, defending world champion Niki Lauda had a horrifying accident. His Ferrari went off the track, through several rows of catch fencing and then exploded into a fireball when it hit a dirt embankment. The burning car then rebounded back onto the racetrack into the path of oncoming traffic. Both Brett Lunger and Harald Ertl hit the already-battered Ferrari. Lunger, Ertl, Guy Edwards and Arturo Merzario stopped their cars and ran to Lauda's aid, pulling him from the remains of his racecar, which was completely engulfed in flames. The Austrian sustained grievous injuries, including extensive lung damage caused by inhalation of toxic fumes from the fire. So severe was the damage that the doctors prepared Lauda's family for the near certainty that he would not live through the night. He was administered last rites. Defying his doctors' prognosis, Lauda lay in intensive care for the next three days battling for his life. Less than six weeks later, he was carefully lifted into the cockpit of a new Ferrari and he drove to a courageous 4th place finish in the Italian Grand Prix. Niki Lauda would fall

short of defending his world championship by just a single point in 1976, but he would return the following year to win it back convincingly.

Although the end result didn't show it, the Dutch Grand Prix on August 29th was the breakthrough event for the Penske Formula-1 program. John Watson qualified the PC-4 in fourth place. In the race, he quickly moved to second, pushing first Ronnie Peterson's Lotus and then James Hunt's McLaren for the lead until being sidelined with a gearbox problem on lap 48 of 75. It was the first time that the Penske entry was legitimately able to challenge for a Formula-1 victory. It had taken just two years, a remarkably short period of time, for the Penske Racing Team to become a serious contender in the most elite auto racing series in the world. This was an extraordinary accomplishment.

Full of confidence, optimism, and perhaps a bit of vengeance, the Penske team headed back to Austria, the site of Mark Donohue's fatal accident a year earlier. In fairytale fashion, John Watson put the Penske PC-4 on the front row of the grid, the team's best-ever qualifying result. In a light rain, Watson jumped into the lead immediately at the start of the race. He dropped back as far as third place in the early laps, but passed Ronnie Peterson for the lead on lap 12 and never looked back. John Watson took the Penske-built PC-4 to the team's first Formula-1 victory at the very same track where they had experienced their greatest loss just one year earlier. It was a bittersweet triumph. Captain Nice would have been pleased.

Although elated by his first F1 victory, John Watson had a painful debt to settle with Roger Penske after this race. The Ulsterman's beard didn't quite fit the Penske team's crew-cut image, so Watson had reluctantly agreed to lose the facial hair after his first win. Following Austria, it was time to settle up.

A clean-shaven John Watson qualified 8th on the grid for the Italian Grand Prix at Monza, but then had his time disqualified when a routine fuel sample revealed that his gasoline was slightly above the allowable 101 octane specification. Forced to start from the back of the field in 27th position, Watson managed to work his way back up to a 12th place finish—certainly a letdown coming off the Austrian win.

That wrapped up the European season and the teams all headed to North America for the Canadian and U.S. races. Watson and the PC-4 struggled all weekend in Mosport, qualifying a disappointing 14th and finishing 10th. Things went a little better a week later at Watkins Glen, where he started 8th and finished sixth, picking up another championship point. The season ended in Japan on a mixed note. Watson had a strong showing in qualifying, taking 4th spot on the grid and jumping up to second place at the start of the race. Weather conditions were terrible, however, with heavy rain causing problems for several drivers, including Watson who had to take an escape road on the second lap. This effectively took him out of contention for the day and he eventually dropped out before the halfway mark with an engine problem. Mario Andretti, who had started from pole position, went on to win the race in a Lotus. The Parnelli Jones Formula-1 program had folded after running only three races at the beginning of the 1976 season, and Mario Andretti had moved to Team Lotus, where he would go on to win the world championship two years later.

It seemed, after the strong year-end showing, that Penske Racing was poised to make a serious assault on the world title in 1977. So it was a shock to almost everyone when Roger Penske announced that he would be discontinuing his Formula-1 program effective immediately. His reasoning was that the predominantly ex-U.S. series was no longer consistent with his business interests. It was an unpopular decision with many fans, and an even more unpopular rationale. After all, was this about winning the World Driving Championship for the United States or was it just a line item on the Penske Enterprises business plan? Of course, the answer was both. And all emotions aside, it was perfectly logical reasoning at the time.

Although the team had done an extraordinary job developing a competitive new chassis—even winning an F1 race—in a remarkably short period of time, challenging for the championship could have been a different story entirely. By the end of the 1976 season, on any given Sunday John Watson and the Penske PC-4 might have been a contender for a Grand Prix victory. But as their weak performance in Canada reminded, there was also still work to be done before they could count on being a contender every Sunday. And it's that kind of consistency that is necessary, week after week, to seriously challenge for the world title.

Another issue was that First National City Bank was interested in shifting its advertising support from the European-based F1 series to something in the U.S. market. Even before the 1976 season, they had inquired about sponsoring the team's Indy-car and NASCAR programs, but Roger Penske was in the enviable position of already having primary sponsors for both of those series. A year later, the First National City logos would turn up on Johnny Rutherford's Team McLaren Indy-car. But for Roger Penske, staying in F1 at the time would have meant finding a new primary sponsor.

And finally, there was an enormous logistics issue associated with competing in Formula-1. Over a season that spanned more than three quarters of the year, F1 raced in more than a dozen countries all around the world. Roger Penske has always enjoyed being actively involved in his racing programs, and this was nearly impossible for him in F1 because of the travel involved. Not only did he have a quickly growing business empire to tend to in the United States, but he was also committed to his USAC Indy-car and NASCAR programs. There were weekends when he had cars running in three different races at the same time. And even for the Captain, this was an unmanageable situation.

Taking all this into consideration, Roger Penske made the difficult but completely understandable decision to withdraw from Formula-1 and focus on his U.S. racing programs. When Tom Sneva won Penske his first USAC Indy-car national championship just one year later, the wisdom of this decision was plainly apparent. Over the years, it has become evident that Roger Penske doesn't make many bad business decisions, and this was no exception.

As for the Formula-1 fabrication shop he had purchased in England, Penske quickly found a much more lucrative use for this facility—building his own Indy-Cars.

CHAPTER 10
CART Indy Cars
The Rick Mears Era
(1979 – 1992)

"This kid is something special. Most of the good drivers in this sport are getting old—well into their late 30s if not their 40s. But Rick [Mears] is only 27, a natural study, and as cooperative a driver as I have ever worked with. Watch him."
—Roger Penske, May 12, 1979

Prior to 1955, the Indianapolis 500 and its supporting races, which collectively represented the highest level of auto racing in the United States, had been sanctioned by the Automobile Association of America (AAA). But after a number of driver fatalities in the early 1950s, including Bill Vukovich's high-profile death in the 1955 Indy 500, AAA felt that it could no longer afford to be associated with the dangerous sport. To replace the sanctioning body, Tony Hulman, owner of the Indianapolis Motor Speedway, helped to organize the United States Auto Club (USAC) to assume responsibility for management of the "Indy-car" series. From that time through the late 1970s, USAC crowned the annual U.S. National Driving Champion based on points accumulated in the Indianapolis 500 and a series of smaller races held primarily in the Midwest and eastern part of the United States. In reality, USAC was a series created by and for the Indianapolis 500. All the other races were there simply to fill out the calendar, and that was not a problem in the early days. But as racing became more sophisticated, more professional, and most importantly, much more expensive, that business model was no longer effective, and the race team owners started to demand change.

Three-time Formula-1 World Driving Champion Jackie Stewart summarized the situation in 1979: "In many ways, this is a very backward segment of the sport. This is not something that's new, it's been like this for years. You can see it in USAC's attempts to keep the 40-year-old Offenhauser engine competitive. You can see it in many of the cars that fill out the field which are no more than service station specials! Here we have the most sophisticated racing cars in America, and yet they race in dilapidated, unattractive old stadiums while tennis, football, golf and all kinds of other, newer sports enjoy brand new, clean stadiums where you can eat and drink in comfort and enjoy the day."

In 1978, as the situation was approaching a crisis level, former driver and respected team owner Dan Gurney drafted his now-infamous "White Paper," basically a state-of-the-union review of the status of Indy-car racing. This letter was addressed to the other team owners, and served as a catalyst to finally bring about a much-needed dramatic change. Gurney wrote:

"Over the past 3 or 4 years I've had conversations with almost all of the car owners and team directors. I've had talks with drivers, with sanctioning body directors, with track owners and promoters and big sponsors and fans and

other interested parties. Generally there is agreement that something is wrong with our sport—it is not reaching its full potential by any means, and there is great need for a change!

"Early in my discussions I realized that we are so intent upon racing each other that we do not stop to look and analyze our situation. In frustration I decided that things must get worse before we will all wake up. Our sport has the potential to be financially rewarding and healthy from a business standpoint for all participants. Many of the car owners and team directors are excellent and very successful businessmen in their own lives outside of racing. We as businessmen should be ashamed of ourselves for being involved in a prestigious sport such as Championship racing with all of its potential while it is as weak and disorganized as it presently is. It is truly strange that with all these "Heavyweights" involved, we still do not have our act together. ('Divide and Conquer' still seems to be working, doesn't it?)

"OK! What shall we do about it?

"First let us digress for a moment. Let's study some history. Back in the early '70s, the status of Formula 1 Grand Prix racing was similar to our own USAC Championship racing right now. The crowds were quite small, sponsors were hard to find, the news media was not overly interested, expenses were high and going higher and the entire scene was one of disorganization.

"It was at this moment in time that the desperateness of the situation made the various 'teams' (constructors) unite and form an organization called the Formula One Constructors Association (FOCA). They appointed a man named Bernie Ecclestone as the chief of operations officer and negotiator and they made a solemn pledge to abide by his decisions 100 percent. They rolled up their sleeves and proceeded to upgrade the entire sport to the point where the paying spectator crowds are much, much larger. Sponsors are numerous and happy to be involved. The media is vigorous in covering all the events on TV and so are weekly magazines and daily newspapers on a worldwide basis. And money is coming back to the constructors and track owners in the form of larger ticket sales, more sponsorship, more prize money and expense money and the spectator is getting a much bigger, better spectacle for his ticket money.

"The obvious fact is that the FOCA has transformed the Formula 1 Grand Prix racing scene from what was a weak and scattered group of teams without any bargaining or negotiating strength into a bona fide business. They did it by uniting and making that "no turning back" commitment. They speak with one voice (that of the chief negotiator) and that voice has gained authority by leaps and bounds.

"Now, it is true that the Championship racing scene is somewhat different from Grand Prix racing and therefore it will require a slightly different organization to bring about an improvement. I only mention the FOCA organization as an example of something that has succeeded, on no uncertain terms. I think everyone agrees that the cost of Championship racing has escalated to the point where it is virtually ridiculous. And at the same time, many of the rewards have not increased at all, but have actually declined when you consider the effects of the general inflation in the U.S. economy.

"At the moment, we the car owners are the ones who have put forth by far the most effort, by far the most financial stake with little or no chance for return. And yet, because we have been so busy fighting each other, we have let the track owners or promoters and the sanctioning body lead us around by the nose while they reap the benefits.

"It is obvious that if Long Beach can afford to pay approximately $1 million per [Formula One] race after only five years of existence and [a] maximum paid attendance of 70,000 [then] Indy with its 600,000 plus audience and its 60-year tradition and international television coverage [can] afford to spend over $2 million on the purse, if it [is] to be fair.

"As Mr. Lindsey Hopkins said, 'We are the ones who did more to build the stands at Indianapolis than anyone else. IMS should thank us each year, in addition to our thanking them.'

"In all of our discussions, as car owners and team leaders, we have agreed that it is essential that we continue to support USAC as the sanctioning body for Championship racing. The only improvement will be that USAC will work for us and support our causes and our policies.

"It should be clearly understood that the purpose of this organization is to make racing better in an overall way.

Not just for the car owners and drivers, but also for the track owners and promoters and the sanctioning body and the sponsors and supporters and last but certainly not least, the racing fans and paying spectators.

"In the final analysis, of course, large crowds of paying spectators are the keys to success for all. Track owners (the sanctioning body must help also) who aggressively promote these big events—which by contract will feature the teams and driving star—will get the crowds, etc., thereby upgrading the entire sport/business. It is my firm belief that rather than cutting the cost of racing, which in itself is nearly impossible, it is far more important to make money more readily available by increasing the popularity and prestige of the sport with the general public.

"Tracks that refuse to put forth the necessary enterprise and promotion in order to meet the minimum purses should not be allowed to hold races. Another alternative is to allow our organization (this idea borrowed from the FOCA) to take over the track on a reasonable lease arrangement and we can do the promotion and the running of the race where we feel it can be successful. Still USAC-sanctioned, of course. For instance, the German GP at Hockenheim will be promoted by the FOCA this year [1978].

"Now, how do we get there from here? As I see it, the first step is to analyze the situation, get together and form the organization. (Let's call it C.A.R.T. or Championship Auto Racing Teams.)

"Once we agree to the fact that CART is needed, then we must outline what we want to do and how we should accomplish it.

"I believe that the organization can be operated by a staff of three people. One director/negotiator, one secretary and a staff accountant and gopher if needed. [The director/negotiator] will need an air travel card, a telephone credit card and an expense account. It is rumored that Bernie [Ecclestone] takes none of this. He only works on a 2 percent commission of everything that is done through the FOCA.

"It appears that a 'showdown' with the Indianapolis Motor Speedway is or should be the first target. They are the ones who can afford it. We should renegotiate the TV contract (our rights—not theirs) and we should double the purse.

"Other tracks should be negotiated with on the basis of what is a reasonable amount of revenue to come from all sources such as TV, gate, receipts, advertising, sponsors, etc. The entire picture should be shared from the standpoint of cooperation rather than killing each other.

"We must work together to learn how to upgrade the overall marketing/advertising. If CART can send in drivers and media material beforehand to the newspapers, the television stations, the Chamber of Commerce as well as various civic organizations and schools, etc., then we should do so. It is vital that we solve the riddle of getting more money coming in from spectators and sponsor/advertisers and TV networks so that there is a bigger pie to carve up. The only way our demands for more money in the form of a prize fund can have any validity is if the money is there in the first place. Unless we reach the point where we can see the books of these various tracks, we will be negotiating from a position of ignorance. It seems to me that we could all be further ahead if we worked together rather than be divided. We must see the tax returns and books.

"With the correct program of exposure, a fuel company can still get the right sort of benefits from being the exclusive Championship series sponsor. Cigarettes, whiskey, banking, unions…we need a very aggressive sales promotion team with super people heading it.

"How do we finance this C.A.R.T. operation? Dues? Memberships? Entry fees? Percentage of the purse?

"Someone (our man from C.A.R.T.) must be part of all Dick King's negotiations with track promoters and television network people and series sponsors, etc."

Dan Gurney was not proposing a revolution. He was not suggesting that the new "CART" organization should replace USAC as the sanctioning body. Rather, he was proposing that CART become a part of the existing system, to operate as an "agent" for the team owners, similar to the Formula One Constructors Association.

Unfortunately, USAC showed little interest in tampering with the status quo. There were a number of factors behind this reluctance. First, the Indianapolis Speedway, which still exerted considerable influence over USAC policy, was doing just fine. Crowds for the "500" were at record levels, and television contracts and gate receipts were far out-pacing prize money payouts. So any changes that might reduce the Speedway's authority over the racing series would, not surprisingly, be resisted.

Secondly, USAC founding member and longtime Indianapolis Speedway president, Tony Hulman, had died in 1977. Because he was so passionately involved in racing, Hulman might have been more open-minded about CART's proposals for the greater good of the sport, recognizing that ultimately this would benefit the Indianapolis Speedway as well. His successors, unfortunately, didn't have that vision.

And finally, adding to USAC's leadership instability at the time was the death of eight club officials in a 1978 plane crash. Certainly, for the remaining members of the United States Auto Club leadership, there was a reluctance to commit to major changes until order had been restored.

Unfortunately, the sport couldn't wait. At a 1978 Christmas party for the employees of Michigan International Speedway, Roger Penske and Pat Patrick met with Dan Gurney and several other team owners to outline CART's 'declaration of independence.' On November 30, 1978, Pat Patrick was elected president of the new organization, and an announcement followed that CART would be presenting its own Indy-car series beginning with the 1979 season. On December 13, CART signed an agreement with the SCCA to serve as the official sanctioning body for the series.

In a remarkably short period of time, the new organization assembled an experienced management team, negotiated with track owners and published a race schedule for the 1979 season, arranged television contracts, established the rules and regulations, and attended to the thousands of other details necessary to launch a high-caliper championship racing series. This extraordinary effort had Roger Penske's fingerprints all over it. The man who had arrived at Indianapolis nine years earlier and rattled the establishment with his efficient, professional and businesslike approach to racing, was now doing it again on a much larger scale. The Penske-led CART organization now was the establishment, and they were going to do it right.

Unlike the 1996 creation of the Indy Racing League (IRL), CART immediately gained the support of almost all the major race teams. The single noteworthy exception was A.J. Foyt, who had been a long-time ally of Tony Hulman and USAC. While all of the other top drivers pledged their allegiance to CART, Foyt and a field of perennial back-markers remained with USAC for the 1979 season. While both CART and USAC suffered with smaller car counts during the first couple of seasons, USAC went so far as to open some races to dangerously uncompetitive front-engine dirt track cars just to have a reasonable number of entries on the grid.

Of course, USAC did hold one very precious trump card—The Indianapolis 500. And when it became apparent that CART was going to be a threat to the very survival of the United States Auto Club, they decided to play that card for all it was worth. In an unprecedented action, the Indianapolis Motor Speedway rejected the 1979 Indy 500 entry applications of Penske Racing, Patrick Racing, Dan Gurney's All American Racers, Team McLaren, Jim Hall's Chaparral Racing, and Fletcher Racing. These teams, the Speedway contended, were not in good standing with the United States Auto Club. It was a cutthroat maneuver, but fortunately one that didn't stand up in court. Following a four-day trial, a U.S. District Court ruled that the Speedway had no grounds to exclude these teams, and the show went on.

CART and USAC ran separate series in 1979 and both crowned a national champion, but there was no doubt that it was the CART title that really counted. In early 1980, there was an attempted reunification between the two bodies, completing five races under the banner of the Championship Racing League. That, however, fell apart by mid-season and CART went on to be the undisputed Indy-car sanctioning organization until the late 1990's.

1979

Penske Racing's Indy-car program had a new look for 1979. After two consecutive championships, Tom Sneva had left the team and was replaced by two-time Indy 500 winner Bobby Unser. Like Mario Andretti before him, Unser was a seasoned veteran, hired to mentor

Penske's latest protégé driver, Rick Mears. Mears, who had alternated driving duty with Andretti the previous year, was promoted to full-time co-number one driver while Andretti opted to focus completely on defending his Formula-1 title. The team retained primary sponsorship from Norton Industries and Gould.

Roger Penske introduced his third-generation Indy-Car, the Geoff Ferris designed PC-7, at the beginning of the season, although Rick Mears elected to run the old PC-6 in several events, including the Indy 500. Pat Patrick had abandoned his own Wildcat chassis in favor of used Penske PC-6's for Gordon Johncock and Wally Dallenbach. Johnny Rutherford was still with McLaren, for what turned out to be the team's last season in Indy-cars. The biggest new competitive threat came from Al Unser in Jim Hall's radical new "ground-effects" Chapar-

ral that debuted at Indianapolis. Throughout the 1979 season, Al Unser would often be the fast qualifier and the early race leader, but reliability problems prevented him from seriously challenging for the championship. Danny Ongais' Parnelli and ex-Penske champion Tom Sneva in a McLaren often challenged, but reliability issues also prevented them from being serious title threats.

In the season opener at Phoenix, CART's inaugural race, Gordon Johncock drove his Patrick Racing Penske PC-6 to victory over Rick Mears' PC-7 Cosworth. Bobby Unser, who had started from the pole, finished fifth in his Penske Racing debut.

Second on the 1979 calendar was Atlanta, which included a pair of independent 125-mile races. Both events were won from pole by Johnny Rutherford's McLaren. Rick Mears finished 5th and 2nd in his PC-7.

Bobby Unser was already a two-time Indy 500 champion when hired by Roger Penske in 1979 to replace Tom Sneva in the Norton Spirit. Unser would win 11 races, including the 1981 Indy 500, while driving for the team over the next 3 years.

Two-time Indy winner Gordon Johncock drove for Penske Racing once in 1972, substituting for the injured Gary Bettenhausen. Driving for Pat Patrick in 1979, he won the inaugural race of the new CART series with a year-old Penske PC-6 chassis. *Alan Hummel*

Bobby Unser was 7th in the first race and 4th in the second. For the Penske team, this new season was off to a modest start.

With the legal battle settled, the Indianapolis 500 was billed as a showdown between CART and USAC, the first time that the two series would be competing head-to-head. As qualifying would quickly confirm, USAC had very little to offer aside from A.J. Foyt. In practice, it looked like the pole challenge might come down to the fiery old USAC veteran, Foyt, against Roger Penske's 27-year-old sophomore, Rick Mears. Al Unser was the first of the real challengers to make a qualifying run, posting a respectable time that ultimately netted him third on the starting grid. Bobby Unser's run was a little disappointing, but good enough for row two. Late in the afternoon, when Tom Sneva made his run, Roger Penske was on the verge of eating crow. The ex-Penske driver who had put Penske Racing's cars on the Indy pole the previous two years turned in the best one- and four-lap times of the day, and now looked like a good bet to be the first driver in Indianapolis history to take the honor three times in a row. After A.J. Foyt turned in a disappointing run, that left only Rick Mears with a shot at knocking Sneva out of the top spot.

At breakfast that morning, Roger Penske told reporters, "This kid is something special. Most of the good drivers in this sport are getting old—well into their late 30s if not their 40s. But Rick is only 27, a natural study, and as cooperative a driver as I have ever worked with. Watch him." When Mears finally got his chance near the end of the qualifying session, he did not disappoint. With a fast lap of 194.847 mph and a 4-lap average nearly one mph better than Sneva's speed, Roger Penske's sophomore sensation put his red, white and blue Gould Charge Penske PC-6 on the pole. So it was not Tom Sneva that ended up with three-straight Indy poles, it was Penske Racing.

In the race, Al Unser's Chaparral jumped out in front early, leading 85 of the first 97 laps before developing a transmission seal leak that put him out just past the halfway mark. Bobby Unser, in Penske's Norton Spirit PC-7 then took control, leading laps 97 through 181 and looking like a sure winner. In fact, at that point,

In his second Indy 500 with Penske Racing, Rick Mears put his year-old PC6 on the pole in 1979, bumping ex-Penske driver Tom Sneva to the middle of row one. Al Unser started third in Jim Hall's Chaparral. *Alan Hummel*

Jim Hall's 1979 Chaparral, driven by Al Unser, was Indy's first "ground effects" design. Using air flowing beneath the racecar to create a negative pressure, this design caused the car to be sucked to the ground allowing higher cornering speeds. *Alan Hummel*

Rick Mears was running second, directly behind his Penske teammate and the two were a full lap ahead of the rest of the field. But then, just 18 laps from victory, Unser lost top gear and had to nurse his car home in third gear.

It looked, then, like Mears would cruise to an uncontested victory, but there was one last bit of excitement when Tom Sneva, who had run in the top five for most of the race, made hard contact with the turn-4 wall on lap 188. That brought out the caution flag, allowing the field to bunch up and putting A.J. Foyt within striking distance. But Foyt was already suffering with an engine problem, and when the green flag dropped, Mears pulled away to a 45-second win as Foyt's engine nearly died on the final lap. Danny Ongais was third

Roger Penske had competed with Jim Hall since they were both driving sports cars back in the early 1960s. Hall was one of the great technical innovators in the sport, most famous for his early Can-Am Chaparrals. Again in 1979, he was using aerodynamics to make his racecars go faster than the competition. *Alan Hummel*

Rick Mears is seen here leading teammate Bobby Unser during the 1979 Indianapolis 500 race. Unser had led earlier, but lost top gear and fell to a 4th place finish while Rick Mears went on to victory. *Alan Hummel*

Former Penske driver Tom Sneva ran well in his "SUGARIPE PRUNE" McLaren, but his day ended with hard contact against the 4th turn wall just 12 laps from the finish of the race. *Alan Hummel*

and Bobby Unser limped home in fourth place with the Norton Spirit. Although Foyt made it interesting, there was no doubt that CART won the battle. "It's just incredible," Mears said after winning the world's greatest race in only his second attempt. "I really can't believe all this has happened so fast. And like they say, it seems like a fairy tale."

After Indy, the USAC teams made their traditional journey to Milwaukee while the CART teams headed for the fairgrounds in Trenton, New Jersey. Here again, CART presented a twin-race format, running back-to-back 100-mile events that counted as two separate races. After being upstaged by his junior teammate at Indy, Bobby Unser asserted himself on the 1-1/2 mile dog-legged track, winning both events. Mears, still choosing to drive the year-old PC-6 chassis, managed only 5th and 7th-place finishes here.

After seeing Bobby Unser run better in the new car, Mears switched back to his PC-7 for the pair of 126-

mile events at Penske's Michigan International Speedway. Unser qualified on the pole but had problems in the first race before coming back to win the second. Mears turned in solid 4th and 5th place finishes. Consistency was positioning him for a strong run at the championship.

On the road course at Watkins Glen, Unser and Mears gave Penske his first one-two finish of the season. They repeated the trick at Trenton, this time with

Rick Mears heads for the winner's circle in only his second attempt at Indianapolis. Rick would win two more times in 1979 and finish outside the top-5 only once en route to becoming the first-ever CART National Champion. *Alan Hummel*

Bobby Unser's Trenton-winning Penske PC7 was considered a partial ground-effects design. Although Rick Mears chose to drive the older PC6 at Indy, the PC7 proved to be a very successful design, winning 8 times in 1979. *Alan Hummel*

Rick Mears points to the spot where his likeness will be added to the Borg-Warner Trophy after his 1979 Indy victory. Mears was the first new winner at the Speedway since Gordon Johncock scored his initial "500" victory in 1973.

Mears beating Unser. And then in the Ontario 500, with Mario Andretti making a one-time appearance in a third team entry, Roger Penske got a triple play with Unser winning, Mears second and Mario third. When they went back to Michigan, Unser won again while Mears claimed third-place points. Then, almost as if it was orchestrated, the two swapped positions and Mears won in Atlanta with Unser finishing third. At this stage, Penske Racing had won six consecutive races and nine of the 13 for the season. The streak was finally broken when Al Unser took the season finale at Phoenix, followed by his brother Bobby in second place and Rick Mears in third.

It was a remarkably strong showing for the Penske team in this first CART season. Rick Mears, with three race victories including the Indianapolis 500, won the national title with 4,060 points. Bobby Unser, with six wins and seven pole positions, made it a one-two Penske Racing championship, finishing the year with 3,780 points. In a distant third position was Gordon Johncock with 2,211 points, driving Pat Patrick's independent Penske PC-6 chassis. Ten years after first showing up at Indianapolis, Roger Penske had established his team as the dominant force in Indy-car racing. His drivers were winning, his cars were winning, and the new Indy-car series that he co-founded was an unqualified success in its debut season.

1980

Penske Racing stayed with the same driver lineup for the 1980 season, running a new PC-9 chassis and Cosworth engine. The strongest competition this year came from Johnny Rutherford, who had switched to the now more reliable Jim Hall Chaparral team; and Tom Sneva, who was driving an outdated independent McLaren for Johnny O'Connell Racing.

In the season-opener at Phoenix, the only CART race before the Indy 500 this year, Rutherford and Sneva finished one-two, while the Penske teammates both suffered mechanical woes, finishing 21st and 23rd.

Penske went to Indianapolis with an all-star lineup. In addition to defending champ Rick Mears and two-time winner Bobby Unser, Mario Andretti was back in an additional Penske entry after missing the 1979 race. In qualifying, Rutherford put his Chaparral on the pole at 192.256 mph, but Andretti was close behind to take the middle of the front row at 191.012. Bobby Unser filled out the first row at 189.994 mph and Rick

Mears was directly behind him in sixth starting spot at 187.490.

In the race, Rutherford's Chaparral was just about untouchable. The three Penskes ran in the top-five for as long as they lasted, leading a combined total of 45 laps, but it was a tough day for the Captain's team. Andretti was out first, after 71 laps, with an engine problem. Bobby Unser lasted 126 laps before a bad magneto eliminated him too. Rick Mears made it to the end, but had to settle for 5th spot. He was challenging Tom Sneva for third late in the race when a cut tire forced an unscheduled pit stop. Sneva went on to finish second after a remarkable run that saw him charge from 33rd and last spot on the starting grid, driving a five-year-old backup car. The ex-Penske driver would be keeping his old boss honest for the next few years anyway.

With CART and USAC temporarily reunited, everybody got to go to the Milwaukee Mile again after Indy. Bobby Unser qualified fifth and went on to win the race over runner-up Johnny Rutherford and pole-sitter Gordon Johncock. Rick Mears started 4th but fell to 5th place, three laps behind the leaders.

Next up was the Pocono 500 and Mario Andretti was back in the third Penske car for this event. Bobby Unser qualified on the pole, Andretti was on the out-

In 1980, Penske Racing introduced the PC9, driven here by Bobby Unser in the Indianapolis 500. Unser won four poles and four races with this design, while Rick Mears won once. *Alan Hummel*

Still driving part-time for Penske Racing in 1980, Mario Andretti climbs from his PC9 after dropping out of the Pocono 500. Mario was sometimes accused of being hard on equipment. A rival team owner once suggested that "he could break an anvil with a rubber mallet." *Alan Hummel*

side of the front row and A.J. Foyt in the middle. Rick Mears started 7th. In the race, Andretti had another short day, dropping out just past the halfway mark with a transmission problem.

At that point in his career, Mario had a well-deserved reputation for being very hard on equipment. A rival team owner once suggested that he could break an anvil with a rubber mallet. Mears, who was generally known for being fairly easy on equipment, also suffered a rare mechanical failure at Pocono, losing an engine on lap 163.

Fortunately, the lone remaining Penske didn't falter. Bobby Unser claimed the lead after Foyt dropped out before the halfway point, and went on to lead a race-high 116 laps and take the win. Rutherford and Sneva finished second and third, continuing to bank points for the championship.

Following Pocono, CART went to a new venue, the Mid-Ohio road course in Lexington, Ohio. When CART opened for business in 1979, it raced on mostly the same oval tracks that had previously been used in the USAC series. Over the next several years, however, CART would transform the traditionally oval-based series into a mix of ovals, road courses, and temporary street circuits. Initially, that was a culture shock for many of the established drivers, most who had graduated from the short dirt tracks and never had to be concerned about turning right. Ultimately, as CART's format shifted more and more toward road racing, new drivers started coming into the series from the Can-Am and other road racing programs. This also had the effect of bringing in a lot of foreign drivers, including ex-Formula-1 competitors, who had strong road racing backgrounds.

Bobby Unser put Penske's Norton Spirit on the outside of the front row at Mid-Ohio, but dropped out of the race with an engine problem. Rick Mears started third in the Gould Charge, and led a race-high 32 laps before crashing out just 12 laps from the end, while Johnny Rutherford went on to score another win in his Chaparral. Back on the more familiar high-banked oval at Michigan, Unser and Mears finished second and fourth respectively, while Rutherford took top honors again, padding his lead in the championship.

The Captain's drivers redeemed themselves at Watkins Glen, posting their first one-two finish of the year, with Unser leading Mears to the checkered flag. Then Johnny Rutherford won from the pole at Milwaukee, with Mears and Unser finishing second and third, respectively. The same three drivers took the podium positions in the Ontario 500, with Bobby U. claiming the win from pole, Rutherford finishing second and Mears third. They were the only three drivers to lead in the race, with Unser out front for 182 of the 200 laps.

In the 150-mile fall Michigan race, the Penske team had a perfect day. Andretti claimed the pole in the third team car. Bobby Unser qualified second fastest, with Rick Mears fourth on the grid. Mario dominated the race, leading 53 of the 75 laps and taking the win. He was followed to the flag by Unser and Mears. It was a great home-track 1-2-3 showing for Penske Racing.

The next race took the CART teams to another new venue, a 2.5-mile road course in Mexico City. Mears found his way back to the winner's circle here, finishing ahead of teammate Unser. Unfortunately by that time,

Rick Mears, wearing the number "1" as defending CART champion, starts on the front row next to Al Unser's Longhorn-Cosworth at Watkins Glen in 1980. Mears finished second to teammate Bobby Unser. *Alan Hummel*

Johnny Rutherford was so far ahead in the championship that it really didn't matter.

Penske Racing had three cars entered for the season's final race at Phoenix, but Unser crashed in practice and did not start the race. Mario Andretti took the pole and went on to be the only challenger to a notably dominant Tom Sneva, the eventual race winner. Sneva and Andretti finished four laps ahead of third-place Gary Bettenhausen. Mears finished 7th after being penalized two laps for a pit violation. This last race of the year was full of action, topped by Johnny Rutherford's front-straight flip, in which the Texan landed on his trademark lone-star helmet beneath the yellow Chaparral. Fortunately he was not hurt, and despite his DNF, Rutherford easily won the points championship for 1980. He was followed in the final standings by Bobby Unser, Tom Sneva and Rick Mears. Collectively, these four drivers won 11 of the season's 12 events. The remaining victory belonged to Penske's Mario Andretti.

1981

Penske Racing started the 1981 CART season with the same primary drivers and an updated PC-9B81 chassis. Mario Andretti had decided to leave Formula-1 and was back in Indy-cars on a full-time basis, this year driving for Patrick Racing. For his traditional "extra" driver at Indianapolis, Roger Penske selected unlikely rookie, Bill Alsup. At 42 years of age, Alsup was a late bloomer in racing. He had tried and failed to make the Indy 500 starting field the two previous years, but was running a surprisingly successful independent CART effort in 1980 and early '81 using a Penske PC-7 chassis. After Indy, Penske signed Alsup to drive for the remainder of the season.

There was very little competition for the Penske chassis in 1981. Johnny Rutherford's Jim Hall Chaparral, which had been so fast and reliable a year earlier, was neither in 1981. New Patrick Racing Wildcats for Andretti and Gordon Johncock showed potential, but never made it to victory lane. A Penske-built car would win 8 of 12 races run this season. Tom Sneva's March 81C would take two of the other four events, signaling the beginning of the 1980s "kit car" era. Dan

Bill Alsup was an unlikely candidate when hired by Roger Penske to drive the team's third car in 1981. At age 42, with no Indy 500 starts, the former independent driver proved to be a good choice. Though never scoring a win, he finished second to Penske teammate Rick Mears in the '81 CART standings.

Bill Alsup qualified his AB Dick Penske PC9 7th on the Indy 500 grid and finished 11th in the race, his only start at the Speedway. *Alan Hummel*

Gurney's radical new Eagle design would take one of the remaining races and Johnny Rutherford's Chaparral the other."

As usual, the season opened on the Phoenix mile. Johnny Rutherford scored what would turn out to be his only win of the season, with Bobby Unser finishing second and Rick Mears fourth.

Unser put his Penske PC-9B on the pole at Indy, although he didn't have the fastest qualifying time. That honor went to Tom Sneva, who posted his speed of 200.691 mph, on the second day of qualifying. Rick Mears also failed to qualify on pole day and had to start back in the 8th row. Bill Alsup placed the third Penske team entry on the inside of row 3.

The 1981 Indianapolis 500 was marred by injuries and controversy. It began well enough, with Bobby Unser leading a clean start and staying out front for the first 32 laps until Tom Sneva had charged through the field from his 21st starting position to take control. Sneva would lead fairly easily until experiencing clutch problems on his second pit stop at lap 56. Mears then took the lead, but pitted on the very next lap for what was supposed to be routine service. A fuel coupling malfunction, however, allowed a large amount of methanol to spill over Mears' car and his entire pit box erupted into flames. Mears scrambled out of his flaming racecar and was doused with water and fire extinguishers by the crew and safety team. He ended up with first and second degree burns on his face and hands. Six Penske team crew members were also burned, two requiring hospital treatment. Bobby Unser would have a similar, but thankfully less serious incident later in the race, as would Gary Bettenhausen. These occurrences would contribute to eventual changes in safety regulations, leading to today's requirement for all over-the-wall crew members to wear full fireproof gear, including helmets.

With Mears out, Danny "the Flyin' Hawaiian" Ongais moved into the lead. But after leading only three laps, he too had a pit problem, stalling the car as he was trying to pull away following his stop. After getting restarted, a presumably aggravated Ongais charged back into the race. Halfway around the racetrack, with tires that were still cold, Ongais lost control of his Inter-

Bobby Unser won the pole at Indy in 1981 with his Penske PC-9B, although the fastest qualifier that year would actually be former Norton Spirit driver Tom Sneva who qualified on the second weekend. Unser went on to lead almost half of the incident-marred race en route to his third "500" title. *Alan Hummel*

One of several scary moments during the 1981 Indianapolis 500 occurred when Rick Mears' car erupted in invisible flames during a routine pit stop. Mears sustained first and second degree burns in the incident. *Alan Hummel*

scope Parnelli racecar and crashed nearly head-on into the third turn wall. Full of fuel from the pit stop, the car exploded into flames as it slid and spun along the concrete wall, shedding wheels, body panels, wings, and suspension parts. The crash was described as the most severe impact since Swede Savage's fatal accident in the 1973 race. When the flaming wreckage finally

Roger Penske, leaning over the wall in front of the Norton Spirit, controls pit action during one of Bobby Unser's stops in the 1981 Indy 500. Unser's mistake leaving pit lane nearly cost him the race victory. *Alan Hummel*

ground to a stop in the north chute, Danny Ongais lay motionless in the cockpit, his head slumped forward, his arm dangling outside car, and his left leg protruding at a grotesque angle from what had once been the front of a beautiful black racecar. It took rescue workers 15 minutes to cut the badly burned and broken driver from the wreckage. Ongais would spend many months in rehabilitation, but would return to race again, until a frighteningly similar accident in practice for the 1987 Indy race would convince him to retire.

For the remainder of the race, Bobby Unser, Mario Andretti, and Gordon Johncock would share the lead, but it was Unser who seemed to have the upper hand. Yet despite having the fastest remaining car, Roger Penske's "experienced" driver nearly lost the race on a technicality. Under a caution period on lap 149, Unser, Andretti and most of the other lead cars pitted for fuel and tires. Exiting the pits, Andretti was right behind Unser as they came upon the procession of cars still on the racetrack that were bunched behind the pace car heading into the first turn. The rulebook stipulates that a driver, in this situation, must merge into the line of traffic without gaining an advantage by passing any cars. Andretti did just that, but Unser clearly stayed on the pit apron and went by six other cars before merging

into the field. It was a blatant and indefensible violation of the rules by the veteran Penske driver. Andretti immediately radioed in to report the infraction, but the USAC race officials took no action. According to the book, the appropriate punishment would have been a one-lap penalty that should have been imposed immediately after the violation was committed.

The race ended with Unser in the lead and a very irate Mario Andretti second. While Roger Penske and Bobby Unser were in victory lane, both celebrating their third Indy 500 victories, Mario Andretti and his teammate Gordon Johncock, one of the cars Unser had passed in the pit incident, were starting the process of filing a formal protest. When the official race results were posted at 8:00 AM the next morning, Andretti and Johncock filed the paperwork. To almost everyone's surprise, the protest was upheld. Bobby Unser was penalized one lap for passing cars under the yellow flag, and Mario Andretti was declared the winner of the 1981 Indianapolis 500. It seemed that Mario had finally won his second "500," twelve years after his famous 1969 victory.

Roger Penske is seen here on the pit wall reacting to Bobby Unser's 1981 Indianapolis 500 victory. What Penske didn't know at the time was that he would have to go to court to get this victory reinstated after USAC officials levied a post-race penalty against Unser and tried to give the win to Mario Andretti. *Alan Hummel*

But Roger Penske wasn't going to give up that easily. Penske filed an appeal on the grounds that the penalty should have been levied during the race, theoretically giving Unser the chance to make up the lost distance on the track. Months after the race was over, the USAC Appeals Board, by a 2-1 vote, reinstated Bobby Unser as the winner. It wasn't the Speedway's finest hour, but it did return the controversial victory to Penske Racing.

Rick Mears missed the Milwaukee race because of his Indy injuries and Bobby Unser was the lone Penske Racing entry for this event. He qualified second and led the first 33 laps of the race, but spun and made contact with the wall just before the halfway point, ending his day.

Mears was back in the car for the twin Atlanta races just four weeks after his injuries. Bill Alsup was also back in a third Penske car for this event. Johnny Rutherford won the pole and dominated the first race, leading 64 of the first 79 laps, but Rick Mears was never far behind. On lap 80, Mears passed Rutherford for the lead and stayed ahead for the final four laps to win by only three seconds over the Chaparral. Bill Alsup finished a lap down in eighth position, and Unser fell back two laps to finish 13th. In the second heat, Mears proved it wasn't a fluke, leading 62 of the 83 laps to take the win over Mario Andretti and Johnny Rutherford. Bobby Unser finished 6th and Alsup came home 8th again.

With the demise of the Ontario Motor Speedway, CART upgraded its summer Michigan race to a 500-mile event. Ironically, the Penske team had a remarkably mediocre weekend at the boss' track. Mears, Alsup and Unser qualified 3rd, 7th, and 9th respectively, and combined to lead a grand total of only four laps in the race. The first half of the event was dominated alternately by Tom Sneva, Johnny Rutherford and Mike Mosley, until each experienced mechanical problems. Al Unser and Pancho Carter then traded the lead over the next 100 laps until Unser's engine expired, leaving Carter, who was driving a two-year-old Penske PC-7, to go on to a popular underdog victory. Mears and Alsup, who were never serious factors in the race, went on to finish third and fourth. Bobby Unser dropped out with an engine problem and finished 16th.

On the road course at Riverside, Rick Mears put the Penske team back on top. He took the lead when Al Unser's gearbox failed on the 45th lap and stayed in front until the end, claiming his third victory of the season. Bill Alsup drove a solid race to finish third behind Mears and Gordon Johncock. Bobby Unser continued to struggle, coming in 11 laps down in 9th place.

There was a period between 1981 and 1984 when Tom Sneva, regardless of what he was driving, was virtually untouchable on the one-mile bullrings at Milwaukee and Phoenix. For the September Milwaukee race, Sneva qualified third behind Rutherford and Bobby Unser, but he took the lead on the second lap and never looked back, leading 186 of the 200 laps for the victory. Mears and Unser drove good races, but had nothing for the former Penske Racing driver that day. They finished second and third, respectively. Alsup was 11th.

Back in Michigan for the fall 150-miler, Rick Mears won from the pole over Mario Andretti, with Bill Alsup 4th and Bobby Unser 7th. Mears came home first again in the next race at Watkins Glen. On this 3.4-mile road course, Mears finished an incredible 1 lap and 10 seconds ahead of runner-up Johnny Rutherford. Penske's young driver was quickly proving to be a very capable road-racer, an invaluable talent as CART began shifting away from the oval tracks to more road courses. Bill

Rick Mears leads #20 Gordon Johncock and the rest of the field en route to victory at Watkins Glen in 1981. Penske Racing won the only three CART races ever run at Watkins Glen, with Bobby Unser taking the honors in '79 and '80. *Alan Hummel*

Alsup finished third at the Glen, but he was driving in his own private PC-7 for this race. Bobby Unser's car had been disqualified after qualifying, so Penske bumped Alsup and put Unser in his car. As it would turn out, Bobby U. would last just 23 laps before losing a piston. Except for the dubious Indy win, he was having a dismal year.

Mears made it three-in-a-row at Mexico City, finishing ahead of Al Unser and Gordon Johncock. Mears and Bobby Unser combined to lead all but two laps of this race, but Unser crashed seven laps from the finish, to continue his disappointing string of poor results. Bill Alsup piloted the third Penske PC-9B to fifth place.

The season ended where it began, on the Phoenix mile. Having his best race since Indy, Unser qualified on the pole and battled all day with Tom Sneva, ultimately settling for second place to his Penske Racing predecessor. Rick Mears had a slight brush with the wall, but managed to continue and finished 8th, five laps behind the leaders. Alsup dropped out with a fuel pump problem.

Despite missing the Milwaukee race because of his Indy injuries, Rick Mears won six of the 12 CART races run in 1981, taking his second championship in three years by a wide margin over runner-up Bill Alsup.

Although Alsup never won a race and led only three laps all season, he completed more miles than any other driver and scored his points on consistency. Bobby Unser finished a disappointing 7th in the title chase. At the end of the season, with a little encouragement from Roger Penske, Unser decided to call it quits, leaving a prized seat vacant at Penske Racing. The Captain's team had now won four of the last five national championships.

1982

With Rick Mears already performing like a seasoned veteran, Roger Penske looked for youth to fill the vacancy left by Bobby Unser's retirement. Penske picked Kevin Cogan, a 27-year-old ex-Formula Atlantic champion from California. Cogan had run six Indy-car races for O'Connell Racing in 1981, including a second place finish in his Milwaukee debut and an impressive 4th in the Indianapolis 500.

Mears and Cogan drove all-new Penske PC-10s for the new season. Back in the early days, when Roger Penske and Mark Donohue were simultaneously running in four or five different racing series, Donohue often complained that things were too rushed and there wasn't adequate time for testing. Now that the Captain

Driving the Penske PC9B, Rick Mears won at Watkins Glen by a full lap over second-place Johnny Rutherford. It was one of six victories for Mears in 1981 as he marched toward his second CART title in three years. *Alan Hummel*

Rick Mears and Roger Penske would enjoy one of the most enduring partnerships in motor sports. Mears would drive his entire Indy car career for Penske Racing, giving the Captain three CART championships and four Indy 500 wins.

was focusing his full attention on the Indy-car series, that was no longer the case. In fact, the new Penske PC-10 had been ready since October of 1981. Before the 1982 season ever started, the new Penske car had seen more than 3,000 test miles. At Indianapolis, A.J. Foyt would comment enviously, "The rest of us are trying to do as much in six days as Penske took six months to do." And it showed.

At many of the races on the CART circuit this year, half the field was comprised of older Penske-built chassis, although that wasn't the only competition. Marches driven by Tom Sneva and rookies Bobby Rahal and Geoff Brabham were formidable challengers. And Mario Andretti and Gordon Johncock were strong again in Pat Patrick's Wildcats. Johnny Rutherford's aging Chaparral would be parked in favor of a new March by mid-season.

Rick Mears dominated the season opening Phoenix 150, starting from pole and leading 139 of the 150 laps. Mario Andretti was second and Penske rookie Kevin Cogan had an impressive debut finishing third. Mears gave a similarly dominating performance at Atlanta, winning from the pole again, this time pacing 123 of the 132 laps. Cogan lasted only 27 laps here before being sidelined with a bad wheel bearing.

Going into the Indianapolis 500 in 1982, it would

Penske Racing introduced an all-new PC10 chassis in 1982 and hired promising sophomore Kevin Cogan to replace Bobby Unser in the Norton Spirit. Rick Mears won four races and 8 poles with the Penske PC10, taking his third CART title in four years. *Alan Hummel*

have been foolish to bet against Rick Mears and Penske Racing. Qualifying did nothing to change that outlook, as Mears put his Gould Charge PC-10 on the pole with a record speed of 207.004 mph, nearly 3 miles-per-hour faster than teammate Kevin Cogan who took the second spot on the grid. A.J. Foyt filled out the front row with a speed of 203.332.

But the celebration of Penske's one-two qualifying sweep didn't last long; not because anyone would go faster—in fact, nobody would come close—but for a much more serious reason. There was a horrific accident involving driver Gordon Smiley that resulted in the first Speedway death since the tragedy-filled 1973 event. "One hour after Mears and Cogan had made their record runs," wrote Sam Moses in his *Sports Illustrated* account, "Smiley, 33, a Texan in his third Indy appearance, began to slide out in Turn 3 as he tried to get a flying start for the first of his four qualifying laps. When Smiley corrected, his March-Cosworth shot head-on into the wall at about 190 mph. The car disintegrated into little pieces of metal and big balls of fire, and with it went the life of a man who was doing what he wanted to do." It was a sad, but increasingly rare reminder that auto racing was still a dangerous sport.

At the start of the 66th running of the "500," Roger Penske had every reason to be optimistic, even arrogant about his prospects for scoring a fourth Speedway victory. But as soon as the green flag dropped, those prospects dimmed. "It was, without a doubt, the sorriest start and the finest finish there has ever been at the Indianapolis Motor Speedway," wrote Indianapolis Star reporter Robin Miller.

From his starting spot in the middle of the front row, Penske's new driver, Kevin Cogan, lost control of his car as he accelerated down the front straightaway to the green flag. It may have been simple inexperience or it may have been a mechanical failure, but the result was a mess. Cogan veered sharply to his right, clipping A.J. Foyt's car. He then bounced back and shot across the track, collecting hard-luck Mario Andretti on the way. Fortunately, unlike the disastrous 1973 start, injuries were limited to mechanical equipment and drivers' egos. Kevin Cogan took abuse from all directions. The always

Kevin Cogan's promising career was derailed when he triggered a multi-car accident at the start of the 1982 Indy 500. Cogan's failure to accept responsibility for the incident contributed to his release after one unsuccessful season with the team. *Alan Hummel*

subtle and understanding A.J. Foyt was quick to offer his input saying, "The guy had his head up his ass." Mario Andretti was also vocal, but made the mistake of dragging Roger Penske's name into his criticism saying, "He couldn't handle the responsibility of being in the front row. Roger Penske had him in a car too good for the kid." Penske didn't appreciate Andretti's comments, but replied with characteristic diplomacy saying, "Mario should realize he's had some ups and downs, too." He then added a much-needed vote of confidence for his rookie driver, saying, "Kevin is going to continue to drive for us."

It took nearly an hour to get the race restarted. Foyt's car was repaired but Cogan and Andretti were done for the day. For the first time in several years, Roger Penske had not entered a third car at Indy. So Cogan's first-lap departure left Penske Racing with just one hope and a full 500 miles to go. Foyt jumped into the lead on the restart and stayed there for the first 23 laps. Then Rick Mears, Tom Sneva and Gordon Johncock battled for the front spot for the remainder of the race. Final pit

stops played a deciding role in the outcome of the race. First, Mears and Sneva pitted together 17 laps from the finish. Mears was caught off-guard by the slower car of Herm Johnson in pit lane. He locked up his brakes but bumped the back of Johnson's car before he could slow down enough. Fortunately there was no serious damage, but the incident cost him priceless time in pit lane. Sneva's stop went smoothly, but the new tires put on his car upset the handling balance, and he was no longer able to challenge for the lead. Johncock pitted three laps later without incident and came out with an 11-second advantage over Mears with only 10 laps remaining—seemingly a secure margin. But Rick Mears wasn't done yet. In three laps, he cut the gap to 7 seconds. Two laps later, it was four seconds. At the white flag, they were side-by-side—the new Penske PC-10 and its driver were that good. Going into the first turn, Johncock had the outside line and Mears had to ease slightly. He followed behind Johncock's Wildcat until the final turn of the final lap; then he dived below the yellow line trying to pass on the inside. But Johncock moved low too, cutting off Rick's momentum. At the finish line, Johncock led by 16 hundredths of a second, the closest winning margin in Speedway history. "I knew when I took the white flag," Mears said, "I probably didn't have enough steam to get by him on that lap. If I'd have had a couple more laps, I think I might have been able to get by. But I've got nothing to complain about. I guess we put on a pretty good race." None of the 350,000 paying customers disagreed.

Mears and Cogan finished third and fifth at Milwaukee, in a race dominated by Gordon Johncock's Wildcat. Cogan, however, was pushing his luck, crashing another one of Roger Penske's PC-10s in practice. He tried hard to redeem himself on the road course at Cleveland, qualifying on the pole and leading a race-high 48 laps before encountering problems and finishing nine laps off the pace. Mears also led at Cleveland, but ended up finishing fourth. Rookie Bobby Rahal scored his first Indy-car win in this race.

Roger Penske didn't have much to celebrate when the CART circuit came to his track for the July Michigan 500. Rick Mears did win the pole and dueled with

Gordon Johncock for more than half the race, but an accident on the 181st lap ended his day. Teammate Cogan dropped out with a water leak 10 laps later and Johncock went on to win the race. This was significant because Mears and Johncock were in a close battle for the championship at this point, and Michigan gave the lead to Pat Patrick's driver.

Back at Milwaukee, the CART series suffered its first fatality when rookie Jim Hickman died following a practice crash. Hickman had run only three Indy-car races previously, including a respectable 7th place finish in the Indianapolis 500 just two months earlier. Although it was the first death attributed to the CART organization, it was, alarmingly, the second Indy-car fatality of the year.

In qualifying for the Milwaukee race, the two Penske cars claimed the front row. Mears then led from the green flag without much challenge for the first half of the race. Through the third quarter, he battled with Tom Sneva, trading the lead back-and-forth until the Penske's Cosworth engine quit on lap 146, leaving Sneva to cruise to a one-lap victory over Bobby Rahal. Kevin Cogan finished 5th, three laps down.

Things improved dramatically for the Penske team at Pocono. Rick Mears and Kevin Cogan qualified first and second. Mears led 142 of the 200 laps; Cogan led 10. At the end of the 500-mile race, the two Penske cars were still out front, three full laps ahead of the field. This race demonstrated the rarely seen awesome potential of the PC-10. Most importantly, it put Rick Mears back into the championship points lead for good.

Kevin Cogan displayed his road racing talents again by taking the pole at Riverside. Mario Andretti jumped into the lead from his second-place starting spot at the beginning of the race, but lasted only 10 laps before he broke his transmission. Cogan took control at that point and led for the next 40 laps until his engine quit. It was certainly his best drive of the year, while it lasted. When Cogan disappeared, Rick Mears inherited the lead and stayed out front for the remaining 45 laps, holding off Tom Sneva to take another victory.

At Elkhart Lake in mid-September, Mears won another pole, but led only the first lap before Bobby

Rahal and Mario Andretti took over. Cogan dropped out with another engine problem on the very first lap, but Mears stayed in the hunt until just before the end when he ran out of fuel and had to settle for a 5th place finish. The unlikely winner of this race was Mexican rookie Hector Rebaque.

When CART returned to Michigan for the 150-miler in late September, Mears and Cogan recorded another one-two qualifying performance. Cogan jumped into the lead at the start, battling with a very racy A.J. Foyt. That lasted eight laps, until the two came together, ending the day for both of them. In the meantime, Rick Mears had stopped on the first lap; apparently it was his turn to have the engine trouble this day. The impressive rookie Bobby Rahal went on to win the race over veteran Mario Andretti.

The season ended back in Phoenix. Rick Mears took his 9th pole of the year and battled all afternoon with Tom Sneva, before settling for the runner-up spot again. Andretti was third and Kevin Cogan fourth, two laps down.

After the mid-season challenge from Gordon Johncock, Mears finished strong to take his third CART championship in four seasons. That made five Indy-car titles for Penske Racing in six years—a dynasty was born. Rookie Bobby Rahal had a very impressive season and ultimately finished second to Mears in the championship race. Roger Penske's embattled number-two driver, Kevin Cogan, ended up a disappointing 6th in the title chase without ever winning a race. Even more damaging for the young Californian was the fact that he continued to blame his controversial Indy crash on mechanical failure even after the Penske team found no evidence to support that claim. Under the circumstances, nobody was really surprised when Cogan's contract with Penske Racing was not renewed for the following season.

1983

A year earlier, when Roger Penske went shopping for a driver, he looked for youth. No doubt he was hoping to discover another Rick Mears, and probably at a bargain price. When that didn't work out as planned, the Captain reevaluated his strategy and turned to one of the most experienced and successful drivers on the circuit, 44-year-old Al Unser. Bobby's younger brother was a three-time Indianapolis 500 winner, a former USAC national champion, and a veteran of 17 Indy 500s. Al won the 1978 Indianapolis race, but the CART years had not been kind to him. In 1979, he struggled with the fast but unreliable Chaparral, managing only one victory and finishing 5th in the championship. Then he spent three years driving for the upstart Longhorn Racing team without scoring a single win. But Roger Penske had competed against Al Unser for many years and he knew it wasn't for lack of effort or talent.

Unser and teammate Rick Mears would be driving the new Penske PC-11, which was theoretically a refinement of the extremely successful PC-10. The cars would have a new look this year. With long-time sponsors Norton and Gould replaced by Pennzoil and Hertz, both PC-11s would now by dressed in brilliant-yellow fiberglass.

The competition was noticeably stronger this year. Italian rookie Teo Fabi, a Formula-1 refugee, came from nowhere to be a constant threat throughout the 1983 season. Mario Andretti had moved to the newly-established Newman-Haas team, co-owned by actor/racer Paul Newman and Lola distributor Carl Haas. Driving a new Lola T700 Cosworth, Andretti was an immediate challenger. Tom Sneva and Bobby Rahal were back with new March 83Cs. And then there were a couple of 20-year-old kids on the circuit this year, and both arrived with some impressive family connections. Their names were Al Unser Jr. and Michael Andretti, sons of Al and Mario. 1983 was destined to be a good year for CART.

The season began in Atlanta rather than the traditional Phoenix stop this year. Rick Mears started out on a strong note, breaking his own track record to take the pole at a speed just under 205 mph on this high-banked 1.5-mile oval. Gordon Johncock went on to win the race over Al Unser Sr. This was the last victory for Pat Patrick's American-built Wildcat chassis, and as it would turn out, the last win for driver Gordon Johncock.

In 1983, the Indianapolis 500, although still officially sanctioned by the United States Auto Club, became a part of the CART national championship.

Roger Penske turned to Al Unser, already a 3-time Indy 500 winner and former national champion, to partner with Rick Mears in 1983. Unser would drive for Penske Racing through the 1989 season, contributing 3 victories and two CART titles.

This organizational alignment would remain until the 1996 CART/IRL split. Roger Penske gambled again by entering just two cars for the Indy 500, but the drivers of those cars were no gamble at all. Rick Mears, in only five seasons on the Indy-car circuit, already owned one Indianapolis 500 title and three national championships. Al Unser had won Indy three times, in addition to his 1970 USAC national championship. Roger Penske had almost every reason to be confident going into the month of May.

The first sign of trouble came during practice when,

The 1983 Penske PC11s were both painted in bold yellow because of new sponsorship packages—Al Unser with Hertz and Rick Mears carrying Pennzoil colors. The PC11 chassis struggled to be competitive with a new wave of March kit-cars. By mid-season, both Unser and Mears were back in their old PC10s looking for more speed. *Alan Hummel*

unlike the previous years, it was not the Penske cars that were continually raising the speed bar, but rather the March 83Cs. The March chassis had first appeared in 1981 with Tom Sneva and the George Bignotti team. There were a couple more in 1982, but this year they would fill more than half of the Indy starting grid. And they would be fast. With March factory support, Italian rookie Teo Fabi, driving for Forsythe Racing, surprised everyone by taking the pole at a speed of 207.395 mph. Mike Mosely claimed the middle of the front row in another March. Rick Mears managed to put a Penske PC-11 on the outside of row one, but he qualified 2.7 mph slower than his 1982 pole speed. The second row was comprised of the Marches of Tom Sneva and Bobby Rahal and the Eagle of Al Unser, Jr. Al Sr., in the second Penske, was in row three, 0.2 mph slower than his rookie son. In total, there were only six Penske chassis in the field this year compared to 18 Marches.

At the start of the race, pole-sitter Teo Fabi jumped into the lead and pulled away with apparent ease until the first round of pit stops at lap 23. When Fabi dropped out 24 laps later, the race became a battle between the two Penske team cars and the Marches of Bobby Rahal and Tom Sneva. Rahal dropped out with a radiator problem just past the midpoint of the race, but by then, Rick Mears was already having serious handling trouble. The Penske team tried to make adjustments on pit stops, but nothing seemed to really help. After the race, Mears would say, "I about spun the thing 15 times today." Roger Penske added, "We just didn't have the car as ready as we should have. Last week we tested and worked on durability, so we couldn't foresee what happened today."

Mears ran in the top five all day, but had his hands full just keeping the car off the concrete walls; unfortunately, he was in no position to challenge for the win. Al Unser also had a less-than-perfect car, although his was not nearly as difficult as his teammate's. With Sneva leading handily in the closing stages of the race, front-row starter Mike Mosely pounded the Turn-One wall, bringing out the caution flag. Penske gambled on a quick pit stop, adding fuel only, to get Unser into the lead. At the restart on lap 177, the order behind the pace car was Unser Sr., Sneva, and then Al Unser, Jr., who was actually several laps behind the leaders. Before the green flag even dropped, Al Jr. blew past both Sneva and his father, setting up one of the most fascinating finishes in Indy history. Although Al Jr. had no chance of winning the race, he was in the interesting position of being able to directly influence the outcome between the two legitimate contenders, one of them being his father.

Al Unser, Jr. immediately let his father go by, but then his Eagle racecar got very wide, noticeably weaving back-and-forth across the track in tandem with every movement made by the white March running on his tail. For 14 laps, Tom Sneva struggled to find a way around "Little Al," but even with the USAC scoring stand waving the "passing" flag, warning him to allow the faster car to pass, he continued blocking. In the meantime, Al Sr. had pulled out a several second lead, and the laps were winding down. Finally, with only 9 laps remaining, Sneva pulled along Al Jr. on the front straightaway and held the line into the first turn, running all four wheels below the yellow line to pull ahead. He carried

Al Unser Jr.'s first Indy 500 was exciting and controversial. After a late-race restart, the younger Unser blatantly blocked eventual winner Tom Sneva, allowing his father's Penske to pull out a 12 second lead. Ten years later, Roger Penske would make Al Unser Jr. the third family member to drive for the Penske team. *Alan Hummel*

Ex-Penske driver Tom Sneva, racing George Bignotti's March-Cosworth, spoiled the Captain's party, winning the 1983 Indianapolis 500 over Al Unser and Rick Mears. *Alan Hummel*

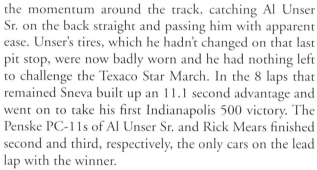

the momentum around the track, catching Al Unser Sr. on the back straight and passing him with apparent ease. Unser's tires, which he hadn't changed on that last pit stop, were now badly worn and he had nothing left to challenge the Texaco Star March. In the 8 laps that remained Sneva built up an 11.1 second advantage and went on to take his first Indianapolis 500 victory. The Penske PC-11s of Al Unser Sr. and Rick Mears finished second and third, respectively, the only cars on the lead lap with the winner.

Tom Sneva's victory was a popular one. There was a general consensus that, after three runner-up finishes and two poles at the Speedway, plus two USAC National Championships, he was due. The fact that he won by beating the two Penske cars was not overlooked by his fans or the racing press. *Auto Week's* headline read: "Sneva thumbs the Penske boys after three second-bests." And the *Indianapolis Star* noted, "The victory could have been extra sweet for Sneva had he wanted to look at it that way. It was Penske Racing for whom he won those two national championships—and still got fired. And it

was Penske Racing with Unser Sr. and Rick Mears that finished second and third Sunday." When questioned about this after the race, Sneva couldn't completely conceal the grin as he responded, "They were two yellow cars. I didn't notice who was the owner." Roger Penske took it in stride. "I think Tom really did a great job, he said. "We got beat fair and square." To Penske, it was just another white car. What was more disconcerting for the Captain was the realization that his PC-11 was obviously not as good as the March chassis. And that was going to be a real problem.

Al Unser Sr., unlike many of the USAC-bred championship drivers, was reasonably comfortable on a road course. That came in handy in the next race on the airport runways in Cleveland. Although Mario Andretti qualified on the pole and led convincingly until being sidelined with an overheating problem, Unser went on to lead a race-high 55 laps to take the victory. Mears continued to struggle, starting sixth and finishing 7th,

Next on the schedule was the Michigan 500, and Penske Racing came away with a lot of championship points but not a victory. Teo Fabi qualified on the pole again and would be one of 11 drivers to lead throughout the day. The surprise winner of this event was rookie John Paul Jr. driving a year-old Penske PC-10. Rick Mears and Al Unser led a combined total of 52 laps in the 250-lap event, and both were in contention with Paul and Mario Andretti right to the end. Mears took the lead from Unser on lap 239 and led until the last lap when he crashed with the lapped car of Chris Kniefel. That left Paul in the lead with Al Unser second, and Andretti third as the race ended under the yellow flag. With no other cars on the lead lap, Mears was still credited with fourth place, but it should have been a win. Gordon Johncock's accident in this race effectively ended his driving career. He would be out for the remainder of this season recovering from a broken leg and other injuries. He'd return for the 1984 season but would go winless until announcing his retirement before the 1985 Indianapolis 500.

Next, on the road course at Elkhart Lake, Mario Andretti in the Newman-Haas Lola scored the first of what would be many victories for this new team. Rick Mears had a terrible weekend, qualifying 11th and crashing out of the race early. Al Unser did better, hanging on for a third place finish behind Andretti and his own 21-year-old son. Al Sr. was making the best of a less-than-perfect situation. It was obvious that the Penske cars were not the class of the field in 1983, but Al was quietly racking up the points with top-five finishes, making the most of the equipment he had to work with.

For the mid-August Pocono 500, Roger Penske put Rick Mears in a year-old PC-10, leaving Al Unser in the new PC-11. Mears qualified 4th, behind three Marches but four spots ahead of Unser's PC-11. In the race, Mears led 26 of the 200 laps and finished third behind Teo Fabi and Al Unser Jr., who had by then abandoned Dan Gurney's Eagle chassis in favor of the dominant March. Al Sr. finished 8th.

Riverside was a terrible weekend for the Penske team. Both cars qualified poorly and dropped out of the race with transmission problems. For Mid-Ohio, Penske found another PC-10 for Al Unser, but it didn't make much difference. His drivers qualified 10th and 11th, and neither led a lap. Unser managed to hang on for a fourth place finish, a lap behind the leaders. Mears crashed three laps from the end and was credited with

9th. It was shaping up to be a disappointing year for the three-time CART champion.

But just as things started looking bleak, Rick Mears found a rabbit in the hat at Michigan. From his mediocre 11th place staring position, Mears led 55 of the 100 laps and held off Bobby Rahal to score his first victory of the season. Al Unser, two laps behind, banked 5th place points.

The next race was on a new 1.1-mile street circuit in Las Vegas. This was a part of CART's business strategy to bring their racing to the customer in major market areas. Unfortunately, this strategy often resulted in dull "parade" races on short, narrow temporary street courses, where speeds were low and passing was next to impossible. The drivers didn't like these tracks, nor did most of the "real" fans; but it seemed to be good for the sponsors and it did open Indy-car racing to a new breed of urban fan who was used to commuting minutes, not hours, to attend a sporting event.

This first Las Vegas visit resulted in another unspectacular weekend for Penske Racing. Al Unser finished fourth behind Mario Andretti, John Paul Jr., and Chip Ganassi, but he was never in contention for the win. Rick Mears finished 12 laps down in 13th position. It was another race in which neither Penske car led a single lap. At Laguna Seca, it was even worse, both cars dropping out early with mechanical problems.

Going into the season finale at Phoenix, Al Unser Sr. held a slim lead over Teo Fabi and Mario Andretti in the championship point's battle. Despite scoring only one win all season, Unser had managed to accumulate points through consistency, but Fabi and Andretti had been closing fast. In qualifying, Fabi and Andretti took the first two spots. Rick Mears was third fastest, and Unser started 8th. The key for Al Unser in this race was to do what he'd done so well all season—stay out of trouble and go for a top-five finish. If he could do that, it wouldn't matter what Fabi and Andretti did. And that's exactly how it played out. Fabi won the race with Andretti second. Al Unser finished fourth, good enough to hold a 5-point margin over Fabi in the final championship standings. Andretti was third in the title chase, Tom Sneva fourth, Bobby Rahal fifth, and defending champion Rick Mears, a disappointing sixth. In the record book, it was another national championship for Penske Racing—making it now an unthinkable six titles in seven years—but there was plenty of reason for concern. For the first time in several years, the Penske dynasty was looking vulnerable.

1984

For 1984, Roger Penske rolled out his new PC-12 chassis, hoping that the PC-11's successor would be more competitive with the army of March "kit-cars" that were now dominating the starting grids. Before the season started, Penske was confident, saying, "The engineering that's gone into this car is well beyond anything we've done in the past." But the March challenge was going to be formidable. In fact, the March chassis had become so popular because of its success that a remarkable 47 March 84Cs were ordered from the factory for the new season.

The Penske Racing driver lineup remained intact for the new season. Rick Mears' car retained sponsorship from Pennzoil Motor Oil, while Roger Penske inked a new deal with Miller Brewing Company to support Al Unser's entry. This was to become one of the most enduring partnerships in auto racing, with Miller still sponsoring Penske South entries in the NASCAR Nextel Cup Championship more than 20 years later.

The principal competition in the 1984 championship included Tom Sneva, Bobby Rahal, Al Unser Jr., and Michael Andretti in Marches, and Mario Andretti and Danny Sullivan in Lolas. The older Penske chassis, along with the Wildcats and Eagles, were no longer serious contenders.

The season opened on the street circuit in Long Beach, California. This course had been the site of the U.S. Grand Prix West Formula-1 race since 1976, an American version of the Grand Prix of Monte Carlo. But promoter Chris Pook grew tired of dealing with Formula-One's bureaucracy and prohibitive costs, so he worked out a deal to host CART races beginning in 1984. This track, by far the most suitable of the temporary street circuits used by CART over the years, soon became the cornerstone of the racing series. It has always been one of the most successful races on the calendar, in terms of both attendance and profitability.

Mario Andretti had an incredible advantage at Long Beach this first year, not only because of his general road racing talent, but also because he had raced on this course several times during his Formula-1 career. Not surprisingly, Andretti qualified on the pole and then led

In 1984, Penske picked up sponsorship from Miller Brewing for Al Unser's PC12. Unser carried the number "1" as the defending CART champion. The Penske PC12 chassis lasted only two races before being replaced by Marches.

every single lap of the race, finishing more that a minute ahead of runner-up Geoff Brabham. The Penske PC-12s had a dismal debut, finishing 21st and 22nd after dropping out with mechanical problems.

Back on the more familiar Phoenix mile, the Penske team fared no better. In a race dominated again by Tom Sneva, Rick Mears and Al Unser Sr. finished 18th and 21st respectively, both sidelined with engine failures.

Heading into the Indianapolis 500, Roger Penske had a real dilemma. It was clear that the PC-12 had a problem. To hedge his bet, Penske purchased a pair of March 84Cs and entered them along with his PC-12s for the Indianapolis race. On the official 1984 Entry List, the Marches were listed as the "T" entries for Mears and Unser, designating them as backup cars. But when it quickly became apparent that the PC-12s weren't going to be any better at Indy than in their previous two outings, Roger Penske swallowed his pride and put his drivers in the Marches for the race. It was a good decision.

Qualifying speeds broke the 210 mph barrier for the first time this year, and it was Tom Sneva, who seven years earlier had been the first driver to officially run 200 mph, who was setting the records again. Throughout his career, Tom Sneva was known as a great qualifier. In this run, he started at 209.113 mph and got faster on each successive lap, ending up with a four-lap average of 210.029. Sports Illustrated wrote, "Progressively faster laps are almost unheard of in qualifying: A driver can't hold his breath that long, and the tires get hot, causing handling to deteriorate. Sneva's car was set up "loose," so that when the tires heated, the car's handling would improve. It wasn't a secret strategy; explaining why everyone doesn't employ it, Teddy Mayer, co-owner of Sneva's team, said, "There aren't many drivers who are brave enough to drive the first lap that loose." He added, "I've had world champions like Niki Lauda drive for me, and Sneva's as good as any of them in his understanding of the car." This was the one that Roger Penske let get away—one of the few mistakes in his 40 years as a team owner.

Sneva's relatively unknown teammate, Howdy Holmes, took the second spot, and Rick Mears captured the

At Indianapolis, Al Unser was driving a Penske-prepared March 84C rather than the uncompetitive PC12. Because Indy was not a CART-sanctioned race, he wears the number "2" here reflecting his second-place finish in the 1983 "500." *Greenfield Gallery*

remaining front row position in his Penske Racing March. Al Unser Sr. qualified on the fourth row in 10th position. Mario Andretti, who had been running the fastest in practice all week, ended up in 6th spot after his engine died coming to the flag on the last lap. When the 33-car field was filled, it contained 30 Marches, two Lolas, and one Eagle. It was easily the fasted field to start an Indy 500, with every car qualifying over 200 mph. And it was also one of the most competitive grids, with less than 9 mph separating the fastest and slowest cars.

Rick Mears jumped into the lead on the first lap of the race and stayed there until the first round of pit stops. After that, Mario Andretti and Tom Sneva took turns leading while Mears stayed close enough to challenge. Al Unser Sr. didn't run well from the start. Although he would finish the race and end up with a solid third place, he was never a factor for the win. When Andretti began to experience problems, Mears moved back into the lead, pursued by Sneva. Moving toward the closing stages of the race, Sneva was closing steadily on Mears

After switching from the Penske chassis to a March, Rick Mears qualified on the front row for the 1984 Indy 500. The starting field for this year's race consisted of 30 Marches, two Lolas and an Eagle. *Greenfield Gallery*

After former teammates Mario Andretti and Tom Sneva experienced problems, Rick Mears went on to win his second Indianapolis 500 in 1984, finishing two laps ahead of runner-up Roberto Guerrero and Penske teammate Al Unser. *Greenfield Gallery*

when a caution flag came out on lap 163, setting up what should have been a great shootout to the finish. During the caution period, however, Sneva's March developed a problem with a constant-velocity joint, and the defending champion's day was over. Mears went on to an easy two-lap victory over rookie Roberto Guerrero and teammate Unser.

In the process of winning his second Indy title, Rick Mears broke a 12-year-old record for the fastest Indianapolis 500 ever run, a record set by Mark Donohue when he scored Penske Racing's first "500" victory back in 1972. For those who had followed the Penske team since its earlier days, it seemed particularly fitting that it was the talented, quiet and likeable Rick Mears who finally eclipsed Donohue's record. "Captain Nice" would have been pleased.

In Victory Lane, Mears was emotional about his sec-

ond Indy win, saying, "The first time, I was too young to appreciate what winning this race means. It was a week or two before it set in last time. This year, it started soaking in in the last few laps and I had to calm myself down until it was over." For Roger Penske, it was a remarkable turnaround. Without making the bold and expensive decision to scrap his own PC-12s in favor of the Marches, it is extremely unlikely that Mears or Al Unser would have made the top-10 in this race. "I had to eat a little crow," Penske said after it was over, "but it really paid off."

After tasting success with the March, there was no turning back to the hopeless PC-12. Rick Mears showed up in Milwaukee a week after his Indy triumph and duly planted his Pennzoil Penske-March-Cosworth on the pole. Mears battled the entire race with Tom Sneva, the two being the only drivers to lead a lap that day. Mears got ahead of Sneva on lap 138 and stayed there until Sneva made his pass for the win on the very last lap. Al Unser Jr. finished third, the only other car to complete the 200 miles, followed by Michael Andretti and then Al Unser Sr. in the second Penske March.

Next on the CART schedule was a new road course in Portland Oregon. This turned out to be a forgettable weekend for the Penske team, with Mears finishing 10th and Unser dropping out on the first lap with an engine failure. It was memorable for another reason, however, as it would mark the first of many Indy-car victories for future Penske team driver, Al Unser Jr.

Portland was followed by another new track at the Meadowlands, New Jersey. This temporary "street" course, which was actually laid out in the parking lot of the Meadowlands Sports Complex, must be regarded as the worst racetrack ever to present a modern-era Indy-car event. The idea was simple—put a racetrack within shouting distance of New York City, open up a huge new market for the sport, and then just sit back and count the money. Unfortunately, this particular track was more suitable for go-karts than Indy-cars, and neither new fans nor old ones could find much entertainment value in watching these exotic 200-mph racecars parade single-file through the parking lot at less than half that speed.

This first event at the Meadowlands was particularly unimpressive, as rain fell sporadically throughout the race, slowing speeds to a crawl and making passing virtually impossible. In fact, Mario Andretti started from the pole and led all 100 laps, finishing more than a minute ahead of second-place survivor, Danny Sullivan. Al Unser finished two laps off the pace in 8th place, and Rick Mears was four laps behind in 10th. But much more memorable than his finishing position that day was a simple gesture that Rick Mears made during that race, a gesture that personified this man who was known as much for his class as he was for his incredible driving talent. It happened midway through the race, after a particularly heavy rain shower had created a sizable puddle at the exit of pit road. One by one, as drivers came charging out of the pits, they would hit that puddle and execute an embarrassing slow-motion

spin, coming to rest in a spot where they needed the assistance of the track corner workers to get turned around and back into the race. Some drivers would sit calmly and patiently, waiting until those corner workers could safely come to their assistance. Others would wave and gesture frantically, as if it were the duty of the track personnel to run through racing traffic without regard for their own safety. Rick Mears was one of the many who fell victim to the "puddle" that afternoon. After he spun, the reigning Indianapolis 500 champion waited patiently until help arrived and got him moving. The next time around, as he came past that spot on the track, Mears slowed and raised his arm from the cockpit of his Penske Pennzoil March, waving "thank you" to those track workers who had come to his aid. Most people who were there on that soggy afternoon over 20 years ago wouldn't even remember that Mario Andretti won the race that day, but they will remember that hand waving in the air. Auto racing, like all sports, has its share of good guys and bad guys. Rick Mears was one of the all-time greats; a class act all the way.

Next on the CART schedule was the Cleveland road course. Neither Penske entry did particularly well in this event that marked the first win for another future Penske driver, Danny Sullivan. Mears qualified a dismal 23rd but worked his way up to a respectable fourth place finish. Al Unser started and finished in 10th position.

Penske Racing also had a rather lackluster showing in the Michigan 500. Mears and Unser each led just one of the 250 laps at the boss's track. Mears had qualified fourth and stayed with the leaders all day to finish third behind Andretti and Sneva, while Unser dropped out with an overheating problem early in the race. This event will be remembered for one of the most spectacular racing accidents ever to unfold on live television. A little past the halfway point, Al Unser Jr. and then-driver Chip Ganassi got together in the fourth turn on this extremely high-speed racetrack. Both cars shot down off the steep banking and into the infield, skating across the grass like it was ice. Both cars hit an infield dirt embankment with violent force. Parts of racecars flew everywhere. What was left of Ganassi's March chas-

The inaugural CART race at the Meadowlands Sports Complex in 1984 was a slow, soggy and generally unimpressive spectacle. Heavy rains caused numerous spins and off-track excursions. Geoff Brabham (#18) recovered to finish third, but Roberto Guerrero and Howdy Holmes were not as fortunate. *Alan Hummel*

Like many of his competitors, Rick Mears spun in a water puddle at pit exit. Track workers are seen here getting him restarted and back into the race. Mears went on to finish 10th. *Alan Hummel*

Alan Hummel

Alan Hummel

sis finally came to rest upside-down. Given the brutality of the impact, it seemed inconceivable at first that either driver could have survived. Thankfully, that was not the case. Safety engineering had obviously come a long way. There was no fuel fire—despite the fact that the cars were shattered into thousands of little pieces, the fuel bladders remained intact. The March chassis somehow withstood the incredible force of the impact, protecting both drivers from serious injury. Al Unser Jr. would not even miss a race. Ganassi would sit out the remainder of the season, and then competed in only four more CART races over the next two years before following in Roger Penske's footsteps and becoming a successful team owner.

Back at the scenic Road America road course in Elkhart Lake, Wisconsin, Mario Andretti had another dominating day. From the pole, he led two-thirds of the race to take a convincing win over Bobby Rahal. Al Unser and Rick Mears finished third and fourth respectively. They were consistent, but not particularly fast. By now, two things were becoming apparent. First, the Lola chassis had an inherent advantage over the March, especially on road courses. And second, when all the March teams had the same exact equipment to work with, it was very difficult to gain an unfair advantage, even for the once-invincible Penske Racing team.

Going into the Pocono 500, there was reason for hope. Rick Mears had traditionally done well in this race. In fact, Mears generally did well in most long races. He was, above all else, a smart driver. He understood the importance of pacing himself and the equipment to make sure there would be enough left to finish the race. Some called it sand-bagging, but in reality, it was just smart, disciplined driving. An old racing adage says: "To finish first, you first have to finish." Nobody understood that better than Rick Mears.

Mears broke the Lola streak by qualifying his Penske-March Cosworth on the pole at a speed of 202.87 mph. He then led a race-high 74 laps, battling all afternoon with Danny Sullivan, Bobby Rahal and Tom Sneva. In the end, Sullivan pulled out the win, with Mears less than three-tenths of a second behind at the checkered flag. Even though it wasn't a victory, it was a real shot in the arm to be that competitive. Al Unser, unfortunately, continued to struggle, finishing in 8th position, a lap off the pace.

Next time out, at Mid-Ohio, Mears and Unser qualified second and third, respectively. But the race was a battle between Andretti and Bobby Rahal, who finished a lap ahead of the rest of the field. The Penske drivers ran decent races, finishing 5th and 8th, but they were not really competitive. With Danny Sullivan third and ex-Formula-1 champion Emerson Fittipaldi in fourth, the value of that road racing experience was becoming painfully obvious to those who didn't have it.

Normally, any year that you win the Indianapolis 500 would have to be considered a good year. But at this point in the season, with Indy being the only win in the record book and the competition looking stronger with every race, the Penske gang was feeling the pressure. And unfortunately, things were about to get a lot worse as the CART parade headed north of the border for a new race at Sanair in Quebec, Canada. This track was a short oval, less than a mile in length. It should have been a good opportunity for Rick Mears

and Al Unser to get the Penske effort back on track, but it didn't work out that way.

Maybe Rick Mears was trying too hard, knowing how important it was to have a good showing here. In the Friday practice, he made a rare mistake, clipping another car as he was trying to execute a pass. Mears spun and crashed head-on into the steel guardrail on the inside of the racetrack. It was one of those accidents that, at first, didn't look like it should have been that serious. Because the track was so short, overall speeds were not nearly as fast as on the super speedways. The car didn't flip or explode into pieces as in some of the other memorable crashes of the time. But a couple of factors combined to make this a very serious incident. First, the barrier was steel guardrail rather than a concrete wall. The nose of Mears' March punched between the steel rails, getting tangled and shredded rather than just hitting and bouncing off. Secondly, the design of the racecar—not just the March, but all Indy-cars of the era—positioned the driver dangerously forward in the chassis. In fact, the drivers' feet were actually in front of the centerline of the front wheels, making them extremely vulnerable to injury, even in minor front-end contact incidents. And this wasn't minor contact.

Rick Mears sustained serious injuries to both of his feet and lower legs. He was rushed, semi-conscious, to a local hospital while CART's medical director, Dr. Steve Olvey, administered first aid. Local doctors initially believed that his feet needed to be amputated. Fortunately, Roger Penske and Dr. Olvey insisted on a second opinion. Penske immediately sent his private Lear jet to Indianapolis to pick up orthopedic surgeon, Dr. Terry Trammel, who ultimately saved Mears' feet. As a result of this incident, Trammel would become a valuable, permanent part of the CART safety team.

Rick Mears had a long and painful recuperation, not racing again for the remainder of the 1984 season. He would return the following year, but only for the five oval-track races on the schedule, his feet still not strong enough to tolerate all the gear-shifting, accelerating and braking necessary to navigate the road courses. Finally, in 1986, he did return to a full schedule, but he never regained full movement and reflexes in his feet.

Although he would continue to be a major force on the ovals for many more years, Rick Mears never again was a serious threat on road courses.

Two days after Mears' crash, Roger Penske had Johnny Rutherford in the backup Pennzoil Penske-March for the Sanair race. Rutherford was already a three-time Indianapolis 500 winner, but he hadn't enjoyed much success since the Jim Hall Chaparral program ended a couple years earlier. But with little preparation time, he qualified 10th and finished 5th in the race. Al Unser, meanwhile, dropped out with a transmission problem. He was surely not enjoying his season as the defending CART champion.

Penske kept Rutherford on the payroll for the Michigan 200, and J.R. responded by winning the pole at a speed of 215 mph. In race that spanned two days because of rain, Rutherford led 46 laps, but crashed just six miles from the end, causing the race to finish under a yellow flag. Al Unser ran a strong race too, leading 14 laps and going on to finish in 4th position, behind winner Mario Andretti, Tom Sneva and Danny Ongais.

Phoenix wasn't the last race of the season this year, although Roger Penske and the whole team would have probably been happier if it was. Johnny Rutherford got one more chance with the team. He started third, but fell four laps down and finished 11th. Unser's day was worse, starting 12th and then getting caught up in a four-car pile-up midway through the race. The Penske mechanics were working overtime putting wrecked cars back together after almost every race.

Laguna Seca followed Phoenix this fall, providing road-racers Bobby Rahal and Mario Andretti another opportunity to showcase their talents, the two being the only leaders in the race. Roger Penske picked up a relatively unknown driver named Mike Thackwell to fill the Pennzoil March seat for the final two events. At Laguna, he qualified mid-field and dropped out with an oil fitting leak. Al Unser started fifth, but finished 6th, a lap behind the leaders.

The long and difficult season finally ended at Las Vegas in mid-November. This race was fairly anti-climatic for the Penske team because Unser had long since been out of the championship battle. Coming into this weekend, Mario Andretti held a slim points lead over Tom Sneva. In order for Sneva to take the title, he had to win the race and hope that Andretti finished out of the top ten. That scenario seemed unlikely because Tom Sneva had never won on a road or street course before, while Andretti was the undisputed master on these tracks. But it turned out to be an interesting day. Andretti drove a conservative race, protecting his car and staying out of trouble to make sure he got that top-10 finish. Sneva, on the other hand, drove the race of his life, surprising almost everyone by leading a race-high 53 laps and beating Andretti to the flag by 7 seconds to win the battle but lose the war. Midway through the race, Sneva and Al Unser got together at one point; Sneva recovered but Unser did not, ending his dismal season with a 14th place DNF. Mike Thackwell, in the other Penske Racing entry, dropped out with an overheating problem. And with that, thankfully, the frustrating and painful 1984 season was finally over!

1985

In planning his 1985 driver lineup, Roger Penske had several factors to consider. First, Rick Mears' status was still uncertain. He was expected to be back for Indy, but whether he'd be fit to drive on the road courses immediately was still very much in question. Second, with more than half of the 1985 CART races scheduled on road or street courses, it would be prudent to have at least one driver on the team that excelled in this type of racing. And finally, at 45 years of age, Al Unser Sr. was obviously approaching the twilight of his career. After winning the 1983 CART championship by consistency rather than speed, he'd had a dismal season in 1984. Penske had to be thinking that maybe he was just about done.

Processing all these considerations, along with the ever-changing status of free-agent driving talent, Roger Penske devised his plan. He hired Danny Sullivan, who had won three races in 1984, to drive the Miller-sponsored entry. Sullivan was relatively young, he had a road racing background, including some Formula-1 experience, and he had demonstrated the ability and desire to win races. Al Unser Sr. would drive the Pennzoil car while Mears was still recuperating. After Mears returned, Unser would drive a third Penske entry in just the 500-mile races. That was the plan. Of course, as it turned out, it would be Mears who would drive only a handful of races while Unser would run the full schedule, feeding his boss another healthy serving of crow in the process.

Although Roger Penske would soon be building his own racecars again, he recognized that this wasn't the time to jump back in. For 1985, everyone had either a March or a Lola. Rather than risk wasting valuable time developing another in-house car that might not match up, the Captain decided to commit to the March 85C from the outset, and put his team's talents to work finding that famous Penske Racing unfair advantage.

The strongest competition this year would come from Mario Andretti and a quickly maturing Al Unser Jr. in Lolas; and Bobby Rahal, former F1 World Champion Emerson Fittapaldi, Johnny Rutherford, and Michael Andretti in Marches. Tom Sneva started the season with promise in Dan Gurney's new Eagle, but team problems prevented him from mounting any serious challenge.

The 1985 season started again in Long Beach, California, with Al Unser Sr. in the Pennzoil March and Danny Sullivan in the Miller car. Mario Andretti won the race, but Sullivan had a strong day in his Penske Racing debut, the only driver other than Andretti to lead a lap. He ran out of fuel on the last lap and ended up third for the day. Unser also ran a solid race, starting 12th and finishing fifth. For the team, it was certainly a much better start than a year earlier.

The spring Phoenix race was cancelled because of heavy rains and flooding, so Indianapolis was the second stop on the 1985 schedule. Even though Indy was a part of the CART championship, it was the one race on the calendar that was still sanctioned by the United States Auto Club. USAC and the Indianapolis Motor Speedway still disagreed with CART on several issues, one being their dependence on ex-U.S. engine manufacturers. In the interest of trying to make American stock-block engines competitive with the more exotic and expensive Cosworths, USAC allowed stock block "pushrod" engines to run with a higher turbocharger

With Rick Mears recovering slowly from serious foot injuries and Al Unser struggling to be competitive, Roger Penske added ex-Formula-1 driver Danny Sullivan to the roster for 1985. Sullivan would be with the team through the 1990 season, claiming one CART title and 12 race victories, including the 1985 Indianapolis 500.

Danny Sullivan drove the Miller-sponsored Penske March-Cosworth while Al Unser Sr. and Rick Mears shared driving duties in the Pennzoil-sponsored March for 1985.

boost pressure than their overhead camshaft counterparts. Several years later, Roger Penske would capitalize on a loophole in this regulation to fashion his greatest unfair advantage of all time. For this year, however, Penske's cars continued with the proven Cosworth powerplant, though several smaller teams did take advantage of the new pushrod incentive, running turbocharged V-6 Buick and Chevrolet engines. This made for an interesting starting grid.

Penske Racing had a three-car team at Indianapolis for the first time in several years, with Rick Mears back in the cockpit for his first appearance since the terrible accident. He was far from fully recovered, but strong enough to navigate the less-demanding oval track. Al Unser Sr. was the fastest Penske driver in qualifying, taking 7th spot on the grid with a speed of 210.523 mph. Right next to him, in the middle of the third row, was Danny Sullivan at 210.298. Rick Mears was on the inside of row 4 at 209.796. Buick V-6's stole the show in qualifying. Duane "Pancho" Carter, driving for Galles Racing, took the pole with a record speed of 212.583 mph. Next to him was another Buick-powered March, driven by Scott Brayton. The stock block engines were certainly fast, but few observers expected them to be able to tolerate 500 miles on race day. As it turned out, neither lasted 20 laps.

From his third-place starting position, Bobby Rahal jumped into the lead at the drop of the green flag and stayed out front for the first 14 laps. Scott Brayton's Buick then took the lead for one lap before his turbocharger quit, leaving Mario Andretti in control. Danny Sullivan came into the picture about a quarter of the way into the race, trading the lead back and forth with Andretti over the next 100 laps. On lap 120, while running second to Andretti, Sullivan misunderstood a radio message from his pit crew. He thought he was told that there were only 19 laps remaining in the race when, in fact, there were still 80 to go. Thinking that he had to make his move quickly, Sullivan made a daring pass on Andretti, getting all four wheels below the yellow line going through the first turn. It looked like he'd gotten away with it until the Miller Penske March wiggled slightly and then snapped loose, executing a complete 200-mph, 360-degree pirouette in the short chute between turns one and two. By some miracle he did not hit the wall. By another miracle, Mario Andretti, who was following directly behind, somehow managed to avoid the racecar spinning in front of him, which was completely engulfed in a cloud of tire smoke. Sullivan never even came to a stop. At the end of the spin, finding himself looking at turn two with the engine still running, he shifted into a lower gear and took off after Andretti. Pitting under the caution flag that he initiated, Sullivan got four fresh tires and charged back into the hunt, still in second place. Unbelievably, he had lost only one position.

By this point in the race, Rick Mears had already dropped out with a gear linkage failure, which followed a couple of other smaller problems that had plagued him earlier in the day. The good news was that his feet held up well, and despite the end result, Mears was happy to be back. Al Unser was also experiencing problems. Although his car was fairly strong, he had been penalized a lap early in the race because of a pit violation and was never able to make that up. He would go on to a fourth place finish, a lap down to the leaders.

Twenty laps after Danny Sullivan's now-infamous spin, he completed a much more cautious pass on Mario Andretti to take the lead of the race for good. The Penske-prepared March was clearly working better than Andretti's Lola, and everything else still on the track for that matter. Sullivan had pulled out a 15-second lead when Don Whittington hit the wall, bringing out a yellow flag seven laps from the finish, thus giving Andretti one last shot. But when the green flag waved on lap 198, Sullivan pulled away again to win the Indianapolis 500 in only his third attempt. It was Penske Racing's 5th Indy title. But even more impressive than the absolute number of wins, it was their fourth visit to Indy's Victory Lane in a span of just seven years.

In keeping with Roger Penske's pre-season game plan, Al Unser sat out the Milwaukee race while Rick Mears teamed with Danny Sullivan on the one-mile oval track. Later in the season, the Captain surely second-guessed himself on that decision, as Unser wound up in the points battle for the CART championship. Andretti

Danny Sullivan had an exciting and memorable Indianapolis 500, spinning midway through the race but recovering to win over Mario Andretti. Sullivan's whole career was defined by his Indy "Spin and Win."

won the Milwaukee pole and gave another dominating race performance, being challenged only by Tom Sneva's Dan Gurney Eagle. This would be the Eagle's best showing of the year and, unfortunately, one of Sneva's last noteworthy races. Rick Mears drove a superb race, being the only other car on the lead lap with Andretti and Sneva. And Danny Sullivan continued his strong run with a fourth place finish.

Mario Andretti won again at Portland, making it three victories in four races. Danny Sullivan qualified on the pole and led the first five laps, but his day ended early with a steering problem. Al Unser qualified poorly, but drove a steady race to finish in 4th position, a lap

behind the leaders. Next, at the Meadowlands, Al Unser Jr. began to assert himself, setting up what would be an interesting family battle later in the season. Little Al won the race over Emerson Fittapaldi, with Al Sr. finishing third. Sullivan led early but was sidelined with a turbocharger problem. Al Unser Jr. and his father finished first and third again at Cleveland, this time separated by Geoff Brabham. Sullivan suffered another early departure, this time because of transmission problems.

Penske Racing was back to a three-car effort for the Michigan 500, with Rick Mears punctuating his comeback by winning the pole position. Unfortunately, the fun lasted only seven laps in the race before transmission problems ended his day. Danny Sullivan started next to Mears on the front row and was in the hunt for most of the race, but radiator trouble eventually sidelined the Miller Penske March. Al Unser, in the third Penske entry, was in the fight all afternoon. From his 8th place starting spot, he led 81 of the 250 laps, more than any of the other 11 race leaders. But Emerson Fittipaldi came on strong at the end, scoring his first Indy-car win and relegating Unser to second place.

Elkhart Lake produced an interesting and foretelling result. Jacques Villeneuve, brother of Formula-1 driver Gilles and uncle of future Indy winner and world champion Jacques Villeneuve, scored his only Indy-car win, holding off Michael Andretti, Alan Jones, Bobby Rahal, Emerson Fittipaldi, and Arie Luyendyk. Al Unser did well to finish 7th behind this dean's list of experienced road racers. It was clearly a preview of CART's non-oval future.

The Pocono 500 was next on the schedule, and Rick Mears was back in the lineup for just his fourth race of the season. As he had done at Michigan, the man who had earned the nickname "Rocket Rick" claimed another pole position in his Pennzoil Penske March. Driving a signature Rick Mears race, he paced himself and the car throughout the long day, charging hard at the end when it counted to score a gratifying win over Al Unser Jr. Al Sr. was third and Danny Sullivan fifth in the other Penske entries, making it a great day for Pennsylvania's home team.

At Mid-Ohio, Danny Sullivan had his best result since Indianapolis, finishing second to Bobby Rahal who dominated the race. Unser had a short day, dropping out after just 12 laps with a broken suspension. Next was Sanair, Ontario, site of Mears' accident a year earlier. Although this was an oval track, Mears opted not to participate—who could blame him? It turned out to be a frustrating day for the Penske team anyway. Al Unser had a good race going and seemed to be on the way to his first victory of the season when he crashed while leading 25 laps from the end. Johnny Rutherford went on to pick up his first win in several years, while Danny Sullivan claimed fifth place.

The next event was the fall 200-miler at Michigan.

By this time, Al Unser Sr. was in the hunt for the championship, so with Rick Mears back for this oval race, Penske had to enter a third car. Mears gave another impressive performance, finishing second to Bobby Rahal. Sullivan and Unser finished 8th and 12th respectively in the other Penske entries. Rahal did it again two weeks later at Laguna Seca, winning comfortably from pole position. This time, Al Unser Sr. claimed the number-two spot for Penske Racing, despite a mid-race tangle with Tom Sneva, which left Sneva's Eagle on the sidelines. Danny Sullivan started second at Laguna, but dropped to an 8th place finish.

By this point in the season, with just two races remaining, the championship had come down to a father and son battle between Al Unser Sr. and Al Jr. As he had done two years earlier, Al Sr. reached this position through consistency and top-5 finishes rather than raw speed and race victories. At Phoenix, the elder Unser stepped it up a notch, driving his best race of the season. Starting from the pole, he led 112 of the 150 laps to take his first victory since early 1983. And he won it convincingly, by a full lap over runner-up, Al Jr. That gave Penske's "substitute" driver a three-point advantage over his son going into the season finale.

The 1985 CART season closed on a new street circuit in Miami, Florida. Although the focus of this race was the championship battle between the two Unsers, Danny Sullivan found his way back into the winner's circle for the first time since Indy. Sullivan started in fourth position, and moved ahead of early leader Bobby Rahal two-thirds of the way through the race to score the long-overdue win. But it was what was happening behind Sullivan and Rahal that everyone was watching. For most of the race, Al Jr. was far enough ahead of his father to make up the 3-point differential and take the championship. In the closing stages of the race, however, with Little Al running in third position, his father passed Roberto Moreno and moved into the fourth spot, which is how they crossed the finish line. That gave Al Unser Sr. the championship by a single point—151 to 150—over his son. CART couldn't have hoped for a more exciting Hollywood ending. And neither could Roger Penske, who ended up with his 7th national championship in nine years. Danny Sullivan finished fourth in the standings, behind the two Unsers and Bobby Rahal. Rick Mears, who ran only five of the season's 15 races, still managed to land 10th in the final points.

1986

Despite his team's continuing success, as measured by national championships and Indy 500 victories, Roger Penske wasn't content fielding "kit-cars" and spec engines. He knew that the only way to achieve a genuine advantage was to have equipment that was inherently better than that of the competition. To that end, Penske embarked on two ambitious projects for the 1986 season.

The first project involved engines. Penske Racing, like all the other serious contenders in CART, had been using V-8 Cosworth racing engines since the late 1970's. When Roger Penske received a hand-written letter in late 1983 from two Cosworth engineers who wanted to start their own company, he recognized a golden opportunity. The engineers, Mario Illien and Paul Morgan, were frustrated that Cosworth's monopoly in CART racing had diminished the company's motivation for continuing innovation and improvement. They believed that they could build a better and faster engine than the one currently offered by Cosworth Engineering, and Roger Penske liked that idea—but only under his terms and conditions.

Illian and Morgan needed a big financial backer and they needed a credible, high-profile customer. Roger Penske would help them on both counts, but in return, he had a couple of requirements. First, he insisted on being a partner in the company, which would become known as "Ilmor Engineering." And second, he wanted exclusive use of the new engine for its first season. For that, Penske provided $130,000 in startup capital and committed to finding a full financial backer for the project. He quickly located that backer in General Motors, which was attracted by the prospect of challenging Cosworth's dynasty in the prestigious Indy-car series. The new engine, which ultimately became known as the Ilmor-Chevrolet, saw occasional action in Penske's cars during the 1986 season, but early reliability problems kept it from having a big impact until the following year.

The second project that the Penske team undertook for 1986 was development of the first new in-house chassis since the unsuccessful PC-12 was abandoned at the start of the 1984 season. Penske hired a new designer, Alan Jenkins, to pen the new PC-15. The original plan was to begin the 1986 season with the all-new Penske-Chevrolet package, but a variety of teething problems with both components would make that impractical. When Rick Mears and Danny Sullivan arrived in Phoenix for the season opener, they were both piloting March 86Cs with "conventional" Cosworth power. Penske used defending CART champion Al Unser Sr. as the guinea pig, assigning him the task of debuting the "work-in-progress" PC-15 Chevy.

For 1986, the CART grids were still dominated by March-Cosworths, although there was also a healthy representation of Lola chassis. This would be the year that a new generation of drivers would come to the forefront. Bobby Rahal, Michael Andretti, Al Unser Jr. and Kevin Cogan would present the strongest competition for the Penske team. What was left of the "old school" contingent would be represented by aging former champions Mario Andretti and Emerson Fittipaldi.

The Phoenix season-opener was not a raging success for the Penske team. Former Penske driver, Kevin Cogan, scored his first and only CART victory, beating Tom Sneva and Emerson Fittipaldi, with Danny Sullivan finishing fourth. Rick Mears had qualified third-fastest and led 16 laps early in the race before being sidelined with an oil leak. Al Unser Sr. started 7th in the new Penske-Chevrolet, but ended his day against the turn-two wall at the halfway mark.

On the streets of Long Beach, Sullivan qualified a March-Cosworth on the pole and led a third of the race, but retired with an ignition problem. Rick Mears ran the new PC-15/Chevy in this race, qualifying 9th, but dropping out early with engine trouble. This race was definitely a sign of things to come, with Michael Andretti taking his first CART victory, followed by Al Unser Jr. in second place. Michael's dad finished back in fifth spot, while Al's father was not even invited by Roger Penske to participate that day.

Penske Racing entered three cars in the Indianapolis 500, with Mears and Sullivan in March-Cosworths and Al Unser Sr. in a Penske PC-15/Chevrolet. Qualifying for the "500" got back to normal this year. Although three stock-block Buick-powered cars made the field, the fastest one started well back in the fifth row and none of them were factors in the race. Every other car to make the field had a Cosworth engine, expect for Al Unser's Ilmor Chevrolet. Rick Mears shattered the track record with a four-lap average speed of 216.828 mph. Penske teammate Danny Sullivan took the second spot and Michael Andretti filled out the front row. Al Unser Sr. and the PC-15/Chevy made a very respectable showing, claiming fifth spot on the starting grid with a speed of 212.295 mph.

Getting the 1986 race started turned into a major ordeal. Heavy rain caused a two-day postponement, pushing the start back to the following Saturday. Then, before the green flag fell, there were more problems. There used to be a superstition about green racecars at Indianapolis. They were supposedly bad luck, and for many years, a green car was never seen in the field. Maybe Tom Sneva could blame it on that, because there really wasn't any other good explanation for what he did on the pace lap of the 1986 race. Starting in 7th spot, with every expectation of being competitive in his March-Cosworth Skoal Bandit, the former winner lost control of his car on the back straightaway while warming up the tires for the start. He spun into the inside retaining wall hard enough to take him out of the race before it even started. It was as big an embarrassment as it was a disappointment. Roberto Guerrero would do the very same thing three years later, and it would be even worse for him because he'd do it from the pole. And what color was the car he would be driving? Green, of course!

When the race finally did get started, Michael Andretti jumped out front and led through the first 42 laps. After pit stop shuffling, Rick Mears moved ahead from laps 49 through 74. From that point through the end of the race, Mears battled with Bobby Rahal, passing the lead back-and-forth several times, while Kevin

Cogan tagged along closely in third position. Just 12 laps from the end of the race, Cogan made his move, passing Mears for second place and then getting by Rahal to take the lead. Suddenly, it looked like the ex-Penske driver was finally going to redeem himself for the 1982 first-lap debacle when he brought the race to a stop at the drop of the green flag. But then, on lap 195, Arie Luyendyk tagged the wall in turn four, bringing out the pace car. At first, it seemed that the race would finish under the yellow flag, guaranteeing Cogan of the win. But the accident was cleared quickly and the race went green again on lap 198 for a 5-mile shootout to the end. Kevin Cogan got caught sleeping on the restart and Bobby Rahal shot past on the inside going into turn one to take the lead—which he would hold to the finish. They came across the line: Rahal—Cogan—Mears, all separated by just 1.88 seconds, the closest 1-2-3 finish in the race's history.

Bobby Rahal dedicated his first, and only, Indianapolis 500 victory to his car-owner, Jim Trueman, who was terminally ill with cancer. Just eleven days after this race, Trueman passed away.

Penske's other two cars had a less-than-successful day in the 1986 '500.' Defending race champion Danny Sullivan was never really in the hunt, and ended up finishing in 9th spot, three laps off the pace. Al Unser Sr. finally retired the troublesome PC-15/Chevy three quarters of the way through the race because of a vibration problem.

Michael Andretti won again at Milwaukee, over Tom Sneva and Rick Mears. Sullivan finished 11th. Penske Racing ran just the two March-Cosworths in this race. Then on the road course at Portland, the Andretti family took top honors, with Mario scoring his first victory of the year and Michael finishing 7 seconds behind. Penske Racing had a difficult day, with both drivers finishing out of the top 10.

Danny Sullivan rebounded nicely with a great drive in the March-Cosworth that resulted in a win at the Meadowlands. Rick Mears, meanwhile, struggled with the PC-15/Chevy and dropped out after an uncompetitive 25 laps. What was happening here, unfortunately, was that problems with the PC-15 chassis were masking the true potential of the Ilmor-Chevrolet engine. Regrettably, the team didn't recognize this fact until it was too late to salvage any real advantage during its first-year exclusive-use period with the Chevy powerplant.

Danny Sullivan had another strong showing a week later at Cleveland, starting from the pole and winning convincingly over Michael Andretti. Mario Andretti was third and Rick Mears, back in a March-Cosworth, finished a respectable fourth. Sullivan almost made it three-in-a-row, finishing second to Bobby Rahal on a new road course in Toronto. Rick Mears, who was still having considerable difficulty adapting to road courses because of limited movement and strength in his injured feet, struggled to an 8th-place finish, three laps down to the leaders.

Next was the Michigan 500, and Roger Penske brought Al Unser back to run a third car with the Ilmor-Chevy engine. But this time, it wasn't in a handicapped PC-15 chassis; this time it was powering a competitive March 86C. Although Rick Mears qualified on the pole in a March-Cosworth, Unser took the second starting spot with the Chevy-powered March. That really showed the potential of the new engine for the first time. In the race, Mears, Michael Andretti and Bobby Rahal battled for the lead through the first 400 miles. Danny Sullivan survived only 33 laps before he was out with a broken suspension. Al Unser lasted 164 laps until clutch failure ended the Chevy's strong run. Then, within a span of 40 laps, the three main contenders, Mears, Rahal, and Andretti, all retired with engine trouble. That left Johnny Rutherford to take what would be the last victory of his career over Mexican rookie Joselé Garza. Attrition was extremely high in this race. Only Rutherford and Garza finished on the lead lap. Third-place finisher Pancho Carter was two laps down and fourth-place Geoff Brabham was 11 laps behind.

With only two weeks to rebuild all those blown engines, the CART teams arrived in northeastern Pennsylvania for their second-straight 500-mile race. The Penske team lineup was the same as at Michigan, with Al Unser in the March-Chevy again. Rick Mears led about a quarter of this race, but eventually dropped back to an 8th-place finish. Danny Sullivan retired at the halfway mark with a bad water pump, and Al Unser was involved in an accident with rookie Ed Pimm, ending his day after just 25 laps. Mario Andretti, a resident of Nazareth Pennsylvania, just 30 miles from the racetrack, was the popular hometown winner.

Danny Sullivan came back to lead the most laps at Mid-Ohio, but ended up finishing third to Bobby Rahal and Roberto Guerrero. Rick Mears lost an engine and finished out of the points. Sullivan was staying within site of the championship battle, but Mears was having an uncharacteristically poor season.

The next race was Sanair, Canada. In his first appearance here since his accident, Mears made a dramatic statement, winning the pole with the previously uncompetitive Penske PC-15/Chevrolet combination. He then led the first 23 laps of the race, before retiring with engine trouble, but it was good while it lasted—and it was a sign of things to come. Danny Sullivan drove the March-Cosworth to a solid fifth-place finish at Sanair, but, unfortunately, his principal championship competitor, Bobby Rahal, won the race.

Next, CART returned to Michigan for the September race, which this year was extended to 250 miles. Rick Mears claimed another pole, this time with the Chevy engine in a March chassis. He led the first 18 laps of the race, but eventually fell a lap behind and finished in 8th position. But the good news was that the Ilmor-Chevrolet had finally made it to the end of a race. Danny Sullivan, still driving the March-Cosworth combination, had a difficult day, ultimately finishing in 12th spot, two laps behind winner Bobby Rahal.

At Elkhart Lake in early October, Mears and Sullivan both drove March-Cosworths. This race actually took two weeks to complete. It started on September 21st but was stopped after five laps because of heavy rain. It couldn't be completed the following weekend because that date was already scheduled for Michigan, so the balance of the race ran on October 4th. Mears had one of his better post-accident road course efforts here, finishing third behind Emerson Fittapaldi and Michael Andretti. Sullivan led for 10 laps early in the race before slipping to a 6th place finish.

With three races remaining in the 1986 season,

Danny Sullivan was still a long-shot contender for the championship, along with Bobby Rahal and Michael Andretti. At Laguna Seca, Sullivan finished second to Bobby Rahal, with Michael Andretti one spot behind him in third place. Rick Mears, driving the March-Chevy, out-qualified his teammate, starting third on the grid, but a minor accident just past the halfway mark ended his day.

Michael Andretti dominated on the mile-oval at Phoenix, with Danny Sullivan finishing second again and Bobby Rahal third. This left Rahal with a very slim lead over Andretti in the points chase, but Sullivan was, by then, effectively eliminated. Rick Mears ran the March-Chevy again at Phoenix, qualifying second but dropping out early with an electrical problem.

The season ended on the street circuit in Miami, with Al Unser Jr. scoring his only win of the year. Rick Mears drove a solid race in the Penske PC-15/Chevy, claiming the third spot on the podium, behind Little Al and Roberto Guerrero. Danny Sullivan was also at the wheel of a PC-15/Chevy for this last race, but his day ended very early with an electrical problem. Roger Penske had Al Unser Sr. entered in a March-Chevy too, but he also had problems and ended up in 15th spot, many laps behind the leaders. Bobby Rahal won the 1986 CART championship with his 8th place finish at Miami when Michael Andretti dropped out at the halfway mark and didn't gain any points. Danny Sullivan finished third in the season championship and Rick Mears was 8th, going winless for the first time in his career. Al Unser Sr., who had driven five races during the season, did not score a single point, undoubtedly reinforcing Roger Penske's opinion that "Big Al" was ready for retirement.

1987

For the new season, Roger Penske had Alan Jenkins design another new chassis, designated the Penske PC-16, but he didn't get rid of his old March 86Cs—just in case. In the engine compartment, Penske committed to the Ilmor-Chevy, as did Patrick Racing and Newman-Haas. Roger Penske's plan was to run a two-car team for the full season, with a third car entered at Indy in a one-race deal in which Danny Ongais brought his own sponsorship.

The competition looked a lot like it did the year before, with just a little bit of equipment shuffling. Bobby Rahal was back with Truesports Racing, having switched to a Lola chassis. Michael Andretti was still in a March-Cosworth at Kraco Racing and Al Unser Jr. had traded his Lola for a March-Cosworth at Shierson Racing. Roberto Guerrero, who'd had some impressive performances over the previous two seasons, was back with a reorganized team in a March-Cosworth. Mario

The final Alan Jenkins designed Penske chassis—the PC16—was another mediocre racecar. Throughout the 1987 season, drivers Rick Mears, Danny Sullivan and Al Unser alternated between the PC16 and the old March 86C. Unfortunately, the under-performing PC16 masked the considerable potential of Penske's new Ilmor engine.

Andretti was still in the Newman-Haas Lola and Pat Patrick had Emerson Fittipaldi and Kevin Cogan in his March-Chevrolets. The big news at Patrick was the arrival of big money from Marlboro cigarette sponsorship.

At the Long Beach CART season opener, 47-year-old Mario Andretti set the tone for the year by taking the pole and leading all 95 laps of the race to win by two miles over runner-up Al Unser Jr. Andretti would win 8 poles in the 15 races during the 1987 season, and was usually the man to beat when his car stayed together. His win at Long Beach marked the first victory for the Ilmor-Chevrolet engine. Rick Mears and Danny Sullivan both drove Penske's new PC-16s, without much success. Sullivan qualified 9th but lasted only 28 laps. Mears started back in 18th, and eventually finished a lackluster 9th, five laps behind the leaders. Phoenix wasn't any better for the Penske team. In a race won by relative newcomer Roberto Guerrero, Sullivan finished a disappointing 11th and Mears dropped out early with an engine problem.

Heading for Indianapolis, the situation looked much like it had three years earlier. It was apparent that the Penske PC-16 chassis was not competitive, and Roger Penske wasn't going to handicap his team with inferior equipment in this race. So, although the entry form listed PC-16s for Mears, Sullivan and Danny Ongais, those Penske chassis would be replaced by year-old March 86Cs before qualifying was over. On the Thursday before Pole Day, still struggling to find speed in his Penske PC-16, Ongais crashed heavily and sustained a concussion. This was enough to convice Roger Penske to put Rick Mears in a March-Chevrolet so that he would have at least one shot at the pole.

As anticipated, Mario Andretti took the number-one starting position in his Newman-Haas Lola Chevrolet. Bobby Rahal grabbed the second spot in a Lola Cosworth and Rick Mears—thankfully—filled out row one in a Penske March Chevrolet. Danny Sullivan qualified a PC-16 at 205.288 mph, the slowest of 11 cars to post times on the first day of qualifying—more than 10 mph behind pole-sitter Mario Andretti. Another seven cars took official times on Sunday, while everyone else waited for the second weekend. After Sullivan's disappointing run, Roger Penske sent for another March 86C—just in case.

Because of his concussion, Danny Ongais didn't receive medical clearance to participate on the first weekend of qualifying, but he was initially expected back in time to make the race. After further examination, however, it was determined that the concussion was more serious, and Ongais was barred from driving for the remainder of the month, which left Penske Racing scrambling with a last-minute vacancy to fill. Roger Penske immediately signed the unemployed Al Unser Sr. to take the seat; but the dilemma was that there wasn't actually a seat available. By this time it was obvious that the PC-16 just wasn't going to be at all competitive and Sullivan would have to re-qualify in the second Penske March 86C. Unfortunately, this was the only other car that was readily available to the team.

With only a few days to get a car together so that Al Unser could qualify on the second weekend, Roger Penske re-commissioned an old March 86C that was on display in a Pennsylvania hotel lobby and had it rushed to Indianapolis. Because this car had not been modified to accommodate an Ilmor-Chevy engine, Al Unser had to settle for an old, but reliable Cosworth. On the second Saturday of qualifying, Danny Sullivan took the middle of the 6th row in his March-Chevy and Al Unser Sr. claimed the outside of row seven. Once again, Penske Racing had three good cars in the starting field—but this year, they really did it the hard way.

Mario Andretti absolutely dominated the 1987 race, leading from the start and staying out front for 170 of the first 177 laps. In the meantime, Rick Mears dropped out after 75 laps with an ignition problem; Danny Sullivan stayed near the front, leading a handful of laps before his engine expired at 160 laps; and Al Unser Sr., driving the former "hotel planter" was just hanging in there, a lap behind the leaders in third position going into the closing stages of the race. Then, the infamous Andretti Indy curse struck again. Despite having many good opportunities over the years, Mario had been denied another win since taking the 1969 "500" early in his career. Now, after one of the most dominating performances ever witnessed at the Speedway, he would be bitten again, sidelined with an ignition problem only 22 laps from certain victory.

The apparent beneficiary of Andretti's bad luck was Roberto Guerrero, who had been in second place, a lap ahead of Al Unser Sr. After holding the lead for only four laps, Guerrero pitted for what should have been his final routine fuel stop. But when he released the clutch to leave his pit, the engine stalled. The crew got it re-fired, but it died again—the clutch was shot. Finally, after a painfully long time, Guerrero's crew got the car push-started and sent the distraught Columbian back into the race. But by then, he had lost a lap and was running second to non-other than Al Unser Sr. Big Al led only 18 laps in the race, but they were the ones that counted most. Unser claimed his fourth Indianapolis 500 victory, tying him with A.J. Foyt, the only other four-time winner at that time. It was Roger Penske's 6th Indy 500 title, making him the most-successful car owner ever to compete at Indy. But it was by the most implausible scenario that anyone could have imagined earlier in the month.

Following Indianapolis, the CART action resumed, as usual, on the one-mile oval at the Milwaukee State Fairgrounds. It was a forgettable weekend for the Penske team, with Rick Mears crashing his March-Chevy and Danny Sullivan hanging on for an 11th-place finish. It got a little better, two weeks later in Portland, where Mears drove the PC-16 Chevy to a podium finish, albeit two laps behind winner Bobby Rahal and runner-up Michael Andretti. Sullivan finished 11th again, this time going off-course halfway through the race. The Meadowlands was another bad weekend for the team, with Sullivan out early because of a broken wheel and Mears sidelined after hitting debris on the track. As the Penske drivers were having all these problems, Bobby Rahal and Michael Andretti were steadily pulling away from everyone else in the championship battle.

Emerson Fittipaldi won the July 4th weekend race at Cleveland, while Danny Sullivan finished fourth and Rick Mears 7th. Fittipaldi won again in Toronto, but this time Sullivan was on his tail in second place. Rick Mears, still struggling with the unstable PC-16, ended

up 10th after dropping out with a radiator problem. After Toronto, Roger Penske decided that he'd had enough. He scrapped the PC-16 altogether and focused on the more reliable and faster March chassis for the remainder of the season.

Al Unser was back in the Penske lineup for the Michigan 500, driving his Indy-winning March 86C-Cosworth. Mears and Sullivan were in March-Chevys. Championship contender Michael Andretti won the race, with Al Sr. leading the Penske Racing challenge in second place. Bobby Rahal finished third and Danny Sullivan was fourth. Rick Mears suffered another Chevy engine failure, dropping out early in the race. Mears was having the worst slump of his career.

Penske's number-one driver finally broke back into the win column with a victory in the mid-August Pocono 500. It had been two years since Rick's last tri-umph, which came in the 1985 Pocono race. Mears qualified second fastest and drove a smart race, moving into command when early-leader Emerson Fittipaldi dropped out with engine trouble. Penske's other two drivers didn't fare as well. Sullivan departed early with a gearbox failure and Unser crashed on lap 158.

After Pocono, there wasn't much to get excited about for Penske Racing fans. There would be no more wins to celebrate in the last five races of the 1987 season. Rick Mears would make the podium with a couple of third-place finishes, one at the new Penske-owned Nazareth Speedway and the other at Laguna Seca. Danny Sullivan would score a third at Mid-Ohio and a second at Laguna. But Penske Racing would end the year with only two victories—Indy and Pocono. Bobby Rahal repeated as CART champion, beating Michael Andretti for the sec-ond year in a row. Rick Mears finished 5th in the final standings, and Danny Sullivan 9th. Penske Racing obvi-ously had some homework to do in the off-season.

1988

By the end of the 1987 season, it was apparent that the Ilmor-Chevy had become the engine of choice in CART. The Chevy was clearly faster than the Cosworth on both ovals and road courses; and most importantly, the early reliability problems had been resolved. Roger

Rick Mears ended a two-year winless streak, returning to victory lane in the 1987 Pocono 500. It was one of only two victories for Penske Racing this season, the other being Al Unser's unlikely win at Indianapolis. *Alan Hummel*

Penske could have taken the safe approach, which would have been to put his Chevy engine into a proven March or Lola chassis, and then focus the team's formidable talents and resources on developing unfair advantages to give them an edge over the competition. But even after two years of struggling through unsuccessful in-house designs, Penske still wasn't ready to give up on the idea of developing his own car. What he would give up on was designer Alan Jenkins, who had created the flawed PC-15 and PC-16 designs. Penske later said of Jenkins, "while he had a lot of great ideas, he never really got it together. He was just not flexible at all, and he just didn't understand that there are some practical things that take

place when you do a race car." To replace Jenkins, Penske hired proven talent Nigel Bennett. Bennett had worked for several Formula-1 teams, including Lotus, and most recently as chief designer for Lola's CART program. This would prove to be a brilliant move, as the new PC-17 would become the first successful Penske-built chassis since the 1982 Ferris-designed PC-10.

Penske's driver lineup remained intact for 1988, with Mears and Sullivan running the full schedule and Al Unser Sr. making guest appearances in the three 500-mile races. Al Unser Jr., Bobby Rahal, Mario and Michael Andretti, and Emerson Fittipaldi would represent the chief competition again this year. Aside from the Penske team's new PC-17s, only Marches and Lolas would score championship points in the 1988 season. Cosworth engines still outnumbered the Ilmor-Chevys by a 4-to-1 margin, but there were other engine manufacturers on the grid this year as well. Teo Fabi was driving for the new Porsche team, with a March chassis and Porsche engine. Bobby Rahal, Scott Brayton, and Ludwig Heimrath Jr. were powered by the new Honda-based Judd engine. And once again, several stock-block Buicks were entered in the Indianapolis 500, where they were still permitted a turbo boost advantage over the "pure" racing engines.

When the 1988 season opened at Phoenix in early April, it was immediately obvious that the new Penske chassis was going to be a winner. Rick Mears took the pole and dominated the early part of the race until making contact with another car that he was lapping after just 22 miles. Danny Sullivan, unfortunately, was already out with an oil pressure problem, so the PC-17 wouldn't see Victory Lane that day, but it wouldn't be long. In the second race of the season, on the Long Beach street course, Danny Sullivan put his PC-17/Chevy on the pole and battled for the lead with Al Unser Jr. for most of the race before losing an engine in the closing laps. Mears qualified third, but also had problems and finished 8th.

Although Roger Penske didn't have much to show for the first two races, he knew the team was in a strong position going into the Indianapolis 500. But even he probably couldn't have imagined just how strong that position would turn out to be. Penske Racing did something in 1988 that had never been accomplished in the 71-year history of the world's greatest auto race. When qualifications were completed, the starting field was comprised of 18 Lolas, 12 Marches, and 3 Penske PC-17s. What made it historic was the fact that those three Penskes were all sitting on the front row of the grid. Rick Mears won the pole, his fourth at Indy, at 219.198 mph; Danny Sullivan took the second spot at 216.214; and defending champion Al Unser Sr. filled out the row at 215.270 mph. No team had ever swept the full front row of the Indianapolis 500 before.

If the competition wasn't demoralized enough by the time qualifying was finished, they certainly must have lost all hope for the remainder of the season before the race was done. To cap off the most dominating performance ever seen in the history of the Indy 500, Penske's cars led 192 of the race's 200 laps. Danny Sullivan controlled most of the first half of the event while Rick Mears struggled to get his handling balanced, at one point actually falling a lap down to the leaders. Then on lap 101, Sullivan's front wing broke as he was coming out of turn one, throwing his car hard into the concrete wall. Fortunately, the driver was unhurt, but his impressive day was done.

By the time Sullivan had his accident, Mears had the handling problems resolved in his PC-17, and he was right there to pick up the lead of the race. Mears dominated the second half of the afternoon, leading 89 of the final 100 laps. Al Unser Sr. ran a steady race, leading a total of 12 laps over the course of the event, although he was never a strong contender for the win. The 1988 race was slowed by a record 14 caution periods accounting for 79 laps. But between each caution, the Penske cars seemed able to pull away from the competition with ease. Mears was running away with it when Michael Andretti lost a wing three laps from the finish, causing the race to end under the yellow flag. For Rick Mears, it was his third Indianapolis 500 victory in 11 attempts. For car-owner Roger Penske, it was a record 7th Indy win for his 20-year anniversary at the Speedway. Al Unser Sr. finished third in the other Penske, behind runner-up Emerson Fittipaldi. All in all, it was an incredible month for the Penske Racing team.

A week later, on the Milwaukee mile, it was just as one-sided. Although the Andretti family grabbed the top two spots on the starting grid, Rick Mears went on to lead 129 of the 200 laps to win by six seconds over teammate Danny Sullivan. The two Penske cars were alone on the lead lap at the end. Then on the Portland road course, it was Sullivan's turn to shine, as he took the pole and won the race convincingly over ex-Formula-1 contender Arie Luyendyk. Mears also drove a strong race, finishing sixth behind Mario Andretti. Cleveland didn't work out quite as well, although Sullivan did win the pole and led a race-high 39 laps, he ultimately finished third behind Mario Andretti and Bobby Rahal. Mears experienced gearbox problems and dropped out early.

Danny Sullivan claimed another pole in Toronto. He pushed Al Unser Jr. all day before settling for second place. Mears had another respectable road race, finishing in 6th spot. Unser Jr. won again at the Meadowlands, followed by Mario Andretti and then the two Penskes of Mears and Sullivan.

Sullivan scored his second win of the season in the Michigan 500. Rick Mears started on the pole and traded the lead with his teammate throughout most of the race before suffering a rare engine failure. After Mears departed, Sullivan led the final 60 laps of the race and finished more than a full lap ahead of Bobby Rahal. Al Unser Sr. was driving a third team car in this race, and he too experienced engine trouble after driving a solid race from his front-row starting position.

The Penske team had an uncharacteristically poor showing in the Pocono 500, even though they clearly had the fastest cars on the track. Rick Mears started from the pole again and ran well in the early going, but got caught up in a wreck with back-marker Phil Krueger on lap 42, ending his day. Danny Sullivan was also having a good race, challenging Mario Andretti for the lead when Mario and Dick Simon got together in front of him. Sullivan ended up in the wall and out of the race. Al Unser Sr. led a race-high 79 laps, but suffered an ignition problem in the closing stages and dropped out on lap 182. Bobby Rahal ended up winning the event over Al Unser, Jr.

Heading into the last quarter of the season, both Sullivan and Mears were still in contention for the championship, along with Al Unser Jr., Mario and Michael Andretti, and Bobby Rahal. At Mid-Ohio, Sullivan won another pole, his 5th of the season. Emerson Fittipaldi won the race over Mario Andretti, while Rick Mears led the Penske team with a third place finish and Sullivan ended up fifth. But this 5th place result put Danny Sullivan one point ahead of Al Unser Jr. in the championship battle, a dramatic turnaround considering that he did not score one single point in the first three races of the season. In the remaining four events, he would

steadily pad his lead on the way to a CART series title.

At Elkhart Lake, the Penske drivers qualified first and second. Sullivan led from his pole position for the first 15 laps, but slipped to a fourth-place finish behind Fittipaldi, Rahal and Mario Andretti. Mears fell several laps down and finished 12th. On the one-mile oval at Nazareth, Sullivan won from the pole. Rick Mears had led the majority of the race before problems dropped him to 7th place. Danny Sullivan was unstoppable at this point. He took his 8th pole of the season a Laguna Seca, then led 70 of the 84 laps to score his 4th win of the year, locking up the championship in the process. Rick Mears also had a good day at Laguna, leading a handful of laps and finishing 5th on this demanding road course.

In the season finale at Miami, Sullivan won his 5th consecutive pole, making it a remarkable 9 out of 15 for the season. The race got off to a wild start, with a first turn pile-up that eliminated seven cars immediately. Rick Mears drove a great street race, finishing second to Al Unser, Jr., while Sullivan closed his championship season with a 5th place finish.

For Roger Penske, winning his 8th national championship was especially sweet because he did it with his own car powered by his own engine. The combined six wins recorded by Sullivan and Mears hardly did justice to the superiority of the Penske-Chevrolet combination. But the front-row sweep at Indy and 13 poles in 15 races told the real story. After struggling through several years of less-than-satisfactory results, Penske Racing was back in the driver's seat. For Roger Penske, who is fond of saying that you're only as good as your next race, it had to be as much relief as it was gratification.

1989

Roger Penske learned a valuable lesson from Team McLaren way back in the early Can-Am days—when you're in the car-building business, never sell your newest design to the competition. For the businessman Penske, that was sometimes a difficult temptation to resist, but to the racer in him, it was obvious. Why would you go to the effort and expense of developing a competitive advantage, only to share it with your rivals? From the time his first successful PC-5 Indy-car rolled out of the Poole fabrication shop, Roger Penske lived by that philosophy.

But something happened before the 1989 season that enticed Penske to break his golden rule, just once. Pat Patrick, who had been an Indy-car team owner since 1969, and was the first president of the CART organization, had decided that he was ready to sell his racing team. But he wanted to go out a winner. Patrick's team had seen its greatest successes in the 1970s and early '80s with Gordon Johncock bringing Indianapolis 500 titles in 1973 and 1982. But even with two-time World Driving Champion Emerson Fittipaldi at the wheel, the team had been struggling to find a competitive edge in the kit-car era of the late 1980s. Patrick had purchased year-old Penske cars in the past and could have bought the PC-17s that took Danny Sullivan to the 1988 championship, but he wanted to put Fittipaldi in Roger Penske's new PC-18 design for the 1989 season. Normally that would have been out of the question, but he had something that Penske truly coveted—the extremely lucrative sponsorship package with Marlboro cigarettes. So Roger Penske, Pat Patrick and Phillip-Morris Tobacco worked out a deal that gave Patrick Racing a PC-18 chassis for the 1989 season. In return, Penske would get Marlboro's support for Al Unser's entry in the three 500-mile races that season, and more importantly, would inherit both Emerson Fittipaldi and the Marlboro sponsorship package a year later. Penske was risking one season in return for a long-term financial arrangement that turned out to be one of the most enduring and mutually beneficial partnerships in auto racing. As an added benefit, this deal also set up a great battle for the 1989 CART championship.

Penske Racing returned for the new season with the same driver lineup—Rick Mears and Danny Sullivan running the full schedule and Al Unser Sr. signed for the three 500s. The strongest competition came from Emerson Fittipaldi in the lone Patrick Racing PC-18 Chevy, Michael Andretti, who had now joined his father at Newman-Haas, Teo Fabi in the Porsche, and Al Unser Jr. at Galles Racing.

The season got off to a great start for the Penske team, with Rick Mears taking the pole and the race at Phoenix, winning by more than a lap over Al Unser Jr. as Danny Sullivan finished third. Long Beach was a little less successful, but Mears and Sullivan managed to take 5th and 8th place points respectively. Heading to Indianapolis, the Penske team was in the familiar position of being the odds-on favorite.

Mears dominated in practice, turning a lap of 226 mph on opening day and never looking back. Al Unser Sr. had a less spectacular month, but was fast when it counted on pole day. Danny Sullivan, unfortunately, had a huge crash in practice. The engine cowling ripped off the car, sending his PC-18 hard into the concrete. Sullivan suffered a mild concussion and a broken forearm, but he would return to qualify on the second weekend despite his injuries. Mears took his 5th Indy pole, another record, with a "modest" speed of 223.885 mph. Al Unser Sr., in the Marlboro-sponsored Penske, qualified second fastest, at 223.471. Had Sullivan not been eliminated from the pole day competition, it might well have been another all-Penske Racing front row. It certainly looked like the Captain's team was set for another

Collectively, Rick Mears, A. J. Foyt, Al Unser Sr., and Johnny Rutherford—seen here during Indy practice in 1989—would retire from racing with a total of 15 Indianapolis 500 victories. *Only Classics*

dominating performance on Memorial Day weekend.

But when the green flag fell on the 73rd running of the Greatest Spectacle, the Penske challenge fell apart in a hurry. Emerson Fittipaldi, in his Patrick Racing PC-18, jumped into the lead from his number-three starting position, and led all but seven of the first 100 laps. By that point, Al Unser Sr. and Danny Sullivan were already out of the race, both victims of clutch trouble. Rick Mears lasted 113 laps before he was eliminated with an engine failure. By just past the halfway point of the race, all three Penske Racing entries were out, having never led a single lap. It was the first time since 1975 that the Penske team didn't have at least one car running at the finish of the Indy 500.

For the remainder of the race, Michael Andretti traded the lead with Fittipaldi until his engine quit at lap 163. Al Unser Jr. stayed with Fittipaldi to the end, taking the lead four laps from the finish. At this point, these two drivers were an unbelievable six laps ahead of the third-place car of Raul Boesel. On the 199th lap, Fittipaldi dived under Little Al going into the third turn. It was an impossible pass but neither driver lifted, not one lap from the end of the Indianapolis 500. When the inevitable happened and wheels touched, Unser Jr. spun up into the concrete wall, while Fittipaldi wobbled and then recovered to go on to the checkered flag. Al Jr. was surprisingly gracious, calling it an unavoidable racing accident and even giving Fittipaldi a congratulatory wave as he came around on his victory lap. But while all this was happening, the Penske team was back in the garage area packing up their broken equipment. It was little consolation that it was a Penske PC-18 chassis that won the race.

When the CART party reconvened in Milwaukee a week later, Penske Racing was ready for vindication. Although Danny Sullivan was still struggling with his Indy injuries, Rick Mears took the pole and led 120 of 200 laps on his way to a convincing victory. Unfortunately, it was a different story the next time out, on the streets of downtown Detroit. Mears was still handicapped on road courses because of his 1984 injuries. And now Sullivan was also playing hurt, his broken arm unable to withstand the abuse of the bumpy street circuit. Mears drove a decent race to score a 5th place finish, but Sullivan was forced to withdraw in pain after only 16 laps. With the next two races scheduled for road courses at Portland and Cleveland, it was apparent that Danny Sullivan would need a hiatus to let his arm heal properly.

For Portland, Roger Penske signed Geoff Brabham, son of Formula-1 legend Jack Brabham, to drive Sullivan's Miller PC-18. It turned out to be another unrewarding weekend for the team, with Mears finishing a distant 8th while Brabham was sidelined with radiator problems. Cleveland was only marginally better, with Al Unser Sr. driving Sullivan's car to a 10th place result while Mears hung with the leaders to finish 5th. Sullivan returned for the mid-July Meadowlands race, struggling to an 8th place result, four places behind teammate Mears. The Penske team was suffering an uncharacteristic streak of mediocrity, even though Rick Mears was quietly accumulating championship points.

In Toronto a week later, Danny Sullivan had his first strong race since the injury, leading 35 laps and ultimately finishing third behind Michael Andretti and Emerson Fittipaldi. Mears ran his typical steady road-course race, taking 5th place points. The Michigan 500 should have been a better story for the Penske team. In fact, Rick Mears led a good portion of the event and was in contention for the win until a problem in the closing stages relegated him to 7th place. Al Unser Sr. and Danny Sullivan also had their troubles, Unser finishing nine laps down in 8th position and Sullivan dropping out early with bad handling. Michael Andretti went on to score his second consecutive victory.

By this point in the season, Penske Racing really needed a boost, and fortunately they got it at Pocono. Rick Mears led a race-high 64 laps and ultimately finished second to teammate Danny Sullivan, who came on strong at the end. Al Unser Sr. was 7th in the third team car. Mears' second-place points, coupled with Emerson Fittipaldi's early exit, tightened up the championship battle between the two. With his damaged feet preventing him from being a serious contender on the road courses, Rick Mears had been unable to challenge for the CART championship since his 1984 accident.

This year, however, consistent top-10 finishes on the road courses coupled with wins and other strong results on the ovals kept him in the championship hunt until the very end.

Next, on the Mid-Ohio road course, Mears gave up just three points to Fittipaldi, finishing in 6th position, behind teammate Sullivan in 5th and Fittipaldi in 4th. Then at Road America, Sullivan drove to an impressive win from the pole, with Mears finishing a strong third and gaining four points back on 5th-place finisher Fittipaldi.

Mears had his best shot at taking command of the championship as they went to the one-mile tri-oval at Nazareth. After starting from the pole, he trailed Fittipaldi for most of the first half of the race, before moving to the front in the later stages. Pitting from the lead just 11 miles from the end of the race, Rick Mears made a rare, but costly mistake. In his excitement to get out of the pits ahead of Fittipaldi, Mears popped the clutch too early and pulled away with the fuel vent hose still connected to the car. Fortunately, it didn't cause any damage, but it resulted in a black flag for a pit violation, costing Mears the race and the championship. He recovered to finish second to Fittipaldi, but that put him 22 points behind the former world champion with a maximum of 21 points available from the one remaining race of the season. Displaying his typical sportsmanship and integrity, Mears readily admitted the error. "I messed up in the end," he said. "I tried to get out of the pits too quick. It just killed us."

As if to redeem himself, Mears did the near-impossible in the season finale on the difficult Laguna Seca road course. After winning the pole, he led a race-high 47 laps on his way to a convincing victory over world champions Mario Andretti (second) and Emerson Fittipaldi (fifth), as well as Al Unser Jr., Michael Andretti and Bobby Rahal. With the championship already out of reach, most drivers wouldn't have made the valiant effort. But then, Rick Mears just wasn't like "most" drivers.

Ironically, Roger Penske's decision to break his long-standing policy against selling new cars to his competitors ultimately cost Mears the championship, as his finished in second place, just ten points behind Emerson

Fittipaldi's Patrick Racing Penske PC-18. But, business is business. Now 17 years later, Roger Penske's Indy-car program is still funded by Phillip-Morris Tobacco. Rick Mears might beg to differ, but the Captain would undoubtedly say that it was worth it.

1990

In 1990, Penske Racing ran a three-car team for the entire schedule. It was, by any definition, a super team. Three-time Indy 500 winner and three-time CART national champion Rick Mears was back for his 12th season with Roger Penske. Indy winner and national champion Danny Sullivan was returning for his 6th year with the team. And two-time former world champion, Emerson Fittipaldi, who also happened to be the reigning Indianapolis 500 and CART title-holder, was joining them. Penske's shop rolled out another new chassis design, the PC-19, powered by the now-dominant Ilmor-Chevrolet engine. Rick Mears was again sponsored by Pennzoil motor oil, although this would be the last year for the relationship that dated back to 1983. The price of funding CART's top team was becoming too expensive for the "little" oil company. Sullivan and Fittipaldi were both sponsored by Marlboro cigarettes, in what was generally believed to be the most lucrative sponsorship package ever seen in American auto racing.

While it was widely anticipated that the Penske super-team might dominate the competition in the 1990 season, that would not turn out to be the case. This would be the year of second-generation drivers, Al Unser Jr. and Michael Andretti. Unser Jr. was paired with Bobby Rahal on the Galles Team, driving a Lola-Chevy package. Andretti was partnered again with his father at Newman-Haas, and they were also campaigning Lola-Chevys. Pat Patrick had sold his team to former driver Chip Ganassi. With Eddie Cheever at the wheel of the Target-sponsored entry, Ganassi didn't find immediate success, but that would come soon enough. Pat Patrick, however, did not retire as originally expected. Instead, he entered into what might have been a significant partnership with Italian automaker Alfa Romeo, which wanted to get into the popular and competitive

Penske Racing rolled out the Nigel Bennett designed Penske PC19-Chevrolet for its drivers in 1990. The PC19 claimed 9 poles but only four wins among its three drivers in a very competitive CART season. The 1990 championship was contested by Penske, March and Lola chassis powered by a diverse mix of Ilmor-Chevrolet, Cosworth, Porsche, Alfa Romeo and Judd engines. *Alan Hummel*

Former two-time World Champion and defending CART champ Emerson Fittipaldi joined Penske Racing in 1990, teaming with Rick Mears and Danny Sullivan. "Emmo" had driven Patrick Racing's PC18 to the 1989 title. *Greenfield Gallery*

CART series. The Alfa program, however, was plagued with problems from the start and never amounted to much of a threat. Porsche was back again with Teo Fabi at the wheel of a Porsche-powered March, but they too struggled to find speed and reliability in 1990.

The Penske team got off to a good start as the season opened in Phoenix. Rick Mears broke his own track record to take the pole, and then went on to lead 132 of the race's 200 laps, en route to a 7-second victory over Bobby Rahal and Al Unser Jr. Emerson Fittipaldi and Danny Sullivan also had good runs, finishing 5th and 6th respectively. The Penske teammates collected a lot of points at Long Beach too, with Fittipaldi and Sullivan finishing second and third to the untouchable Al Unser Jr., while Rick Mears gave a respectable street-course performance, finishing 6th.

Despite the all-star lineup, Penske's drivers were not at the top of the speed charts in practice for the Indy 500. That honor went to Al Unser Jr. But when pole day came, a day late because of rain, it was the Captain's newest driver, Emerson Fittipaldi, setting new track records to earn the number-1 starting spot. Rick Mears was close behind to take the second starting position, while Danny Sullivan was a little slower, ending up 9th on the grid. On the outside of row one, next to Rick Mears, was Arie Luyendyk. The Dutchman was a veteran of 76 Indy-car races, including five Indianapolis-500s, but was still without a victory.

At the start of the race, Fittipaldi jumped into the lead, a position he did not relinquish for 92 laps. In total, he would lead a race-high 128 laps, but tire problems forced him to make two unplanned green-flag pit stops, and that ultimately cost him any chance of winning. He ended up finishing a disappointing third. Rick Mears struggled with handling problems and never led a lap in the race. He would finish two laps behind the leaders, in 5th place. Danny Sullivan, who had crashed in practice at Indy a year earlier, did it in the race this year, taking himself out on just the 19th lap. This may have been the beginning of the end of his Penske Racing career. The race came down to a battle between 1986 winner Bobby Rahal and a surprisingly competitive Arie Luyendyk. In the end, it was the flying Dutchman who crossed the finish line first. For the generously funded and normally flawless Penske team, there was little consolation in two top-five finishes.

Rick Mears tried to reassert himself, taking the pole a week later in Milwaukee. But in a race that was dominated by Al Unser Jr. and Michael Andretti, the best Rick could do was hold on for a second-place finish. Fittipaldi took third and Sullivan was 8th. Michael Andretti led every lap to win in Detroit, while all three Penske team cars struggled, with a best showing of fourth by Rick Mears. Danny Sullivan rebounded to take the pole at Portland with a new track record, but he went on to finish 4th, one spot ahead of teammate Mears. The podium consisted of Michael and Mario Andretti and Al Unser Jr.

Danny Sullivan continued to run strong at Cleveland, taking over the front spot when early leader Unser Jr. was eliminated because of a pit fire, and holding on for the win over Bobby Rahal and Emerson Fittipaldi. With Mears coming home 8th despite an overheating problem, it was a pretty good day for the team. At the Meadowlands, Mears and Fittipaldi finished second and 6th respectively while Michael Andretti dominated. Then in Toronto, the Penske team's only top-ten result was Danny Sullivan's 4th place finish. It got even worse at Michigan, where Emerson Fittipaldi dominated the first half of the race before exiting with an engine problem, while Mears and Sullivan also failed to finish. By this point in the season, it was becoming apparent that there was not going to be a championship in the cards for Penske Racing this year. The title chase would come down to a battle between the two famous sons, Michael Andretti and Al Unser Jr.

As CART continued on its business strategy of expanding into new markets by racing on temporary street circuits, some traditional oval venues fell by the wayside. Sadly, in 1990 the series did not return to the 2.5-mile tri-oval in the Pocono Mountains, site of Penske Racing's very first Indy-car victory in 1971. The Pocono track had suffered from neglect in recent years, and CART decided that it was no longer fit to host a race. In reality, it may have had more to do with the declining attendance figures than the bumps in the racetrack, but 1989 would go down in history as the last time that Indy-cars ran at Pocono. Fittingly, it was Penske Racing's Danny Sullivan who won that last race, just as Penske's Mark Donohue won the very first Pocono 500 some 18 years earlier.

The Pocono slot on the calendar was filled by a new street course in Denver, where Danny Sullivan managed a second place finish behind Al Unser Jr. Rick Mears was a lap down in 7th spot, and Emerson Fittipaldi dropped out with a broken half shaft. Following Denver, CART went to yet another new track, this one on the streets of Vancouver. The U.S.-based series was beginning to broaden its horizons, and was finding Canada to be a very lucrative market. Throughout the 1990s, CART would continue to add ex-U.S. venues to its schedule, and by the end of the decade the series would find itself, not surprisingly, dominated by non-American drivers. While some of this diversity was good for business, it eventually led to a declining U.S. fan base, ultimately opening the door to the Indy Racing League and another Indy-car civil war.

In the 1990 Vancouver race, Sullivan placed second to Al Unser Jr. again, while Mears took 4th and Fittipaldi 6th. Mid-Ohio was a disappointment too, with Sullivan's fifth-place finish being the best showing for the Penske team. Elkhart Lake was a little better, with Fittipaldi and Mears on the podium with winner Michael Andretti; but by that point it was a humiliating seven races since the powerhouse Penske Racing team had last tasted victory. Fortunately that slide was halted in the next race on the Nazareth mile. Although Danny Sullivan crashed after a suspension failure halfway through the race, Emerson Fittipaldi and Rick Mears went on to a dominating one-two finish, four-tenths of a second apart and a full lap ahead of the rest of the field. Then, in a textbook demonstration of "too little, too late," the Penske teammates scored again in the season finale at Laguna Seca, with Sullivan taking his second win of the year, while Rick Mears finished 4th and Fittipaldi 6th.

Rick Mears ended the year with a single win and third place in the CART championship behind Al Unser Jr. and Michael Andretti. Emerson Fittipaldi also scored just one victory and ended up 5th in the standings.

In his final season with Penske Racing, Danny Sullivan, seen here at Road America, was part of a super team that also included Rick Mears and Emerson Fittipaldi. Sullivan won two races and four poles, but was released at the end of the season when Penske scaled back to a two-car program for 1991. *Greenfield Gallery*

Two-time winner Danny Sullivan finished in 6th position. So much more was expected of this "super team" when the season began. While many deliberated over what went wrong, the objective observer might have recognized that this season's "unexpected" outcome was simply the result of a new reality—a reality that Roger Penske himself was principally responsible for defining. Remembering the 1979 words of World Champion Jackie Stewart, the "old" Indy-car reality consisted of one or two dominant teams leading a field filled with 'service station specials' racing in dilapidated facilities for minimal prize money. When Roger Penske shaped CART, he established a business model that attracted widespread corporate financial support, which fostered increased competition among a greater number of teams and attracted talented drivers and new fans from around the world. He raised the bar. While Roger Penske's "head start" gave his team an inherent advantage throughout much of the 1980s, others had now caught up. Unlike the artificially manufactured parity of the modern-day IRL series, CART had achieved a genuine free-market competitive environment. Although this meant that the Penske Racing Team would have to work harder than ever for its successes, this transformation of the sport had to be one of Roger Penske's most gratifying personal accomplishments.

1991

For the 1991 season, the Pennzoil sponsorship was gone and Marlboro was interested in running just two cars, so Roger Penske had a dilemma. He had three outstanding drivers, but he had only two seats available. Fittipaldi was assured a spot because of his association with Marlboro. Rick Mears, though he had some limitations as a result of his 1984 injuries, still managed to outperform Danny Sullivan over the long-term. Mears also had more history with Penske, and he was the ultimate team player. In reality, it wasn't a difficult decision for the Captain—Danny Sullivan was the odd man out.

He ended up driving for the struggling Patrick Racing Alfa Romero program for the '91 season, unfortunately without much success.

Rick Mears and Emerson Fittipaldi would be piloting new Nigel Bennett-designed Penske PC-20 chassis with Ilmor-Chevrolet power. The list of top challengers again included Michael and Mario Andretti at Newman-Haas, and Bobby Rahal and Al Unser Jr. at Galles Racing. There were also a couple of new contenders this year. Defending Indy 500 winner Arie Luyendyk had moved to a much-improved Vince Granatelli team, which had finally replaced its hopelessly uncompeti-

After 8 years of Pennzoil sponsorship, Rick Mears was in Marlboro colors for the 1991 season. Mears and teammate Emerson Fittipaldi combined to win three races in their Penske PC20-Chevys, finishing 4th and 5th in the CART championship. *Alan Hummel*

tive Buick engines with Ilmor-Chevrolet power. Also, returning to CART after an 8-year absence was Jim Hall Racing with driver John Andretti, nephew of Mario. Hall's program picked up the Pennzoil funding that Penske had forfeited.

The 1991 season opened on the new street circuit in Surfer's Paradise, Australia, one of three ex-U.S. sites on the CART tour this year. In Cinderella fashion, John Andretti and the Jim Hall team won in their very first outing, edging Bobby Rahal to the flag. Rick Mears drove a good race to take the last spot on the podium. Fittipaldi suffered a broken driveshaft early in the race and finished out of the points.

Back on the more familiar streets of Long Beach, California, Mears scored a 4th-place finish while Fittipaldi was eliminated in a pit lane incident involving Michael Andretti. On the first oval race of the season, Arie Luyendyk gave team owner Vince Granatelli his first Indy-car win, while Fittipaldi finally got on the scoreboard with a third-place finish. Mears was fifth.

Heading into the 1991 Indianapolis 500, the Penske team looked strong, but by no means dominating. In fact, the competition looked stronger and deeper than ever. Mears and Fittipaldi set the fast laps in the early practice sessions, but Michael Andretti, Bobby Rahal, part-time driver Jim Crawford and Kevin Cogan all topped the speed charts as the days went on. On the Friday before pole day, Rick Mears had a suspension failure and crashed hard into the concrete, cracking a bone in his foot. Incredibly, this was the first time in his 15 years at the Speedway that Mears had ever made contact with a wall. Driving his backup car the next day, in windy weather conditions on a slippery racetrack, the incomparable Rick Mears recovered to win his sixth Indianapolis 500 pole with a speed of 224.1 mph. Anyone who may have questioned why Roger Penske chose to retain Mears over Danny Sullivan now had a definitive answer. Emerson Fittipaldi got caught out by rain later that afternoon and had to qualify on the second day, ending up 15th on the starting grid even though he ran over 223 mph. Mears had some pretty impressive company on the front row, with A.J. Foyt and Mario Andretti filling the other two spots. Combined, these

After winning the 1990 Indy Lights championship, Paul Tracy was hired as a test driver for Penske Racing. He drove his first race for the team in 1991 and would ultimately score 11 victories before leaving after the 1997 season. Roger Penske can attribute more than a few of his gray hairs to Tracy's wild driving style and his maverick attitude.

three drivers had a total of 8 Indianapolis 500 wins to their credit.

Uncharacteristically, Mears jumped into the lead at the start of the race. He led for the first 11 laps, followed closely by Mario and Michael Andretti, Al Unser Jr. and A.J. Foyt. But as the leaders came up on back-markers already by lap 12, Mears began to experience handling problems in traffic and Mario Andretti passed him for the lead. Based on his experiences over the previous couple of years, Mears had intentionally set his car up with a lot of understeer. Unfortunately, although the car handled well that way in clean air, it was almost uncontrollable when running in heavy traffic. As Michael Andretti then took the lead from his father, Mears continued to fall back, until at one point midway through the race he was almost lapped by Andretti. Fortunately, a cut tire sent Michael to the pits before that happened, giving the Penske crew time to make adjustments on Mears' car, ultimately getting him back into contention. In the meantime, Emerson Fittipaldi had moved through the field and claimed the lead from Andretti on the 109th lap. Fittipaldi led throughout most of the third quarter of the race until he was sidelined with a broken gearbox. But by that time, Mears had his handling problems resolved, and the stage was set for a down-to-the-wire battle between Penske's three-time champion and the still-winless Michael Andretti. Thanks to quick work by the Penske crew, Mears took the lead during a late-race caution period. When the green flag waved with only 14 laps remaining, Michael Andretti made a daring pass on the outside of Mears going through Turn One. But Mears stayed right on Andretti's tail and as they came around the next time, he returned the favor. These are generally regarded as two of the most memorable passes ever made in Indy history.

Once in front on lap 188, Mears never looked back, leading Michael Andretti over the line by three seconds. "Rocket" Rick had won his fourth Indianapolis 500, tying the record held by two of the sport's most esteemed drivers—A.J. Foyt and Al Unser Sr. What made this achievement even more remarkable was the fact that he'd amassed these four wins in only 14 starts, an astounding .286 batting average against not one, but

32 opponents each time. The headline in The Indianapolis Star said it all: "MEARS JUST TOO GOOD TO BE TRUE."

After winning the pole at Milwaukee, Mears dropped out of the race with an electrical problem, while Fittipaldi had his own troubles and finished a disappointing 8th. Detroit was much better for both Penske drivers as Fittipaldi led the most laps and won over Bobby Rahal, Arie Luyendyk and Al Unser Jr., with Mears finishing fifth. Unfortunately, that would turn out to be Fittipaldi's lone victory of the season, although he would pick up second-place finishes in the next two events at Portland and Cleveland, and later in the season, two more at Denver and Mid-Ohio.

The only other highlight for the team that year was the Michigan 500, which was notable for a couple of reasons. First, Roger Penske entered a third car in this race for rookie Paul Tracy. The 22-year-old Canadian was the run-away winner of the 1990 Indy Lights championship, CART's "training" series. He had driven for Dale Coyne Racing in one CART event, the Grand Prix of Long Beach, earlier in the '91 season and had been testing for Penske Racing since then. Penske decided to put the young charger in a car at Michigan because the field was very thin that year. Only 20 other cars were entered, compared to a typical count of 26 or 28, and Penske wanted to make sure there was a good show for the fans at his racetrack. Tracy would go on to drive for Penske Racing in five of the next six seasons, but it would prove to be a turbulent relationship. The young Canadian had enormous talent behind the wheel, but he was not a team player. There was a time when Roger Penske would not tolerate the slightest hint of dissention from his drivers, regardless of their talent or potential. But he seemed to make an exception for Tracy, surely hoping that the situation would improve with time as Tracy matured.

At Michigan, Rick Mears started from the pole, his 5th of the season, with teammate Fittipaldi alongside in the second spot and Paul Tracy starting a respectable 8th. Unfortunately, the rookie's day lasted only three laps until he stuffed his PC-19 into the Turn 4 wall, breaking a leg in the process. His experienced teammate

Fittipaldi followed suit, crashing his PC-20 on lap 22, thus securing the last two finishing positions for the Penske team. Michael Andretti led a good part of the race until his engine expired on lap 143 of 250. From that point on, Rick Mears traded the lead with Arie Luyendyk, Mears finally taking control with 30 laps remaining and holding on for a rewarding three-second victory over the 1990 Indy winner.

Michigan marked the third and last victory for the Penske team in 1991. Paul Tracy returned from his injuries to join Mears and Fittipaldi for the final two events of the season at Nazareth and Laguna Seca, where he finished 7th and 25th. By winning his 6th pole of the year at Nazareth, Rick Mears had taken honors at all five of the ovals plus the Meadowlands street course. By 1991, the one-time all-oval series was comprised of 12 road/street courses and only five oval tracks. Rick Mears had everybody covered on those ovals, but the numbers were working against him.

Michael Andretti won the championship over Bobby Rahal and Al Unser Jr. in 1991. Penske drivers Rick Mears and Emerson Fittipaldi finished 4th and 5th respectively. Although any season that includes an Indy 500 victory has to be considered a success, this was, at best, just a mediocre year for the team.

1992

1992 was a transition year for Penske Racing, although that certainly wasn't the plan as the season began. Penske started the year with veteran drivers Rick Mears and Emerson Fittipaldi back for a full assault on the CART championship under Marlboro colors, while test driver Paul Tracy would be called upon to run selected events with Mobil-1 sponsorship. New PC-21 chassis with Chevrolet engines would be ready for Mears and Fittipaldi, while Tracy would have to make due with a year-old PC-20.

There were some notable changes in the competition for 1992. Bobby Rahal left Galles Racing to form his own team in partnership with St. Louis businessman Carl Hogan. Former Penske driver Danny Sullivan joined Al Unser Jr. in the Galles lineup. They would be driving an in-house chassis called the "Galmer." Third-year driver Scott Goodyear would become a frequent threat, taking one win and almost stealing the Indianapolis 500. Michael and Mario Andretti were together again at Newman-Haas, but there was other news there. After being pushed aside by Penske's Ilmor-Chevrolet engine in the late '80s, a new Ford-badged Cosworth emerged in 1992 as a serious contender. The Newman-Hass team and Ganassi Racing, with drivers Eddie Cheever and Robby Gordon were the initial beneficiaries of the new Cosworth powerplant.

When the season opened on March 22nd in Australia, the Penske team jumped out to a strong start with Emerson Fittipaldi taking the win two seconds ahead of teammate Rick Mears. Bobby Rahal then dominated at Phoenix, leading all 200 laps and giving early notice that his new team was going to be a strong threat. Penske drivers Fittipaldi, Paul Tracy and Mears finished third, fourth and eighth respectively at Phoenix. Then at Long Beach, Danny Sullivan scored his first win since departing from Penske Racing, giving the new Galmer chassis its initial victory. He was followed by Rahal and Fittipaldi, with Rick Mears taking sixth place.

Heading for May at Indy, Penske and his drivers had reason to be hopeful, but the Penske/Chevrolet combination clearly wasn't showing the dominating speed of past years. The Buick-powered entries of Roberto Guerrero, Jim Crawford and Gary Bettenhausen hovered at the top of the speed charts during the week preceding qualifications. The other development that was more concerning to the Penske camp was the obvious straight-line speed advantage enjoyed by the new Cosworths over the Chevy engines. Then, to make matters worse, on the Wednesday before Pole Day, Rick Mears crashed heavily after spinning in fluid from his own car. Mears broke a bone in his foot and suffered a severe wrist sprain, but somehow still managed to take the green flag for qualifying on Saturday. Despite considerable pain, Mears managed to post the ninth best speed on pole day, two positions ahead of Fittipaldi, while rookie Paul Tracy landed three rows farther back, 19th on the grid. Roberto Guerrero won the pole in a Buick, but the real concern for the Penske team was the speed of the Cosworth-powered competition. The fastest Chevy in the field belonged to Danny Sullivan, who was just one spot ahead of Mears on the starting grid and nearly 8 mph off the pole-sitter's pace.

While Penske Racing and the other Chevy teams struggled to find more speed in practice the following week, 27-year-old rookie Jovy Marcelo of the Philippines became the Speedway's first fatality in 10 years. The defending Formula Atlantic champion was attempting to qualify for only his fourth Indy car race when he lost control and hit the wall in a single-car incident.

Race day 1992 was overcast, windy and unseasonably cold, leading to a rash of cold-tire incidents. The misfortunes started before the green flag even waved, as pole-sitter Roberto Guerrero spun his Quaker State Lola-Buick on the backstretch while trying to warm his tires. Tom Sneva was next to pound the concrete. By this point in his career, Sneva was running an Indy-only schedule, and he later admitted that it was his lack of familiarity with the car that caught him off guard, letting it get away from him without warning. Although he was lucky to escape with only minor injuries, this would be the last race for the popular and always-exciting 1983 winner who had given Penske racing its first two national championships back in 1977 and 1978.

As the rest of the race unfolded, it looked like it was going to be a Michael Andretti rout. After his father was effectively eliminated with an early ignition problem, the younger Andretti went on to lead 160 of the first 189 laps. During that time, a lot of things were happening, and most of them were not good. On a lap 75 restart, Jim Crawford spun and crashed in the northwest turn. Rick Mears, following closely behind, had no place to go and rammed into Crawford's wreckage, bruising his already damaged feet and breaking his sprained right wrist. In a separate incident on the very same lap, Emerson Fittipaldi took himself out of the race with a spin into the wall, leaving only rookie Paul Tracy to uphold the Penske team honor. On the lap 84 restart, Mario Andretti went almost head-on into the Turn 4 wall, earning himself a trip to the hospital with broken bones in both feet. It wasn't long after that that Paul Tracy retired the last remaining Penske with a blown engine.

Several more spins and crashes followed, the most serious involving rookie Jeff Andretti, Mario's youngest son. This accident, triggered by a mechanical failure, sent a second Andretti head-on into the concrete. Unfortunately, Jeff's injuries were much more severe than his father's. He would spend more than three months in the hospital recuperating from shattered legs and feet. Then, as if this race hadn't already been cruel enough to the Andretti family, just 11 laps from the end of his dominating performance Michael Andretti lost a fuel pump belt and coasted his Newman-Haas Lola-Cosworth to stop on the track.

Michael's misfortune, however, set up one of the most exciting finishes in the history of the Speedway. Al Unser Jr. and Scott Goodyear, who had been battling for second place in the late stages of the race, suddenly found themselves fighting nose to tail for victory in the Indianapolis 500. Unser Jr. led the final seven laps, strategically weaving his Galmer-Chevy back and forth on the straightaways to keep Goodyear behind him. On the last turn of the last lap, Unser got loose and had to lift just slightly, giving Goodyear one last hope to get by. The Canadian shot to the inside and pulled alongside Unser, but Little Al pinched him to the bottom of the track, and crossed the line 0.043 seconds ahead of his challenger. It was the closest finish in the 76-year history of the 500, eclipsing the 1982 record 0.16-second margin between Gordon Johncock and Rick Mears. Unfortunately, there were no Penskes involved in this excitement. It was a disappointing ending to a less-than-spectacular month for the Penske Racing team.

After Indy, CART broke tradition and went to Detroit instead of Milwaukee. Rick Mears sat this race out, recovering from his Indy injuries, and Penske put Paul Tracy into the second Marlboro seat. Surprisingly, rookie Tracy out-qualified his much more experienced teammate, taking 4th spot on the grid with Fittipaldi starting 5th. Then in the race itself, Tracy moved into the lead by the midpoint, and looked to be a serious contender for the win until his gearbox let go in the closing stages. Fittipaldi, meanwhile, never led, but held on for an 8th place finish, a lap behind winner Bobby Rahal.

Mears returned for the Portland race two weeks later, but pain from his injured wrist prevented him from being very competitive. Fittipaldi, meanwhile, took the pole and dogged Michael Andretti the entire race, ultimately finishing a strong second. Next up was Milwaukee, where Andretti dominated again to take his second consecutive win. Mears qualified second and ran well, but retired early with a water leak. Emerson Fittipaldi drove an unremarkable race there, finishing in 4th place, three laps behind the leaders.

Next on the schedule was a new one-mile oval track in Loudon, New Hampshire. Neither of the Penske drivers qualified well, and in the race, Fittipaldi would be the first retiree, sidelined with an engine problem on lap 56 of 200. Bobby Rahal and Michael Andretti controlled the event, finishing first and second, followed by Scott Goodyear and Rick Mears. Mears then decided to sit out the bumpy Toronto street circuit, giving Canadian Paul Tracy a chance to race in front of a hometown crowd. Michael Andretti was unstoppable again, leading flag-to-flag, and beating pole-sitter Bobby Rahal to the finish by some 21 seconds. Emerson Fittipaldi qualified second, but was out of the race just past the midway point with an electrical problem. Paul Tracy was gone even earlier with a broken gearbox.

Rick Mears was back in the cockpit for the Michigan 500, but after a respectable 5th-place qualifying effort, he was forced to withdraw less than halfway through the race because of continuing pain from his broken wrist. Paul Tracy was the star of the Penske team at Michigan, qualifying 6th, leading 67 laps, and finishing a close second to fellow Canadian Scott Goodyear. Emerson Fittipaldi, meanwhile, started 7th but parked his Penske-Chevy after 133 laps with unmanageable handling.

Following his Michigan experience, Rick Mears decided to stay out of the racecar until he was more fully recuperated. As it turned out, he would be out for the remainder of the season—and then some. Fortunately for the team, Paul Tracy was available and apparently ready to step in. He would pilot the second Marlboro Penske-Chevy for the rest of 1992.

Heading to Cleveland, it had been 9 races and 5 months since the Penske team had seen victory lane.

Fortunately, this race would break that winless streak, as Emerson Fittipaldi would take the pole and score a convincing victory over Michael Andretti. Paul Tracy, unfortunately, had a less satisfying day, starting fourth but dropping out early with an overheating problem.

Now that the 1992 season was almost over, the Penske team apparently had finally figured out how to make a PC-21/Chevrolet go fast. On the road course at Elkhart Lake, rookie Paul Tracy had an excellent qualifying run to take the pole position away from Emerson Fittipaldi, who would start beside him on the front row. Tracy led the first five laps before being passed by his teammate. Fittipaldi went on to lead 41 of the remaining 45 laps to log his second consecutive victory. By this time, however, the championship battle had come down to a two-man race between Bobby Rahal and Michael Andretti. Fittipaldi looked strong again at Vancouver, but was sidelined early with a broken transmission. Paul Tracy missed another opportunity to shine on his home soil, crashing on the 8th lap to finish dead last.

Both Penske drivers rebounded at Mid-Ohio, posting a one-two finish with Fittipaldi at the top of the podium. It was his third win in four races. At Nazareth, Tracy led 35 laps before settling for a respectable third-place finish, four positions ahead of his teammate. The CART championship went down to the wire in the last race of the season at Laguna Seca, with Bobby Rahal prevailing over Michael Andretti by just four points. Andretti did everything he could, taking the pole and leading flag-to-flag in the final race, but Rahal's third place finish was just enough to keep him out front. While the championship was being decided in the final laps at Laguna, the Penske team was loading another one of Paul Tracy's wrecked racecars onto the transporter and Emerson Fittipaldi was limping home to a 19th-place finish. It was a fitting end to a strange and unrewarding season.

It certainly wasn't a bad year. The team posted four victories, all of them by Emerson Fittipaldi who ended up 4th in the final championship standings. Fittipaldi's late-season surge certainly put some much-needed life into the struggling Penske team. But with three of his four wins coming long after he was eliminated from the

championship battle, they seemed somehow less significant. Rookie Paul Tracy showed moments of brilliance
and other moments of baffling stupidity, the later of
which were prematurely attributed to youthful exuber-
ance. Over the many years since his rookie season, Tracy's forceful driving style and the associated inconsistent
results have become trademarks of his career. Certainly,
Roger Penske must have had mixed feelings about this
young driver after his first year. As it turned out, however, because of unexpected circumstances that would
not become evident until December, Tracy would find
himself back in a Marlboro Penske racecar for the 1993
CART season.

The unexpected circumstance that precipitated
Tracy's return was a retirement announcement by Rick
Mears; an announcement made not at a high-profile
press conference, but among his friends at the annual
Penske Christmas party. It was, at first, a shocking and
disappointing development for his many fans. Only a
year after winning his record-tying 4th Indianapolis
500, and still relatively young by Indy driver standards,
it seemed inconceivable that Mears would be ready to
hang up his helmet already. At 40 years of age, he still
had possibly another five or even 10 years to score a
5th Indy win, a feat that would have guaranteed him
immortality. The immediate question at the time was:
how could he walk away from that destiny?

But for Rick Mears, the answer to that question was
really quite simple. He was never racing for the fame or
the records in the first place. For him, it was all about
the thrill of competition; and that just wasn't there anymore. "You hear a lot of drivers say they'll quit when
they're not enjoying it," he said. "That's pretty much
what happened to me. It was a combination of things,
but mostly it was losing that enthusiasm I always felt
before."

There were at least a couple of obvious reasons why
it hadn't been as much fun for Mears lately. First, after
avoiding contact with the unforgiving concrete walls of
Indianapolis Motor Speedway throughout his first 14
years of competition there, he'd now had the unfortunate
experience of crashing heavily three times in two years.
And all three of those accidents resulted in painful injuries. Secondly, although is was rarely highlighted because
of his outstanding overall record, Rick was struggling
desperately to be competitive on road and street courses,
as his 1984 foot injuries were becoming more debilitating
with age. By 1992, with 10 of CART's 16 races held on
such tracks, Mears was playing at a tremendous disadvantage. Given this handicap, he had virtually no prospect of
challenging for the championship.

He could have continued on a limited schedule, racing only the oval tracks or even just the Indianapolis
500. This is a path that many veteran drivers take as
they ease into retirement, but this strategy has its drawbacks. In a sport that demands unparalleled focus and
concentration, not just to be competitive but sometimes
simply to survive, running only a handful of races in a
season can't possibly keep a driver on that fine edge.
Rick Mears certainly didn't want to become a statistic.
And so he did what he felt was right for him. He walked
away while he was still at the top. And like everything
else he'd done in his career, he did it with a lot of class.

Rick Mears left a legacy that will doubtfully ever be
approached in Indy-car racing. His list of accomplishments is daunting. He started on the front row in his
very first race at the Speedway, and went on to win the
World's Greatest Spectacle four times, joining A.J. Foyt
and Al Unser Sr. as the only drivers to ever accomplish
that feat. Of course, Foyt was 42 years old and Unser 48
when they scored their fourth victories. Mears was just
39. In addition to the wins, the Indy record book will
show that Rick Mears claimed the pole position a record
six times in his 15 appearances.

He logged a total of 29 Indy-car victories in his
17-year career. He won 40 poles, and captured three
CART national championships. In 1990, he was named
"Driver of the Decade" by the *Associated Press*. In 1997,
just five years after his retirement, he was inducted into
the International Motorsports Hall of Fame. But more
importantly than all the records, Rick Mears was the
ultimate ambassador for his sport. Intelligent, articulate,
gracious, and modest to a fault, he was a quiet champion who let his accomplishments speak for themselves.
He was the consummate team player, and above all, a
genuinely likeable guy.

The *Associated Press* called him "Driver of the Decade." Fans called him "Rocket Rick." Roger Penske would later say that Rick Mears was his favorite driver of all those that had worn a Penske Racing uniform over the years. At the end of the 1992 season, Rick Mears ended his celebrated driving career at the age of 40, marking the end of an era for the Penske Racing team.

Rick Mears' retirement marked the end of an era for Penske Racing. It was an era that began in the late 1970s, actually just before Mears joined the team. It was an era that saw the Captain's organization transformed from the upstart, crew-cut, college boy challengers, into the mainstream, defining team in American open-wheel racing. It started with Tom Sneva at the wheel, but when he didn't fit the Penske mold, Rick Mears quickly became the key player of this "second generation" Penske Racing team. There were other notable drivers, including Bobby Unser, Al Unser Sr., Danny Sullivan, Mario Andretti, Kevin Cogan, Bill Alsup, and now Emerson Fittipaldi. But Rick Mears was the constant; he was the backbone of the team throughout these extraordinary years. With Rick gone from the driver's seat, Penske Racing was clearly moving on to a new chapter in its history.

Fortunately, Mears chose to remain involved with Penske Racing in a coaching and consulting capacity, working with new drivers and always promoting the sport. He continues in this role today, now more than 14 years after his retirement as a driver.

Pat Smith

CHAPTER 11
Penske South
(1992 – 2006)

"We probably have 15,000 trucks running in the NAS-CAR market area. I love to see the truckers come in the plant in Detroit and say, 'We can't wait to see you run on the NASCAR circuit.'"
—Roger Penske

When the Penske team competed in NASCAR during the early 1970s, American stock car racing was in the early stages of a transition from its "moonshine" origins into the respectable, family-oriented commercial phenomenon that it is today. Roger Penske's interest in NASCAR at that time was driven by a lucrative financial arrangement with American Motors, a company that was willing to spend generously to make a name for itself in a sport dominated by its rivals—Ford, General Motors and Chrysler. When AMC lost interest in the mid 1970s, Penske Racing briefly campaigned Mercurys and Chevrolets without much success. By

that time Roger Penske was consolidating his racing efforts around his increasingly successful Indy-car program, and in 1977, he withdrew from NASCAR altogether. With the exception of a brief "experiment" in 1980, Penske Racing would not return to the NASCAR circuit until 1991.

In 1978, Roger Penske held a Christmas party for his employees and business associates, and out of it, the CART Indy-car series was born. A year later, the unanticipated product of the Captain's holiday gathering was the birth of Penske Racing South. What started out as an uncharacteristically impulsive move by Roger Penske would, years later, evolve into one of the most successful programs in the new NASCAR era.

Penske had a conversation at that party with Don Miller, an 8-year employee of the Penske Corporation. Miller was a former drag racer from St. Louis who had been the unfortunate victim of a pit road accident while helping out on the team's AMC Matador crew in the 1974 Talladega 500. As a result of that accident, Miller lost a leg, but he never lost his enthusiasm for racing. In addition to his St. Louis-based job with the Penske Corporation, Miller was actively involved in managing the early racing career of a talented young stock car driver

At a 1979 Christmas party, Don Miller talked Roger Penske into putting together one of his leftover NASCAR Chevy chassis for an unknown rookie named Rusty Wallace. Rusty made his NASCAR debut in the Penske car at Atlanta in 1980, qualifying 7th and finishing second to Dale Earnhardt. Penske Racing ran Wallace two more times that season with less successful results. It would then be 11 years before the team returned to NASCAR. *High Bank Slope Classic Race Photos*

named Rusty Wallace. Wallace, a St. Louis native, was tearing up the short tracks across the Midwest in the mid and late 1970s. By 1979, he was competing in the now-defunct USAC stock car division against names such as A.J. Foyt and Bobby Allison. Miller approached Roger Penske with a proposition to help field a car for Rusty Wallace in some NASCAR Winston Cup races during the upcoming 1980 season. In retrospect, this sounds like a pretty far-fetched proposal—to ask the team that had just won three consecutive Indy-car national championships to spend its time and resources on some unknown rookie who thought he wanted to go big-time stock-car racing. But Miller knew that Roger Penske had a two-year old Chevrolet chassis just sitting around collecting dust since the team's exit from

NASCAR in 1977. And somehow, he managed to convince Penske that it was worth investing a little time, effort and money to find out what this kid could do. Ultimately, Penske agreed to let Miller put the Chevy together for Rusty Wallace to drive in the Atlanta 500 and a handful of other NASCAR races in 1980.

With sponsorship from Roger Penske's Chevrolet dealership in Detroit, Rusty Wallace made his NASCAR Winston Cup debut in the Atlanta 500 on March 16, 1980. The rookie stunned everyone by qualifying the Penske-Chevrolet 7th on the starting grid, one position ahead of NASCAR's all-time most successful driver, Richard Petty. In the race, Wallace had just one significant problem, a minor pit-road incident with Benny Parsons. At the end of the day, he found himself in second place behind winner Dale Earnhardt, the driver who would go on to win the championship that year. For Rusty Wallace and his Don Miller/Penske Racing team, it was the ultimate Cinderella story—finishing second in their very first Winston Cup appearance, behind only the series champion.

Later that summer, in his second outing with the Penske-Chevrolet, Wallace had a drive-shaft snap while exiting the pits, ending his day early. Then in the October National 500 at Charlotte, Wallace had a difficult and disappointing run, finishing 14th, many laps behind the leaders. After such a promising start, this unlikely experiment ended with frustration and disappointment. Roger Penske decided that he really couldn't afford the distraction from his Indy-car program, and opted to discontinue the arrangement after Charlotte. "I had so many other programs I was doing," Penske said, "it was difficult to do an all-out attack on NASCAR. What I did was I gave him kind of a kick start. Rusty got some visibility. He picked it up from there."

With that, Roger Penske walked away from NASCAR and did not return until 1991. In the meantime, Rusty Wallace, with the benefit of that Penske kickstart, went on to become a major force in the Winston Cup series, ultimately winning the national championship in 1989.

During the decade of the 1980s, NASCAR completed a metamorphosis, transforming itself into the premiere auto racing series, if not the premiere sport in the United States. Purist racing fans downplayed the significance of this technologically deficient "spec-car" series. After all, these racecars were built with carburetors, pushrod engines, conventional distributors, and other outdated technology while their modern-day production counterparts had fuel injection, overhead camshafts, electronic ignition and many other technical innovations. NASCAR had intentionally frozen its specifications with 1960s technology for the sake of simplicity and ease of rules enforcement. But for the NASCAR fans, this did not seem to matter in the least. In fact, the new NASCAR follower was just as likely to be a minivan-driving soccer mom as the conventional auto-enthusiast, gear-head male. In one of the most

successful marketing strategies ever executed, NASCAR had managed to transform the dirty, unruly and dangerous world of southern stock car racing into the new middle-American pastime, with a fan base that couldn't care less about what was under those non-stock body panels with painted-on headlights.

By 1990, NASCAR had surpassed CART and all other forms of American auto racing in every measure of popularity and success. They had more races, bigger starting fields, more sponsors, better television ratings, and most important of all, more paying spectators in the grandstands. There was a business opportunity there that Roger Penske really could not afford to ignore for much longer.

Since he had helped launch Rusty Wallace's NASCAR career back in 1980, Penske had kept a watchful eye on the St. Louis native's progress. After Rusty won the 1989 Winston Cup championship, Penske had an opportunity to use his influence to help Blue Max Racing, the team for which Wallace was then driving, secure a new sponsorship deal with Miller Brewing for the 1990 season. Although that was the extent of his official involvement at that point, Penske seemed to take a considerable interest in Wallace's performance during the next season. Rusty later recalled that he would get notes from Penske congratulating him on good races and letting him know that the Captain was keeping an eye on him.

Rusty Wallace and his long-time friend/manager Don Miller, who was still on the Penske Enterprises payroll, were busy making plans in the fall of 1990 to launch their own new Winston Cup team. When Miller told Roger Penske that he was going to resign so that he could move to North Carolina to be general manager of this new enterprise, Penske got the push he needed. "[Are] you really serious about this," Penske asked Miller. When Miller said, "Yes," Penske's response was, "Then lets do it together." And with that, "Penske Racing South" was born as a three-way partnership between Roger Penske, Rusty Wallace and Don Miller. Penske was the majority owner with 52% of the pie, while Wallace and Miller each held 24%. By the 1991 season, Roger Penske was back in the stock car racing business.

"We're using this as a business venture," Penske said. "One of our strongest markets is the Southeast for our truck leasing business. We probably have 15,000 trucks running in the NASCAR market area. I love to see the truckers come in the plant in Detroit and say, 'We can't wait to see you run on the NASCAR circuit.' And we use it as a customer entertainment medium. Racing has been a common thread throughout our businesses for years."

Pontiac Grand Prix, 1991-1993

NASCAR Winston Cup had changed dramatically since Penske Racing's last serious involvement some 15 years earlier. Most significantly, it had become infinitely more commercialized, with everything focused on creating more parity for the sake of closer and more exciting competition. When Penske Racing campaigned the aerodynamically-challenged, boxy Matador in the early 1970s, they were pretty much stuck with the dysfunctional shape that the misguided AMC design engineers had created for the general public. By the 1990s, however, NASCAR worked with all manufacturers to ensure that whatever production model they wanted to showcase in the series would not be handicapped by the simple technicalities inherent to its basic production-model design. If "adjustments" were needed to make a car competitive, those adjustments were not only permitted, they were factored into the specifications. The cars looked less and less like their production model namesakes, with only the painted-on headlights and front fascia bodywork distinguishing one brand from another. Different models were permitted different spoiler sizes, ride heights, and other modifications to make them competitive. It was a new and more complex world down south now; and that's exactly why Roger Penske decided not to take the challenge alone, but to do it with an established organization that understood both the politics and the engineering subtleties involved in fielding a competitive team in this new NASCAR era.

The other dramatic change since Penske's previous participation was the natural turnover of personalities in the sport—in fact, there was basically an entirely new generation of drivers and many new teams at the front of the field now. When Penske Racing brought the Matador to Winston Cup in 1972, they raced against some of the all-time legends of stock car racing: Richard Petty, Bobby and Donnie Allison, David Pearson, Cale Yarborough, and Buddy Baker. Many were second-generation drivers to NASCAR's founding fathers, such as Lee Petty and Buck Baker.

By 1991, there was a whole new crop of talent at the head of the field. Bobby Allison's son, Davy, was a formidable competitor, as was Allison's protégé from Alabama, Neil Bonnet. Richard Petty's son, Kyle, was also now a serious challenger. And then there was Dale

Rusty Wallace was a native of St. Louis, where he started his racing career on the short dirt tracks in the 1970s. He made his NASCAR debut in 1980 and was a regular on the "Winston Cup" circuit by 1984, going on to win the championship in 1989. Wallace became a minority partner in the new PENSKE SOUTH NASCAR team in 1991 and would be the team's lead driver until his retirement after the 2005 season. *Miller Racing Press Kit*

PENSKE SOUTH raced a Pontiac Grand Prix from 1991 through 1993. Driver Rusty Wallace is seen here posing with the car at Daytona Speedway. *Greenfield Gallery*

Earnhardt, who had been around for over a decade by then and had decisively established his unrepentant "Intimidator" reputation. Other notable competitors included Alan Kulwicki, Ernie Irvin, Mark Martin, Bill Elliott and Dale Jarrett. And of course, on any given Sunday, Russell William Wallace Jr. could run with the best of them. It was a different era, with different faces, different rules, and in many ways, a totally different purpose; but in almost every sense, NASCAR was more interesting and more successful than ever before, and Penske Racing was now a part of it again.

Penske Racing South campaigned a Pontiac Grand Prix on the Winston Cup circuit from 1991 through 1993. This was the model that Rusty Wallace had

driven for the previous several seasons and, lacking any particular reason to change, Don Miller and crew chief Jimmy Makar decided to stick with the known commodity. Wallace's sponsorship arrangement with Miller Brewing remained intact for the remainder of his driving career, making it one of the most enduring partnerships in the history of the sport.

Penske Racing's first year back in NASCAR was not exactly an unqualified success. Rusty Wallace did win two races, at Bristol and Pocono, and he scored a total of 14 top-ten finishes during the 29-race 1991 season. Unfortunately, 10 DNFs, due mostly to reliability issues, prevented the team from making any serious challenge for the championship. To make matters worse, crew chief Jimmy Makar left by mid-season to join a new team that was being formed by Washington Redskins coach Joe Gibbs. Makar's brother-in-law, Dale Jarrett, was to be the driver for the new Gibbs operation, which went on to become one of the strongest new teams in NASCAR. The loss of Makar virtually paralyzed the Penske South program for the remainder of the '91 season and well into the following year.

By August of 1992, Rusty Wallace had not won a single race, and had only two top-five finishes all season. It was a situation that had the former champion very concerned; he knew he had all the resources at his disposal, but the team just couldn't seem to pull everything together. The turning point came when veteran crew chief Buddy Parrott was hired in August. Parrott had previously worked with Richard Petty, Darrell Waltrip and Derrike Cope, all highly regarded NASCAR teams. But when he saw the Penske South operation, he was dumbfounded. "I'd never had anything like that to work with," he said later. "It was just unbelievable. The resources. The beautiful shop. And I saw that all we needed to do was just stir the people up a little bit." In less than a month, Rusty Wallace and Penske South were in the winner's circle at Richmond. Although that would turn out to be the only victory celebration for the entire 1992 season, the groundwork had been laid for a strong comeback the following year.

1993 would turn out to be a brutal season, both physically and emotionally, for NASCAR in general and for Rusty Wallace in particular. It was a year that started with great promise and confidence for the Penske South team. In a pre-season press conference, new crew chief Buddy Parrott boldly proclaimed that he expected Wallace to win 10 races that year. Given that this team had managed to score a total of only three victories over the previous two seasons, that seemed to be an unrealistically optimistic prediction. But Parrott knew what he had to work with, and he had no doubt that it was a completely attainable goal.

Rusty Wallace started out looking strong in the season-opening Daytona 500, running with the leaders throughout most of the race. But 30 laps from the finish, all hell broke loose. Two cars got together in front of him coming off of turn two. In trying to avoid the accident, Rusty got sideways, and then things got really frightening. The #2 Penske Pontiac got airborne and started doing barrel rolls at nearly 200 mph into the Daytona Speedway infield. The replay showed that Wallace rolled twice, flipped end-over-end one and a half times, and then rolled another four times, shedding wheels, sheet-metal and other miscellaneous components as he flew and bounced helplessly. As spectacular as the accident appeared, the driver was very fortunate that nothing prevented the car from flipping and turning freely until it had safely dissipated its 200-mph reserve of kinetic energy. When he crawled out of the crumpled wreckage of Roger Penske's destroyed racecar, Wallace was more mad than hurt, suffering only bruises and a couple of nasty cuts on his face. It was a tough way to start the season.

Rather than dwelling on the Daytona disaster, however, Wallace focused his anger on the goal of winning the championship. He won the next race at Rockingham, and then ticked off three top-fives at Richmond, Atlanta and Darlington before taking another victory at Bristol. But there were no celebrations after this second win. On the Thursday before that race, defending Winston Cup champion Alan Kulwicki was killed in a private plane crash en route to the track. It was devastating for the close-knit NASCAR community and for Rusty Wallace, who had raced against Kulwicki throughout much of his career and considered him a friend.

A week after Bristol, Rusty Wallace and Penske South took the checkered flag again, this time at North Wilkesboro; and in the process, they assumed the lead in the championship battle. When Wallace made it three in a row with his victory at Martinsville, it started to look like Buddy Parrott's prediction of 10 wins might not be so far-fetched after all. But unfortunately, there were some serious bumps in the road just ahead.

Next on the schedule was Talladega, the first superspeedway race since Wallace's wild ride at Daytona. Up until the last 200 yards of the 500-mile event, Rusty was having a great day. But a late-race caution had set up a wild two-lap charge to the finish, and Wallace didn't quite make it. Coming to the checkered flag, he made a poorly-judged block on Dale Earnhardt, and suddenly, it was Daytona all over again. The Penske Pontiac got sideways and then went up in the air, flipping and crashing to the ground a total of nine times before coming to a rest. In the process, Wallace's car crossed the finish line in a nearly vertical position, with its nose in the ground and the tail of the Pontiac pointing into the sky. This time, however, the driver was not as fortunate as he had been at Daytona. The car bounced violently rather than rolling freely, pounding the ground with brutal force on each turn. Wallace, half conscious, had to be cut out of the wreckage. He ended up with a broken wrist and a lot of painful bruises. It was much more physically damaging than the Daytona crash. The good news was that he was credited with a 6th place finish as he literally flew across the start-finish line.

Wallace did not miss a race after this accident, jumping back into the car two weeks later for the demanding road race at Sears Point, which was a particular challenge with his broken wrist. Unfortunately, he would struggle through six more painful races with only one top-five finish before scoring another win at New Hampshire in early July. But before the celebrating was even over for that victory, NASCAR was devastated again by the loss of another of its talented young drivers. Davey Allison, son of former Penske Racing driver Bobby Allison, died in a helicopter crash while landing in the Talladega Speedway infield the day after the New Hampshire race. For Bobby Allison and his wife, this was an unimaginable tragedy, coming just 11 months after losing their older son, Clifford, in a racing accident at Michigan Speedway.

Wallace struggled through the rest of the summer before stringing together a second-place at Bristol, a third at Darlington, and then two straight victories at Richmond and Dover, which propelled him into second place in points behind Dale Earnhardt. He then went on to win three of the last six races of the season, but still fell short of Earnhardt by a mere 80 points at the end of the year. Despite not taking the title, Rusty Wallace did, amazingly, make good on Buddy Parrott's pre-season prediction by winning a total of 10 races. That was four more victories than the champion Earn-

hardt had claimed, but the two big crashes took their toll. Wallace lost a lot of points by not finishing at Daytona, and the after-affects of his brutal Talladega accident cost him dearly throughout the summer.

Rusty Wallace's two wild accidents during the 1993 season highlighted a serious problem that NASCAR was struggling with on their high-speed tracks. Aerodynamic engineering advancements had created a racecar that sliced through the air and stuck to the track far better than ever before, provided it was moving in the intended direction. But when that car got sideways, these same aerodynamic forces could instantly turn the vehicle into an out-of-control flying machine. Wallace's two horrifying demonstrations of this new phenomenon were key in prompting NASCAR to mandate essential safety design changes. These changes included hinged roof flaps that automatically lift when a car gets sideways or backwards, disrupting the airflow pattern that could cause the vehicle to be launched into the sky. Once implemented and perfected, these improvements virtually eliminated the frightening site of 3,500-pound stock cars doing somersaults through the air.

Ford Thunderbird, 1994 – 1997

Despite their remarkable record of 10 victories with the Pontiac in 1993, Penske South switched to a Ford Thunderbird for the 1994 season, believing that they would get more factory support than was being offered by General Motors, which seemed to be focusing most of its attention on the Chevrolet teams.

The NASCAR season got off to a bad start, with popular driver Neil Bonnett being killed just 20 minutes into the first practice session for the Daytona 500. Then three days later, Rodney Orr also died in a practice crash on the Daytona racetrack. Rusty Wallace was clearly shaken by these tragedies and the apparent callousness he saw in some of his fellow drivers. At the pre-race driver's meeting, he made an impassioned plea to his competitors to drive responsibly. "These cars just don't flip by themselves or spin out by themselves," he said. "I've been upside down at Daytona and I've been upside down at Talladega, and I'm telling you, it hurts…I think everybody in this room is running scared. I'll tell you,

Looking for more factory support than they were receiving from GM, PENSKE SOUTH switched from Pontiac to the Ford Thunderbird for 1994. Rusty Wallace is seen here in the Miller Splash Thunderbird in 1996. *Greenfield Gallery*

my wife is damn scared. So use your heads, please."

Wallace's bad luck in the Daytona 500 continued. He started fourth in the field, but lasted only 63 laps before he was once again the innocent victim of somebody else's mistake. Fortunately, this time it wasn't a big wild wreck, but it had the same effect on his championship ambitions, leaving him 41st in the points-standings as the NASCAR convoy pulled out of Daytona. "It was just one of those deals," he said with frustration later. "Two weeks of all this stuff always ends up for me this way."

But just a week later, Wallace took the new Penske Ford Thunderbird to a dominating victory in the Goodwrench 500 at Rockingham, one of his favorite tracks. He followed that up with a second-place at Richmond, moving back up to 8th place in the championship battle after three races. Then after a couple of less successful weekends, a 7th-place finish at Bristol followed by a second at North Wilksboro and a win at Martinsville vaulted him up to 4th spot in the standings.

On Memorial Day, Wallace's Penske Ford was runner-up to Jeff Gordon in the Coca-Cola 600 at Charlotte, and that pushed Rusty to third position in the championship race, where he would stay even after three

consecutive victories at Dover, Pocono, and Michigan in June. His 6th win of the season came at the end of August back at Bristol. A 7th-place result the following weekend at Darlington was enough to move him into second place behind only defending champion Dale Earnhardt, but unfortunately, that was as far as he was going to get. Even with back-to-back wins at Dover and Martinsville in September, a string of four poor finishes at the end of the season dropped the Penske driver to third place in the final standings behind the Intimidator and Mark Martin.

It was unfortunate that Rusty Wallace and Penske South didn't get a Winston Cup title out of the 1993 or '94 seasons because they were clearly the team to beat almost every weekend. With a total of 18 wins over those two years, Wallace had seen victory lane eight more times than Dale Earnhardt, who won both of those championships. But in NASCAR, consistency is everything, and again in 1994, Wallace's 20 top-ten finishes couldn't match up to the 25 posted by Earnhardt.

1995 brought significant change for Penske South as crew chief Buddy Parrott departed for a new Winston Cup team. Parrott had been the catalyst that pulled the Penske program together two years earlier and he

For 1987, Rusty Wallace's Penske Ford Thunderbird had a new look, promoting Miller Brewing Company's "Lite" brand beer. While racing the Thunderbird, PENSKE SOUTH did most of the development and testing work on the new Taurus, which would be Ford's NASCAR entry for 1988. *Pat Smith*

deserved a lot of the credit for Wallace's two spectacular seasons. Roger Penske and Don Miller hired Robin Pemberton to take Parrott's place, but it took a good part of the 1995 season before the relationships between Wallace, Pemberton, and the rest of the team really started to click.

The season opening Daytona 500 was typically disappointing, as Wallace was eliminated in another accident and finished 34th. That was followed by a mechanical DNF before the team put together a string of five top-ten finishes in seven races, culminating with a win at Martinsville that moved Rusty to 5th-place in the points. Unfortunately, there wasn't much more to get excited about over the next couple of months. A third-place at Pocono in July, a second to Jeff Gordon at Indianapolis in early August, and a 5th at Michigan later that month kept Wallace from ever dropping below 7th-place in the standings, but he was clearly out of the battle for the championship by the time the season was half over. This was particularly unfortunate

because when everything finally did come together by Labor Day, the team finished out the season with an impressive string of 9 consecutive top-ten finishes, eight of which were top-fives, including a victory at Richmond. But by that time, unfortunately, the hole was just too deep, and Rusty Wallace ended the 1995 season in 5th position behind rising superstar Jeff Gordon, Dale Earnhardt, Sterling Marlin and Mark Martin.

Following the strong finish in 1995, there was good reason for optimism as Penske South opened the new season with no significant changes in personnel or equipment. But Wallace would manage only two top-ten finishes in the first six races of 1996 before breaking through with a win at Martinsville in late April. Then after a DNF at Talladega, he rebounded with another victory on the Infineon Raceway road course to move up to 7th-place in the points. There would be two more wins, at Michigan in June and Bristol in August, but the 1996 season was a model of inconsistency for the Penske South team. Wallace would never manage to get higher than 6th in the points chase and would ultimately finish 7th in the championship battle with a total of four wins for the season.

The 1997 season began with the traditional disappointment at Daytona, but then rebounded nicely with Rusty Wallace finishing 6th at Rockingham and taking the win at Richmond. But that would turn out to be the team's only victory for the entire season. Wallace would go on to score only 12 top-ten finishes and ended the season a very disappointing 9th in the championship points. It had now been three years since Wallace and the Penske South team had really challenged for the Winston Cup title. And this was apparently enough to make Roger Penske start thinking about making some significant changes.

1998 – 2002, Ford Taurus

For 1998, the Ford Motor Company changed its NASCAR Winston Cup entry from the Thunderbird to its newer Taurus model. One of the things that may have hurt the Penske team's effort in '97 was the fact that they had taken on the burden of developing this new car for Ford. Ultimately, that should have proven to be an advantage, but it was certainly an unneeded distraction while they were struggling through the difficult 1997 campaign.

The bigger change, however, was the addition of a teammate for Rusty Wallace in 1998. During the off-season, Roger Penske had purchased a 50% interest in the existing Michael Kranefuss Cup team, complete with driver Jeremy Mayfield and sponsorship from Mobil 1 Oil. Kranefuss, who had been head of Ford's worldwide racing operations for 25 years, had been campaigning a Ford in the NASCAR series since 1995. Roger Penske was certainly thinking that the second team would essentially double the development and testing capabilities of the organization. He may have also been starting to hedge his bets on the aging Rusty Wallace, who recently seemed to be losing a little of the competitive fire he had demonstrated in the 1980s and early '90s. This was a somewhat delicate situation considering that Wallace was still an owner in the Penske South partnership. But the Captain was intent on winning a Winston Cup title, and if he had concerns that Rusty Wallace might no longer be able to deliver on that goal, changes would have to be made.

The new teammate relationship seemed to be a good thing, as Rusty Wallace opened the season with five straight top-five finishes. This was good enough to keep him on top of the championship points battle through the first third of the season. He would not actually pick up a win until three races from the end of the year, however, and by that time he'd dropped back to 4th-place in the standings where he would ultimately finish the season. Despite the disappointment of scoring only one victory, his 21 top-ten finishes represented a considerable improvement over the previous year's statistics and he made it pretty clear that he wasn't ready to be put out to pasture just yet.

The other half of the team had a pretty respectable 1998 season as well. Jeremy Mayfield also won a single race, the Pocono 500 midway through the year, and ended up 7th in the title chase. This was, by far, the best showing of the young driver's 4-year NASCAR Winston Cup career. Once again, the Penske South team seemed to have laid a solid foundation for the following

Driver Jeremy Mayfield came to the team as part of a package deal when Roger Penske bought a 50% interest in the Michael Kranefuss Cup team before the 1998 season. Mayfield would win three Winston Cup races in his three seasons with PENSKE SOUTH.

season.

Rusty Wallace actually completed the Daytona 500 in 1999, posting an 8th-place finish. It likely would have been even stronger had it not been for some questionable driving tactics by eventual winner Jeff Gordon. Wallace and the new kid had developed a sometimes-dangerous rivalry on the racetrack, and neither would give the other an inch, especially 10 laps from the end of the Daytona 500. Still, with the 8th at Daytona and 10th and 9th-place results in the next two events, Rusty found himself sitting in second-place in the championship points three races into the season. Unfortunately, that was as high as he would get. Winning just one race again this year and posting only 16 top-ten results, Wallace sank to 8th-place in the year-end championship standings. Jeremy Mayfield fared even worse, not winning a single event and finishing in the top-ten only 12 times. He ended up 11th in the points. Overall, it was a discouraging season for Penske Racing South.

The Penske team returned with the same lineup for the 2000 season, with drivers Rusty Wallace and Jeremy Mayfield still piloting Ford Taurus'. Given the team's recent struggles, it would not have been surprising if Roger Penske had made some changes; but in 2000, he was in the process of doing just that with his CART

Indy-car program, so any overhaul of the NASCAR operation would have to wait until that job was completed.

Rusty Wallace's luck was improving at Daytona. After years of early exits, often dramatic and painful, he followed his 1999 8th-place result with a very impressive 4th-place finish in 2000. Unfortunately, that was followed by four consecutive finishes outside of the top-ten, dropping him quickly to 10th in the standings. A win at Bristol and a 4th-place finish at Texas Speedway brought him back up to 5th position, but that's as high as he would climb for the rest of the year. Wallace's Taurus was fast all season, claiming a total of 9 pole positions. That was more than double his nearest competitor, teammate Jeremy Mayfield, who took pole honors four times. Rusty won four races during the season, second only to Tony Stewart's six victories, but his 20 top-ten finishes were not good enough to keep him in the hunt for the title. Despite what appeared to be a pretty strong season, he ultimately finished 7th in the championship standings. Jeremy Mayfield scored two victories, but managed to land in the top-ten only 10 other times, leaving him a very disappointing 24th in the final standings. By that time, however, Mayfield was probably already on his way out the door.

The 2000 season was a difficult time for the NASCAR community. In May, 20-year-old Adam Petty, a fourth-generation representative of the first family of the sport, was killed in practice on the one-mile Loudon Speedway in New Hampshire. Exactly eight weeks later, 1998 Winston Cup Rookie-of-the-Year Kenny Irwin died in a similar practice crash at the same track. A day after Irwin's death, Rusty Wallace won the pole for that weekend's race, but he was clearly shaken. "These are the days that make you really sit back and look at yourself in the mirror and ask, 'Why do I do this?'" he said.

Jeremy Mayfield's eventual replacement at Penske South was going to be a 22-year-old Purdue University engineering student from Indiana named Ryan Newman. Newman had been racing open-wheel sprint cars with impressive results in the Midwest, but as early as 1997 he began looking for opportunities to move into NASCAR. At Daytona in February of 2000, he got the

chance to meet with Roger Penske and Don Miller, and that started the ball rolling quickly. Penske and Miller must have been extremely impressed, because they agreed to test the ambitious young driver that June. This led to an initial ARCA entry at Penske's Michigan track in August and Newman was already in a Winston Cup car for the Phoenix race in November of that same year. Roger Penske realized, however, that his promising new talent still needed time to mature and gain experience, so for the 2001 season he planned to have Newman run a combination of ARCA, Busch, and Winston Cup events while Rusty Wallace and Jeremy Mayfield would continue as the team's primary Winston Cup drivers.

In October of 2000, Roger Penske completed a deal to purchase the remaining 50% share of the Jeremy Mayfield/Mobil1 entry from the team's original owner, Michael Kranefuss. From that point forward, Penske and Don Miller would have full control over both of the Penske South entries. In the announcement of this deal, Penske also revealed his plans for Newman, indicating that he would be running selected ARCA, Busch and Winston Cup races throughout the following season in preparation for becoming Rusty Wallace's teammate in 2002. This effectively made Mayfield a lame duck at Penske South for the 2001 championship.

After having one of his best seasons of recent years in 2000, Rusty Wallace struggled again in 2001. His new-found Daytona luck continued, however, as he moved from his 12th place starting position to finish third in NASCAR's biggest event. Of course, that was the day that NASCAR was changed forever with the death of Dale Earnhardt. In a strange last-lap accident, Earnhardt was apparently nudged from behind as he blocked Sterling Marlin to protect his position. His infamous black #3 Chevrolet veered into the outside concrete wall, although not apparently with a force that would have typically caused serious injury. But as Michael Waltrip took the checkered flag followed by Dale Earnhardt Jr. just a couple hundred yards away, the man who proudly answered to the nickname "the Intimidator" was probably already dead.

Although Earnhardt couldn't match the overall statistics of all-time series great Richard Petty, there's no doubt that in this new era of unprecedented NASCAR popularity, he was a legend in his own time. His death rattled American auto racing like none other before. His millions of fans mourned their fallen hero with bumper stickers and "#3" window murals on their vehicles, dedicated websites, country songs, memorial clothing and more. In their grief, some even made death threats against fellow driver Sterling Marlin and businessman Bill Simpson, owner of the safety equipment company that manufactured the seat belts in Earnhardt's racecar. Ironically, Dale Earnhardt was notorious for bumping and nudging other drivers, when "necessary," to make a winning pass. Although everyone associated with American auto racing agreed that this was a tragedy and a terrible blow to the sport, many quietly suggested that the Intimidator may have ultimately gotten a taste of his own deadly medicine.

When the badly shaken NASCAR community returned to business a week later at Rockingham, Rusty Wallace managed a 7th-place finish. He had three more top-ten finishes in the first 11 races, including an impressive win at Roger Penske's California Speedway, which boosted him as high as third place in the championship points. But once again, he was unable to build on his early-season successes, and ultimately slid back to 7th-position in the final standings without ever winning another race that year. Ironically, it was the same final result as a year earlier, but with just one victory, no poles, and only 14 top-ten finishes, it didn't seem nearly as rewarding. Jeremy Mayfield, who had very little incentive and probably even less team support, had a dismal season, with no wins and only 7 top-ten finishes, ending up 35th in the final championship standings.

Ryan Newman, meanwhile, had a storybook year as he bounced between ARCA, Busch and Winston Cup, all while completing his engineering studies at Purdue University. He won the ARCA season-opener at Daytona and a Busch event at Michigan. He scored two top-five finishes in his 7 Winston Cup starts, and claimed a pole position in only his third race. It was apparent to everyone that this young driver had great potential. Newman was clearly not the typical NASCAR personality, if there even was such a thing anymore. General

Manager Don Miller described him like this: "He is a balls-to-the-wall kind of driver like Cale Yarborough or Junior Johnson, but a thinker like David Pearson. He's also an educated, resourceful individual on the racetrack and quiet and educated like Mark Donohue. But he's not like those guys; he's like himself." And that was something else!

For the 2002 season, Jeremy Mayfield was released, as expected, and Rusty Wallace and Ryan Newman were full-time teammates in the Penske South Ford Taurus'. Wallace had a disappointing start with an 18th-place finish in the Daytona 500; but with four top-10s in the next five races, he found himself in third position in the early championship standings. Newman, meanwhile, started strong with a 7th-place finish in his rookie Daytona 500, and followed that with a 14th at Rockingham and then three top-tens, which put him up to second-place in the points. Penske South was looking pretty impressive early in the season.

After his decent start, however, Wallace really struggled for the remainder of the year. He would score a top-five finish and then be out of the top-ten for the next three or four races. That went on for much of the season, as the veteran slowly lost ground in the championship battle, eventually finishing in that familiar 7th position for the third year in a row. Although he had several runner-up finishes, Wallace did not win a single Winston Cup race in 2002, breaking a record string of 16 consecutive seasons of scoring at least one victory in NASCAR's top series.

While Rusty was struggling, Ryan Newman was coming on strong in the latter part of the season. After his good start, Penske's rookie suffered through a string of six poor finishes in the next seven races, dropping him from second place to 17th in the points before things really turned around. From the midpoint of the season, however, Newman looked very impressive. He ended the year with just one victory, in the fall race at Loudon, New Hampshire; but he captured a series-leading 6 pole positions, 22 top-ten finishes and 14 top-fives along the way. Penske's new star ended his rookie season 6th in the NASCAR Winston Cup points, one spot ahead of his veteran teammate, and it appeared that the Captain

Ryan Newman made his first "Cup" start for Penske Racing at Phoenix in 2000 driving a Ford Taurus and ran 7 more races in 2001 with the number "02." He moved to the "12" car for 2002 after Jeremy Mayfield left the team. *Greenfield Gallery*

had made his best discovery since hiring Rick Mears to drive his Indy-cars back in 1978.

2003-2004, Dodge Intrepid

After a 25-year hiatus from the sport, Chrysler Corporation had returned to NASCAR in 2001 with a Dodge Intrepid entry fielded by a new factory team under the direction of Ray Evernham. The highly-respected Evernham had served as Jeff Gordon's crew chief during Gordon's meteoric rise to the top of Winston Cup, winning three Cup titles in the previous four years. During the 2001 and 2002 seasons, Evernham's new team, along with independent Dodge entries fielded by Petty Enterprises, Ganassi/Sabates Racing and other teams, had won races and demonstrated considerable promise.

After Dodge had proved to be a legitimate contender, Roger Penske decided to switch to an Intrepid for the 2003 Winston Cup season. "This just wasn't a

deal where we said we're going to switch because we want to switch or it's a money situation. We looked at the technology that was available to us and the opportunities to go forward. In less than 24 months, Dodge has become a major player in the NASCAR Winston Cup Series. They've won key races. They've led the drivers' points standings most of the year. And just as importantly, they have incredible resources and an enviable, unique approach."

Rusty Wallace and Ryan Newman were back as the team's two drivers, but it wasn't long before it would become apparent that it was now going to be the young Newman, not his veteran teammate, who would most likely bring Penske Racing its first NASCAR title. Newman got off to a rough start, crashing and finishing last at Daytona, and then not managing to score a top-five finish until winning at Texas in the 7th race of the season. He had, however, already won two poles and started in the first two rows in five of those seven races,

After Dodge had been back in NASCAR for a couple of years and proved to be a serious contender, Roger Penske made the decision to move from Ford to the Intrepid. "They have incredible resources and an enviable, unique approach," he said. Ryan Newman's series-leading 8 victories and 11 poles in 2003 validated the Captain's decision.

proving that the Dodge Intrepid was indeed a competitive racecar. Unfortunately, after the Texas win, Newman failed to finish the next four events, plummeting to 27th-place in the Winston Cup standings and virtually eliminating himself from the championship battle before the season was one-third over. But beginning with the Memorial Day Coca-Cola 600, Penske's sophomore driver went on a tear. He racked up seven top-fives in the next nine events, including wins at Dover, Chicagoland and Pocono, which rocketed him back up to 9th in the standings. He then recorded 12 top-ten finishes, including victories at Michigan, Richmond, Dover and Kansas in the remaining 16 races of the year. It was an impressive charge that would certainly have netted him a championship had it not been for the horrendous start that he experienced. As it was, he got as high as 4th position in the standings before being involved in an early accident during the season finale at Homestead

that dropped him to 6th spot in the final results.

In addition to a series-leading 8 wins, twice as many as any other driver, Newman also claimed a remarkable 11 pole positions, seven more than his nearest challengers. Unfortunately, NASCAR's system of awarding championship points, which had been in existence since 1972, heavily favored mediocre consistency over exceptional performance. Although it had often been challenged over the years, it took this dramatic scenario in 2003 to finally force a change. Even NASCAR found it difficult to rationalize crowning a champion who scored just one win when another driver with 8 victories ended up in 6th position. For the 2004 season, things would be different—not necessarily better, but different.

While Newman was doing almost everything right in his second full year with Penske South, team partner Rusty Wallace was struggling. Throughout the 36-race season, he managed only 12 top-ten finishes, with no victories and no poles. Ultimately, he finished 14th in the championship standings. What was most disconcerting about these unspectacular statistics was that his teammate, with the very same equipment and resources, was regularly the class of the field. But the difference was that Wallace and Newman were at opposite ends of their careers. Unburdened by many of the responsibilities that come with years of success in racing, Newman had the luxury of being 110% focused on driving the racecar, while Wallace had a lot of other things on his plate. "The competition is just so much tougher," Rusty said. "You look at Winston Cup qualifying, and everybody is bumper to bumper on the speed chart. You can run every lap and finish twenty-fifth or thirtieth. We think we're trying hard, but down deep I know there's probably some left. Unfortunately, the requests on my time—whether its from the media, the businesses I'm involved in, family, or whatever—the demands are greater right now than they ever have been. I'm doing more right now than I ever did in my life. It's easy for car owners and people to say, 'Hey, you need to get off that and pay more attention to the car.' But how do you do it? I'm the one who's supposed to take care of the sponsors and all that stuff." It would be almost another year before Rusty Wallace would announce his plans to retire, but surely he was seriously contemplating this decision by the end of his very disheartening 2003 season.

For 2004, there were a couple of high-profile changes in NASCAR's top-level series. The first involved the championship points system. Although most critics of the old system believed that a new model should do more to reward victories and top-five finishes over mere "participation," that wasn't the outcome of the much-anticipated overhaul. NASCAR did not actually change the way points were distributed on a race-by-race basis. What they did, to create an exciting playoff-style shoot-out at the end of the season, was to eliminate all but the top-10 drivers from contention for the title after the 26th race on the schedule. Then they reset the point totals for those select drivers that made the cut, separating them by just five championship points each as they headed into the final 10 races. It is, unquestionably, a unique scoring system; but not surprisingly, totally consistent with NASCAR's guiding strategy of enhancing the show—even if they have to artificially manufacture the competition to accomplish that goal.

The second major change for the 2004 season was the series title sponsor. Since 1972, R.J. Reynolds Tobacco had supported NASCAR's top-level championship through its Winston cigarette brand. For over 30 years, the series was universally known as the "Winston Cup." But with legislation mandating the phased elimination of tobacco advertising from all U.S. sporting events by 2006, R.J. Reynolds decided to discontinue its long and mutually beneficial relationship with NASCAR at the end of the 2003 season. Taking its place as title-sponsor of America's number-one spectator sport was Nextel Communications.

Apparently encouraged by his success with Ryan Newman, and probably anticipating the imminent retirement of Rusty Wallace, Roger Penske decided to run a third Nextel Cup team for the 2004 season. He hired promising young Californian Brendan Gaughan, who was cut from the same mold as Newman—educated, athletic, focused, and at a very young age, already a proven racing talent. Gaughan had won the Winston West championship in 2000 and 2001 and then took

rookie-of-the-year honors in the Craftsman Truck series in 2002. In 2003, he scored 6 victories in the truck series and finished fourth in the final standings. With the veteran Rusty Wallace and his two young guns, Newman and Gaughan, Roger Penske appeared to have a stacked deck going into the 2004 season.

Unfortunately, the Gaughan experiment turned out to be a relative failure. During the 36-race season, the rookie would produce just four top-10 finishes, with a single showing in the top-five. He finished a disappointing 28th in the championship standings. By the end of the year, Roger Penske would decide to cut his losses and Gaughan would not be invited to return.

Ryan Newman once again proved to be the fastest driver on the circuit, winning a total of 9 poles over the season, three more than his nearest rival. But Newman's season was plagued by inconsistency. He did not find his way to victory lane until late June when he won the Michigan 400. And he struggled constantly to stay within reach of the top-ten in points to ensure his place in the "Chase for the Nextel Cup," the new 10-race shootout that would crown the 2004 champion. After climbing to 8th place following the Pocono 500 at the beginning of August, consecutive poor finishes at Indianapolis, Watkins Glen and Michigan dropped Newman to 13th with only three races remaining to claw his way back into the top-10. He finished second at Bristol, 5th at California and 20th at Richmond, just good enough to claim the 10th and last slot in the "Chase."

After losing an engine and finishing 33rd at New Hampshire, Newman rebounded with an impressive victory at Dover, moving him to 8th in the standings. But, with the exception of a third-place at Martinsville and a second at Phoenix, there were no more top-10 finishes in the remaining races. At the end of NASCAR's inaugural "Chase for the Nextel Cup," Newman was in 7th position.

Rusty Wallace had an even more frustrating 2004 season. He did finally break a 105-race winless streak by taking an emotional victory at Martinsville early in the season. Unfortunately, the rest of his year was pretty unremarkable, with only three top-fives and 11 top-ten finishes in total. Following his Martinsville win, Wallace had moved to 8th place in the standings, but there was a long and painful slide after that. He fell back to 17th place after Richmond, the point at which the line was drawn between the challengers for the "Chase" and everyone else.

By late August, at age 48, Rusty Wallace decided that it was just about time to close the curtain on his celebrated driving career. With 55 victories, 36 poles and one Winston Cup title to his credit over a 24-year NASCAR career, the kid from St. Louis had accomplished a lot. "I want to go out on the top of my game," Wallace said. "I want to go out a champion, a front-runner. I still feel like I'm at the top of my game. I've had a wonderful career. I'm proud of all of my accomplishments."

Rather than retire immediately, however, Wallace announced that he would compete through the end of the 2005 season. With support from his longtime backer, Miller Brewing, this farewell tour was known as "Rusty's Last Call," and it gave the popular driver an opportunity to say goodbye and thank-you to the legions of fans that had enthusiastically supported him throughout his career. "I've made a lot of fans happy but there's one thing I know for sure," he said. "Without me spending a lot of time with the fans and the fans supporting me, I couldn't have got where I am today, so I want to thank all the fans for supporting me. A lot of them have pleaded with me not to retire, but it's time. I feel it. It's the right time and I know I'm doing the right thing, and I feel good about it."

The only thing that threatened to put a damper on Wallace's farewell season was an unfortunate rift that had surfaced between Rusty and teammate Ryan Newman. If there had been any problems between the two of them before the end of the 2004 season, they were well concealed. But an on-track incident in the fall Martinsville race led to an ugly post-race fender-banging episode between the two Penske drivers. "Above all, what I want is some respect," Wallace said of the situation. "I remember when this thing was a dirt field with 20 guys working and now it's a team bringing in a lot of money, employing a lot of people. I'm not in the mood for dealing with no respect." Wallace was referring, of course, to the fact that he, along with Don Miller and

Roger Penske had built the Penske-South program from scratch. He had an enormous amount of sweat equity invested in this team, and while he certainly didn't expect Newman to do him any favors on the racetrack, he also didn't expect to be getting pushed around by his junior teammate. One thing was certain—Roger Penske wouldn't let the situation be a problem that threatened his prospects for winning a Nextel Cup title.

2005-2006, Dodge Charger

Penske Racing South again fielded three Nextel Cup teams for the 2005 season. Chrysler Corporation was reintroducing its famous "Charger" nameplate, and elected to run this new model in NASCAR, replacing the Intrepid, although the model change should have been virtually insignificant under NASCAR's modern-day template specifications. Rusty Wallace was back for his final season in the familiar #2 Miller-Lite Dodge and Ryan Newman returned in his #12 Alltel-sponsored Charger. Roger Penske signed 2001 Craftsman Truck series Rookie-of-the-Year Travis Kvapil to replace Brendan Gaughan in his third car. In addition to preparing for Wallace's impending retirement, it was becoming imperative to run multiple cars to be competitive in Nextel Cup, where other top teams were fielding four and even five entries.

NASCAR's "Chase for the Nextel Cup" concept, which seemed to be generally successful at meeting the corporate objectives in its debut season, was back again in 2005; and this time, it obviously played a greater role in the racing strategy. Clearly, there were two distinct components to the new season. First, there was the regular-season "Race-for-the-Chase," which more than ever, put a premium on consistent top-10 finishes that would be necessary to earn a berth in the "playoffs." Then there was the much-hyped 10-race chase for the title at the end of the season.

The 2005 NASCAR season produced a number of surprises, not just for Penske Racing, but also for several of the other top Cup contenders. At Penske, probably the biggest surprise was an unexpectedly strong showing by the retiring Rusty Wallace. While some had written his final season off as a self-indulging farewell tour, the

For 2005, Dodge's NASCAR entry was the new Charger. Wallace's car sported a "Rusty's Last Call" logo, as long-time sponsor Miller Brewing saluted their driver in his final NASCAR season. *Pat Smith*

Penske-South founding partner showed that he still had the right stuff to be competitive against challengers half his age. Although he would close out his career without claiming another victory, Rusty impressed almost everyone in 2005 by running near the front of the field all year. By mid-season, he had climbed to fourth place in the standings, and at the 26-race cutoff point for the "Race for the Cup," the 48-year-old veteran found himself in third spot, just 10 points behind championship leader Tony Stewart and solidly positioned to challenge for a long-overdue second NASCAR title.

Ryan Newman, who was theoretically the more viable Penske championship contender, had a much more rocky season. Although he again led all challengers in number of pole positions by claiming the top starting spot eight times, Newman's season was another frustrat-

ing picture of inconsistency, as mechanical problems, numerous tire failures and other misfortunes regularly robbed him of certain top-10 results. Without a race victory through the first 25 events of the season, Newman found himself in 11th place in the standings with little hope of getting into the Chase. But this time luck intervened on his behalf, and with only a 12th place finish in the final pre-chase event at Richmond, Newman squeaked past a disappointed Jamie McMurray to claim the 10th and last slot in the "playoffs."

While Newman was struggling through the 2005 Cup season, he was having a field day in the NASCAR Busch Series, where he made nine appearances when scheduling allowed. In those nine starts, he claimed four poles, won six races, and recorded a total of eight top-10 finishes. It was a remarkable display of appar-

Ryan Newman had a frustrating 2005 season in the Alltel/Sony HDTV Penske Charger. He made the Chase for the Nextel Cup, but a string of late-season accidents, tire problems and engine failures derailed his championship hopes. *Pat Smith*

ently effortless domination, and probably a very gratifying reprieve from the frustration he was experiencing in the Cup series.

First-year Penske driver Travis Kvapil had a completely mediocre season. With only three top-10 finishes, Penske South's third wheel finished a very disappointing 33rd in the final Cup standings. After the end of the year, Roger Penske would announce that he planned to field only two cars in 2006, leaving Kvapil out of a job, and possibly putting Penske South's two-car operation at a disadvantage to the three-, four-, and five-car programs fielded by Roush Racing, Hendrick Motorsports, and other top teams.

The 2005 Chase for the Nextel Cup got off to a great start for the Penske team at Loudon, New Hampshire. Ryan Newman finally scored his first victory of the season, vaulting him from 10th to third position in the championship standings. Rusty Wallace also had a strong race at Loudon, finishing 6th but getting bumped from third to fourth on the charts. At Dover the following weekend, the good news continued. After winning the pole for the Cup race and scoring another Busch series victory on Saturday, Newman drove to a fifth-place finish on Sunday afternoon. Rusty Wallace fared even better, finishing third and jumping into second place in the standings, leaving only former champion Tony Stewart ahead of the two Penske teammates in the championship battle.

Newman kept the pressure on, finishing fourth at Charlotte and moving to within a hair of first place in the points. And even with his 25th-place finish, Rusty Wallace still clung to third position after Charlotte. Unfortunately, it was all downhill for both Penske drivers from that point on. Newman picked up only three more top-10 results in the remaining six races. It wasn't for lack of speed, as NASCAR's best qualifier earned front row starting positions in four of those six races. But when the green flag dropped, the No. 12 Alltel Dodge consistently faded back through the field. According to the Penske organization, as well as most of the other Dodge teams, there was an inherent problem with the front-end aerodynamics of the 2005 Charger. This problem was obviously not a factor when the Dodges were running in clean air, as witnessed by Ryan Newman's eight pole positions. But in traffic, it seemed to be a different story. Well before the end of the season, Dodge campaigners were petitioning NASCAR for some relief in the way of changes to the Charger's approved nose design, but the sanctioning body declined. To prove a point, Penske South parked the '05 Charger and put Ryan Newman in a 2004 Dodge Intrepid for the final race of the season at Homestead, and they were rewarded with a 7th-place finish. By that time, however, the game was long lost, as Newman had dropped back the 6th position in the final standings. An apparently matured Tony Stewart went on to win his second NASCAR Cup title.

Rusty Wallace wrapped up his season, along with his 25-year NASCAR Cup career, finishing 8th in the championship points. It was a very solid season for the departing veteran, who had rightfully earned the position of NASCAR's elder statesman. By this stage of his career, fans and competitors alike demonstrated a universal respect and affection for Wallace that is rarely witnessed in the sport of auto racing; in fact, it was vaguely reminiscent of the sentiment displayed toward Rick Mears near the end of his storied career.

Although he never won a championship in his 15 years with Penske Racing, Rusty Wallace was undoubtedly responsible more than anyone for the overall essence of Penske Racing South. Like Mark Donohue and Rick Mears before him, Rusty's combination of dedication, raw talent, and personal character contributed more to the success of the team than could ever be measured in mere dollars or racing championships. Once again, the Captain had been blessed to find exactly the right person at the right time.

Filling Wallace's driving suit would be no easy task. Midway through the 2005 season, Roger Penske announced that he had signed '04 Nextel Cup Champion Kurt Busch to join the team beginning with the 2007 season. Busch was still under contract with Roush Racing through 2006, and Jack Roush initially expressed no interest in releasing his champion driver any earlier than necessary. But prior to the end of the year, other driver moves fell into place, and Busch was able to gain an early release from his contract after all.

Kurt Busch was an improbable choice to replace Rusty Wallace. Although his talent was never a question, Busch's attitude and behavior had not exactly been exemplary during his NASCAR career. He'd had a less-than-perfect relationship with the Roush Racing organization, which ended with Busch being benched for the final two races of the 2005 season after a high-profile traffic arrest. "Kurt was a challenge at one time or another for everyone on this team," Jack Roush said afterward. "He had used up his equity with his sponsors and he had used up his equity with me….He is an extraordinary talent, but he has had trouble dealing with the realities of normal social behavior." That is hardly the description of a typical Penske team driver. There was no doubt that Mr. Busch would either get his act together quickly or find that he'd have a very short-lived career with the Captain.

After logging just one Nextel Cup victory during the entire 2005 season, there was a renewed sense of urgency to get the Penske NASCAR program back on track. Unfortunately, the much-anticipated turnaround was not going to be aided in any way by the Dodge Charger equipment that Ryan Newman and Kurt Busch would be campaigning. "It is almost unfathomable that an aerodynamically challenged Dodge can take anyone to the Cup." This was the discouraging, but widely shared pre-season prediction offered by writer Al Pearce in *Auto Week's* 2006 NASCAR Preview. As the season played out, the Dodge handicap would prove to be less dramatic than originally expected, but unfortunately, that wasn't going to mean that the Penske Racing Chargers would be spending a lot of time in the winner's circle.

As the new season opened in Daytona, the NASCAR community reflected on the five-year anniversary of the loss of Dale Earnhardt. Thankfully, the sport's safety record had been very good since that tragic final-lap accident in the 2001 "500." But defending series champion Tony Stewart, not normally known for his cautious or patient driving style, was making a lot of noise before the 2006 Daytona race about potentially deadly consequences of the unchecked practice of bump-drafting on NASCAR's big tracks. Stewart's comments prompted NASCAR officials to take action to implement penalties against drivers who were observed "intentionally" bumping others on the track. Ironically, Stewart would be one of the first victims of the new NASCAR rule, but his point was valid and appropriate.

For the Penske team, Daytona had to be considered an overall success. Ryan Newman and new teammate Kurt Busch ran near the front of the field for almost the entire race. Busch was ultimately eliminated just 12 laps from the scheduled finish after getting nudged into the wall by Jamie McMurray. McMurray then suffered a similar fate 10 laps later, bringing out a final caution flag and forcing the race into overtime. After the restart, Newman was running second behind Jimmie Johnson with Casey Mears on his back bumper as the leaders entered the final turn of the race. Hoping that fellow Dodge driver Mears would work with him, Newman attempted to pass Johnson on the outside, but Mears didn't go. He stayed in line behind the leader, effectively pushing Johnson's Chevrolet to victory and bumping Ryan Newman back to third. It was a missed opportunity for the much-maligned Dodge brand to shine. But on the positive side, this strong showing proved that the Dodge teams didn't need to be conceding anything just yet in terms of their 2006 championship ambitions.

A week after Daytona, Kurt Busch put his Charger on the pole at California Speedway, but finished a mediocre 16th, four spots ahead of teammate Newman. Las Vegas and Atlanta were forgettable, but then Bristol turned out to be a season highlight, albeit a controversial one. In the closing stages of the race, Kurt Busch found himself running second to Matt Kenseth and he admittedly bumped his former teammate, putting him sideways, to make the winning pass. "That's short-track racing at Bristol," Busch said afterward. With Ryan Newman not too far behind in 9th place, it was a rare good day for the whole team. Unfortunately, neither of the Penske drivers would see another top-10 finish until Busch took 7th at Talladega four races later. Newman picked up an 8th and a 6th the following two weeks, but then both cars were involved in accidents in the World 600 at Charlotte. Newman came back to win the pole at Dover—probably his favorite track on the circuit—but in the race he could only manage 14th place.

Kurt Busch had a mid-season streak of six top-10 finishes in the next seven races, including impressive second-place runs in both of the Pocono events. At that point Busch was 13th in the standings with still six races remaining to pick up three more spots and get himself into the Chase for the Nextel Cup. Unfortunately, his best result in those six races would be a 12th place at the Brickyard, ending his hopes of a 2006 championship run. Busch closed out the season with four top-10 finishes in the 10 Chase races, but still ended up 16th in the final Nextel Cup standings.

Ryan Newman's year turned out even worse than his new teammate's. Other than two poles, the third place at Daytona and a runner-up finish in June on the Infineon road course, Newman had little to get excited about, ending the year with only 7 top-10 results. For the first time in his five years with Penske he failed to win a race, and he ended up a dismal 18th in the final Cup standings.

How much of Penske South's disappointing 2006 performance could be blamed on the Dodge Charger was debatable. Although Chevrolet was the winningest manufacturer overall, young Kasey Kahne had a series-leading six victories on the season driving a Dodge, so the Charger was clearly capable of winning races. The challenge for the Penske team looking toward 2007 would be to understand why they couldn't get the same results from their Chrysler product.

Greenfield Gallery

CHAPTER 12
CART Indy Cars
Triumph to Tragedy
(1993 – 1999)

"With the PC-23, the [Penske] team achieved a dominance never previously seen in CART, or for that matter in the entire history of Championship Car racing in the United States." —Rick Shaffer, *CART, the First 20 Years*

As Penske Racing's Indy-car program entered the post-Rick Mears era in 1993, the team would be represented by an aging former champion and an unpredictable young charger. Emerson Fittipaldi was 46 years old now, and surely he was not far from his second and final retirement. Roger Penske certainly was hoping that Paul Tracy, despite his shaky start the previous year, could be groomed to fill the huge vacancy left by Mears. Only

time would tell. But for this season, the Captain was going to rely on these two interestingly diverse drivers to carry on the Penske Racing mission.

1993

For the new season, the Penske challenge would depend on an updated Penske-built chassis, the PC-22, powered by a new version of the Ilmor-Chevrolet engine. Although the Chevy struggled to run with the reincarnated Cosworth in the early part of the '92 season, diligent work by the Ilmor engineers and the Penske team had closed the gap considerably by the end of the season. The new Ilmor-Chevrolet Indy V-8C incorporated all the lessons learned during the difficult 1992 season and, hopefully, a couple more. The most noticeable change at Penske Racing, going into the 1993 season, was in the actual name of the team. From that point forward, they would be known as "Marlboro Team Penske," adopting the European convention of incorporating the sponsor's name.

CART gained a tremendous amount of credibility within the international racing community when reigning Formula-1 World Champion Nigel Mansell made the unprecedented decision to drive in the U.S.-based CART series rather than defend his world title in 1993. Mansell was a popular British champion, whose unconscionable defection to the "second-rate" Indy-car series was widely believed to be more the unintended result of an ugly Formula-1 power struggle than any burning passion on his part to drive in CART. But once the deal was done, he clearly decided to make the best of the situation. The end result was a wonderfully competitive and entertaining season that was witnessed by a world audience, instantly propelling CART to a status almost comparable to Formula One on the world stage. This was undoubtedly the pinnacle of series' existence.

Mansell drove for the Newmann-Haas team, replacing Michael Andretti who had parlayed his CART successes into an offer to drive as Ayrton Senna's teammate on the McLaren Formula-One team. Unfortunately for Michael, because of poor timing and a number of unfavorable circumstances that were beyond his control, his F1 career would be brief and undistinguished.

Penske Racing rolled out the evolutionary PC22 chassis for 1993 with an updated version of their Ilmor-Chevrolet engine. After enjoying several years of engine superiority with the Ilmor powerplant, a revitalized Cosworth motor had Penske Racing and the other Chevy teams scrambling. *Laini Peterson*

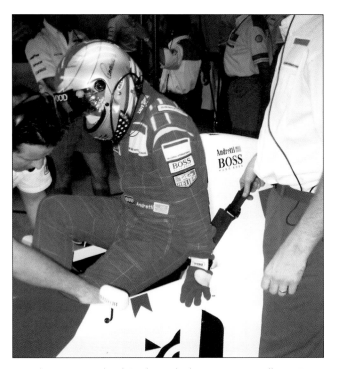

No, that's not Michael Andretti climbing into a Marlboro Team Penske Indy car. In 1993, Mario's son headed to Formula-1 in Europe where he teamed with Ayrton Senna at Marlboro-McLaren. Reigning World Champion Nigel Mansell replaced Andretti at Newman-Haas, focusing international attention on the CART series. *Alan Hummel*

At Newman-Haas, Mansell was teamed with the aging Mario Andretti, who was now 53 years old and clearly nearing the end of his storied career. Other than Mansell, the only other serious new contender was Brazilian Raul Boesel, racing for ex-Indy-car driver Dick Simon. Boesel, who was in his second CART season, would not manage to win a race, but he would make the podium several times and finish high in the championship standings.

The season opened as it had for the previous several years in Surfer's Paradise, Australia. Nigel Mansell made it known immediately that he was to be taken very seriously, winning the pole position and taking victory in his first ever Indy car race. Emerson Fittipaldi also served notice that he was not going to concede anything to his fellow ex-World Champion competitor. Fittipaldi qualified second on the grid and led 33 laps in the race, one more than Mansell, before settling for second place at the finish. Paul Tracy started in third spot, reinforcing the strong Team Penske position, but he fell out early with an electrical problem.

On the Phoenix mile, Mario Andretti came through to win what would turn out to be the last Indy-car victory of his career, making it two in a row for the Newman-Haas Lola-Cosworth combination. Rookie Mansell found the unfamiliar short oval to be more tricky than he expected, crashing heavily in practice and missing the race altogether with the resulting back injury. Paul Tracy started 5th and moved quickly to the front to lead 151 of the race's 200 laps. Unfortunately, he crashed while leading on the 161st lap. That left Emerson Fittipaldi in command until he too smacked the concrete just 10 laps later—two big missed opportunities for the Penske team.

Mansell was back to take the pole at Long Beach in April, but Paul Tracy finally came through to score his first CART win with an impressive victory over defending CART champion Bobby Rahal. Mansell was third, while Fittipaldi lost three laps and finished out of the points.

For Team Penske, practice and qualifying for the 1993 Indianapolis 500 went a lot like it did a year earlier. The Penske-Chevrolets were good, but didn't have

In 1993—his first full year with Penske Racing—Paul Tracy won two poles and scored a series-leading five races victories. Unfortunately, he let a lot of other good finishes get away because of avoidable mistakes. *Laini Peterson*

With former team leader Rick Mears in retirement and a young Paul Tracy searching for balance between fast and reckless, 46-year-old Emerson Fittalpaldi was the team's stabilizing influence in 1993. Emmo was motivated by the opportunity to race against defending F1 champion Nigel Mansell. *Laini Peterson*

quite enough to run with the Ford-Cosworths. On pole day, it would be the Target-Ganassi Racing Lola-Ford of 1990 winner Arie Luyendyk that would post the best time, nipping Mario Andretti's Lola-Ford by a half mile per hour. Next would be Raul Boesel and Scott Goodyear, both also piloting the popular Lola-Ford combination. The first Chevy-powered car on the grid was Al Unser Jr. in 5th spot. He was followed by the Penske-Chevrolet of Stefan Johansson, driving for Bettenhausen Racing. Paul Tracy started 7th and Emerson Fittipaldi, 9th, sandwiching rookie Nigel Mansell in the third row.

Unlike in many years past, no one dominated the '93 Indy 500. More than a dozen drivers moved in and out of the lead battle over the course of the race as yellow flags, pit stop strategies and changing handling shifted the balance of power. Mario Andretti moved to the front at the second round of pit stops and went on to lead the most laps in the race, but he faded late when his final set of tires didn't perform well. Nigel Mansell led the second-highest number of laps, but in the closing stages of the race, he was out-foxed on a restart, costing him any chance of victory. Neither of the Penske drivers led during the first half of the event, but they were never out of the hunt, although Fittipaldi did get a bad break on the timing of a yellow flag, falling almost a lap down to the leaders at one point. Just short of mid-race, Paul Tracy was battling for position with Scott Brayton when they touched, sending Tracy into the wall. The good news, aside from the fact that Tracy was unhurt, was that the resulting yellow flag allowed Emerson Fittipaldi to move back into contention.

In the late stages of the race, Nigel Mansell found himself in the lead, with Fittipaldi closing fast. Over his radio, Fittipaldi said to Roger Penske, "Don't talk to me anymore. Now I go racing!" On lap 181, Lyn St. James stalled on the track and the yellow light came out again to tow her car into the pits. On the restart, Emerson Fittipaldi and Arie Luyendyk gave Nigel Mansell a freshmen initiation he would never forget. As the green flag waved, Fittipaldi went to the inside of Mansell while Luyendyk shot to the outside, leaving the dazed rookie hanging on in third place. But he wasn't ready to concede just yet. Pushing as hard as he could, Mansell got a little wide in Turn Two on lap 193 and just brushed the wall. The yellow flag flew again, but Mansell didn't even pit; he just hoped his car would stay together for seven more laps. When the race went green for the last time on the 195th lap, Fittipaldi pulled away to his second and Team Penske's 9th Indianapolis 500 title. Luyendyk was second, Nigel Mansell third, Raul Boesel 4th and Mario Andretti 5th. This finishing order was representative of what was happening in Indy-car racing at that point in history, with non-American drivers moving to the forefront of the championship.

Milwaukee reclaimed its rightful spot following Indy on the schedule this year, and Nigel Mansell resumed his surprising rookie charge, taking the win over Raul Boesel and Emerson Fittipaldi. Paul Tracy led more than a quarter of the race, until he got together with Arie Luyendyk and Adrian Fernandez on lap 141 to end his day. Then Detroit was pretty much a write-off for the Penske team. Fittipaldi led the first 12 laps of the race, but later crashed and finished out of the points. Tracy led a third of the race, but he lost a lap with a blown tire and ended up finishing 9th. Things got better at Portland, where Fittipaldi, Mansell, and Tracy fought a spirited battle to finish in that order, a lap ahead of the remaining competition. Then, on the bumpy Cleveland runways, the Penske drivers came through with their first one-two finish of the season, with Paul Tracy dominating the day to score an 18-second victory over Emerson Fittipaldi. Championship frontrunner Nigel Mansell was third. By Toronto, the Penske team was beginning to look pretty intimidating again, with Tracy and Fittipaldi scoring a second consecutive one-two finish, keeping both drivers solidly in the battle for the CART title.

Home-track didn't prove to be any advantage at Michigan this year, with both Penske cars experiencing problems and finishing out of the points, giving winner Nigel Mansell a big boost in the points race. Then on the one-mile oval at Loudon, New Hampshire, Tracy led the most laps but followed Mansell across the line at the end, while Fittipaldi came home third. Tracy took another victory, his third in five races, at Elkhart Lake, with Mansell second and Fittipaldi losing points in 5th

spot. Then Al Unser Jr. won his first and only race of the season at Vancouver while Tracy, Fittipaldi, and Mansell all had less than banner days.

With just three races left, Emerson Fittipaldi turned up the heat at Mid-Ohio, taking his third win of the year over Robby Gordon, Scott Goodyear and Raul Boesel. Paul Tracy led the first 20 laps, but once again managed to crash while in front, ending his day early. Going into the penultimate race of the season at Nazareth, Paul Tracy was already mathematically eliminated from the title chase, which by that point had come down to a battle between the two former world champions, Nigel Mansell and Emerson Fittipaldi. Mansell locked up the title by winning Nazareth when Fittipaldi finished 5th. But the Penske team closed the season on a high note with another one-two finish at Laguna Seca, with Tracy again besting his senior teammate.

Overall, 1993 was a very good year for Team Penske, with 8 race wins between the two drivers, including the Indianapolis 500. Fittipaldi and Tracy finished second and third respectively in the CART title chase. Unfortunately, there were many missed opportunities, several of which could have propelled either Penske driver to the championship. Paul Tracy in particular, with 5 victories for the season, could easily have had two or three more wins had he managed to keep the car on the racetrack. But then, as would become apparent in the years that followed, that just wouldn't be Paul Tracy's style. And that was a problem that Roger Penske would eventually have to deal with.

1994

For 1994, both Emerson Fittipaldi and Paul Tracy were back in Marlboro-Penskes, but the Captain had managed to make it even more interesting, convincing Phillip-Morris to bankroll a third entry for the new season. By this time Penske had probably already realized that Paul Tracy, though an exciting and talented driver, was never going to fill the "lead driver" role that had been vacated by Rick Mears a year earlier. To do that, he turned to yet another member of the Unser family, Al Jr. "Little Al," at 31 years of age, had already won the Indianapolis 500 and a CART national championship. Over

Al Unser Jr. became the third member of the famous racing family to drive for the Penske team. At the still-young age of 31, "Little Al" was already a 10-year Indy car veteran with an Indianapolis 500 ring and a CART national championship to his credit. Unser would go on to be the team leader through the end of the decade.

Laini Peterson

the previous two seasons, however, the Galles Racing Team had struggled, and Al Jr. had managed only two wins. He was ready for a better opportunity, and Roger Penske believed that this young charger could bring the stability necessary not only to win races, but hopefully the team's first CART championship in 8 years.

In the chassis department, the Penske team would field the new PC-23, a considerably improved redesign of the 1993 car. For the 15 CART-sanctioned races, the three Marlboro-Penske PC-23's would be powered by an updated version of the Ilmor V-8, although it would no longer be called a "Chevrolet," as GM had decided to drop its support of the program. For the one USAC-sanctioned race, the Indianapolis 500, Roger Penske executed a top-secret design and development program that resulted in the most incredible unfair advantage in the history of his team. In partnership with Mercedes-Benz and Ilmor Engineering, Team Penske created an engine exclusively for the Indianapolis 500, taking advantage of a loophole in the rulebook that allowed pushrod engines to operate with a higher turbocharger pressure than "conventional" overhead camshaft racing engines. This rule was designed by USAC as a handicap for stock-block based engines in an effort to encourage more involvement from U.S. automakers and to help control escalating technology costs. The loophole that Penske exploited was the fact that the rules did not specifically limit the pushrod advantage to only stock-block engines. There was nothing but cost that prevented a team from developing its own new racing engine based on antiquated pushrod technology. Of course, the prospect of someone actually doing this, when the design could be used for only one race, the Indy 500, seemed implausible—to everyone but Roger Penske. After watching the low-budget Buick-powered entries steal the spotlight in Indy qualifying over the previous several years, the Captain hatched a plan to build a brand new engine, called the Mercedes-Benz V-8, which would turn Indy upside-down in 1994.

The project was a collaborative effort between Penske's Ilmor Engineering team and the German automaker. All work was carried out with utmost secrecy, with even Penske team members being informed on a need-to-know basis. In late January of 1994, the engine was ready to be tested in a racecar for the first time. "We didn't have transient dynos in those days, so we had to run that car," said Penske. "I think one thing we have to give Paul [Tracy] a lot of credit for….He was out running that car with a snowmobile suit on." This initial testing was done at the Penske-owned Nazareth Speedway in weather that was so bad that they had to plow two feet of snow from the track before they could even start. The new engine immediately showed incredible potential, but suffered from typical reliability problems. In the relatively short time that remained before its Indianapolis debut, however, these problems were addressed and resolved. It wasn't until mid-April, the very last possible moment, that Penske announced this program to the world. By then, it was too late for anyone to do anything about it.

While auto racing's version of the Manhattan Project was unfolding behind closed doors at Penske's shop, the regular CART season launched on March 20th in Surfers Paradise, Australia. In a race that was delayed and then shortened because of heavy rains, Michael Andretti, who was back in CART after an unhappy and unsuccessful year in Formula-1, prevailed over Emerson Fittipaldi and his father, Mario. Paul Tracy and Al Unser Jr. both experienced electrical problems and did not finish. The results of this race would prove to be atypical of the 1994 CART season.

The Penske steamroller hit its stride in the season's second race, on the Phoenix mile. Emerson Fittipaldi led the most laps and took the victory over his new teammate, Al Unser Jr. Paul Tracy led the second-highest number of laps, but as he had done so many times before, managed to crash while leading the race. Otherwise, it might well have been a Team Penske 1-2-3 finish.

Next on the calendar was Long Beach, a track that Al Unser Jr. loved. The Penske teammates qualified 1-2-3 with Tracy on the pole, Unser second and Fittipaldi third. Together, they led 103 of the race's 105 laps. Both Tracy and Fittipaldi would experience early gearbox problems, but Unser survived to score a fairly easy victory over Nigel Mansell.

Emerson Fittipaldi leads Paul Tracy at Long Beach in 1994. Both would retire with gearbox problems, but new teammate Al Unser Jr. went on to win the race. *Laini Peterson*

Emerson Fittipaldi's Penske PC23-Chevy races with Davy Jones in A.J. Foyt's Lola-Ford at Long Beach. *Laini Peterson*

In the first three races of the season, the Penske team had already scored two convincing victories, which normally would have made them the favorites going into Indianapolis. And this year, they had the secret weapon—the 209 cid Mercedes-Benz V-8 pushrod engine, with its 55 inches of turbocharger boost pressure. This month of May appeared from the beginning to be nothing less than a Team Penske landslide. After Raul Boesel posted a 230+ mph lap early in practice, Emerson Fittipaldi came back with a speed of 230.438, which held as the fastest unofficial speed of the month. Going into the first weekend of qualifying, it looked entirely possible, almost probable, that Team Penske would repeat the unique feat of putting three cars on the front row of the Indy starting grid, as they had done in 1988 with Mears, Sullivan and Al Unser Sr. Unfortunately, Paul Tracy threw a monkey wrench into that plan with a Friday-the-13th practice crash the day before qualifying started. He didn't receive medical clearance to drive until two days later, making him ineligible to challenge for the front spots on the grid.

Al Unser Jr., who Roger Penske would later admit was never a particularly good qualifier, turned in the early fast time in pole day qualifying, with a four-lap average speed of 228.011 mph. Raul Boesel, who had been very quick all week, was right behind him at 227.618. But weather would intervene, as rains would close the track before the final 12 drivers in the initial qualifying line got a chance to make their runs. Therefore, under the Indianapolis 500's unique and complex qualifying rules, these 12 drivers, which included Emerson Fittipaldi, would still be eligible as "first-day" qualifiers when time trials resumed on Sunday. Fittipaldi had been the odds-on favorite to win the pole based on his consistently fast practice times during the preceding week. Weather on Sunday, however, was hot and humid, conditions that just choke the horsepower out of the turbocharged racing engines. A very disappointed Fittipaldi could manage no better than 227.303 mph when he made his run, good enough for the outside of the front row, but not the pole. Paul Tracy later completed a very respectable run at 222.7 mph, but would start well back in 25th position because he was not an official "Day-1" qualifier.

The race, which Roger Penske would years later cite as his favorite Indianapolis 500 victory, was a display of total domination by the red and white Marlboro-Team Penske cars. Paul Tracy, unfortunately, encountered a turbocharger problem and dropped out early, but the other two Penske entries had the field covered from start to finish. With the exception of 7 laps that were led by future world champion Jacques Villeneuve, Emerson Fittipalid and Al Unser Jr. were in control for

the entire race. Fittipaldi seemed to have the strongest hand, pacing 145 laps compared to Unser's 48. With 20 laps remaining in the event, Fittipaldi put a lap on his teammate and the rest of the field. But two laps later, Unser came back in traffic and unlapped himself. Fittipaldi followed his younger teammate for the next three circuits, waiting for the right opportunity to repass. Then, going into turn 4 on lap 185, the Brazilian made a foolish mistake. He went too low and hit the "rumble strips" that are designed to keep cars from running on the safety apron at the bottom of the racetrack. Fittipaldi's car broke loose and he slid up and smacked the outside concrete wall, ending one of the most dominating runs in Indy history. Had it not been for the fact that there was another Penske entry right there to inherit the lead, it would have been a devastating blow for the team. But Al Unser Jr. wouldn't make any mistakes. He cautiously threaded his way through one more yellow flag to take his second Indy 500 victory. It was the second in a row for the Penske team, and their 10th overall. It was a very gratifying reward for the extraordinary effort and cost that went into the special Mercedes-Ilmor engine program, a classic Team Penske unfair advantage, executed to perfection. It was so perfect in fact that the United States Auto Club and the Indianapolis Motor Speedway acted immediately to ban the engine from future competition. The rules were changed to exclude the turbocharger boost advantage from non-stock-block engines. Surely the Captain was disappointed by the decision, but probably not completely surprised. It wasn't the first time that a rulebook had been rewritten solely to constrain the ingenuity of the Team Penske engineers. As with the Can-Am turbo-Porsche and the single-seat Zerex Special, this was simply a case of the sanctioning organization struggling to maintain a competitive environment in the face of Penske's extraordinary technological innovation. It's like a high-stakes game of poker—a game that Roger Penske wins more often than not.

When the CART schedule picked up at Milwaukee, the Penske cars were refitted with their "conventional" Ilmor engines, theoretically eliminating the overwhelming advantage they'd enjoyed during the month of May

The PC23—seen here in road course trim at Elkhart Lake—was the most successful Penske-designed chassis ever. With it, drivers Al Unser Jr., Emerson Fittipaldi and Paul Tracy won 12 of 16 races and finished 1-2-3 in the 1994 CART championship. Five times they swept the podium, finishing first, second and third. Collectively, they won 10 poles and they qualified 1-2-3 seven times. *Larry Arnt*

at Indy. But when Al Unser Jr., Emerson Fittipaldi, and Paul Tracy combined to lead every single lap on their way to a 1-2-3 Penske finish at the historic one-mile track, it became immediately apparent that this was not going to be just any ordinary season. Rick Shaffer later wrote in his book, *CART, the First 20 Years*, "With the PC-23, the [Penske] team achieved a dominance never previously seen in CART, or for that matter in the entire history of Championship Car racing in the United States." Milwaukee made it four wins in a row for the Penske team. Paul Tracy continued the streak at Detroit, winning over Fittipaldi. Then it was another 1-2-3 Penske finish at Portland, with Unser Jr. leading the way, Fittipaldi second and Tracy in third. Unser won again at Cleveland, his fourth of the season and an unbelievable 7th consecutive victory for the team.

The winning streak was finally broken in Toronto where Michael Andretti prevailed over Bobby Rahal,

with Emerson Fittipaldi third and Paul Tracy 5th. Unser lasted only two laps there before losing an engine. The temporary setback continued at Michigan, where all three Penske drivers suffered mechanical problems and finished poorly. But on the road course at Mid-Ohio, the team came back with a vengeance, posting its third 1-2-3 finish of the season, with Unser winning over Tracy and Fittipaldi. Then, to prove that they could do it at any time and any track, they repeated the sweep on the mile oval in Loudon, New Hampshire. Al Unser Jr. won his third in a row and 8th of the season at Vancouver, while both Emerson Fittipaldi and Paul Tracy were sidelined as a result of contact with Nigel Mansell in two separate incidents.

Young Canadian Jacques Villeneuve won at Elkhart Lake over Unser Jr. and Fittipaldi. But the Penske drivers responded with force at Nazareth, scoring the team's 5th 1-2-3 finish of the year, with Paul Tracy taking the victory over teammates Unser Jr. and Fittipaldi. Tracy then continued his late-season charge, taking the pole and leading every lap to win the final race at Laguna Seca. Fittipaldi came home 4th and Unser dropped out with a gearbox problem.

Al Unser Jr. won the CART championship. Emerson Fittipaldi was second and Paul Tracy third in the standings. The statistics for the season were remarkable. The Penske team won 12 of the 16 races. Five times they swept the podium, finishing first, second and third. Collectively, they won 10 poles and they qualified 1-2-3 seven times. It was a season of domination reminiscent of Penske Racing's old Trans-Am and Can-Am days. It seemed at the end of 1994 that Team Penske was invincible. Betting against a similar outcome for the following year would have seemed imprudent. Nobody could have foreseen the problems that lay just ahead.

1995

1995 was a season of change for both Team Penske and CART. Coming off his team's most successful year ever, Roger Penske scaled back his effort to two drivers for the new season. Paul Tracy, despite his three victories, four poles and third-place in the 1994 CART championship, was out of a job—sort of. Penske was convinced that the hard-charging, accident-prone sophomore had raw talent, but he was getting tired of paying the repair bills while Tracy matured and refined that talent to the point that he could consistently keep his car off the concrete walls. Fortunately, the Captain was able to work out a deal whereby Tracy was "loaned" to Newman-Haas Racing for the 1995 season, retaining the option to bring the him back the following year. Tracy would take Nigel Mansell's seat at Newman-Haas, as the 1993 rookie champion decided to return to Europe after a less-than-gratifying second year in the U.S. series. Tracy's teammate would be Michael Andretti, who was back at Newman-Haas after spending the '94 season with the Target-Ganassi team. Mario Andretti, at age of 54, had finally decided to end his illustrious career at the end of the 1994 season, vacating that prized seat at Newman-Haas.

Al Unser Jr. and Emerson Fittipaldi would be pilot-ing new Penske PC-24s with Mercedes-Ilmor engines, as the German automaker's 3-point star badge now replaced Chevrolet's bowtie on the Ilmor engine's valve covers. In addition to the formidable Newman-Haas team, other competition in 1995 came from Canadian Jacques Villeneuve with Players-Team Green, Robby Gordon who was driving for former Team Penske crew chief Derrick Walker, and former series champion Bobby Rahal.

In addition to the variety of new teams and drivers that were coming to the forefront in the Indy-car series, CART also saw new engine, chassis and tire manufacturers entering the fray in 1995. The Ford-Cosworth was now the most prevalent engine in the series, with the Mercedes-Ilmor losing ground fast. In 1994, Japanese automaker Honda had debuted its new Indy-car engine in the Rahal-Hogan team cars with limited success. For '95, the Honda program moved to the new Tasman and Comptech teams. Although the end-of-season statistics would not be overly impressive, a Honda-powered racecar driven by Scott Goodyear very nearly won the Indianapolis 500, taking the checkered flag ahead of official winner Jacques Villeneuve only to be disqualified for passing the pace car on a late-race restart that was botched by the Speedway. But despite that disappointment, Honda's day was just around the corner.

Also in its second year of competition was the Reynard chassis. Like March and Lola, Reynard was a European "kit-car" manufacturer of open-wheel racecars that had enjoyed success in many lower-level racing classes. Michael Andretti had driven a Reynard to two victories in 1994, although these successes were overshadowed in the season of Penske domination. By '95 however, the Reynard would be the new chassis of choice, accounting for almost half of the Indianapolis 500 starting grid.

The final significant equipment development for the new season was the return of the Firestone Tire Company after a 20-year absence from Indy-car racing. Over that period of time, Goodyear had enjoyed a total monopoly in the sport. Shortly after Japanese tire manufacturer Bridgestone acquired Firestone in 1990 they embarked on an ambitious program to bring the Firestone brand back to its former glory in Indy-car racing. To ensure that their return was an immediate and unqualified success, Bridgestone-Firestone contracted with Patrick Racing and driver Scott Pruett to take a one-year sabbatical from CART in order to devote full attention to the development and testing of its new tires. For the first season, Firestone supplied only four full-time teams, with Patrick Racing being the only established contender. Yet by the end of the year, it would be apparent that Firestone had done its homework, and by 1996, starting grids would be nearly evenly split between Goodyear and Firestone-shod racecars.

The 1995 season opened on a new 1.8-mile road course running through the city streets of Miami, Florida. From the vantage point of the Penske Racing team, the change from CART's season finale at Laguna Seca just 4 months earlier could not have been more dramatic. Al Unser Jr. and Emerson Fittipaldi qualified their Mercedes-powered Penskes 9th and 16th respectively, while the Ford-Cosworths and Reynards dominated the front of the field. Jacques Villeneuve won the race over Mauricio Gugelmin, both driving Ford-powered Reynards. Unser Jr. struggled to a 15th-place finish while Fittipaldi dropped out early with an engine problem. It was a disappointing start to what was going to be a difficult year for Team Penske.

Australia was a little better, as Unser and Fittipaldi qualified third and fourth, but failed to show much in the race itself. Unser finished 6th while Fittipaldi dropped out again, this time with electrical problems. To make matters worse, Team Penske reject, Paul Tracy, won the event for the Newman-Haas team. Emerson Fittipaldi finally finished a race at Phoenix, leading 78 laps and coming home in third place behind Robby Gordon and Michael Andretti. Unser finished 8th, three laps off the pace.

Finally at Long Beach, a track where Al Unser Jr. always seemed to be at his best, Team Penske found its way into the winner's circle for the first time in 1995. Unser led nearly three-quarters of the race, posting a convincing 23-second victory over the Firestone-shod Lola-Ford of Scott Pruett. Fittipaldi had another tough day, losing an engine 20 laps from the end of the race and finishing out of the points.

In what could have been considered a Team Penske rally, Fittipaldi came back two weeks later to win on the Nazareth one-mile tri-oval. It was a less-than-convincing victory, however, as he inherited the lead on the very last lap when Eddie Cheever ran out of fuel. Al Jr. had a bad day, finishing two laps off the pace in 13th spot.

Then came Indy. A year earlier, with the now-banned pushrod Mercedes-Ilmor, Team Penske had dominated the month of May as no team had ever done in the 78-year history of the world's greatest auto race. But it would be an unimaginably different story in 1995. With five races already in the record books before the CART teams arrived for opening day of Indy 500 practice, it was clear that the Penske team would not have the advantage they'd enjoyed the year before. But, with two wins in those five races, nobody could have anticipated that the Penske drivers would have trouble just qualifying for the 33-car starting field. It was going to be a very unusual month.

Roger Penske entered four PC-24 Mercedes-Ilmor cars for the 500, two each for drivers Al Unser Jr. and Emerson Fittipaldi. Once again, the Buick stock-block-powered cars posted the fastest laps in practice. John Menard's drivers, Scott Brayton and 1990 winner Arie Luyendyk ran over 234 mph, while the Penske drivers struggled in the low 220s. Eventually, Brayton and Luyendyk would take the top two spots on the grid and Scott Goodyear, driving a Honda-powered Reynard with Firestone tires, would fill out the front row. The highest-qualifying Mercedes-Ilmor car was Roberto Guerrero, who started in the fifth row in 13th position. In total, only five Mercedes-Ilmor cars made the field, and none of them belonged to Roger Penske.

In this new era of Indy-car technology, there were three components that determined the competitiveness of a racecar: chassis, engine, and now tires. It quickly became apparent that the best package for Indianapolis, discounting the fast but notoriously unreliable Buick-powered entries, was a Honda-powered Reynard on Firestone rubber. Roger Penske's problem was that he didn't have any of those components. In fact, Penske's cars, it seemed, had the weakest of the available options in every category. The Reynards and Lolas both looked superior to the PC-24 chassis. Honda and Ford-Cosworth had the power advantage over the aging Mercedes-Ilmor engine. And newcomer Firestone had clearly provided a tire that was better suited for the Indianapolis Speedway than Goodyear. Handicapped with all these weak links, Al Unser Jr. and Emerson Fittipaldi could not find enough speed to assure them a starting spot in the field, let alone any possibility of making a run for the pole.

Faced with this problem that he had encountered twice before, Roger Penske did what he had done so successfully on both of those previous occasions. He reluctantly scrapped his own equipment and purchased kit-car chassis from his competitors. First, he tried the Mercedes engine in a Reynard. When that didn't show immediate promise, he purchased Bobby Rahal's two backup Lolas. On the second weekend of qualifying, Unser and Fittipaldi both made qualifying attempts below 225 mph, too slow to make the field. In the final hour on "Bump Day," Fittipaldi ran three laps at just over 225, but Roger Penske waved off the run, believing that it was still not fast enough and thinking they could find a few more tenths of a mile-per-hour as the track cooled in the closing minutes of the final session. Unfortunately, with other cars already in the qualifying line, Fittipaldi never got the chance to get back on the track before the day ended at 5:00 PM. It was almost beyond comprehension—Team Penske, winner of a record 10 Indianapolis 500s including the previous two, had failed to qualify for the race. Ironically, the speed that Fittipaldi had been running on his aborted final attempt would have been just fast enough to put him in the show after all. Roger Penske had made a judgment call, and it turned out to be a costly mistake. Fittipaldi was furious. The emotional Brazilian blamed Penske, and the relationship between the two men was never quite the same afterwards. It was one of the team's darkest hours. And unfortunately, because of political circumstances that were just beginning to develop, it would turn out to be a long time before Roger Penske and his team got the chance to make things right again at the Speedway.

Lesser teams might have been demoralized by the adversity of the Indy failure, but Team Penske responded with typical professionalism and class. A week after being a "500" spectator for the first time since 1968, Roger Penske took his team, with their PC-24 chassis and Mercedes-Ilmor engines to Milwaukee and very nearly won the race. Al Unser Jr. led 120 of the 200 laps before ultimately finishing a close second to Paul Tracy. Fittipaldi qualified well at Milwaukee, but never led and took himself out with a single-car crash on lap 122. Unser had another respectable race in Detroit, leading nearly half of the event before dropping back to a 5th place finish. Fittipaldi, meanwhile, gave another uninspired performance, qualifying 17th and finishing 10th.

Portland was an interesting race. Al Unser Jr. qualified third on the grid, led a race-high 76 laps, and scored a decisive 28-second win over Jimmy Vasser's Target-Ganassi Reynard-Ford. With the very same team and equipment, Emerson Fittipaldi qualified 15th and was never a factor in the race before dropping out by the halfway point. While the PC-24/Mercedes/Goodyear combination was clearly not the package of choice in the 1995 CART season, Unser had obviously resolved to make the best of it while his teammate, apparently still seething over the Indy debacle, couldn't seem to get his focus back. Unfortunately for Emerson Fittipaldi and the team that supported him, it was not a problem that would be resolved anytime soon. As the rest of the '95 CART season played out, Al Unser Jr. was normally competitive and would be in the championship battle to the end. Emerson Fittipaldi, on the other hand, would not have another podium finish for the remainder of the year. In fact, as it would turn out, Fittipaldi had already won the last race of his career.

After early wrecks at Elkhart Lake and Toronto and a transmission failure at Cleveland, Al Unser rebounded with a strong runner-up finish in the Michigan 500 followed by a solid win on the road course at Mid-Ohio. Then there was a third-place podium at Loudon, New Hampshire, and another impressive road course win in Vancouver. Going into the final race of the season at Laguna Seca, Unser Jr. still had a mathematical chance of catching Jacques Villeneuve for the championship.

His 6th place finish, however, wasn't quite enough, and the '94 champion fell 11 points short of defending his CART title. All in all, that really wasn't a bad outcome considering the desperate position that the team was in earlier in the season. Overall, Unser and Fittipaldi combined to score 5 victories for the season—a far cry from the 12 wins posted one year earlier, but in a season when the team failed to even qualify for the Indy 500, this was a fairly commendable achievement.

By the time that Jacques Villeneuve was crowned the 1995 CART champion, there was a new civil war reaching crisis proportions in Indy-car racing. And unlike the relatively quick and bloodless coup that resulted in CART taking control of the sport from the United States Auto Club 18 years earlier, this new conflict was going to be long, costly, and extremely detrimental to the health of American open-wheel racing. After enjoying its most successful seasons ever in 1993 and 1994, CART now began a downward spiral that would ultimately lead to its demise some ten years later. How things got to this point is sad story of ego, greed and gross miscalculation on the part of many players.

It's hard to say specifically where this latest unrest actually originated. As with most major conflicts, it was a complex situation that was driven by a variety of legitimate issues and visions, all related to the future of American Indy-car racing. When CART was formed and took control of the Indy-car series in 1979, almost everyone, including the drivers, team owners, promoters, sponsors, and fans, immediately sided with the new organization, realizing that CART truly offered a better future for their sport. USAC had allowed the series to deteriorate into little more than a state fair sideshow, with the exception of its crown jewel, the Indianapolis 500. There was an imminent danger in the late 1970s that America's once-premiere auto racing series might simply vanish for lack of interest and leadership.

In 1994, when the real potential of another Indy-car split first surfaced, there was no such imminent danger. In fact, CART's business was booming. Coming off of the boost provided by Nigel Mansell's two seasons with Newman-Haas, CART had a healthy new international fan base, new drivers, new teams, new manufacturers,

and more available venues than the schedule could realistically accommodate. From a business standpoint, it was hard to imagine a better situation for almost all concerned. Even the Indianapolis Motor Speedway, which was still operating independently, but in "cooperation" with CART, was flourishing as never before. All 250,000+ seats were sold out every year. These tickets were in such high demand that they were handed down in wills, like family heirlooms. In addition to the grandstand seats, another 150,000 or more infield tickets were sold annually, making the Indianapolis 500 the world's biggest single-day spectator event year after year. The world's second biggest event, which drew some 250,000 spectators annually, was pole day qualifying for the Indy race. The whole month of May was a phenomenon, which dwarfed everything including the Super Bowl in fan support. So it seemed that the last thing that anybody would want was sweeping change.

But in March of 1994 Tony George, grandson of Tony Hulman Jr. and now president of the Indianapolis Motor Speedway, announced his intention to launch a new Indy-Car championship series that would include the Indianapolis 500. It didn't require a lot of reading between the lines to realize that this new series would be in direct competition with CART. Initially, this "threat" wasn't taken very seriously by anyone in the inner circle of Indy-Car racing. But when it became obvious over the next year that George was dead serious, and he was willing to spend huge amounts of his family's fortune to make this new series a reality, things got ugly fast.

After Tony Hulman died in 1977, there was a huge leadership void in the Indianapolis Motor Speedway front office. Hulman had operated this historic racetrack, which he had rebuilt from the dilapidated ruins of World War II neglect, with a personal passion that could never be replaced after his death. In fact, it was this void in large part, that allowed CART to so quickly take control of Indy-Car racing in the first place. After a year or so of token resistance by the new Speedway management, CART was pretty much able to call the shots regarding rules, specifications and other technical matters that governed the running of the Indianapolis 500. And that's how things remained until the late

1980s. But when Anton "Tony" George was elected president of Indianapolis Motor Speedway in 1990, he quickly signaled his intention to reclaim the authority and control that had been abdicated to CART over the previous decade. As a non-voting member of the CART Board of Directors, George was frequently in conflict with the decisions and general philosophy of the other board members. As CART continually became more biased toward road racing, foreign engine and chassis manufacturers, and ex-U.S. venues, George lobbied for Indy-Car racing to return to its roots. He wanted to see more oval tracks on the schedule, more American manufacturers and drivers involved, and he wanted to overhaul equipment specifications in an effort to contain the rapidly escalating costs associated with fielding a competitive team.

While his actions would ultimately make him the most vilified man in the world of auto racing, Tony George had valid concerns and suggestions. Although CART was apparently flourishing, by 1995 twenty-two of the 34 drivers who earned championship points were non-American. By the late 1990s, there were races in which Michael Andretti and Jimmy Vasser were the only Americans in the field. While diversity is undeniably a good thing, an American-based series would not be able to thrive indefinitely without American participants, and Tony George seemed to be one of the few people in a position of authority who recognized that fact.

CART's leadership, however, never seemed to take George's input very seriously. This was, in part, because of their own arrogance, and in part because of George's often-combative style. George was known for making hostile public statements that only served to further alienate his detractors. In a February 1990 interview in Indycar Racing, he issued his first subtle threat saying, "First and foremost we have to look out for what is in the best interest for the Indianapolis Motor Speedway. In the same way, we have to consider what's good for all motorsports, particularly Indianapolis-type racing. That's what our tradition has been built on—Indianapolis cars….We have to pursue the 500-mile race on it's own. It's our first priority….Only time will tell as to what direction [CART] racing goes. It's our hope that

it will remain a viable series. My guess is that it will. We have to keep all of our options open to us at this point."

Throughout the early 1990s, Tony George and the CART leadership made several attempts to find common ground where they could agree on the future direction of the sport, but little real progress was ever made. In January of 1994, George resigned his seat on CART's Board of Directors, and a month later announced the formation of his own series, which he said would begin with the 1996 season. In July, George announced the Board of Governors and the organizational structure of what he had now named "The Indy Racing League." One alarming detail that was disclosed in this July 1994 announcement was that the Indianapolis 500 would reserve a yet-to-be-determined number of starting positions for competitors who had participated in the other Indy Racing League (IRL) events. This, in effect, said that CART teams might have to take part in George's new series if they wanted to be reasonably assured of getting a spot in the Indy 500.

Over the next year, as George worked toward the launch of his new enterprise, a verbal war waged between the CART faithful and the new IRL contingent. As more details emerged from the Indianapolis Motor Speedway office, it became very clear what Tony George was intending to do. With some conditions, 25 of the 33 starting spots in the "500" were to be allotted to IRL "regulars." That would leave only 8 "at-large" positions for all the CART teams to fight over. Unlike the failed attempt by the Speedway in 1979 to reject the entry applications of specific "unfriendly" CART teams, this new restriction could not be considered an unlawful lockout. Furthermore, if it had worked as George intended, it would have served to create a rift between the CART teams that made the cut and those that did not. It was truly a shrewd move on George's part. But in the end, for better or worse, it didn't work as he had hoped.

In October of 1995, when it was already a certainty that the inaugural IRL season was going to happen beginning with a January race on the brand new oval at Disney World, Tony George was feeling the heat from all directions. What people initially dismissed as an idle threat was now on the brink of being reality. And it was a reality that had the potential to literally destroy American Indy-car racing. In an effort to explain his position and justify this perilous course of action that he had initiated, George wrote this letter to the editor of the *Indianapolis Star*, which was published October 22, 1995:

"It is my hope to provide an understanding of the purpose and motivation behind the formation of the Indy Racing League. There is much controversy in this matter, expressed as anxiety and even animosity by certain members of the Indy racing community, several fans, and more than one journalist.

"In time, I hope the current wounds are healed and that these disagreements ultimately provide for clearer and stronger relationships throughout our sport. Later, I'll get into specific reasons why I believe so strongly in the formation of this league.

"Of immediate concern, though, is the unsettling rhetoric of threats, boycotts and an alternate race on May 26 as leveled by Championship Auto Racing Teams (CART) against both the Indianapolis 500 and the IRL. Other than to once again reiterate our almost daily, sincere invitation to the racing community that we consider all racers friends and that IRL events and the '500' are open to any legitimate team with a legal car and qualified driver, I cannot say how this will all turn out.

"What I can say, very sincerely, is that any and all teams that have competed in past '500s,' many of them CART franchisees, are 100 percent welcome to enter and compete in any of our IRL events. New entrants are welcome too. That said, I'm going to specifically address just a single, highly inaccurate word that has recently surfaced as CART's focal buzzword to describe its self-imposed predicament regarding the '500.' The word is 'lockout.'

"Let's make this clear: There is no lockout. What I believe to be the case is that CART, following an effort to eliminate the IRL and gain control of the Indianapolis 500, is in the uncomfortable position of having created deliberate and unnecessary conflicts from which it will not extricate itself.

"Those conflicts surfaced with CART's announcements

of technical specifications for its 1996 cars and of its 1996 schedule, both of which occurred well after the corresponding IRL information had been made public and put in place for our inaugural season.

"Probably 90 percent or more of the discussion (and cussing) has been aimed at the IRL's 75 percent-of-the-field qualifying incentive, the one that conditionally guarantees 25 spots in the Indianapolis 500 lineup to IRL competitors. Although we have not changed any of the four-day, speed-seeded qualifying format for the '500' with the fastest first-day qualifier, whoever it is, still on the pole, let me explain where the new qualifying criteria—which only affects who gets bumped—came from.

"The IRL qualifying incentives, bridging across different events, provide a new and interesting dimension to how starting fields are established because they provide a hard, venue-to-venue continuity. There is a positive side in terms of publicity and race-to-race interdependency to build the league's identity. But the down side is that if the '500' were to be a true league member, then the rule would have to apply to the 33-car Indy field as well. We were on the fence leaning away from that one until the middle of June.

"That was when CART announced its 1996 schedule. The components of our modest, five-race IRL schedule had been announced in January, April and late May, and each announcement was accompanied by an IRL promise not to create conflict with what we understood would be CART's schedule. We obviously hoped they would enter our races.

"On June 10, CART announced its 15-race 1996 schedule. Ultimately, four of its dates appeared to us to have been put deliberately in conflict with three important IRL dates: CART's Brazil and Australia races were placed one week before and one week after the IRL's announced Phoenix date of March 24, 1996; CART's Nazareth race was listed on April 28 against USAC's important Indy Rookie Orientation Program; and inexplicably, CART chose to schedule Elkhart Lake directly opposite the IRL's Aug. 18 New Hampshire race.

"Travel logistics virtually eliminate the possibility of any team running Brazil, Phoenix and Australia on consecutive weekends. While "ROP" (as USAC's rookie program is called) is not a highly publicized event, it is nonetheless well known in racing circles that it occurs a week before

opening day at Indianapolis, when the final preparations to the race track have been completed. All CART could say about its Elkhart Lake date was that it had always raced on that date (it hasn't) and besides, CART stated, it hadn't made any promises that it wouldn't conflict.

"What do you do if you are in our shoes? CART had obviously made a perfectly legal, free-market competition move to prevent its teams from participating in the opportunities presented by the IRL. At that point it became incumbent on us to respond in kind, and we did it with a carrot instead of a stick.

"On July 3, we announced $12 million in prize money for the five-race series, and qualifying criteria weighted toward teams that participate in IRL events. In August, we weighted our season championship points system very heavily toward consistent IRL participation. Plus we already had an agreement in place with ABC Sports for live television coverage of all five IRL races.

"These are strong, attractive incentives for open participation that in no way imply a lockout. Then as now, the IRL is designed for open inclusion of any and all competitors. It is unfortunate CART is forcing its members to choose.

"Then there is the equipment question. On Oct. 11, a CART car owner was quoted in The Star *sports section about the necessity for the IRL to adopt '96 CART equipment rules or else CART will be unable to compete in next year's Indianapolis 500. That is a true statement, sort of. The problem resulted from CART's decision last May to institute sweeping changes in its own '96 chassis specifications that it knew when it made them would effectively eliminate its cars from competing in the 1996 '500.' That was CART's decision, not ours, and I firmly believe the decision was motivated by CART's desire to stifle the development of the IRL by creating the burden on its members of redundant, expensive equipment.*

"It was, in my view, another free-market competition decision. I respect CART's right to compete against the IRL, although it was certainly not our original intent to compete against them. We wanted to coexist and not force anyone to choose sides. That is why in early March the IRL rescinded its own proposed sweeping changes in both chassis and engine specifications.

"At that time, CART told us they felt the IRL's proposed technical changes—which we had announced in 1994—would create hardship because they were too late for 1996 production and too expensive for teams because all new equipment would be required. We did not entirely agree with those assessments, but in the interest of removing obstacles to agreement, the IRL announced March 10 that for 1996 all applicable 1995 USAC and CART specifications would be observed. It was purely a move of appeasement on our part.

"Imagine our surprise when two months later, in mid-May, CART adopted changes in chassis specifications that were very close to what the IRL had rescinded in the interest of keeping peace in the family. While technical and safety improvements are the backbone of auto racing, it was obvious to me that CART's chassis change was motivated less by performance than by its political desire to prevent the IRL from conducting races in 1996. I was very disappointed by this, but it was not of our doing and we will stick to the commitments we made for 1996 rules.

"Chassis incompatibility and schedule conflicts: CART created both these problems after the IRL was on record as sincerely having tried to avoid them. The purpose of the IRL is to provide growth, stability and opportunity for open-wheel, oval track racing. That mission is certainly not intended to harm or control CART.

"In fact, it has nothing to do with CART. We simply do not want the Indianapolis 500 to be controlled by an outside group that does not have as its most important goal the future of Indianapolis type oval track racing. Not to mention a group that is based out of state and is far removed from the significance of the '500' in this community.

"It is often said that I am motivated by power and greed in forming the IRL. It certainly is not greed, because this is a very intense financial commitment for us to build a race track in Florida and establish proper league staffing and resources. The monetary payback, if there is any, will be over the long haul. On the subject of power, my desire is not now and never has been control of CART, IndyCar or the entire series of whatever cars run in the Indianapolis 500. The payback on that side is simply a peace of mind that comes from maintaining the sovereignty of this wonderful event.

"Far from wanting to run the sport, I'd love to see even the IRL develop an autonomy. There is much I would like to do in my life, but I'll be unable to enjoy any of it if the '500' is not secure.

"That's why the Indy Racing League was formed. I felt the long-term protection of the '500' depended on a solid series of top level open-wheel, oval track races. To that end, this league was created because CART provided no long-term guarantees to the '500' or to oval track racing. Nor has CART as an organization exhibited long-term stability, with four different board voting structures and four different chief executives just in the short five years I've been president of the Speedway.

"The Indianapolis 500 will not be controlled by CART. They are welcome to join us as competitors, but not to impose their will or their governing structure on the Speedway.

"Our timing in all of this was pretty good. The threat I feared might someday materialize —a CART sanction in a power move against the Speedway—is evidently upon us. Although you can argue that we brought it on ourselves this time, I am convinced it would have happened over some other issue at some other time. This time, though, we were in the middle of exercising some very important American ideals—those of free competition, open markets and entrepreneurship. We are in a position of strength, and we are steadfastly in a position to defend the future of the '500' with the Indy Racing League.

"It breaks my heart when I see CART drivers quoted as saying the '500' is 'just another race,' and I can't count the number of CART owners who have stated on various occasions that they would prefer to emasculate the month of May, and instead re-make the greatest automobile race meeting in the world into a single-weekend event. I would be ashamed if we let that happen here. It would be an incalculable loss for both the world of racing and the local community."

—Anton Hulman George / Indianapolis Motor Speedway President

In 1996, Roger Penske partnered with St. Louis businessman Carl Hogan to form Hogan-Penske Racing, a single-car program with Emerson Fittipaldi as the driver. Fittipaldi got the Penske PC25 chassis and the latest Ilmor-Mercedes engines, but the team operated independently of Penske Racing. *Peter Burke*

Not an unfamiliar sight in 1996, Paul Tracy takes his Penske PC25 for a spin in the Festival Curve at Portland. His unsuccessful attempt at completing a full 360 resulted in this impressive plume of vaporized Goodyear rubber. *Peter Burke*

In December of 1995, CART announced that, as a result of Tony George's "25/8" qualifying rule, its teams would not participate in the 1996 Indianapolis 500. Instead, they would compete in a new race called the "U.S. 500" to be staged at Roger Penske's Michigan International Speedway on the same date as Indy. While most still hoped that a resolution might be reached before the CART teams actually resorted to boycotting the Indianapolis 500, time was running out quickly. When the 1995 season ended, everyone knew that it could well be the end of an era.

1996

Al Unser Jr. was back in 1996 as Marlboro Team Penske's number-1 driver. During the off-season, Roger Penske had partnered with Carl Hogan, who had previously owned part of Bobby Rahal's operation, to form a new team that would be called Hogan-Penske Racing. This partnership, which lasted for only the 1996 season, operated semi-independently of Team Penske, although it would campaign the same new PC-25 chassis and updated Mercedes engines. Emerson Fittipaldi was named as the Hogan-Penske driver and sponsorship came from Marlboro-Latin America. Roger Penske's motivation for this venture may have been to find a way to distance the disgruntled Fittipaldi from his core operations, and at the same time, to open a seat so that he could bring Paul Tracy back from Newman-Haas.

Although much of it would be overlooked because of the ongoing political battle that commanded center stage throughout the 1996 season, this would be one of CART's most competitive championships ever. Several new teams and drivers would share the spotlight; and Target-Ganassi Racing, after several years of knocking at the door, would assert itself as a new dominant force in the series. Even more than in 1995, the combination of chassis, engine and tires played a critical role in the competitiveness of any team. Unfortunately, although there were improvements made to Penske's chassis and the Mercedes engine, when coupled with Goodyear tires, the new package as a whole seemed to be at a net loss relative to what many other teams rolled off the transporters at the beginning of the '96 season.

Target-Ganassi drivers Jimmy Vasser and Alex Zanardi had what seemed to be the optimum combination with a Reynard chassis, Honda engine and Firestone tires. Michael Andretti and his new teammate Christian Fittipaldi, nephew of Emerson, had Goodyear-shod Lola Fords. Gil de Ferran, who would drive for Team Penske in the not-too-distant future, was running Jim Hall's Reynard-Honda on Goodyear tires, while Bobby Rahal and his new teammate, Bryan Herta, went with a Reynard-Mercedes-Goodyear package. Outside of this group, the only other team to score a victory in the 1996 season was Tasman Racing, with its drivers Andre Ribeiro and Adrian Fernandez in Lola-Hondas with Firestone rubber.

Well before CART's season opened at the new 1.5-mile high-banked oval in Homestead, Florida, the Indy Racing League had already run its inaugural event, what might have been called the "Mickey Mouse 200," at Disney World. Twenty cars took the green flag, led by Buddy Lazier who was driving for Hemelgarn Racing. Other ex-CART drivers included Roberto Guerrero, Arie Luyendyk, Mike Groff, Lyn St. James, John Paul Jr., Eddie Cheever, Scott Sharp, and Scott Brayton. Of this group, only Guerrero, Paul and Luyendyk had ever won a CART race. The rest of the field was filled with a bunch of unknowns, including eventual winner Buzz Calkins, a 22-year-old college student. When CART started a healthy field of 27 cars at Homestead, very few people doubted that it would be only a matter of time before Tony George's IRL project would disappear for lack of interest.

Homestead started on a high note for Team Penske, as Paul Tracy won the pole and dominated the first 82 laps before being sidelined with a broken transmission. Al Unser Jr. never found the speed that Tracy had, qualifying a disappointing 13th and finishing 8th. Emerson Fittipaldi had a similarly unspectacular race in his debut with Hogan-Penske Racing, starting 12th and finishing 13th.

Although CART lost a couple of its traditional venues to the IRL, it had no trouble finding new tracks to host its events. The second race on the 1996 schedule took place on the new 1.8-mile oval in Rio de Janiero,

Brazil. Al Unser Jr. drove a steady, though not particularly competitive race here, finishing second to surprise winner Andre Ribeiro, who gave the passionate Brazilian fans a hometown winner, even if it wasn't a Fittipaldi. Tracy crashed and ended up 19th while Emerson Fittipaldi struggled to finish 11th.

After one more disappointing weekend in Australia, where Paul Tracy tore up yet another racecar, the Penske program rebounded somewhat at Long Beach. On his favorite track, Al Jr. managed a third-place podium finish, one spot ahead of teammate Tracy. Fittipaldi continued to struggle. Tracy then won his second pole of the season at Nazareth. He went on to lead most of the first half of the race before slipping to a 5th place finish, behind Unser and Fittipaldi. Michael Andretti won the race over rookie Greg Moore. But it was encouraging to see three Penske cars in the top five.

Then came Memorial Day weekend, and instead of going to Indiana, the CART crowd all headed to Brooklyn, Michigan, for the inaugural U.S. 500. This was a day that everyone, on both sides of the battle, had hoped would never come. But threatening rhetoric and actions from both camps had ensured that there would be no quick and easy resolution this time. During the month of May, Indy filled its 33-car field with a collection of second-string CART drivers and a bunch of lucky and daring wannabees. The Indy 500 starting field was comprised of 17 rookies, more than at any time in history except for the inaugural race in 1911. Many were not just Indy rookies, but were driving in their very first Indy-car race ever! It looked like a recipe for certain disaster.

There was tragedy, although maybe not where it might have been expected. Having already won the pole position, 14-year Indy veteran Scott Brayton was killed in a single-car practice crash, giving the IRL its first fatality. Almost surprisingly, the race itself started without incident, which is more than could be said for CART's Michigan event. A final lap crash at Indy, however, left Alessandro Zampedri in critical condition as Buddy Lazier was taking the checkered flag. Following Lazier in the final results were such household names as Davy Jones, Richie Hearn, Alessandro Zampedri,

Roberto Guerrero and Eliseo Salazar, the last three of which were involved in the last-lap wreck that nearly killed Zampedri.

Meanwhile, in Michigan, the "real" race drivers were embarrassing themselves with a 12-car pile-up on the first lap of the U.S. 500. The race was red-flagged before a lap was completed, which allowed for backup cars to be used on the restart. Fortunately all but one of the drivers involved were able to restart, avoiding what could have been a real public relations nightmare for CART. The Target-Ganassi team dominated the race, with Alex Zanardi leading 134 laps before his engine quit. Then Jimmy Vasser came on strong at the end to take the win, his fourth in the first six events. Paul Tracy and Al Unser Jr. both drove unremarkable races, finishing 7th and 8th respectively, while Emerson Fittipaldi posted a disappointing 10th-place result.

The Penske package seemed to work much better on the short ovals, with Tracy taking the pole on the Milwaukee mile and Fittipaldi starting second. Unser and Tracy combined to lead two thirds of the race, but it was Michael Andretti out in front when it really counted. Still, Unser finished second, Tracy third, and Fittipaldi fourth. It was definitely the best team showing in the first half of the season. There were still no checkmarks in the "win" column, but Al Jr.'s consistency was keeping him in the championship battle even with the undeniable equipment handicap.

Detroit was a bust, with all three Penske entries finishing out of the points. Unser came back to finish fourth at Portland, gaining ground on championship leader Jimmy Vasser who finished out of the points there. Then with another fourth place run at Cleveland, Unser pulled to within just three points of Vasser in the standings. But that would be as close as he'd get. At Toronto, Paul Tracy led the Penske team with his 5th-place finish, while Unser and Fittipaldi finished out of the top-12. Mexican driver Adrian Fernandez scored his first CART victory in this race, but there wasn't much celebrating when it was over. Rookie Jeff Krosnoff had a violent accident that brought the race to an early conclusion. Krosnoff and an unlucky course worker were both killed. It was CART's first driver fatality in 14 years, adding another black mark to this already difficult season.

Back in Michigan for the regular Michigan 500, the Penske team took a hit with driver injuries. First Paul Tracy crashed in practice, keeping him out of this race and Mid-Ohio two weeks later. Then on the first lap of the race, Emerson Fittipaldi had a career-ending accident, breaking his back and narrowly escaping paralysis. Although he considered returning after his recovery, he injured himself seriously again in an ultra-light flying accident back home in Brazil, and that ended any thoughts of a comeback. At the not-so-tender age of 49, "Emmo" retired from racing for the second and final time.

Al Unser Jr. went on to finish fourth at Michigan behind winner Andre Ribeiro, Bryan Herta, and Mauricio Gugelmin. At Mid-Ohio, Alex Zanardi dominated, leading all but four laps, which were covered by his teammate Jimmy Vasser. Roger Penske brought in Jan Magnussen to sub for the injured Paul Tracy, while Fittipaldi's car sat this one out. It was a frustrating weekend for the Penske team, with Unser and Magnussen qualifying 15th and 18th respectively, then struggling to finish 13th and 14th a couple laps behind the leaders. Unser would have placed much better had it not been for an encounter with Parker Johnstone just two laps from the finish. Unfortunately, there would be more days like this.

Paul Tracy was back for the Elkhart Lake race in mid-August, so Penske moved Jan Magnussen into the Penske-Hogan entry. This looked like it was going to be Al Unser's day. After qualifying only 12th, he worked his way to the front of the field by the midpoint of the race, and led most of the remainder of the event. He headed into the last lap with a comfortable lead over Michael Andretti, Bobby Rahal and Alex Zanardi only to have his Mercedes engine expire in a spectacular cloud of white smoke a mile from the checkered flag. He ended up being credited for 10th place, ending any shot he had at the championship. Magnussen crashed on the first lap and was scored in last place. Tracy had a less-terminal off-course excursion, losing time and settling for a 12th place finish.

With only two chances left for the Penske team to pick up a victory in 1996, CART headed for the streets of Vancouver. Al Unser turned in a strong performance again, but could do no better than 5th in a race that was dominated by Michael Andretti and Alex Zanardi. Both Tracy and Magnussen finished out of the points. Then in the finale at Laguna-Seca, Paul Tracy crashed once again while Unser struggled home in 16th spot, and Jan Magnussen led the Penske team with an undistinguished 8th-place finish. Although the Penske players had nothing to do with it, the finish of this Laguna race went down as one of the most exciting and controversial in racing history. Bobby Rahal's protégé, Brian Herta, had held the lead for 42 laps over the hard-charging rookie Alex Zanardi as they took the white flag. Heading into the "Corkscrew," a twisting, downhill roller coaster corner unlike anything else in auto racing, Zanardi made what has typically been described as a "banzai" dive to the inside of Herta's Reynard. A shocked Herta, who was hard on the brakes entering the apex of the turn, watched Zanardi's red Target-Ganassi Reynard shoot across the nose of his car, bounce over the curbing, through the landscaping, and then back onto the track at the exit of zig-zag corner. Herta, not wanting to be a victim of Zanardi's wild off-track adventure, eased off the throttle enough to let the dust clear. But to his amazement, Zanardi never slowed; and having survived his cross-country shortcut through the turn, he was now in the lead and pulling away to win the race. Fans who witnessed this exhilarating display of aerobatic driving were about evenly split between those who thought it was the greatest pass in the history of the sport and those who thought Zanardi should have been penalized for gaining positions by going off the racetrack. By any reasonable interpretation of the rulebook, it should have been the latter, but CART was not about to do anything to stifle exciting racing when they were in a heated battle for their very survival with the IRL, so "The Pass," as it would come to be known, would stand.

Jimmy Vasser won the 1996 CART title over Michael Andretti and Alex Zanardi, while Al Unser Jr. ultimately slid to fourth place. Paul Tracy, who had a terrible year, ended up 13th in the final standings. It marked the first time in 20 years that the Penske Team went winless for an entire season. This, in addition to the political turmoil that threatened to overthrow the CART organization that Roger Penske had co-founded, surely made for a long off-season at Team Penske's Reading, Pennsylvania shop.

1997

Penske Racing had faced adversity in the past and, it seemed, always managed to emerge from it faster and stronger each time. This time, however, it was going to take a little longer to work through the problems than it had during those prior dips. The 1997 season would turn out to be a little better than 1996—it couldn't have been worse—but this was not going to be the end of the slump. Unfortunately, the Captain's team was going to have to hit rock bottom before the real recovery would begin.

On the political front, not much had changed going into 1997. Both CART and Tony George's IRL had dug in their heels and prepared for a long battle, both sides believing not only that they were morally justified in their positions, but also that they had the resolve and the resources to outlast their opponent. Although nobody was happy about it, CART had survived its first season without the Indianapolis 500, and seemed to be as healthy as ever. Fans overwhelmingly sided with CART, with new and existing race venues drawing strong crowds. The IRL, on the other hand, was playing to audiences of just 5,000 and 10,000 paying spectators everywhere except Indianapolis. But Tony George had deep pockets and he seemed willing to subsidize his new series for as long as necessary; although in 1997, he probably couldn't have imagined how long that was going to be. So as the new CART season got underway, the Indy 500 was not on the schedule. Rather than running the competing U.S. 500 as they did in '96, CART scheduled a new race on a new 1.5-mile oval track in Gateway, Illinois, across the Mississippi River from the St. Louis arch. This race actually ran on Saturday, the day before the IRL's Indianapolis 500. CART's strategy for this scheduling arrangement was to attract fans that would already be in the Midwest for the "500." Of course, the other result was that it would give teams and drivers the option to run in both events.

Despite his dismal showing in 1996, Paul Tracy was retained by Roger Penske for another season. Tracy was teamed again with Al Unser Jr., with continuing sponsorship from Marlboro cigarettes. The equipment package, unfortunately, was unchanged. The team ran Penske PC-26 chassis with Mercedes-Ilmor engines and Goodyear tires. Roger Penske may have considered making changes, but he had a vested interest in all three of these equipment components. The chassis, of course, came from his own shops; he was a founding member and still part owner of Ilmor Engineering; and he had long-time business ties to Goodyear Tire & Rubber Company. Penske hoped, obviously, that Goodyear would step up to the new challenge and provide tires that were as good or better than Firestone. Unfortunately, that didn't happen.

Target-Ganassi Racing would continue to be the strongest competition. In fact, some suggested that Chip Ganassi had become the new "Roger Penske." Ganassi had two excellent drivers—Jimmy Vasser and Alex Zanardi—and he had what was again the optimum equipment package with the Reynard-Honda-Firestone combination. Brazilian Gil de Ferran had moved to Walker Racing for the new season, and was a frequent threat in his Reynard-Honda handicapped with Goodyear tires. PacWest teammates Mauricio Gugelmin and Mark Blundell were also solid contenders, scoring the first wins for this fourth-year team. Other notable challengers, who would each win at least one race this season, included Michael Andretti at Newman-Haas, Greg Moore at Forsythe Racing, and Scott Pruett with Pat Patrick's team.

The CART season opened again at Homestead, the South Florida address providing a suitable climate for an early March race date. After decades of loyalty to Lola, Carl Haas switched his Newman-Haas Racing Team to the new American-built "Swift" Indy-car chassis this year, and Michael Andretti wasted no time putting it in the winner's circle in its very first outing. Paul Tracy ran a strong race for the Penske team, finishing second while

In 1997, the Penske/Mercedes/Goodyear package was not the ideal combination to have, but Paul Tracy managed to win three consecutive races with it and appeared to be a championship contender for a good part of the season. Al Unser Jr. was not so fortunate, going winless for the second year in a row. *LAT*

Al Unser Jr. was sidelined early with electrical problems. Next, in Australia, Scott Pruett finally scored a win for Patrick Racing, finishing ahead of Greg Moore, Michael Andretti, and Alex Zanardi. Paul Tracy qualified second-fastest and led a race-high 21 laps before crashing. Al Unser qualified poorly and lasted only 10 laps until loosing a wheel and ending his day.

At Long Beach, where Al Unser Jr. was once unbeatable, the struggling Team Penske lead driver ran a solid race and managed to hold on for a fourth-place finish, while teammate Tracy followed three spots back in 7th. Alex Zanardi won the race, finally starting his much-anticipated assault on the championship. At this point, it had been 20 races and almost 20 months since Penske Racing had tasted victory. Given these statistics, it would have been hard to believe in April of 1997 what was going to happen in the next three events.

At Roger Penske's track in Nazareth, Pennsylvania, Paul Tracy finally did what he was hired to do. He put his #3 PC-26 Mercedes on the pole, ran the fastest lap of the race, led 186 of the 225 total laps including the most important one, to take a 1/2-second win over hometown favorite Michael Andretti. To make it even

sweeter, Al Unser Jr. was also on the podium with a third-place finish. For Roger Penske and everyone on the team, this had to be a tremendous relief. And it was going to get even better.

On May 11th, CART returned for the second time to the oval in Rio de Janeiro and Paul Tracy scored a second-consecutive victory, this time beating Greg Moore and Scott Pruett while Al Unser followed several spots back in 7th position. Suddenly after floundering hopelessly for a year and a half, it looked like Team Penske was finally back on track. That notion was further reinforced on Memorial Day weekend, as CART opened the new Gateway International Speedway in East St. Louis. From his front row starting position, Paul Tracy out-lasted or outran all his competition, taking his third straight win and a commanding lead in the CART championship. This also marked the 99th Indy-car victory for the Penske team, and at the rate things were going, it seemed that number "100" couldn't be far away. Rumor had it that Roger Penske went out and bought the champagne.

Unfortunately, he wasn't going to be popping those corks anytime soon. After Gateway, things fell apart in a hurry. Paul Tracy won the pole at Milwaukee and led nearly half the race before dropping back to a 6th place finish. Al Unser, meanwhile, continued his miserable streak of bad luck, suffering his 4th mechanical DNF of the season. Tracy missed the Detroit race after a practice crash left him with a mild concussion, while Al Unser qualified 16th and persevered to a mediocre 8th place finish. And things would only get worse. Almost unbelievably, after Tracy's three consecutive wins, the Penske team would fail to score a single podium finish in the remaining 11 races of the 1997 season. After looking like a strong championship prospect at mid-season, Paul Tracy plummeted to 5th in the final standings, ending the year with a string of 5 straight DNFs. Al Jr. could do no better, finishing in 13th position with a total of 10 DNFs on the year.

While the Penske effort was unraveling, Alex Zanardi really came to life. With only one victory in the first half of the year, he went on a late-season charge, winning four of five events in one stretch and clinching the championship even before the final race on the schedule. Gil de Ferran drove very consistently all season, finishing second in the points without ever winning a race. Zanardi's Target-Ganassi teammate, Jimmy Vasser, was third and Mauricio Gugelmin fourth.

By the end of the 1997 season, the atmosphere at Team Penske was certainly tense. Everyone seemed to be in agreement that the equipment package left much to be desired, but Tracy's mid-year winning streak proved that it was certainly not hopelessly uncompetitive. Aside from the mechanical variables, there were sensitive personal issues too. Al Unser Jr. hadn't won a race in two seasons now; and although equipment reliability and competitiveness could be blamed for a part of that disappointing statistic, there was more to it than that. It would not become public knowledge until a couple years later, but Al Jr. was struggling with a drug and alcohol abuse problem that not only cost him his marriage, but certainly affected his driving performance to some extent. Roger Penske was either not aware of the situation, or more likely, didn't understand the scope of the problem, as he would keep the struggling Unser on the team for two more seasons.

Paul Tracy was another issue. By the end of his third season with the team, it was apparent that the personality conflicts were insurmountable, though Roger Penske clearly gave the relationship every possible opportunity. Several years later in an interview with John Oreovicz, Penske reflected on Tracy's tenure with the team: "We had a pretty bumpy career with Paul. He won a lot of races for us and did a lot for his career, but it got to the point where if things weren't going right, it was always the team….Basically, he was very unhappy about what we were doing for him, and I think he showed it with the team. The team was in enough trouble—we didn't need the guy driving the car striking out at the team."

1998

By the time the schedule was being developed for the 1998 CART season, the new world order of Indy-car racing was already fairly well established. Tony George and his Indy Racing League were marching ahead, expanding their series into new markets with more oval-track races; but generally, the crowds were still small, as the IRL had failed to lure any of the top teams and drivers away from CART. Aside from the artificial draw of the Indianapolis 500, there was still relatively little fan interest in the new series.

CART, on the other hand, seemed to be healthy and thriving as they continued to expand not just to new U.S. venues, but also into entirely new regions around the world. In 1998, CART hosted races in Japan, South America, Canada, Australia, and of course, the United States. The series was clearly starting to look like a U.S.-based Formula-One. In fact, because of the competitive threat, the organizers of the F1 World Championship had effectively banned CART from operating anywhere in Europe by pressuring those countries that hosted F1 races not to open the door to the American-based series. In a backhanded way, that was a noteworthy complement for the CART teams and drivers.

Something else happened within CART in 1998, which would ultimately prove to be a major contributing factor in the organization's downfall. Caught up in the country's irrational love affair with Wall Street, the CART principals—with one very notable excep-

Roger Penske hired promising young Brazilian Andre Ribeiro to team with Al Jr. in the new PC27 for 1998. Ribeiro had scored three wins driving a Reynard Honda for the Tasman team in 1995 and '96, but he would manage to earn a total of only 13 points in the entire 19-race season with the uncompetitive Penske/Mercedes. *LAT*

tion—decided to take the company public. The dissenting opinion came from Roger Penske, who knew the drawbacks of answering to stockholders and the Securities and Exchange Commission. The move generated a windfall of cash for both CART and the team owners who all ended up with sizeable chunks of stock. Initially, it was just like free money. It allowed CART to purchase the rights to both of its feeder series, the Indy Lights and Toyota Atlantic championships. But it also complicated the management process just at a time when the organization needed flexibility and autonomy to do what was necessary in their battle with the IRL. Over the next six years, CART would go through several CEOs and temporary leaders before eventually succumbing to bankruptcy at the end of the 2003 season. Of course, at the beginning of 1998, nobody could

have predicted that eventuality. In fact, there was every expectation, by CART and most outside observers, that it would only be a matter of time before Tony George waved the white flag and things got back to normal.

For Marlboro Team Penske, there would be just one significant change for the new season. Despite his relatively strong showing in '97, Roger Penske was tired of dealing with the attitude, so Paul Tracy was released from his contract. Tracy would move to Team Green where he would have mixed success, crashing into his own teammate on more than one occasion, but also winning several races. In a somewhat surprising move, Roger Penske hired 32-year-old Brazilian Andre Ribeiro to replace Tracy. Ribeiro had been driving Indy-Cars with the Tasman team for the past three year. He had three wins and four poles to his credit, but was still considered a relative newcomer when hired by the Captain. Ironically, by the time he departed a year later, the talk was that Penske Racing had doomed his once-promising career. Unfortunately, that's the kind of season it was going to be.

Andre Ribeiro and Al Unser Jr. would contest the 1998 CART championship in Penske PC-27/Mercedes/Goodyear packages, which proved again to be the least competitive combination on the circuit. Alex Zanardi and Jimmy Vasser were back at Target-Ganassi Racing, and once more proved to be the strongest competition. Although Paul Tracy didn't show much in his first season with Team KOOL Green, his teammate Dario Franchitti would have a very strong year. The only other drivers to win a race this year would be Adrian Fernandez at Patrick Racing, Greg Moore at Players/Forsythe, Michael Andretti, and Bryan Herta.

The season opened on a hopeful note for Team Penske, as Andre Ribeiro qualified second-fastest on the 1.5-mile Homestead oval. In the race, however, he fell two laps off the pace and finished 17th. Unser managed to qualify only 14th and dropped out with transmission problems. Next, in CART's inaugural race on the 1.55-oval at Motegi, Japan, Unser climbed from his 15th-place starting spot to lead 26 laps and ultimately finish second to Adrian Fernandez. Ribeiro was a lap down in 9th at the end. From there, however, things got really ugly. It would be five races before either Team Penske driver finished in the points again. That was Al Unser Jr., who had a solid third-place finish at Milwaukee, although he never led a lap all day. Unser would finish 5th two races later in Portland, and then 6th at Mid-Ohio, four more events after that. In the meantime, Andre Ribeiro, with the exception of his Moteigi finish, hadn't earned a single point all season until getting on the board with a 10th-place in Ohio. Unser went on to pick up three more top-10 finishes in the remaining six races of the season, while Ribeiro claimed just one. In the end, Al Unser finished 11th in the CART standings with just 72 points. Ribiero was 22nd out of 28 drivers who scored points in 1998, earning just 13 points in the 19-race season. It was by far the Penske team's worst showing in its 32-year history.

When Al Unser Jr. (left) was injured in the opening race of the 1999 season, Roger Penske hired Tarso Marques (right) to fill in. Marques was invited back to team with Little Al in several more races later in the year. The two are seen here at Gateway, where Unser raced a Lola-Mercedes and Marques ran the Penske. *LAT*

Defending champion Alex Zanardi ran away with the CART championship in 1998, winning 7 races and scoring a record 285 points. His Ganassi Racing teammate Jimmy Vasser was a distant second, with 169 points and three wins. Chip Ganassi, who had a brief and undistinguished CART driving career back in the mid-1980s, was finding much more gratification as a team owner. And his successes were prompting more comparisons to the once incomparable Roger Penske.

1999

The top six drivers in the 1998 final standings had been equipped with Reynard chassis and Firestone tires. Greg Moore, in 5th position, was the highest placed Mercedes-powered entry. Michael Andretti was the most successful Goodyear campaigner, finishing 7th in his Ford-powered Swift chassis. Given these statistics, and considering the magnitude of his own team's problems, it's hard to understand why Roger Penske did not make drastic changes going into the new season. In 1984 and again in 1987, when it became apparent that his own chassis wasn't going to be competitive with the Marches and Lolas, Penske's business instinct prompted him to make difficult, but necessary adjustments. After three years of struggling, culminating in an embarrassingly uncompetitive winless season in '98, it would have been more than reasonable to expect Penske to switch to Firestones tires and scrap his own chassis and engine in favor of the obviously superior Reynard-Honda setup. But he didn't do that—not yet.

Everyone, including longtime financial-backer Marlboro, could see that Team Penske was in deep trouble. In fact, because of the team's recent sub-par performance, Marlboro scaled back its support for the 1999 season, forcing Penske to run a one-car program for many of the races. Despite all the signs, Roger Penske went into the new year with Al Unser Jr. driving a Mercedes-powered Penske chassis on Goodyear tires. Andre Ribeiro had unexpectedly announced his retirement at the end of the '98 season, prompting half-joking comments that Penske Racing had destroyed the young Brazilian's promising career. Over the course of the coming season, Roger Penske would test several young drivers in a second car, but Al Unser Jr. was the team's only regular entry.

In the 1999 battle for the CART title, which unfortunately was not going to involve Team Penske, the Target-Ganassi Racing team was again the cream of the crop, although there was a major change there. Zanardi's stunning success during his three years in CART earned him a top Formula-1 ride with the Williams team, so he would not be back to defend his title. To fill the seat of the two-time defending CART champion, Chip Ganassi turned to a relatively unknown young Columbian driver named Juan Montoya. Team KOOL Green would be very strong again, with both Paul Tracy and Dario Franchitti scoring multiple wins and staying in the title race until the end. Other drivers who would visit Victory Lane in 1999 included Michael Andretti, Adrian Fernandez, Christian Fittipaldi, Gil de Ferran, Greg Moore and Tony Kanaan.

CART, as an organization, continued to look relatively solid heading into the 1999 season, but there would be serious problems before the year was over. With the addition of a new one-mile oval track in Chicago, CART's schedule now boasted a nearly unmanageable 20 races. And despite the continuing split that left the CART teams out of the Indianapolis 500, the fields continued to be full, sponsorship was strong, and none of the top teams had decided yet to break the unofficial Indy boycott.

Al Unser Jr. qualified the lone Penske entry midfield in the Homestead opener, but got caught up in a serious three-car wreck on the first lap, not only ending his day but taking him out of the next two races as well with the resulting injuries. Roger Penske hired 23-year old Brazilian Tarso Marques to sub for Unser in Japan and Long Beach. Marques, who had already seen Formula-1 duty, labored to a 14th-place finish in his debut and then crashed at Long Beach in his second outing. Unser was back for Nazareth, but qualified 23rd in a field of 24 cars and finished dead last after spinning on the 44th lap.

For the race in Rio de Janiero, Penske entered cars for both Unser and Marques. Unser actually led 10 laps, the first time a Penske entry had been out front all season. He ended up falling back to a 12th place finish, though still on the lead lap. Marques drove a steady race and finished 8th.

Finally, after scoring a grand total of five points in the first five races of the season, Roger Penske decided to try something different. Even though a Lola chassis hadn't won a race since Michael Andretti's Vancouver victory in 1996, and the vast majority of the teams were now campaigning Reynards, Penske purchased a Lola for Al Unser Jr. to try. With a Mercedes engine and Goodyear tires, Unser qualified at the back of the field on the Gateway 1.27-mile oval. As a result of pit stop shuffling, he managed to lead 11 laps during the first half of the race, but when everything sorted out, he finished well off the pace in 12th position. Tarso Marques out-qualified his senior teammate, starting his Penske/Mercedes 18th but crashing early and finishing next to last.

The day after the Gateway race, Al Unser Jr. was a spectator at the Indianapolis 500, making not-so-subtle remarks about being ready to come back home to Indy. What wasn't common knowledge at the time was that Roger Penske had already informed Unser that he planned to make major changes for the 2000 season, and that Unser wasn't going to be a part of the new plans. Al Jr. would spend the rest of the season shopping for a new job, finishing out the year as a lame duck, with predictable results.

Unser ran the Lola again at Milwaukee, qualifying 22nd and finishing four laps behind the leaders in 19th spot. On the road course at Portland, it wasn't any better. He started 26th and finished 16th in the Lola while Marques' started and finished 18th in the Penske chassis. Finally, on the airport course in Cleveland, there was a hint of improvement. Roger Penske entered both Unser and Marques in Lolas. Although Marques crashed again and would not be invited back thereafter, Unser qualified mid-field and climbed to a then-respectable 5th-place finish. Still driving the Lola, Little Al then turned in consecutive 9th-place results at Elkhart Lake and Toronto.

For the U.S. 500 at his own track in Michigan, Roger Penske hired young American Alex Barron to team with Al Unser. Both drivers ran Penske chassis for this event, although it didn't really matter because they both experienced problems with their Mercedes

Roger Penske wishes Gonzalo Rodriguez good luck as he heads out to practice at Detroit for his CART debut. Penske hired the 27-year-old Formula 3000 veteran to replace Tarso Marques as Al Unser's part time teammate. Rodriguez finished 12th at Detroit, but while preparing for his second race with the team, at Laguna Seca in September, he was fatally injured in a practice crash. *LAT*

217

Typical of Al Unser's 1999 season, his Ilmor-Mercedes engine lets go at Chicago, leaving him to finish 24th. With three mechanical DNFs and four accidents, Unser's final year with Team Penske had very few highlights. *LAT*

engines and did not finish. Two weeks later, for the race in downtown Detroit, there were more changes at Team Penske. Obviously, the Captain had already written off the 1999 season and was using the remaining races to scout potential new drivers. Teamed with Al Unser now was 27 year old Gonzalo Rodriguez from Montevideo, Uruguay, driving in his very first Indy-car race. Penske appeared to be grabbing at straws, looking for that next undiscovered super-talent like Chip Ganassi had found in Alex Zanardi and Juan Montoya.

Both driving Lolas, Rodriguez qualified 16th, four spots better than Unser. In the race, neither was competitive, but both did finish—Rodriguez 12th and Unser 15th. At Mid-Ohio, Unser was by himself again. He started at the back of the field and crashed early

to finish 25th. A week later, on the new one-mile oval near Chicago, Al Jr. qualified the Lola 24th and finished 25th with an engine problem. He followed that with an identical result in Vancouver. This season was already a disaster for Team Penske, and things were about to get unthinkably worse.

For the Laguna Seca race on September 12, Penske entered a pair of Lolas, calling back Gonzalo Rodriguez for his second drive with the team. In the Saturday practice session before qualifying, Rodriguez crashed heavily in the "corkscrew" turn. His car flipped over a barrier and landed upside down. He was killed instantly. It was the second time Roger Penske had to deal with the death of one of his drivers. And although it wasn't the same deep personal loss that Penske and the team experienced when Mark Donohue died in Austria 14 years earlier, it was still nothing less than a tragedy. Penske withdrew Al Unser's entry for the Laguna race and made the difficult phone call to the Rodriguez family in Uruguay.

For the remaining three races on the 1999 CART calendar, Roger Penske went back to his own chassis, apparently seeing that there was no advantage to the Lola when handicapped with the Mercedes engine and Goodyear tires. Unser drove the lone team entry at Houston and Australia, recording two more disappointing results. For the season finale at his Fontana, California, track, Penske put Alex Barron back in a second car. This was really just to fill out the field, because Penske had already announced his plans for the 2000 season, which included a two-car team with drivers Gil de Ferran and young Canadian Greg Moore.

Al Unser Jr. qualified 10th for the Fontana race, and a lot of people were pulling for him to make a good showing in his last outing for the Penske team. Unfortunately, the best he could do was 7th place, a lap behind the leaders. Barron lasted only 27 laps before an accident ended his day.

Barron's crash was already the third big impact of the day. Richie Hearn had crashed hard on the third lap, luckily escaping without serious injury. But one lap after the race was restarted from Hearn's accident, Greg Moore lost control of his Players Forsythe Reynard coming out of the fourth turn. His car came down off the banking and went into the infield at nearly 200 mph. The car bounced and skated across the wet grass, almost appearing to gain speed as it proceeded. Just before reaching the infield concrete wall, Moore's car flipped on its side and rammed into the immovable barrier, with the open cockpit of the car taking the brunt of the hit. It was a horrible site. Auto racing commentator Paul Page, who was covering the live television broadcast of the race that day, uttered an apprehensive "Oh my." It was sickeningly obvious to all who witnessed this crash that Moore could not have survived.

After a lengthy rescue effort and track cleanup, the race resumed with periodic vague updates on Moore's condition from the CART medical staff. At the end of the 500 miles, flags around the racetrack were lowered to half-mast and it was announced, as everyone expected, that Greg Moore had died. There was no victory lane celebration. There was no ceremony to crown the new CART champion. As Moore's fellow drivers were informed of the terrible news, there were tears up and down pit road. Greg Moore was a popular young man. Just two years earlier, he had become the youngest driver to ever win an Indy-Car race. Unlike Gonzalo Rodriguez and Jeff Krosnoff, who were still relative unknowns at the time of their deaths, Greg Moore had already established a significant fan base. He was considered one of CART's brightest new stars, which is precisely why Roger Penske had hired him to drive for his team the following year. Moore's tragic death was not only a great loss for the Penske team, but for the entire sport of Indy-Car racing. CART was still fighting for its very survival in the civil war with the IRL, it was dealing with its own internal management issues, and now it was ending the season on this very sour note, with two deaths in four races. For Team Penske and the entire CART community, 1999 was a season to forget.

For Penske Racing, 1999 was also the end of another chapter, probably most appropriately labeled the Al Unser Jr. era. It was an era that began apprehensively in 1993, after the retirement of long-time team leader Rick Mears; but quickly evolved into another runaway Penske success story. It started with Emerson Fittipaldi's Indy 500 win in 1993 and included the Captain's most gratifying "500" victory the following year, with Al Unser Jr. taking the revolutionary Mercedes "pushrod" engine to the winner's circle. In 1994, Penske's 3-car team generated the most dominating statistics ever witnessed in American racing on the way to an unprecedented 1-2-3 finish in the CART championship. But then things soured quickly. There was the humiliating failure to qualify at Indy in 1995 and then the agonizing, self-imposed absence from the Speedway because of the CART-IRL split. Finally, this strange and incongruous chapter in Penske Racing's history ended with an agonizing two-year winless streak that ultimately witnessed the tragic death of a promising young driver. By the time the 1999 season came to its ugly end, Roger Penske's embattled team had no place to go but up.

LAT

CHAPTER 13
CART Indy Cars
Return to Glory
(2000 – 2001)

"This year when I won the championship, at the moment I crossed the line all I could think of was my team, about how much I love these people….My life is completely happy, from a personal and professional standpoint, and the one thing that makes all of it possible is my association with this team."
—Gil de Ferran, 2001

When Roger Penske finally decided to make changes in his CART Indy-car program, they were sweeping. By this time, that was the only way he could sell his long-time sponsor Marlboro Tobacco on supporting a full

two-car effort again. The Penske chassis were scrapped in favor of proven Reynards. The Ilmor-Mercedes engines were replaced by Hondas. And with Goodyear withdrawing from Indy-car racing altogether, Team Penske would now be running on the same Firestone tires as everyone else.

Greg Moore's tragic death in the final race of the 1999 season left Penske scrambling for another top-tier driver very late in the silly season, but he was fortunate to sign Helio Castroneves to team with Gil de Ferran. These two Brazilians would prove to make ideal team-mates and perfect representatives for the reincarnated Penske team. Of de Ferran, who would come to be known as "the Professor," Roger Penske said: "He's the ultimate professional. To put it into perspective, the first time we walked into Penske Cars together, there was a technical drawing of a gearbox on the wall. He said, 'That's a funny place for reverse gear.' I don't know how many drivers would have even known what it was…. He spends more time than probably any other driver we've had actually talking with the engineers and under-

They called him "the Professor." Gil de Ferran, seen here with Roger Penske, was a technical driver who spent his time working with the engineers to understand and improve the car. More than any other driver in the team's history, de Ferran clearly cherished the opportunity to drive for Penske Racing. *LAT*

If the Penske Racing team sometimes seems to be too "stuffed shirt," it's not the fault of this carefree Brazilian. Nicknamed "Spiderman" for his fence-climbing victory celebrations, Helio Castroneves is as entertaining as he is talented. When Roger Penske was asked what amuses him, his answer was "Helio's antics." *Peter Burke*

standing the setups." But perhaps the biggest compliment Penske had for his new lead driver was this: "He reminds me a lot of [Rick] Mears."

Helio Castroneves was a lot greener than his new teammate, having competed in only two seasons on the CART circuit prior to signing with the team. He was a bigger risk than the proven de Ferran, but Penske obviously saw the potential in this colorful young Brazilian. "His personality and his relationship with Gil was one we couldn't have planned any better," Penske said of Castroneves. "They respect each other. They pull each other and that's important….Helio has got a great future in open-wheel racing. People probably underestimate him."

Both drivers were emotional, but in very different ways. Castroneves was loud and colorful. He would soon earn the nickname "Spiderman" for his trademark fence-climbing ritual performed after each victory. Gil de Ferran, conversely, was soft-spoken and reserved. His emotions would come out later, when he could be brought to tears just talking about how much driving for Team Penske meant to him.

2000

The competitive picture for the 2000 CART season was not significantly changed. Target-Ganassi had won four straight CART championships with drivers Jimmy Vasser, Alex Zanardi and Juan Montoya. Vasser and Montoya would be back with Ganassi for the new season, although this year, they would be driving Lolas powered by Toyota engines rather than the proven Reynard-Honda package. Toyota had been struggling in CART since its debut with Dan Gurney's All-American Racing Eagle program back in 1996. Since then, the Japanese manufacturer had partnered with several second-tier teams without ever finding success, which made Chip Ganassi's move look like a considerable risk. Then again, Toyota surely offered a sizeable financial incentive for that risk, and Ganassi evidently felt that with four straight titles in his pocket, he could afford to take some chances.

Other challengers this season included Max Papis and 1998 Indy 500 winner Kenny Brack in Reynard-Fords, driving for Bobby Rahal; Paul Tracy and Dario Franchitti together again at Team KOOL Green in Reynard-Hondas; Patrick Carpentier and newcomer Alex Tagliani in Reynard-Fords for Player's/Indeck; Adrian Fernandez and Roberto Moreno at Patrick Racing, and finally, Michael Andretti and Christian Fittipaldi in the Newman-Haas Lola-Fords.

There was a considerable amount of pressure on the new Penske team to perform right out of the gate. After all, they now had the best equipment and drivers that money could buy; there were no more excuses. Now it was up to Roger Penske and his organization to execute. It had been almost three years since Paul Tracy had won Team Penske's last pole position. When Gil de Ferran

Team Penske's new look for the 2000 season included the proven combination of Reynard chassis, Honda engines and Firestone tires. At California Speedway, Gil de Ferran won the pole with a speed of 241.44426 mph, establishing a new World Closed Course Speed Record. *LAT*

went out and put his new Penske-prepared Reynard on the pole for the season-opening Marlboro Grand Prix of Miami, the doubters started to back-pedal. De Ferran didn't win that day, and neither did Helio Castroneves, but it was apparent that it would be only a matter of time.

The second race of the 2000 season was scheduled for April 11th at Nazareth, Pennsylvania. Castroneves and de Ferran qualified 3rd and 5th on April 10th, but by the following morning, the one-mile Nazareth Speedway was a winter wonderland, covered by a fluke spring snowstorm. The race had to be postponed, and because of other scheduled events, would not be run until Memorial Day weekend.

A week later, the CART teams reassembled in Long Beach, California, where the new Team Penske again made a good showing but fell short of actually scoring that elusive 100th victory. Gil de Ferran qualified second and jumped into the lead at the green flag. He would stay out front for the first 30 laps and post the fastest lap of the race before eventually dropping to a 7th place finish. In the meantime, teammate Helio Castroneves drove a solid race from his third-place starting position and finished second to winner Paul Tracy.

The team had an off weekend in Rio de Janeiro, as mechanical problems took both cars out early. Japan was another disappointment, de Ferran's 9th-place finish being the best they could claim. But then things finally fell into place. Back in Nazareth, Pennsylvania, on a track that Roger Penske built, just a few miles from the Pocono International Raceway where Mark Donohue had won Penske Racing's first Indy-car race some 29 years earlier, Gil de Ferran delivered the team's long-awaited 100th victory; appropriately, it came on Memorial Day weekend. It had been three long years and 54 CART races since Paul Tracy last took a Penske entry to the winner's circle. "We've had our ups and downs, but never a down like the one we just went through," said Penske after the Nazareth win. Fighting back his tears, Gil de Ferran said after the victory, "Joining this team was an emotional experience for me, because there's a lot of responsibility in these overalls. To win is indescribable. There's a strange feeling in my chest…I don't know. I'm not too eloquent today." There were, in fact, a lot of people with lumps in their throats that day. *Autoweek* wrote, "[Penske's] team pulled out a dusty box of ball caps, embroidered with a big "100," and passed them around. For all the wealth generated by his businesses and the success won by his race teams, there was celebration and real tears around Roger Penske's transporters, and it made those who witnessed it feel good."

The day after this momentous victory, Roger Penske headed to Indianapolis for the first time since the CART/IRL split divided Indy-car racing in 1996. Team Penske wasn't entered in the 2000 "500," but Penske's United Automotive Group was sponsoring an entry driven by Jason Leffler. This gave the Captain an opportunity to get a first-hand look at what was going on with the IRL and Indianapolis—and it immediately started speculation about Penske Racing staging a return to the Brickyard.

The year 2000 marked the first time since the split that there was any significant CART team presence at Indianapolis. Since the 1997 season, the IRL had run with its own chassis and engine specifications, making it cost prohibitive for most CART teams to consider running an Indy-only program. Of course, the four-

When Paul Tracy won the team's 99th Indy car race at Gateway in 1997, few would have believed the Captain would have to wait three years to celebrate number "100." Fittingly, Gil de Ferran finally delivered that milestone victory at Penske's own Nazareth Speedway on Memorial Day weekend. Rick Mears, Roger Penske and Gil de Ferran pose here in front of a "100" banner. *LAT*

was a clear victory for the CART side. It also opened the door to more CART participation in the future.

Back in the CART world, the Penske team would experience frustration at Milwaukee, coming away with just one point for de Ferran's 12th place finish. But then on the streets of Detroit, it was Helio Castroneves' turn to shine. The Penske cars qualified third and fourth, behind Juan Montoya and Dario Franchitti. Montoya would lead the first 60 laps of the race. But when the defending CART champion broke a half-shaft, Castroneves was right there to take command, leading the remaining 24 laps to score his first CART victory and the second win in three races for Team Penske. Gil de Ferran had an early altercation with Christian Fittipaldi, but recovered to finish a lap down in 9th position.

A week later, CART was on the road course in Portland. This time, the Penske drivers swept the front row of the grid, with Castroneves on the pole and de Ferran beside him. Castroneves led the majority of the race but eventually dropped to a 7th place finish. De Ferran, on the other hand, came on strong at the end, taking the lead from his teammate and holding on for his second win of the season. After not winning a race in 54 attempts, Penske Racing had now been victorious in three of the last four events, and Gil de Ferran was suddenly on a march toward the championship.

Cleveland was a bit of a setback, as both Penske cars were involved in accidents and did not finish. Then in Toronto, de Ferran struggled to a 6th place result while Castroneves was sidelined with a mechanical problem. Next was the U.S. 500 at Michigan, a race that the resurgent Roger Penske would have loved to win. Unfortunately, it didn't work out that way, although Helio Castroneves gave it his best shot. After qualifying a disappointing 13th, "Spiderman" climbed to the lead by the 22nd lap and he would go on to pace a race-high 85 laps. In the end, however, he would cross the finish line in 5th spot, three seconds behind winner Juan Montoya. De Ferran had a tougher day, never leading and crashing a little beyond the halfway point.

The Chicago race would see another first-time CART winner, with Cristiano DaMatta taking the victory over Michael Andretti and Gil de Ferran. It was Castroneves

time defending champion Target-Ganassi team was one of the few organizations that had the resources to manage it. In 2000, Chip Ganassi spent an estimated $3 million to purchase four IRL-spec G-Force chassis and 10 Comtech-built Oldsmobile engines to take his two CART drivers, Jimmy Vasser and Juan Montoya to Indy. The investment paid off handsomely, as Montoya dominated the race to become the first rookie winner since Formula-1 World Champion Graham Hill took the honors in 1966. Nobody was shocked that Ganassi Racing was competitive, but the ease with which the CART team walked in and dominated on the IRL's home turf was somewhat surprising. In the ongoing propaganda war between the two Indy-car factions, this who had the problems in Chicago, losing his Honda engine after just 35 laps.

After this four-race losing streak, Team Penske arrived at Mid-Ohio ready for business. Gil de Ferran won the pole, with his teammate qualifying second. De Ferran led from the green flag for the first 28 laps. Helio Castroneves took over on lap 29 and stayed out front for the remainder of the race, with de Ferran close behind, for a convincing Penske Racing one-two sweep. It was the first time since 1994 that Penske drivers had accomplished that feat, and that undoubtedly made the competition more than a little nervous.

Elkhart Lake and Vancouver would not produce wins for the team, but then at Laguna Seca, where just a year earlier Roger Penske had to withdraw his team after the death of his rookie driver, Castroneves and de Ferran came back with another dominating performance. They qualified first and second on the grid, with Castroneves setting a new track qualifying record. He went on to lead 81 of the race's 83 laps, relinquishing the top spot only for his first pit stop. Gil de Ferran turned the fastest lap of the race, but never ran higher than second position, where he ended up finishing, 9 seconds behind his teammate. Except for two laps led by Juan Montoya during pit stop shuffling, it was a Team Penske steamroller just like the good old days.

On the Gateway oval, the Penske cars were a little off the pace, qualifying mid-pack and finishing a disappointing 8th and 9th. It was becoming apparent that Penske's Reynard-Hondas were stronger on the road courses than on the ovals. But that was something the team could work on during the off-season.

With just three races remaining in the season, Gil de Ferran was in a battle with Adrian Fernandez for the CART championship. On the street course in Houston, de Ferran won another pole position and led two-thirds of the race before settling for a third-place finish. Castroneves finished 5th and Fernandez 7th.

In Australia, de Ferran had a chance to lock up the title early, but things didn't go smoothly. After qualifying second on the grid, he was caught up in a first-lap wreck with Juan Montoya and Dario Franchitti, ending his day well out of the points. To make matters

Gil de Ferran gave Roger Penske his first CART championship since 1994. Along the way, de Ferran won two races and five pole positions. Teammate Helio Castroneves added three more wins and three poles, capping off a joyful and well-deserved comeback season for Marlboro Team Penske. *LAT*

worse, challenger Adrian Fernandez charged from his 17th starting position to win the race, sending the close championship battle to the final round in California.

At Roger Penske's beautiful 2-mile oval in Fontana, Gil de Ferran won the pole position with a track record 241.426 mph, more than 2 mph faster than his nearest challenger, Michael Andretti—not bad for a guy who didn't really like the high-speed ovals. Helio Castroneves led 46 laps and looked like a good bet to win until a blown engine took him out in the closing stages. De Ferran led 26 laps during the course of the race and held on to finish third, two spots ahead of his championship challenger, good enough to lock up his first CART title. It was the 10th Indy-car championship for Team Penske, but the first since 1994.

After going two whole seasons without winning a single race, Team Penske scored a total of five victories in 2000, three by Castroneves and two by de Ferran. The Brazilian teammates also combined to win 8 pole positions. This was certainly not the best season Roger Penske's team had ever enjoyed, but considering their desperate position just a year earlier and the totality of the rebuilding effort before the 2000 campaign, it was nothing less than remarkable. For the competition, the message was as clear as it was disheartening: the party was over—Penske Racing was back!

2001

In theory, though the competition may have disagreed, a strong Penske team was a good thing for CART overall. A content and committed Roger Penske was one of the best weapons the CART organization could have in its ongoing battle with Tony George's Indy Racing League. But, in fact, Roger Penske was becoming increasingly disenchanted with the way things were going within the organization he founded. The Captain was not happy with the leadership's 1998 decision to become a public corporation, and his concerns that were largely disregarded at the time were proving to be real problems three years later. The team owners had run off CEO Andrew Craig in mid-2000 because of disputes over who was to blame for CART's dropping attendance figures and poor television ratings. Bobby Rahal reluctantly served as interim CEO for a short time until the under-qualified Joseph Heitzler was hired to fill the top spot. Through all this, the CART team owners continued to push their own personal agendas, making it increasingly difficult to address the growing threat of a stronger, more credible Indy Racing League. Roger Penske watched all this unfold, and eventually made a decision that would signal the demise of the organization that he had created over 20 years earlier. But that wouldn't happen just yet. For 2001, Marlboro Team Penske was back in CART to defend its title. And CART was going to have one more strong and exciting year before the bottom fell out.

For the new season, Gil de Ferran and Helio Castroneves would be together again in Roger Penske's Reynard-Hondas, but by this point, these cars had been considerably modified by the Team Penske engineers.

These modifications went well beyond the normal "tweaking" that all teams performed on their equipment. The Penske shops changed body and suspension parts to such an extent that people started referring to the hybrid chassis as a "Renske."

During the off-season, there was significant driver shuffling among the top teams and some new faces appeared on the scene. Team Green expanded to a three-car program with Michael Andretti joining Paul Tracy and Dario Franchitti. Andretti was replaced at Newman-Haas by Christiano DaMatta. Target-Ganassi Racing had a whole new lineup, with Juan Montoya heading off to Formula-1 fame and Jimmy Vasser moving to Patrick Racing. Chip Ganassi recruited two new young stars, Bruno Junqueira and Nicolas Minassian, to fill his open seats. Kenny Brack and Brian Herta were still together at Team Rahal, as were Patrick Carpentier and Alex Tagliani at Player's-Forsythe Racing. Competition was still intense for CART's last great year.

Besides defending their 2000 CART title, the folks at Marlboro Team Penske took on another significant challenge in 2001. After considerable speculation, Roger Penske finally announced that he would return to the Indianapolis 500 in May of 2001 with his drivers, Gil de Ferran and Helio Castroneves. This effort would require the preparation and development of an entirely separate chassis and engine package to comply with the IRL's specifications. To ensure that they would be race-ready for Indy, Penske also entered de Ferran and Castroneves in the March 18th IRL season opener at Phoenix, which did not conflict with the CART schedule.

The CART schedule opened on the road course in Monterrey, Mexico, where Cristiano DaMatta scored a victory in his first appearance with the Newman-Haas team. Gil de Ferran was not far behind, however, finishing in second place and starting to bank points in defense of his title.

A week later, Team Penske made its IRL debut in Phoenix, with de Ferran and Castroneves driving IRL-spec Oldsmobile-powered Dallaras. Many observers predicted that the powerful Penske team would show up in Phoenix and stomp their under-funded IRL rivals into the ground, but it didn't unfold that way at all.

In qualifying, Gil de Ferran took 5th spot on the grid, while Helio Castroneves could do no better than 17th. In the race, both drivers managed to lead a few laps, but de Ferran's day ended early in a crash with Mark Dismore and Castroneves lost an engine at the three-quarter mark. Roger Penske put his usual spin on the situation, claiming that the team gained a lot of experience that would be invaluable when they got to the Brickyard in May, but this was not the start that the racing world expected.

The second race on CART's schedule, the Toyota Grand Prix of Long Beach, was a Helio Castroneves success story. From pole position, Castroneves led every one of the race's 82 laps, and set fastest lap on his way to a win over Cristiano DaMatta, with Gil de Ferran in third place.

Next on the CART calendar was a new race at Texas Motor Speedway, a high-banked 1.45-mile oval that had hosted some of the IRL's most exciting battles over the previous few years. This event turned out to be one of CART's most embarrassing moments, and it came at a time when the organization could ill afford public displays of incompetence. Even though some CART teams had tested at the track earlier, a serious problem came to light on race weekend. The extremely high g-forces generated on this fast, steeply-banked racetrack were causing some of the drivers to become dizzy and disoriented—not a good thing at 230 mph! With no time to implement any acceptable changes, CART had no choice but to cancel the event. It was a public relations disaster, which not only upset fans and sponsors, but ultimately resulted in more lawsuits for CART to battle.

CART regrouped at Nazareth on May 6th, where Team Penske found itself having an off weekend. Castroneves qualified 5th and ended up finishing 11th after an early spin. De Ferran wasn't as fortunate, getting together with Alex Tagliani at the halfway point and ending his day out of the points.

Immediately after Nazareth, the Penske team had to switch gears and head to Indianapolis to get ready for qualifying the following weekend. Helio Castroneves had never raced at Indy before, so he had a lot to learn in one week. Gil de Ferran had run there just one time,

in 1995, but he was caught up in a 5-car first-lap accident that ended his day almost before it started. So in reality, both Team Penske drivers would be virtual rookies at the Speedway.

The other unknown as Roger Penske and his team rolled back into Indianapolis after a five-year absence was this: how would the politics play out? A lot of unfriendly words had been exchanged during that dark period and although Roger Penske had been professional and diplomatic through it all, he was still viewed by many as CART's unofficial leader. How he would be received by the Speedway and the growing new contingent of IRL-loyal fans was the subject of much speculation as the time approached. As it turned out, however, everyone on both sides of the issue seemed to go out of their way to make this a joyful homecoming. Tony George couldn't have been happier to have Indy's most successful team back home again in Indiana. And while fans and the media played up the CART-IRL showdown for all it was worth, it wasn't done with a bitter or negative tone. And Roger Penske, of course was thrilled to be back. Overall, people were just grateful that things were finally starting to get back to normal.

Getting qualified on the first weekend was critical for the Penske drivers because there was a CART race scheduled the following week in Japan. Both Gil de Ferran and Helio Castroneves were raised on road racing. De Ferran had had six seasons in CART to learn the tricks of getting around the oval tracks quickly and smoothly. He still didn't particularly like racing on the super-speedways, but he could do it with the best of them. Getting up to speed at Indy was not a problem for him. For Helio Castroneves, however, it wasn't quite that easy. Twice during the first week of practice, the Indy rookie brushed the concrete wall in Turn 1. Fortunately, neither incident resulted in any serious damage, although the second one, which occurred the afternoon before pole day, forced him to switch to his backup car for qualifying.

De Ferran was fastest in the early morning practice on pole day, but when it counted, the top spot went to Kelly Racing's Scott Sharp with a speed of 226.037 mph. Former IRL champion Greg Ray was second fastest and

After failing to qualify in 1995, and then skipping the "500" for the next five years because of the CART/IRL split, Team Penske's return to Indianapolis in 2001 couldn't have been much sweeter. Helio Castroneves and Gil de Ferran finished first and second, giving Roger Penske one of the few things that he had not previously achieved at Indy. Before the traditional Winner's Circle celebration, Castroneves climbed from his racecar on Indy's famous yard of bricks and then proceeded to scale the safety fencing in front of an enthusiastic crowd. "Spiderman" was born. *LAT*

Robby Gordon, driving for A.J. Foyt's team, took the outside spot on the front row. Gil de Ferran landed in the middle of row 2 with a speed of 224.406 mph and Castroneves was two rows back at 224.142. The important thing was that they were both solidly in the field.

Between qualifying and race day, there was a significant change made to the Penske cars. It did not affect performance at all, but it was instantly noticeable and extremely expensive. One of the driving forces behind Marlboro Team Penske's return to Indianapolis was that its sponsor, Marlboro-brand cigarettes, wanted to be there. In fact, it was Phillip-Morris that bore the brunt of the cost for Penske's IRL venture, so as expected, the cars were painted in the traditional red and white Marlboro colors with the cigarette brand name boldly displayed on the sidepods. That's how the cars appeared

through the first weekend of qualifying, but then the lawyers apparently got involved. As a part of the Master Settlement Agreement between the tobacco companies and the states' attorneys general, cigarette manufacturers were limited to advertising in just one U.S. auto racing series. And although they were all "Indy-cars," the Indy Racing League and CART were technically two separate series. Roger Penske had to remove the "Marlboro" logos from his cars for the race.

On the weekend between Indy 500 qualifying and the race itself, Gil de Ferran and Helio Castroveves went to Japan for the 500 Km CART event at Motegi. Castroneves seemed much more comfortable on this 1.5-mile oval, taking the pole position and leading the most laps before ultimately finishing second to Kenny Brack. De Ferran had a less rewarding weekend, finishing out of the points with mechanical problems.

The weather for race day in Indianapolis was unseasonably cool, similar to the 1992 event that saw numerous accidents resulting from cold tires. The 2001 race started with similar problems, as pole-sitter Scott Sharp took the green flag and then went into the first turn too fast, ending up in the concrete wall. Just after the restart for that incident, Sarah Fisher spun in Turn 2 and took Scott Goodyear into the wall with her. Fisher was okay, but Goodyear, the two-time Indy runner-up, suffered a broken back. Though he would recover fully, he never raced Indy-cars again. Nine laps later, when the race went green again, Sam Hornish Jr. lost control and spun in Turn 4. While he was fortunate to escape without touching anything, Al Unser Jr. crashed trying to avoid Hornish's spinning car. It was a tough start, particularly for the IRL faithful. *AutoWeek* wrote: "How bad was the IRL's day? After 20 laps, Tony George's series had its all-time winner and race pole-sitter in the first-turn wall (Scott Sharp); its all-time most popular driver and two-time 500 winner in the fourth-turn wall (Al Unser Jr.); its most popular current driver in the second-turn wall (Sarah Fisher); and last year's series runner-up in the hospital (Scott Goodyear). Also, current point-leader Sam Hornish Jr. was out of contention after spinning."

Fortunately, the Penske drivers managed to avoid all of the early excitement, and by the mid-point of the race, both were running solidly in the top five, with Castroneves taking the lead on lap 109. As the rest of the 500 miles played out, Robbie Buhl was the only driver to challenge Castroneves. Buhl eventually spun on lap 166, leaving only Gil de Ferran to push his teammate. When the checkered flag flew, Roger Penske had accomplished something that he had never achieved before—a one-two sweep of the Indianapolis 500. It was a perfect homecoming.

Instead of driving straight to victory lane, Helio Castroneves stopped his winning car at the start-finish line, climbed out and did his Spiderman routine on the safety fencing, as the crowd cheered wildly. Soon the whole Team Penske crew was up on the fence, joining in the celebration. The more reserved Roger Penske waited until his driver made it to victory lane, a place where the Captain felt much more comfortable. When Castroneves was handed the traditional victor's milk, the exuberant Brazilian raised the bottle to his crew and shouted, "Look at this, guys. I've been dreaming of this!" Needless to say, so had Roger Penske, for seven long years to be exact.

After the initial excitement was over, the political scorekeepers were quick to point out that this Indy 500 was a clear victory for the CART visitors over the hosting IRL teams. Following Castroneves and de Ferran across the finish line were Michael Andretti, Jimmy Vasser, Bruno Junqueira, and Tony Stewart, all CART drivers and teams. The highest-placed IRL regular was Eliseo Salazar in 7th position. Although CART was already in big trouble, it was apparent that the strongest teams were still there and not in the Indy Racing League. But Roger Penske did nothing to highlight this statistic. He was just enjoying his victory, and undoubtedly, making plans for next year.

With the Indianapolis distraction behind them, it was time for the Penske team to get down to the business of defending their CART title. Through the early part of the 2001 season, Gil de Ferran had not been looking like a particularly strong prospect to repeat. The Milwaukee race did little to change that outlook, as the Indy runner-up did not manage to lead a lap and ended up with just six points for his 7th place finish. Helio Castroneves fared even worse, crashing on the first lap to finish dead last.

Castroneves rebounded strongly at Detroit, winning the pole and leading the entire race to score his second CART victory of the season. With Gil de Ferran recording another less-than-spectacular 6th place finish, it was starting to look like maybe it would be Helio, not Gil defending the team's title.

Next, in a nasty, rain-shortened race in Portland, neither Penske driver finished in the points. Cleveland, Toronto and Michigan also turned out to be disappointments, with de Ferran's fourth place in Cleveland being the best showing of the three weekends. Michigan was particularly disappointing because CART had already announced that the track, which Roger Penske had resurrected from bankruptcy and built into a showcase racing facility, would be dropped from the schedule after the 2001 season. Although Penske had recently sold the facility, he still felt a strong sense of ownership in its future and he was openly critical of CART's decision. Surely, he would have particularly enjoyed winning here in the track's last CART event.

Things started looking better in Chicago, as Castroneves led a race-high 68 laps before fading to a 7th place finish. Gil de Ferran, meanwhile, drove a steady, lower-profile race and ended up on the podium, behind Kenny Brack and Patrick Carpentier. Then at Mid-Ohio, it was finally Team Penske's weekend. De Ferran and Castroneves swept the front row in qualifying. Helio led the most laps, set the fastest lap of the race, and went on to his third CART win of the season. De Ferran led most of the remaining laps and finished second to his teammate.

Elkhart Lake was another weather-impacted event, with a red-flag delay resulting in the race being shortened by 10 laps. Castroneves led the most laps again, but unfortunately, not the one that really counted. When the messy day was over, Gil was 5th and Helio 7th. Then in Vancouver, De Ferran picked up a lot of points for a second-place finish while Castroneves had a difficult day, bringing out two yellow flags for an early spin and then a stall on the course.

The next race on the calendar was at a new 2-mile oval in Lausitz, Germany. This was part of CART's initiative to bring American oval-style racing to new European fans. The event was scheduled for September 15th, and despite the 9-11 tragedies, CART and the race organizers decided to go ahead as scheduled after renaming the event "The American Memorial." For Team Penske, it wasn't a particularly good weekend, with de Ferran finishing 8th and Castroneves 12th. But this was another one of those races where the outcome seemed insignificant because of tragic circumstances surrounding the event. Alex Zanardi, who had won the 1997 and 1998 CART championships, had returned to the series after a less-than-rewarding season in Formula-1. Driving now for Mo Nunn Racing, Zanardi hadn't had much success all season; but in Germany, he was driving a fantastic race. In the closing stages, Zanardi

moved into the lead for 20 laps before pitting for a splash of fuel with just 13 laps remaining in the race. It was probably the excitement of being competitive for the first time all season, but as Zanardi exited the pit lane, he got on the throttle too fast and the back wheels of his Reynard broke loose, launching the car in a backwards slide across the racetrack. Zanardi's car darted broadside in front of Alex Tagliani who was heading into Turn 1 at 200 mph. There was no time to react. Tagliani hit Zanardi's car at the front wheels, shearing off everything forward of the steering wheel. What was left of Zanardi's car went pin-wheeling clockwise, while Tagliani veered right and slammed into the outer wall. Amazingly, Tagliani was not hurt, but for Alex Zanardi, it was a devastating crash. While it was a miracle that he survived the violent impact at all, he certainly would have died imminently had it not been for the heroic efforts of CART's safety team. Both of Zanardi's legs were virtually severed at the knees on impact, and the former champion was in grave danger of bleeding to death. Dr. Terry Trammel and Dr. Steve Olvey were at the scene of the disaster almost before Zanardi's car stopped spinning. They worked quickly to halt the profuse bleeding, performing emergency procedures on the gravely injured driver as he was rushed to the hospital.

Alex Zanardi was lucky, and he's the first to acknowledge that. The accident cost him both of his legs, but he would survive…and he would race again. In the months that followed, Zanardi displayed remarkable courage. Fitted with artificial legs, he was up and around, making his first public appearance in December, just three months after the accident. And while he could never compete at the CART level again, he has raced in sports sedans equipped with special controls. When CART returned to the Lausitz track two years later, in an emotional pre-race demonstration, Zanardi drove 13 high-speed laps in a specially-equipped Indy-car to symbolically complete that fateful 2001 race that he never got to finish. Even for those who were never Alex Zanardi fans, it was hard not to feel inspired by his courage and determination.

While the CART teams were in Europe, they also raced at the new oval track in Rockingham, England.

By the 2001 season, the Penske Racing engineers had modified their Reynard chassis to the point that people were calling it a "Renske." Teammates Gil de Ferran and Helio Castroneves combined again for five victories and 8 pole positons, including Laguna Seca where the Penske drivers filled the front row. De Ferran went on to win his second consecutive CART title. On that conquering note, Roger Penske abandoned the series that he co-founded 22 years earlier, moving his team to the Indy Racing League for 2002. *LAT*

Going into this race, with five events remaining on the schedule, Gil de Ferran was in second place and Helio Castroneves in fourth place in the championship standings. De Ferran helped his cause considerably, taking the win at Rockingham over Kenny Brack, who was the current points leader. Castroneves finished fourth, although he would have been in contention for the win had he not been penalized a lap for blocking. Unfortunately, although the reigning Indy 500 champion would finish out the season with some decent showings, there would be no more wins.

Back in the United States, Gil de Ferran then had his best race of the season, claiming the pole and leading all 100 laps of the Grand Prix of Houston. Coupled with Kenny Brack's 7th place result, this gave de Ferran a nice lead in the championship with just three races

remaining. De Ferran followed with another pole and a third-place finish in a wild race at Laguna Seca, where Brack finished well out of the points. Gil then wrapped up the year with a 4th place in Australia and a 6th in the California 500 to end the season 36 points ahead of nearest challenger, Kenny Brack. Michael Andretti was third in the final standings and Helio Castroneves fourth, making this another very gratifying year overall for Roger Penske.

But despite the very strong season on the racetrack, Penske was not at all happy with what was going on behind the scenes. The CART-IRL split was as deep and hopeless as ever, and CART's bickering, self-serving Board of Directors seemed incapable of even keeping a constructive dialogue open with Tony George's organization. At the end of the 2001 season, Penske said in an interview: "I told my CART associates at the time that CART becoming a public corporation was a troubling thing. There might be short-term gains but it would end up with leadership divided, one side trying to run racing and the other side trying to satisfy Wall Street. And certainly, that's exactly the position we're in today."

As the 2001 season was drawing to a close, rumors were circulating that Penske Racing and its two-time defending champion driver would not be back in CART for 2002. The idea of CART without Roger Penske and his team was almost unimaginable. Yet, when he was asked at the Australian race about this speculation, Penske was surprisingly non-committal about his future plans. "We'll sit down with our sponsors after Fontana," he said, "and review our options." For the CART faithful, that should have been a startling wakeup call; but there was surprisingly little concern expressed and no apparent effort made to persuade the series' most successful team to stick around. *Autoweek* wrote, "For decades, Penske has been considered not only the most influential figure in American motor-sports, but the most prescient; as has been noted by practically everyone in racing, when the music stops, Roger Penske always has a chair. If history is any indication, if CART is headed in one direction and Penske in another, it probably means CART is going the wrong way."

Gil de Ferran had no doubts about where he would be

the following season. Despite the fact that he was a born road-racer, and much more comfortable on CART's road and street courses than the IRL's super-speedways, de Ferran was sticking with Roger Penske, wherever that turned out to be. "My loyalty is to Roger and the team," he said. "As I said, I feel very strongly about that. But put all that aside for a moment. In my mind, this type of racing is going into some stormy weather. In that case I couldn't choose a better partner to be with. Over the years he has the proven track record for negotiating the stormy weather." *Autoweek* added, "…that record might be worth CART examining as well, even if perhaps it's too late to do any good."

Roger Penske had at least four compelling reasons to consider a move from CART to the Indy Racing League. First, of course, there was the sorry state of affairs within CART's management organization. Second, there was the lure of the Indianapolis 500, still the world's biggest auto race, even if its brilliance had been tarnished slightly by the recent political events. Thanks to generous financial support from Marlboro, flawless execution by the team, and a reasonable dose of racing luck, Team Penske had been able to show up at Indy and walk away with all the marbles in 2001. But it was painfully expensive and a logistical nightmare running an entirely separate program for just that one race. It would be infinitely easier to compete at Indy if they were running the full IRL schedule.

Roger Penske's third reason for interest in the IRL was that he saw a potential opportunity to get back into the racecar-building business. Since abandoning the uncompetitive Penske chassis at the end of the 1999 season, work at Penske's fabrication shop in England had been limited to optimizing the team's so-called "Renske" chassis. By moving to the IRL, Penske saw the prospect of building and selling new chassis to other IRL participants. Tony George, however, would ultimately reject Penske's proposal on the basis of conflict of interest.

Finally, there was the issue of what Phillip-Morris wanted to do with its substantial advertising resources. The company already had a huge international presence through its support of the Ferrari Formula-1 program.

What they really wanted from their Indy-car sponsorship was exposure in the U.S. market, and that was rapidly shrinking as CART was taking more and more of its races elsewhere. Of course, the richest single card on the table was the Indy 500, and given the choice between that one race and the whole CART series, Phillip-Morris/Marlboro ultimately chose Indy. That was all Roger Penske needed to make his final decision. Team Penske was heading to the Indy Racing League.

Without Penske Racing and other teams that had also defected, in part or whole, to the IRL, CART began to fall apart quickly. By the end of the 2002 season, embattled CEO Joe Heitzler was ousted and the organization managed to lure highly-respected promoter Chris Pook to take the top spot. The general consensus was that Pook might be the one person who could still turn things around. In 2002, to fill the starting grids with a reasonable number of competitive racecars, Pook spent all of CART's cash reserves subsidizing existing and new race teams. But in the end, it was too little, too late. With almost all the big-name teams and drivers now gone to the IRL, CART ran out of money by the end of the 2003 season. As the final hour approached, a group of three remaining team owners negotiated with the CART Board of Directors, attempting to save the series from bankruptcy. Ultimately, they decided that it was more advantageous to allow the corporation to go under and then buy the assets in bankruptcy court. The catch-22 in that strategy, however, was that it left the door open for other bidders to make a play for those assets. Not surprisingly, Tony George and the Indy Racing League came forward with a very attractive cash offer, one that was considerably richer than what was offered by the CART owners group. But in the end, the bankruptcy court sided with the CART owners, who had vowed to keep the series afloat and honor existing commitments, thus avoiding a certain flood of lawsuits that would have resulted had George purchased the series and then shut it down. Under the new name "Champ Car World Series," a resurrected CART championship has survived its first three seasons and appears positioned to continue as a rival to the IRL for some time to come.

CHAPTER 14
IRL Indy Cars
(2002 – 2006)

"Roger Penske is the kind of man who lends credibility to whatever venture he chooses to participate in. The IRL stands to benefit greatly from his character, his business sense and his integrity as a team owner."
—Larry Manch, *Racing News Online*

In its early years, the Indy Racing League was rightfully viewed by most motorsports enthusiasts as the "Minor League" of Indy-car racing, while the established CART series was considered the "real thing." The drivers and teams that rose to the top of the IRL during its first few seasons were either opportunistic CART field-fillers or new participants who happened to be in the right place at the right time. Teams like Panther

Racing, Cheever, Kelley, Treadway, Hemelgarn, Menard and A.J. Foyt Racing established themselves as the serious contenders in the upstart series. But when the top CART teams began cherry-picking the Indianapolis 500 in 2000, competing head-to-head against the IRL's best for the first time, it was a little like taking candy from a baby. Juan Montoya won the 2000 Indy 500 for Chip Ganassi Racing and then a year later, Helio Castroneves and Gil de Ferran gave Roger Penske his first-ever one-two finish in the Memorial Day classic. Understandably, when Marlboro Team Penske announced that they would be moving from CART to the Indy Racing League for the 2002 season, many expected nothing less than immediate and total domination.

2002

Reigning CART champion Gil de Ferran and defending Indianapolis 500 winner Helio Castroveves returned for their third season together at Penske Racing in 2002. In the interest of NASCAR-style regulated parity, there were only two approved chassis and two approved engines available to IRL teams. Team Penske chose the Dallara-Chevrolet combination, which was essentially the same package that Castroneves had taken to victory at Indy the previous year.

With the exception of the Indianapolis 500, which would again draw some one-time challengers from CART, the strongest competition was expected to come from defending IRL champion Sam Hornish Jr. at Panther Racing, Al Unser Jr. and Scott Sharp at Kelley Racing, and Jeff Ward who was driving for Chip Ganassi's single-car IRL program. Other drivers who would find their way to victory lane during the 2002 IRL season included Felipe Giaffone, Alex Barron, Airton Dare and Tomas Scheckter, son of 1979 F1 World Champion Jody Scheckter.

When the season opened in early March on the 1.5-mile oval at Homestead, Florida, it became immediately apparent that Team Penske was going to have to work a little harder than many people originally expected. In qualifying for their first "regular" IRL event, Helio Castroneves claimed the second starting position while Gil de Ferran took the 6th spot on the grid. Sam Hornish won the pole and went on to take the victory, leading 166 of the 200 laps. De Ferran and Castroneves led just five laps collectively and finished second and third in the race. Realistically, that wasn't a bad start at all; but expectations were so high that anything less than a one-two Penske sweep was destined to be viewed as an upset.

In Phoenix two weeks later, a lot of premature "I-told-you-so's" could be heard as Helio Castroneves won from the pole, followed by teammate Gil de Ferran. But Sam Hornish still led the most laps, and Al Unser Jr. and Eddie Cheever also provided serious competition, so this was anything but a runaway. It was, in fact, a snapshot of what was to be a typical race in the 2002 IRL season.

Next, the Penske drivers finished a somewhat uncompetitive 4th and 5th in the 400-miler at California Speedway. Then, de Ferran had a strong run at Nazareth, starting from the pole and leading the most laps before ultimately finishing third in the race. Castroneves started second to his teammate and also led a lot of laps before settling for 5th place. What this demonstrated, more than anything, was the remarkable level of competition in this new arena. A driver could qualify fastest, lead the majority of the race, and still find himself relegated to 3rd or 5th position at the end of the day even without experiencing any serious problems.

Next on the schedule was the big one, the Indianapolis 500. This is the event that Penske Racing, more than any other team, knows how to win. But as the long and sometimes tedious month of Indy got underway, it became apparent that the Penske team was going to have to work hard for this one too. In qualifying, Castroneves and de Ferran found themselves two miles-per-hour off the pace set by visiting CART front-runner Bruno Junqueira in an extra Chip Ganassi entry. Unlike many prior years when a 2 mph deficit might have bumped a driver to the second row, in this intensely competitive field that was separated by less than 5 mph between the fastest and slowest qualifiers, the Penske drivers found themselves back in mid-pack.

As the race got underway, Junqueira led from the pole for the first 32 laps until Tomas Scheckter took

over. The South African rookie then controlled most of the next 140 laps until he inexplicably crashed while leading just 28 laps from the finish. Gil de Ferran had led a total of 13 laps earlier in the race, but by the time Scheckter exited, he had fallen to the end of the lead lap and was not a factor. At this point, defending champ Helio Castroneves had not led a single lap all day, but he had driven a steady race and was in position to inherit the top spot when Scheckter eliminated himself on lap 172. Team Penske president, Tim Cindric, did not pit his driver for fuel during the ensuing caution period, meaning that Helio was going to have to nurse 42 laps out of his last tank. That big gamble forced Castroneves to drive conservatively for the remainder of the race, as he was pressed hard in the closing stages by Paul Tracy. The former Penske driver was part of a formidable four-car Team Green assault from CART. With just 1-1/2 laps remaining, Tracy began to make a move on Castroneves as the two charged down the back straight. In all probability, he would have made the pass had it not been for a very well timed incident between rookie Laurent Redon and former winner Buddy Lazier that took place behind the lead battle. As the caution light was displayed, Tracy shot past Castroneves, but the IRL officials ordered him to relinquish the position because the race was already under caution at the time the pass was completed. The race ended under the yellow flag with Helio Castroneves claiming his second-consecutive Indy 500 victory. Amazingly, after his second appearance at Indianapolis, he was still undefeated, something that had never been accomplished before. Gil de Ferran would likely have finished in the top-five also had he not lost a wheel and spun exiting the pits during the Scheckter caution period. He ended up 10th.

The IRL ruling that relegated CART driver Paul Tracy to the runner-up position was controversial and, not surprisingly, it was protested by Team Green. Although all available data seemed to corroborate the original IRL decision, there was considerable skepticism, particularly in the CART community, about the fairness of the appeal process that was entirely under the control of the Indy Racing League. The fact that Tony George and the IRL ultimately ruled in favor of Team

Penske's IRL driver over Team Green's CART driver was the subject of much debate over the next months. But the fact remained that Roger Penske had won his 12th Indianapolis 500, breaking his own record yet again.

A week later in Texas, the Penske team was much less successful. Neither driver was a major factor, with Castroneves leading just 3 laps before ultimately finishing fourth. Gil de Ferran had problems and finished 16th, many laps behind. But a week after that, on the one-mile oval at Pikes Peak, Colorado, de Ferran dominated. Starting from the pole, he led 217 of the 225 laps, taking the checkered flag 1.4 seconds ahead of his Penske teammate.

Gil de Ferran took the pole again at Richmond with a record speed of 168.7 mph on the 3/4-mile racetrack. With Castroneves qualifying second and everybody else at least 3 mph slower, it looked to be a Team Penske blowout. In fact, de Ferran did lead a race-high 168 laps, but ultimately had to settle for second to Sam Hornish Jr.

Then there was a stretch of four races, at Kansas, Nashville, Michigan and Louisville, where the Penske cars were strangely uncompetitive, scoring some top-five finishes but never really in contention for victories. That string was finally broken in late August on the 1.25-mile Gateway oval in East St. Louis. De Ferran and Castroneves qualified first and third respectively, led almost all the laps, and finished one-two ahead of Alex Barron, Buddy Rice, and Sam Hornish Jr.

With each of these random dominating performances by Team Penske, there was speculation that they had finally discovered the secret that was going to allow them to run away with the series as almost everyone had expected them to do from the outset. But two weeks after stomping the field at Gateway, they had another difficult weekend at Chicago. Castroneves qualified 21st in the 25-car field and eventually worked his way up to a 4th place finish. Gil de Ferran qualified 11th but crashed hard early in the race, resulting in injuries that would keep him out of the season finale the following weekend. Up until that point, he was still in contention for the championship, but his season was now over.

Heading into the final race of the year at the very fast Texas World Speedway, Helio Castroneves trailed Sam Hornish Jr. by just 12 points in the championship battle. Roger Penske put former Team Rahal driver Max Papis in de Ferran's car for this one race, just in case he could do anything to help Castroneves by taking points away from Hornish. In order to overtake the defending series champion and win the title, Castroneves obviously had to finish ahead of his rival in the race, but because he also had to gain a net 12 points, even an outright victory wouldn't earn him the title if Hornish managed to take second-place points.

For all the criticism levied against the IRL, some justified and some not, there was no denying that they had managed to present a perfect storybook finish for their 2002 championship. Castroneves and Hornish traded the lead back and forth throughout the afternoon, with the Penske driver leading 92 of the 200 laps while his rival paced 79 circuits. Hornish grabbed the front spot from Castroneves on lap 192. Helio came back to lead the 195th lap, but Hornish got by again the next time around. As the two championship contenders charged past the checkered flag, Hornish held first position by 0.010 seconds. Of course, even if he had nosed ahead at the end, Castroneves would have still fallen just short of the title, but it was academic at that point. Tony George had to be thinking, "It doesn't get any better than this!" And Roger Penske had to be thinking, "We'll get 'em next year!"

2003

As usual, Roger Penske was on the leading edge of the curve when he jumped from CART to the IRL before the 2002 season. Not long after Penske made his move, Honda and Toyota, CART's two biggest financial backers, both announced that they would be building engines exclusively to the IRL's specifications for the 2003 season. That forced CART to choose between conceding to Tony George's long-time call for lower-tech, lower cost powerplants, or letting the two Japanese automakers walk away from the series. As usual, there were multiple complex political issues involved, and in the end, CART opted to stick with its turbo engine formula after negotiating a deal with Cosworth Engineer-

With Toyota power in their Penske Dallaras, Gil de Ferran and Helio Castroneves scored a one-two finish in the 2003 Indianapolis 500 and both drivers were in contention for the IRL championship going down to the final race of the season. *LAT*

ing to provide identical spec-engines for all its teams.

Concurrent with the arrival of Honda and Toyota to the IRL, Infinity, which was one of the original two engine suppliers for the league, opted to bow out. That left Chevrolet alone to battle the new Japanese competition. Team Penske, along with an expanded two-car Ganassi Racing program that included drivers Scott Dixon and Tomas Scheckter, were the flagship teams for Toyota engines. During the off-season, Michael

Andretti had bought a majority interest in Team Green Racing and moved the whole program from CART to the IRL. The new Andretti-Green Racing (AGR) team, with drivers Michael Andretti, Tony Kanaan, and Dario Franchitti, was the strongest Honda effort. Defending series champ Sam Hornish Jr. and Panther Racing stayed with Chevrolet for 2003.

The season opened in Homestead, Florida, on a good note for the Toyota teams. Scott Dixon won the race for Target-Ganassi Racing, while Gil de Ferran led the most laps and finished second, ahead of teammate Helio Castroneves. Panther Racing and the other Chevy teams struggled to keep up with the new Japanese challengers, as they would for most of the year.

Three weeks after the encouraging start at Homestead, Penske Racing suffered a major setback at Phoenix. Although Castroneves ran with the leaders for most of the race, he was never really a serious threat to win and ended up finishing 4th. But the really bad news was that Gil de Ferran was injured again, sustaining a concussion and two broken vertebrae in a late-race accident with Michael Andretti. These injuries would keep him out of the next race and put his bid for an IRL championship in early jeopardy. De Ferran's two serious incidents in three races probably started him thinking about whether he really wanted to be doing this much longer. It was no secret that he really didn't care for the IRL's high-speed oval tracks, but his loyalty to Roger Penske's team had taken priority over his preference to stay on CART's "safer" road courses—so far.

In mid April, the IRL teams made the journey to Japan for the third race of the season, the league's first venture outside of U.S. borders. Roger Penske recruited American Alex Barron, who had done some substitute driving for the Penske CART program a few years earlier, to take de Ferran's car for this one race. It was another tough day for Team Penske, however, with both cars eliminated in separate accidents. Castroneves got together with rookie Roger Yasukawa and Barron was taken out by the always-dangerous Tomas Scheckter.

De Ferran, still a little sore, was back in the car when practice opened at Indianapolis in early May. The field at Indy was much stronger this year than it had been in a long time. AGR had entries for Michael Andretti (who had announced that this would be the final race of his driving career), Tony Kanaan, rookie Dan Weldon, and Robby Gordon, subbing for Dario Franchitti who had been injured in a non-racing accident. The Target-Ganassi entries for Scott Dixon and Tomas Scheckter would be certain threats. Bobby Rahal had regular driver Kenny Brack and CART visitor Jimmy Vasser in his Hondas. Other challengers that could not be over-

looked included defending IRL champion Sam Hornish and former winners Al Unser Jr. and Buddy Lazier.

Against this strengthened field, Helio Castroneves won his first Indy 500 pole, with a speed of 231.725 mph. Teammate Gil de Ferran, maybe still feeling a little sore and cautious, was three mph slower and landed in 10th position, on the inside of the fourth row. Interestingly, Castroneves qualified a Dallara-Toyota while de Ferran chose to run a Panoz G-Force. This wasn't the first time that the team had run two different chassis in the 500, but it was certainly unconventional.

Castroneves jumped into the lead at the start of the race and stayed there until he pitted on lap 16 during a caution period. He led on two other occasions during the afternoon for a total of 58 laps, second only to Tomas Scheckter who set the pace for 63 circuits. Gil de Ferran didn't make his way to the front of the pack until late in the race. Running behind his teammate 30 laps from the finish, de Ferran capitalized on a traffic opportunity as the two Penske cars came upon a slow-moving A.J. Foyt IV. The 19-year-old grandson of the former four-time winner had served as a moving chicane all day long, prompting criticism from a number of competitors that grandpa A.J. had moved the young man into the big leagues a little too soon. As Castroneves closed on Foyt entering turn one, he had to lift slightly, losing critical momentum and giving de Ferran the opportunity to shoot past when they got to the back straight. With no other interferences, that's the way they went on to finish 30 laps later.

Gil de Ferran became the 9th driver to win the Indianapolis 500 for Roger Penske. It was Penske Racing's 13th Indy win overall, their third straight and the second one-two finish in three years. Helio Castroneves fell three-tenths of a second short of becoming the first driver in history to win the "500" in three consecutive years. Despite missing that rare opportunity for immortality, the excitable and terminally joyful Brazilian embraced his victorious teammate. Then, the two Penske drivers climbed the fence together at the start-finish line, much to the delight of the enthusiastic and appreciative crowd, which had now grown accustomed to this site.

The Indy win moved Gil de Ferran to 4th place in the IRL standings, while Castroneves' runner-up finish bumped him to second in the championship battle as the Indy Racing League teams returned to regular business at Texas a week later. In a race that was dominated by Tomas Scheckter until he crashed, and then won by a reinvigorated Al Unser Jr., the Penske teammates struggled to finish 7th and 8th. At Pikes Peak, they combined to lead 118 laps, but de Ferran ended up third and Castroneves 12th. Then on the short track at Richmond, where the Penske cars had been so fast a year earlier, Helio and Gil finished second and third respectively to Target-Ganassi driver Scott Dixon. This moved Dixon to second place in the championship battle behind Tony Kanaan, with Castroneves third and de Ferran fourth. As it would happen, these four drivers would go down to the wire for the season title.

The Penske teammates took second and third in Kansas behind Bryan Herta; then Gil de Ferran came back to win Nashville over Scott Dixon with Castroneves third. Michigan was unkind to Team Penske yet again, with de Ferran's 7th place being the highlight of the weekend. Castroneves rebounded with a strong run at St. Louis, starting from the pole, leading almost half the race and taking the win over Tony Kanaan and Gil de Ferran. But after that, the season took a dramatic turn.

A week later in Kentucky, suddenly Sam Hornish Jr. was back at the front of the field. Handicapped by the relatively under-powered Chevrolet engine, the defending series champion had struggled all season, creating a very sticky situation for Tony George and the IRL. On the one hand, George certainly felt obligated to intervene on behalf of his popular league champion and the only American engine manufacturer in his series. On the other hand, the IRL's equipment stability rules, a cornerstone of George's justification for the creation of the series in the first place, prohibited the kind of mid-season redesign that Chevrolet wanted to make. George also had to consider the reaction of Honda and Toyota, which had invested a lot of money and played by the rules to earn the advantage they enjoyed. Surely they wouldn't be happy if the IRL arbitrarily conceded to let their rival have a "mulligan." Tony George was between a rock and a hard place; and the IRL critics—of which there were still many—couldn't have been more delighted.

With surprisingly few ramifications, however, the IRL ultimately conceded to let Chevrolet make a change. Apparently the Japanese automakers and the IRL teams they supplied were able to appreciate that this was an issue that had the potential to threaten the very future of the series. In the big picture, it was better to lose this battle but win the war for the survival of the IRL series. Chevrolet's new Cosworth-engineered engine was immediately competitive with the Hondas and Toyotas, propelling Hornish back into the championship battle starting with a win at Kentucky, where the Penske entries finished 5th and 9th. A week later at Nazareth, Castroneves came back with a win over Hornish, moving him into first place in the title chase. Gil de Ferran finished fourth at Nazareth to move up to second in the standings with three races remaining in the season. At this point, Roger's Penske's prospects for his first IRL title looked pretty strong.

Unfortunately, a gearbox failure in the next race at Chicagoland probably cost Castroneves the championship. While he retained the lead after this race, the 30 points he lost to eventual champion Scott Dixon proved to be his undoing. Gil de Ferran also had a disappointing weekend in Chicago, finishing 12th in the race and dropping from second to fourth in the points standings.

Next, in the 400-mile race at Fontana, Sam Hornish Jr. scored his second victory in three outings with the new Chevy engine. Helio Castroneves' 6th place finish dropped him into a first-place tie with Scott Dixon, who was runner-up in this race. Gil de Ferran had another frustrating day, finishing 15th and falling to 5th in the standings. None of this was very good news for Team Penske, but for Tony George and the Indy Racing League, it couldn't possibly have been any better. Heading into the season's final event at Texas Motor Speedway, which traditionally produced the most exciting wheel-to-wheel racing on the circuit, often with two and three car photo finishes, there were *five* drivers still

The "Professor," Gil de Ferran, won the Indianapolis 500 in his fourth start, nudging Penske teammate Helio Castroneves by 0.299 seconds. Soon after achieving this goal, de Ferran quietly informed Roger Penske of his decision to retire from driving at the end of the season. *LAT*

onship this season; and to make it even more interesting, it would turn out to be Gil de Ferran's last chance at that title. The "Professor" had quietly informed Roger Penske in July that he planned to retire at the end of the season. De Ferran had won two CART championships for Penske and, earlier in the year, he'd added a coveted Indianapolis 500 Borg-Warner trophy to his impressive collection of awards. With the exception of capturing an IRL title, there really wasn't anything else the quiet and likeable Brazilian felt that he needed to accomplish. Making his decision easier was the fact that he'd suffered two fairly serious injuries over the past year. He had reached a point where the potential remaining rewards couldn't outweigh the associated risks anymore. He made the choice to retire when he was truly at the very peak of his career, something that very few drivers ever manage to accomplish. Mark Donohue did it, but he went back. Formula-1 World Champion Jackie Stewart, who happened to be de Ferran's mentor, quit after winning his third title. He and Rick Mears were the exceptions. Most drivers wait a little too long, hoping to get one more good year—just a couple more wins to end on a high note. Usually, that doesn't happen. Gil de Ferran was lucky, and he was smart. He did it right.

After de Ferran told Penske of his intentions, the Captain immediately went to work behind the scenes to secure the best available driver to fill his vacant seat. Sam Hornish Jr. had been talking about leaving the IRL for an opportunity in NASCAR, following in the footsteps of the IRL's first legitimate home-grown star, Tony Stewart. But when Roger Penske approached him with the chance to work for the team whose drivers he'd idolized as a child, it was an easy decision. For 2004, Sam Hornish Jr. would be on the Penske payroll. But for one more race, he was still the adversary, one of three drivers who could prevent Roger Penske from winning his first IRL title.

The Texas race turned out to be everything that Tony George and the IRL could have hoped for—until 12 laps from the scheduled finish anyway. In typical Texas fashion, the race produced 11 lead changes, with all five of the potential champions except Helio Castroneves leading at some point during the afternoon. With de

in contention for title. With a maximum of 52 points available at Texas, Castroneves and Dixon were tied for the lead with 467, Tony Kanaan was third with 460, Sam Hornish Jr. had climbed to fourth place with 448 points, and Gil de Ferran was the long-shot, with 437 points in 5th spot.

Team Penske still had two shots at an IRL champi-

Ferran in front 30 laps from the finish, the five contenders were running nose-to-tail on the track, ready for the final shootout. But then within the course of a few minutes, three of the five challengers were eliminated from contention for the win. First, Hornish's Chevrolet engine expired, ending his race and his dramatic comeback charge. Then, as Castroneves was attempting to pass Tony Kanaan on the inside line through the first turn, he hit a bump that pushed his car up the banking, banging his right front wheel into Kanaan's left rear. Usually when Indy-car wheels touch in this type of scenario, the consequences are devastating. Usually one or both of the cars involved ends up flying through the air, sometimes with very serious, even deadly results. But this time, fortunately, both Kanaan and Castroneves escaped with just tire damage. They were, however, both forced to make unscheduled pit stops for new rubber and that effectively took them out of contention for the race and the championship.

That left Gil de Ferran and Scott Dixon to fight it out for the race and the IRL title. Although de Ferran was leading, Dixon had the much stronger hand at that point. In order for the Penske driver to gain enough points on his rival, he would have to win the race and hope that Dixon finished lower than 10th position. Gil de Ferran did everything he could have possibly done—he won the bonus points for claiming the pole and leading the most laps in the race, and he did, in fact go on to win the race itself, but he couldn't do anything to prevent Scott Dixon from finishing in second place. That was enough to give the title to Dixon and Chip Ganassi Racing.

But, by the time de Ferran and Dixon took the checkered flag, almost everyone was thinking about something else, something much more serious than the race or even the championship. On the 187th lap, Tomas Scheckter and Kenny Brack, who were battling for position behind the leaders, touched wheels on the back straight. The contact flipped Brack's car into the air where it then slammed into the safety fencing above the concrete retaining wall. Brack's car was shredded into pieces, with the engine completely torn from the cockpit. For a moment after the debris stopped flying,

it was difficult to tell where to even start looking for the driver. It was a vicious and horrifying crash. Almost surprisingly, Kenny Brack was still conscious as he was removed from the wreckage, but he was very seriously injured. He had a fractured spine, sternum and right leg, plus two badly broken ankles. Thankfully, the personable Swede would recover fully, but it would be a long and painful process, and he would not race again until the 2005 Indy 500.

Because of concern over Kenny Brack's condition, Gil de Ferran was robbed of the opportunity to enjoy and celebrate his victory in the final race of his career. On the other hand, if there was ever any doubt in his mind about whether he had made the right decision regarding retirement, this near-tragedy erased that doubt forever.

For the second year in a row, Team Penske just narrowly missed winning the IRL championship. Gil de Ferran ended the season in second place with Helio Castroneves third, reversing their finishing positions from the year before. But with the very talented and hard-charging Sam Hornish Jr. joining Castroneves for the 2004 season, there was every reason to believe that it wouldn't be much longer before Tony George was handing that trophy to Roger Penske.

Kenny Brack's Texas injuries were by far the most serious suffered by any IRL driver during a season that saw an inordinate number of winged racecars flying through the air. Sixty-three year-old Mario Andretti, test-driving for his son's team, started the frightening trend at Indianapolis in April. The senior Andretti, running alone on the track, apparently hit a small piece of debris that lifted the front wing of his car enough to launch him into the air. The car did a backwards flip as it climbed to the height of the front straight retaining fence. Miraculously, Andretti landed right side up and he walked away from the spectacular aerobatic display without injury. Rookie Dan Weldon went airborne and flipped after making wall contact during the Indy 500 race and Helio Castroneves had a similar experience in testing at Richmond in June. Fortunately, they also both escaped injury in these incidents.

Brack's more serious outcome had people talking

Sam Hornish Jr. had been an IRL sensation during his two seasons with Panther Racing. When he continued to excel even against the heightened competition of Penske Racing and other transplanted CART teams, his talent was validated and he went to the top of the Captain's short list of potential replacements for Gil de Ferran. *Alan Hummel*

Helio flashes that trademark Spiderman smile at the fans. With his former archrival now in the other Team Penske car, Castroneves had something to prove heading into the 2005 season. *Alan Hummel*

about the need to do something to address this frightening development that was reminiscent of NASCAR's problem in the early 1990s. Any debate about the need to take some action was tragically settled on October 22nd when 26-year-old Tony Renna, who had just signed to drive for Chip Ganassi Racing the following year, flew into the fencing during tire testing at Indianapolis. Renna's car appeared to lift into the air with absolutely no outside influence. It rammed into the steel fence above the speedway's four-foot-high concrete wall, taking down two steel fence posts. The promising young driver was killed instantly, becoming the first

fatality at the Indianapolis Motor Speedway since Scott Brayton died in practice for the 1996 race.

The IRL could not longer deny that they had a serious problem. With surprising swiftness, the league moved to mandate design changes to the cars for the 2004 season, the most significant of which was the reduction in engine size from 3.5 liters to 3.0 liters. This was expected to cut top speeds by 10 mph. Aerodynamic changes were required at the start of the 2004 season, but to allow the engine manufacturers adequate time for testing and development, the new smaller engine would not be introduced until the Indianapolis 500.

2004

Heading into its third IRL season, Team Penske was the strong favorite to take the championship. The only question seemed to be which driver would finish first and which second. *AutoWeek* picked Helio Castroneves at 2:1 saying, "[He] would get greater odds if the talented Hornish wasn't his teammate." Hornish was the next best bet at 4:1, while defending champion Scott Dixon was the best of the rest at 6:1. Then came the Andretti-Green super-team of Dan Weldon, Tony Kanaan, Dario Franchitti and Bryan Herta. It seemed that the experts were convinced that Penske's IRL teething problems were finally behind him.

The season opening race on the redesigned 1.5-mile Homestead oval did nothing to dissuade those experts. "The rest of the IRL collectively groaned 'uh oh,'" *AutoWeek* wrote after Sam Hornish took the victory by 0.0698 seconds over his Penske teammate, Helio Castroneves. The race saw eight different leaders and 15 lead changes, but Castroneves was in front for 85 of the 200 laps and appeared to be headed for victory until his new teammate slipped by on the inside line on the very last lap. When Hornish claimed this win, he accomplished something that no other driver had managed in the history of the team—winning his very first race in a Penske Racing uniform. It's no wonder that the competition was nervous.

Three weeks later at Phoenix, however, it was a different story. Tony Kanaan, driving one of Michael Andretti's Honda-powered Dallaras, dominated the day, leading all but nine laps to take the win over defending series champ Scott Dixon. Sam Hornish led four of the remaining laps, but brushed the wall midway through the race and was not a factor from that point on. Helio Castroneves stayed close to the leaders all day, but ended up 6th in the very competitive race.

When the IRL returned to Japan for the last event before the Indianapolis 500, there were a couple of very unsettling developments for the Penske effort. First, for the second race in a row, a Honda-powered car won the pole and dominated the race. This time it was Dan Weldon, the sophomore British driver from the AGR team who took the victory over his teammate Tony Kanaan and Helio Castroneves. The second concern for the Penske camp was that the normally unflappable Sam Hornish Jr. took himself out of contention for the second race in a row, making contact with the turn-one concrete. After the third race of what was sup-

posed to be Team Penske's dominating season, Weldon and Kanaan were first and second in the championship standings, with Helio Castroneves third and Sam Hornish Jr. sixth. Things were not going according to plan.

The Indianapolis 500 marked the debut of the smaller 3.0-liter engine formula mandated by the IRL in response to 2003's safety problems. When the track opened for practice on Sunday, May 9th, the Toyota-powered machines of Scott Dixon and Helio Castroneves were at the top of the speed charts. But by the following Saturday, when the cars lined up for Pole Day qualifying, the advantage had decisively shifted to the Honda teams. To almost everyone's surprise, Honda claimed the first seven spots on the starting grid, led by the very improbable Buddy Rice. Bobby Rahal had recruited Rice, who had been fired by Team Cheever in late 2003, to substitute on a race-to-race basis for the injured Kenny Brack. The young Californian was clearly making the best of the opportunity.

Beside Rice on the front row were AGR teammates Dan Weldon and Dario Franchitti. The second row consisted of CART visitor Bruno Junqueira, Tony Kanaan and Adrian Fernandez. Rice's Rahal-Letterman teammate Vitor Meira was 7th on the grid, followed by Helio Castroneves in the fastest non-Honda-powered car. Sam Hornish Jr. was three positions farther back, in 11th spot. Obviously, the Honda engineers had done a better job than their Toyota and Chevrolet-Cosworth counterparts in reworking their engine to meet the new IRL specs. Also apparent was that the Indy Racing League had achieved the desired speed reduction targeted with the new engines, as Rice's pole-winning speed was down nearly 9 mph from the time posted by Helio Castroneves a year earlier.

Despite their relatively weak showing in qualifying, Helio Castroneves and Sam Hornish Jr. still found themselves pegged as the favorites going into the Memorial Day weekend. Penske Racing's staggering record of 13 Indy 500 victories made it difficult to bet against the red-and-white cars, even if they were at a slight horsepower disadvantage. But when the race started, it became apparent fairly quickly that the only way that a Penske Toyota was going to win that day was if all the

In the final Indy-car race at the short-lived Nazareth Speedway, Penske teammates Helio Castroneves and Sam Hornish Jr. claimed the front-row starting spots and appeared set to give the boss one last victory at the track he built. While leading at the 3/4-mark, Hornish left his pit before the fueling hose was disconnected, igniting a frightening pit fire that ended his bid for the win. *LAT*

Hondas broke. With the exception of a few laps during pit stop shuffling, Honda-powered machines controlled the entire race. Sam Hornish worked his way to the front for nine laps, but he got caught in a three-car wreck on the front-straight halfway through the race, ending his day. Helio Castroneves, who had dominated the previous three years at Indy, never led a single lap all day. In a race that was called 20 laps early because of tornadoes in the area, the remaining Team Penske driver hung on for a 9th place finish, one spot behind the highest-placed non-Honda competitor, Scott Dixon. With a quarter of the season now completed, and the Toyota engine looking like a serious handicap, Team Penske's prospects for an IRL title in 2004 were already starting to look pretty grim.

Qualifying for the next race at Texas Motor Speedway further reinforced the fears of the Toyota teams, as Honda-powered cars swept the top five grid positions. Castroneves claimed the 6th spot and Hornish, on a track where he had enjoyed much success in the past,

landed back in 11th. In the race, AGR teammates Tony Kanaan and Dario Franchitti combined to lead 173 of 200 laps, finishing ahead of Alex Barron in a Chevrolet-powered Cheever Racing Dallara, with Sam Hornish in fourth. Hornish may have done better had it not been for another brush against the concrete, this time while avoiding an incident between Buddy Rice and Darren Manning with 21 laps remaining. Castroneves finished three laps off the pace in 12th position, further damaging his prospects for the championship.

Richmond offered the first signs of hope for the struggling Penske team. Helio Castroneves claimed the pole at 171.2 mph on the 3/4-mile track. A Honda and a Chevy took the next two spots, followed by Sam Hornish in 4th. Castroneves led the first 37 laps and then Hornish took over for the next 76 circuits. The Penske teammates stayed in the hunt throughout the evening race until Hornish banged wheels with Tomas Scheckter 60 laps from the finish. After spinning, the junior Penske driver got restarted and rejoined the chase five laps behind the leaders. But when he continued to battle with the lead cars, even though he was clearly out of contention for the win, Hornish drew criticism from Scheckter, Tony Kanaan and Bryan Herta. IRL Chief Steward Brian Barnhart was also concerned, saying, "I'm a little disappointed with his aggressiveness. I wished he would have shown better judgment and little more restraint." This was the fifth straight race in which Sam Hornish Jr. had been involved in some kind of contact. Although most of the incidents were not directly his fault, this was an unsettling statistic for the normally fast but tidy driver. Almost certainly, he was taking unnecessary chances, feeling pressured to produce better results than the new Toyota engine was able to support. Hornish ultimately regained one of his lost laps and finished 13th at Richmond. Helio Castroneves stayed in the hunt and finished third behind the Hondas of Dan Weldon and Vitor Meira.

A week later at Kansas Speedway, in a race controlled by the Hondas of Tony Kanaan and Rahal-Letterman teammates Buddy Rice and Vitor Meira, Castroneves and Hornish could do no better than 7th and 8th in the final standings. If there was any good news, it was that

Hornish didn't hit anything this time. Two weekends later in Nashville, the Penske teammates managed to finish second and third behind Tony Kanaan in a race that saw only four different leaders, all of them driving Hondas. Hornish had another decent run a week after that in Milwaukee, picking up third-place points. Indy 500 champion Buddy Rice took his third win of the season in the Michigan 400, ahead of Tony Kanaan, Dan Weldon and Hornish. Helio Castroneves might have finished better than 10th at Michigan had it not been for a slight altercation with Vitor Meira halfway through the afternoon.

The next four races, at Kentucky, Pikes Peak, Nazareth and Chicagoland were collectively unspectacular for Penske Racing. Nazareth should have been a bright spot for the team. The track that Roger Penske built back in 1987 was hosting its very last race before going under the wrecking ball, a victim of dwindling attendance in open-wheel racing. The Penske cars suddenly found a burst of speed, with Castroneves winning the pole and Hornish grabbing the second starting spot. Castroneves led all but one of the first 100 laps before fading to a fifth place finish. Hornish's day was a little more exciting. After taking the lead from his teammate at lap 102, Hornish stayed out front until pitting during a caution period on lap 145—and then things got a little frightening. Probably excited about being in the lead for the first time in so long, Hornish jumped the gun leaving his pit, taking off before the refueling hose had been disconnected from the car. When the hose ripped loose, several gallons of methanol splashed over Hornish's car and the crewman who was handling the refueling operation. The methanol ignited after contacting the car's hot engine, leaving an invisible ball of fire in the Team Penske pit area. As the fuel-soaked crewman dropped to the ground with his uniform in flames, buckets of water were thrown over the pit wall by fellow crew members. Interestingly, a television replay showed that the first bucket was tossed by a 67-year old white-haired man in short sleeves. It was Roger Penske.

Fortunately, there were no injuries in the very scary incident. Sam Hornish had to pit again, however, to have the hose nozzle removed from the side of his car.

Although he would continue, he could not make it back to the front of the pack, and ultimately finished 11th.

With just two races left in the 2004 season, both Penske drivers were long out of contention for the IRL championship. At this point, the whole team was simply trying to score another victory to salvage something out of this dismal year. In the California 400, it looked for a while like Helio Castroneves was going to do just that. After qualifying on the pole—his fourth of the season and third in a row—Team Penske's senior driver led 145 of the first 177 laps, the closet thing to a dominating performance by either Penske driver all year. Unfortunately, Castroneves had a gearing problem that handicapped him on a couple of restarts after late-race cautions, and he dropped back to a 7th place finish. In the meantime, Sam Hornish drove a strong race, leading just four laps but posting a solid 4th place finish.

That left the struggling Penske drivers with just one last chance to redeem themselves and the much-maligned Toyota engine before the season drew to a close. It was becoming apparent, based on recent qualifying performances at least, that the Toyota was catching up. At Texas, Helio Castroneves kept his pole streak alive, capturing the number-one starting position for the fourth straight time, probably the only notable record claimed by this team the whole year. Sam Hornish Jr. made it an all-Penske front row again, giving the team reason to hope that they might finally be ready to capture their second win of the season in this closing event.

Castroneves led the first 56 laps of the race, and a total of 104 out of 200 for the day. Sam Hornish was in front for another 53 circuits, meaning that Team Penske was in control for more than three quarters of the show. Hornish eventually suffered an electrical problem and dropped out in the closing stages, but Castroneves was strong to the end, taking the lead from Dan Weldon with 20 laps to go and holding on for the win by 0.37 seconds over Tony Kanaan. Finally, after 13 unsuccessful attempts, Team Penske made it back to victory lane—but not without a little controversy. The IRL felt that Castroneves had jumped a restart two laps from the finish and levied a stiff penalty of $50,000 and 15 championship points against him; but the important thing was that the victory stood and the year ended on a positive note.

The 2004 season certainly had to be a disappointment for Roger Penske and his team, with only two wins and a weak showing at Indianapolis after three straight years of impressive performance there. Helio Castroneves finished 4th in the IRL championship behind Tony Kanaan, Dan Weldon and Indy winner Buddy Rice. Sam Hornish, who had a very difficult and frustrating season, ended up 7th in the final standings.

The 2004 spotlight unquestionably belonged to the new Andretti-Green Racing team and their very talented driver, Tony Kanaan. Helio Castroneves' Brazilian buddy did something that had never been accomplished before, finishing every single one of the 3,105 laps run in the season's 15 races. In addition to scoring three victories, Kanaan ended the year with an astounding record of 14 consecutive top-five finishes. Michael Andretti could not have asked for anything more in his first season as a team owner, except for maybe an Indianapolis 500 win. That honor went to Rahal-Letterman Racing, another very strong Honda team with a gifted young driver who was unemployed until he got the opportunity of a lifetime as a result of Kenny Bräck's Texas accident. Buddy Rice won the pole and the race at Indy, earning himself instant job security with the Rahal team.

2005

Despite the late-season turnaround that saw Helio Castroneves collect four pole positions and a race victory, Team Penske's disappointing overall performance in 2004, coupled with the emergence of new and stronger competition, bumped the Captain's team off the pedestal that it had owned since joining the IRL. Going into the 2005 season, for the first time in four years, the Penske drivers were not favored to win the series title. Even more surprisingly, Castroneves and Hornish didn't even make *Auto Week's* top-five picks, a list populated by AGR drivers Dan Weldon, Tony Kanaan and Dario Franchitti plus Rahal-Letterman's Buddy Rice and even Target-Ganassi rookie Ryan Briscoe. This was a bit surprising, considering that Roger Penske still had two of

the league's most experienced and successful drivers in his corner and an inspired engine manufacturer eager to avenge its embarrassing defeat in 2004.

In fact, Penske Racing's Toyota engines would prove to be very competitive with the Hondas and Chevys right from the start of the 2005 season. But the interesting thing is that all of the other Toyota customers continued to struggle, suggesting that the performance improvements demonstrated by the Marlboro cars didn't come from Toyota's engineering department, but rather from Penske's in-house development program. Early in the season, Toyota would announce plans to withdraw from the IRL at the end of 2006, immediately relegating its customers to lame-duck status. With General Motors already committed to exiting following the 2005 season, that left the IRL with only Honda committed to supplying motors in the future, a situation that neither Tony George nor Honda was very happy about.

This was just one more twist in the continuing struggle of American open-wheel racing as it entered its 10th season of civil war. Although the IRL now clearly held most of the cards in the long and bloody battle, Champ Car showed no signs of going away anytime soon. In fact, despite a significant effort by the Indy Racing League in the spring of 2005 to "steal" Champ Car's crown jewel, the Long Beach Grand Prix, city leaders would ultimately opt to stick with the reinvented CART organization. As the IRL began to execute its plans to add road racing and ex-U.S. venues to its schedule, and Champ Car continued transitioning to an all-street-circuit series, the two factions both seemed to be downplaying the significance of the ongoing split, basically suggesting that they were content to move forward as two separate and independent entities. The question that remained, however, was simply this: would there really be enough fans, sponsors, and manufacturers to support that direction? Judging by the relatively small starting fields in both leagues, the answer to that question still appeared to be a definitive: "No."

Yet, despite the continuing bumps in the road, 2005 would turn out to be somewhat of a breakthrough year for IRL. Attendance was up significantly at most races,

With his extensive road racing experience, Helio Castronves was a favorite to win the IRL's first non-oval race, run on the streets of St. Petersburg, Florida. He qualified outside pole, but retired early after contact with A.J. Foyt IV. *Alan Hummel*

Helio Castroneves is seen here leading Andretti-Green teammates Dan Wheldon and Tony Kanaan on the banking at Motegi, Japan. The Penske Toyotas struggled most of the season to run with AGR's more powerful Honda engines, but chassis refinements made to help compensate for this handicap would prove quite beneficial when the engine disparity was eliminated a year later. *LAT*

Both Penske cars were battle-scarred after the St. Pete race. The donut on Sam Hornish's sidepod is a souvenir of early race contact with another car. He was eventually sidelined after a more serious incident with Tomas Enge. *Alan Hummel*

and TV ratings for the 2005 Indianapolis 500 skyrocketed by more than 50% over recent years. The primary reason for this dramatic increase in interest was the presence of Danica Patrick, a 23-year-old rookie sensation driving for Rahal-Letterman Racing. The talented, attractive and personable young lady from Roscoe, Illinois, was not the first woman to compete in Indy cars, but very early in the 2005 season, it would become apparent that she almost certainly would be the first to claim victory. And in the meantime, a phenomenon that became known as "Danica-mania" would elevate Indy-car racing to a public status that it hadn't enjoyed in over a decade.

The new season got off to a strong start for Marlboro Team Penske. After finishing second and fifth at Homestead, Sam Hornish and Helio Castroneves scored a convincing one-two sweep on the Phoenix mile. The IRL then went to St. Petersburg, Florida, for the first non-oval race in series history. Sam Hornish, like many of his IRL-bred counterparts, was understandably a little apprehensive about turning right for the first time in his career, while the former CART drivers, Castroneves among them, were chomping at the bit to get back on a road course. One thing was certain going into this event—it was going to be an entertaining show.

As expected, Castroneves qualified strong, claiming a front-row grid position beside pole-sitter Bryan Herta. Hornish, meanwhile, settled for a mid-pack start. This should have been a great day for Helio, but on just the 12th lap, as he was already starting to encounter lapped traffic, a miscalculation in passing the slow-moving A.J. Foyt IV ended his day prematurely. Hornish ran a respectable race until tangling with rookie Tomas Enge 15 laps from the finish, leaving Team Penske with two DNFs and two bent racecars. At the end of the day, AGR teammates Dan Wheldon, Tony Kanaan, Dario Franchitti, and Bryan Herta gave owner Michael Andretti an unbelievable one-two-three-four sweep, proving the value of Honda power and road racing experience in this new era of the IRL.

After another disappointing weekend in Japan, Team Penske headed for Indianapolis in search of a 14th victory. Under revised qualifying procedures, Sam Horn-

ish and Helio Castroneves claimed the second and fifth spots on the starting grid. The pole went to defending IRL champion Tony Kanaan, but the big story in qualifying was Danica Patrick. The 5-foot, 1-inch, 100-lb rookie, who many had discounted as just a female novelty act, was suddenly at the top of the speed charts in the week preceeding pole day. As Patrick took the track for her first-ever Indy qualifying run, there was the very real possibility that she could win the pole. And in fact, that almost certainly would have been the outcome had it not been for a slight mistake on her first lap. "How she didn't crash is beyond comprehension," said Curt Cavin in his *AutoWeek* report. "Instead, she put her foot to the floor and motored along to a saving lap of 224.920 mph." Her next three laps were all faster than Kanaan's 227.566 average, but that first lap miscue dropped Patrick back to fourth overall. Still, it was a startling performance and a preview of what was to come two weeks later.

The 2005 Indianapolis 500 wasn't a particularly good story for Team Penske, or any other Toyota-powered teams for that matter. Helio Castroneves held on for a 9th-place finish, the highest-placed Toyota and the last car to complete all 200 laps. Sam Hornish was even less fortunate, ending his day with an accident on lap 146. AGR's Dan Wheldon, who had already won two of the first three races in the young IRL season, would ultimately take the checkered flag; but to do it, he had to take the lead away from a very determined Danica Patrick just seven laps from the end of the race. In one of the most impressive rookie performances in years, Patrick ran with the leaders most of the day, recovered brilliantly from two of her own mistakes, and pushed her Rahal-Letterman Honda-powered Panoz past Wheldon to take the lead on a lap-190 restart. But Patrick was running very low on fuel and her tires were not as fresh as Wheldon's, so she finally had to relinquish the position on lap 193 and ultimately faded to fourth place at the finish. It was, nevertheless, a remarkable performance, which not only earned her "Rookie-of-the-Year" honors, but more importantly, put Indy-car racing back on the U.S. sports map. For the remainder of the 2005 season, the spotlight, and all the pressure that went with

it, would be on the 23-year-old rookie from Roscoe, much to the chagrin of Dan Wheldon, his AGR teammates, and anyone else who would achieve any notable success in this unique season of "Danica-Mania."

After Indy, the IRL went to the always-exciting Texas Motor Speedway, a track so fast and so intimidating that it tends to generously reward experience. Panther Racing drivers Tomas Scheckter and Tomas Enge surprised everyone, putting their Dallara-Chevrolets on the front row in qualifying. In the race, the Penske cars were competitive throughout, and Sam Hornish played a key role in the outcome, pushing Scheckter past Tony Kanaan on the last lap, to give the accident-prone South African his first win since 2002. Hornish ended up second while Castroneves finished fifth. Points leader Dan Wheldon finished an inconspicuous sixth.

On the three-quarter-mile bullring at Richmond, the Penske Toyotas finally shined. Helio Castroneves claimed the pole with Sam Hornish beside him on the front row. They might well have finished the race in

that order, were it not for an unfortunate mistake by Hornish as he was attempting an ill-advised pass on his teammate midway through the event. "It was driver error," Hornish admitted. "I was trying to push it too hard trying to get around Helio." Hornish took himself out and had to watch the finish from the sidelines as Castroneves scored his first victory, the team's second, of the 2005 season.

The 1.5-mile tri-oval at Kansas proved to be a Honda track, as the Marlboro Toyotas labored to 8th and 12th-place finishes. Nashville seemed more suited to the Penske package, as both cars were in the hunt all afternoon and Sam Hornish may well have won had it not been for two costly miscues. On his final pit stop, the fuel hose stuck on Hornish's car, resulting in a long stop. In his frustration over this problem, Hornish made the situation worse by pushing too hard into the first turn and nearly sliding up into the wall. As a result, he lost any chance of catching Dario Franchitti, the AGR driver who would take the honors in his adopted American

When the IRL returned to Watkins Glen in 2005, it was the first time that a major open-wheel series had raced at the infamous upstate New York track in 24 years. Penske driver Rick Mears had scored that last Indy-car victory there in 1981, and Helio Castroneves looked to be a good bet to continue the team's winning streak. But after claiming the pole and leading early, Helio faded in the second part of the race and ultimately was eliminated in a last-lap incident with Tomas Enge. *LAT*

hometown. Hornish rebounded for a second place finish and Helio Castroneves ultimately settled for fifth.

When Roger Penske announced toward the end of the 2003 season that Sam Hornish Jr. would be replacing the retiring Gil de Ferran, there was more than a little apprehension about potential clashes between Helio Castroneves and his new teammate. The two had been, after all, fierce rivals in the 2002 championship battle, and while they had always raced each other cleanly, it was common knowledge that they were not the best of friends. There seemed to be a valid concern that these two formidable talents might find it challenging to peacefully coexist on the same team. But to the surprise of many skeptics, that turned out not to be the case at all. In fact, through the 2004 season, Hornish and Castroneves appeared to be perfect teammates, both on and off the racetrack. That apparent tranquility, however, began to exhibit some stress cracking by the middle of the 2005 season. Two races after Sam Hornish put himself out of the Richmond race with an overly

aggressive move on his teammate, he made a similar mistake on the Milwaukee mile. This time, however, Hornish survived the battle and Castroneves did not. "Sam's got a lot of explaining to do, not me," said the openly displeased Castroneves when interviewed following the incident. Fortunately for Hornish, he held on to put his Penske-Toyota in victory lane; otherwise, the Captain might have been less willing to pardon the recurring mistakes. Roger Penske has always been clear that there are no team orders between his drivers. The only rule is that they do not crash into each other—and Sam Hornish had been pushing his luck lately testing that imperative.

Hornish's victory at Milwaukee, coupled with Dan Wheldon's fifth place finish, moved the junior Penske driver into second place in the championship battle, still well within reach of the Indy 500 winner. Unfortunately, that was about as close as he was going to get for the remainder of the season. In the Michigan 400, neither of the Penske cars was particularly strong, with Hornish hanging on for a fifth place finish while Castroneves suffered a DNF. Kentucky produced another mediocre showing for the Penske Toyotas, with Helio and Sam finishing 5th and 7th respectively. Although Hornish was still second in the championship standings, he was slowly losing ground to Wheldon. On the one-mile oval at Pikes Peak, Castroneves claimed the pole and the two Penske entries combined to lead well over half of the race, but in the end, it was Dan Wheldon first to the checkered flag. Sam Hornish followed in second place and Helio Castroneves was fourth. This virtually guaranteed the championship for Dan Wheldon with four races still remaining on the schedule.

Next, the IRL made its second appearance on a road course, this time at Infineon Raceway in California. For the Penske team, it was an altogether forgettable weekend save for another front-row qualifying effort from Castroneves. On just the 19th lap, the lead Penske driver was punted out of the race, along with Danica Patrick, by Target-Ganassi's impatient rookie, Ryan Briscoe. Sam Hornish, still not much of a factor on the road courses, slid off track midway through the event, eliminating the second Penske-Toyota, and any remain-

For the 2006 season, the Marlboro Team Penske Dallaras got a big "H" on their nose cones and the accompanying 50 HP boost under the engine cowling. With Honda power, Hornish and Castroneves would finally be on level ground with Andretti-Green Racing and the other IRL teams. *Alan Hummel*

ing long-shot hope he had of catching Dan Wheldon for the championship.

The Penske teammates, particularly Castroneves, were much more competitive on the 1.5-mile oval at Chicagoland. However, a now-unstoppable Dan Wheldon ended up with yet another victory, his record-breaking sixth of the season, just ahead of Helio Castroneves and Sam Hornish. By this point, defending IRL champion Tony Kanaan had passed Hornish for second place in the standings, but all Dan Wheldon needed to do to clinch his title was to pick up a point by taking a single practice lap in either of the remaining two races.

When the IRL arrived at the Watkins Glen road course for the penultimate event of the 2005 season, the racing seemed almost secondary to a rich sense of nostalgia and tradition that it ignited. It had been 24 years since a major open-wheel race had been contested on this historic track, which for many years had hosted the United States Grand Prix. After losing Formula-1 in the late 1970s, the Glen was home to three CART races in 1979, 1980 and 1981, all of which were won by

Penske Racing; but for purist race fans, there had been a long drought since then. Seeing the IRL machines climb through the "esses" and fly past the site of the infamous "bog" was a long-overdue and welcomed sight to many.

For the third time in as many road races, Helio Castroneves put his Penske-Toyota on the front row, this time claiming pole position. He led the first 21 laps of the race before falling off the pace and ultimately getting tangled up with rookie Tomas Enge in an unfortunate last-lap accident. Sam Hornish finally finished his first road-course race with a steady, if not particularly spectacular, 7th place result. Target-Ganassi driver Scott Dixon, the 2003 IRL champion, broke a 40-race winless streak to score the victory at Watkins Glen. Meanwhile, Dan Wheldon officially clinched the 2005 title.

As the IRL headed to Fontana, California, for the season finale, there really wasn't much left to settle. The championship had been decided, team lineups for 2006 were pretty much set, and Danica Patrick had already locked up rookie-of-the-year honors. The biggest point

Helio Castroneves prepares for his qualifying run at St. Petersburg in 2006. He would start fifth, but moved to the front early and dominated the remainder of the race. *Alan Hummel*

of interest may have been Patrick's last shot at scoring a first victory in her otherwise impressive rookie season. Despite claiming three pole positions, the young lady from Illinois, who had almost single-handedly put Indy-car racing back on the map, seemed to be having trouble translating her qualifying success into race-day results. At Fontana, she had another respectable top-10 run going well into the race before getting tangled up with Jacques Lazier, ending the day for both drivers. Sharing an ambulance ride to the infield hospital for their mandatory post-accident examinations, the two competitors apparently got into a heated discussion

about responsibility for the incident, which ended when Patrick reportedly poked (some reports said "punched") Lazier in the forehead to suggest that he needed to use his head a little more. Whether that act of aggression tarnished Danica's poster-girl image or just spiced things up even more seemed to depend entirely on who was offering the opinion.

Dario Franchitti won the California race with a suspiciously easy last-lap maneuver on teammate Tony Kanaan, while the Penske cars finished with Sam Hornish in fifth and Helio Castroneves in ninth position. Hornish ended the season in third place behind runaway champion Dan Wheldon and runner-up Tony Kanaan. Castroneves was sixth in the final standings. It was another frustrating year for Roger Penske's team. Despite the fact that they had done much more with the Toyota engine than any other team, over the course of a full season, it just proved to be too much of a handicap against the more powerful Hondas.

Throughout the 2005 season, there was a persistent rumor that General Motors was reconsidering its decision to withdraw from the IRL at the end of the year. Following Chevrolet's strong mid-season showing, capped by Tomas Scheckter's win at Texas, A.J. Foyt switched his team from Toyota to Chevy engines. Then there was speculation that Roger Penske was also considering a move to the GM powerplant for 2006. But all this talk was put to rest in August when General Motors executives reconfirmed that they would not be participating in the series beyond 2005. In October, Roger Penske announced that he would switch to Honda power for 2006. Obviously, there was no incentive for remaining with the lame duck Toyota engines for another season. Not long after Penske's crippling defection, Toyota announced that they would exit the series a year earlier than planned, leaving the IRL with Honda as the lone engine supplier for the 2006 season.

2006

Pre-season testing at Phoenix and Homestead quickly confirmed that the Toyota engine had been a huge handicap. Both Team Penske and Target-Ganassi Racing suddenly found themselves at the top of the speed charts with their newfound horsepower boost. Other noteworthy changes for the 2006 season included Dan Wheldon's move from AGR to Target-Ganassi, teaming with 2003 IRL champion Scott Dixon. Filling Wheldon's seat at AGR would be Michael Andretti's 18-year-old son Marco, who had shown great promise in the 2005 IRL Pro Series. Panther Racing, which had twice won the IRL championship with Sam Hornish driving, lost its Pennzoil sponsorship and struggled to field a single-car team for the new season. Tomas Scheckter bolted from Panther to Tony George's Vision Racing, teaming with George's stepson, Ed Carpenter. Panther picked up Vitor Miera who had been released from Rahal-Letterman Racing when 2005 rookie Paul Dana brought the team a lucrative sponsorship package from Ethanol Corporation.

The season opened on the lightning-fast 1.5-mile oval in Homestead, Florida. Qualifying signaled the new

Sam Hornish Jr. consistently set fastest lap times during practice for the 2006 Indy 500 and went on to win his first pole at the speedway with a run of 228.985 mph. Going into the race, Roger Penske said with conviction, "I think it's ours to lose." *Alan Hummel*

world order, with Sam Hornish and Helio Castroneves taking the front row, followed by Scott Dixon's Target-Ganassi Dallara-Honda in third position. The excitement and anticipation of the season-opening green flag was abruptly silenced, however, with a horrible accident in the final practice session on Sunday morning. The incident began when Ed Carpenter spun and hit the outside wall in turn two, then slid down the banking and came to a rest broadside on the racetrack. Immediately after Carpenter's impact, yellow safety lights were activated around the track and in the racecar cockpits. Several drivers slowed and avoided Carpenter's stranded car. But nearly eight full seconds after the incident began, Paul Dana rammed into the unforgiving engine block of Carpenter's motionless Dallara at an estimated speed of 170 mph. Carpenter's car pinwheeled violently on the racetrack while Dana's car was launched verti-

Helio Castroneves started second in the 2006 "500," but struggled with handling problems early in the race and then crashed heavily after contact with 2004 winner Buddy Rice. Helio's honeymoon with the Brickyard was finally over. *Alan Hummel*

cally into the air, its front end completely destroyed. Ed Carpenter was briefly unconscious, but his injuries were otherwise minor. Paul Dana was not so fortunate. Before the season even started, the IRL had a fatality on the books—the third in its 10-year history and the first outside of Indianapolis.

The race went on as scheduled, but it was a somber day. Sam Hornish led the most laps overall and eventually settled for third. Helio Castroneves and Dan Wheldon traded the lead in the closing stages, with Wheldon inching past Helio on the final lap to score the victory for Target-Ganassi Racing.

On the streets of St. Petersburg a week later, Helio Castroneves drove an aggressive race and recorded a gratifying win over Scott Dixon, Tony Kanaan and Bryan Herta. Sam Hornish had an impressive qualifying effort on the street course, starting in fourth position, one spot ahead of his teammate. Hornish ran well in the early part of the race, but ultimately faded to an 8th-place finish.

Castroneves then made it two-in-a-row with a victory in Japan, a track where the Penske team had typically not fared well. Helio started from the pole and led 184 of the 200 laps while Sam Hornish finished fourth. Heading to Indianapolis, Castroneves enjoyed a 42-point lead over Dan Wheldon in the championship standings, with Hornish in third spot another 10 points back.

The Indianapolis 500 always offers special excitement, not only because of the history of the event itself, but also because it presents a starting grid with 50% more cars than the typical IRL race. Making it even more interesting is the fact that those extra cars are generally piloted by drivers from other series or those who have semi-retired and come out once a year just for "the big one." This year, the "extras" line-up included two former champions and the most successful non-winner in Speedway history. Two-time champion Al Unser Jr. was back for his first race since 2004. Eddie Cheever, winner of the 1997 "500," returned after a three-year

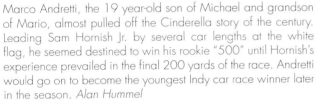

Marco Andretti, the 19 year-old son of Michael and grandson of Mario, almost pulled off the Cinderella story of the century. Leading Sam Hornish Jr. by several car lengths at the white flag, he seemed destined to win his rookie "500" until Hornish's experience prevailed in the final 200 yards of the race. Andretti would go on to become the youngest Indy car race winner later in the season. *Alan Hummel*

Alan Hummel

absence. And Michael Andretti, who had led more laps at Indy than any other non-winner in history, took a holiday from his two-year retirement for the opportunity to race against his teenage son at the Brickyard.

From the day that the gates opened for practice, the only thing more consistent than the rain falling over Indianapolis Motor Speedway was the speed from Sam Hornish's Penske Dallara-Honda. Hornish topped the charts in all but one of the pre-qualifying practice days. Dan Wheldon claimed top honors on that one other occasion, but Helio Castroneves was never far behind.

A one-week rain delay before qualifying opened did nothing to improve the prospects of Hornish's challengers. When the skies finally cleared and qualifying started on the second weekend, Sam Hornish did exactly what everyone expected. With a four-lap average speed of 228.985 mph, he claimed the pole position just ahead of teammate Helio Castroneves, who would start beside him on the front row.

Heading into the 90th running of the "World's Greatest Race," the Penske team was exceedingly confident. When interviewed before the race, Roger Penske said "I think it's our's to lose." And incredibly, until the last 200 yards of the 500-mile spectacle, it looked like they might do just that. After a good start, in which he moved to the front for the first nine laps, Helio Castroneves began to experience handling problems that caused him to fade backward in the standings until he was running 10th midway through the race. Just past the halfway mark the two-time winner's day ended with

Passing under the checkered flag at Indy's famous "yard of bricks," Sam Hornish Jr. scored his first "500" win after a strategic comeback that was orchestrated by Roger Penske after a late-race pit mishap had put him almost a lap down to the leaders with less than 50 laps to recover. Hornish became the first driver in the history of the Indianapolis 500 to win the race when not leading in the fourth turn of the final lap. *LAT*

a very hard impact against the fourth-turn concrete after contact with 2004 winner Buddy Rice. Fortunately, he was unhurt, but this marked the first time in his six Indianapolis 500 starts that Castroneves didn't finish in the top-10 and it would take a big chunk out of his IRL championship lead.

While Helio had been struggling through the first 275 miles, pole-sitter Sam Hornish Jr. was just biding his time, running patiently behind defending "500" champion Dan Wheldon. When the green flag dropped after the Castroneves-Rice caution period, Hornish finally began to assert himself, moving around Wheldon

to take the lead on lap 130. But just when it appeared that the Penske driver had everything under control, a pitstop miscue on lap 151 threatened to take it all away. After what should have been routine fuel and tire service under caution, Roger Penske prematurely signaled his driver to go before the fuel hose coupling was disconnected from the car. When Hornish started to pull away, the fuel hose ripped, spewing methanol and knocking the hose man to the ground. Hornish sat stationary for several seconds until the crew regrouped, removed the broken coupling and got him moving again. By the time he got back on the track, Hornish had dropped to 8th position, but the more serious damage came when race officials levied a drive-through penalty for the pit infraction. That would cost Sam Hornish three quarters of a lap and, presumably, any chance of winning the race.

But Roger Penske has won the Indianapolis 500 in just about every conceivable fashion, and he wasn't done with this one yet. Even before Hornish took his drive-through penalty, Penske had his driver make a quick pit stop to top off fuel while the field was still under the yellow flag, giving him just enough methanol to complete the race. At that point, most of the other front-runners would still require one more stop. Hornish and Penske got the final break they needed ten laps from the checked flag when Felipe Giaffone brushed the wall and brought out the pace car for the last time. As Wheldon, Tony Kanaan, Marco Andretti and Scott Dixon made their final splash-and-go pit stops, Hornish moved up to fourth position, erasing the 3/4-lap deficit and putting himself into contention for victory again.

As the field lined up for a restart on lap 195, the scene looked like something from a Hollywood movie. After runningly solidly in the top-10 all afternoon, suddenly crowd-favorite Michael Andretti found himself sitting at the front of the pack. In his mirrors were three lapped cars and then his 19-year-old son Marco, who was having the most extraordinary rookie run since… well…Danica Patrick a year earlier. Behind Marco sat Scott Dixon followed by fourth-place Sam Hornish Jr.

When the green flag flew, Marco Andretti and Sam Hornish began to move quickly. On lap 197, Marco executed a daring outside pass on his father to take the lead. In the meantime, Sam Hornish had moved around Scott Dixon and the lapped traffic before blowing by Michael Andretti on lap 198. He then made a run on young Marco in turn three, but the rookie skillfully closed the door and Hornish had to back out of the throttle, losing critical momentum. As they raced to the white flag, Hornish still trailed Andretti by several car lengths and it appeared unlikely that he would have enough time to take another shot. Not until the short chute between turns three and four did the Penske driver start to show his hand, quickly closing the gap between himself and Marco. As the two cars shot onto the front straight, Hornish faked to the outside and then darted underneath Andretti's Dallara. Marco tried to move back down the track, but it was too late—Hornish was already there. Less than 200 yards from the end of the 500-mile contest, Sam Hornish poked his nose into the lead. At the yard of bricks, the margin was 0.0635 seconds, the second closest finish in the 90-year history of the "500." Sam Hornish Jr. had won the Indianapolis 500—his first, Penske Racing's 14th.

In the six years since Roger Penske had returned to the Brickyard, his drivers had reached the winner's circle four times. Obviously, the Captain's Indianapolis 500 magic was stronger than ever.

Heading to the Watkins Glen road course, Team Penske had won three of the season's first five races and Helio Castroneves held a slim lead over Sam Hornish Jr. in the championship standings. Road racing was still an unnatural thing for most of the IRL drivers, and wet conditions at the Glen made this race even more interesting. Castroneves started from pole position, but was passed by Tony Kanaan on the first lap. Helio would come back to lead 7 laps midway through the event, but he didn't have the best car on this day, ultimately finishing seventh. Sam Hornish started sixth, but spun early in the race, losing a lap and any chance of contesting for a win. He went on to a 12th place finish. Marco Andretti had another very strong race going until being blind-sided by an oblivious Eddie Cheever Jr. Marco and father Michael were both very critical of Cheever's driving, actually accusing the former Indy winner of intentionally causing the accident. Ultimately, Target-

Ganassi's Scott Dixon took the checkerd flag, making it two Glen victories in a row for the quiet New Zealander. Fortunately, Dixon's championship contending teammate, Dan Wheldon, suffered mechanical problems and finished a harmless 15th.

Sam Hornish came back to win the pole at Texas and may well have won the race had not it not been for an uncharacteristic fuel calculation error by the Captain. Hornish pitted nine laps from the end of the race for what was supposed to be a quick splash-and-go, but his engine died before the crew could get fuel into the car. That turned out to be the difference between first and fourth place. Both of the Target-Ganassi drivers also had late-race pit miscues, leaving Helio Castroneves to take his third victory of the season and extend his lead in the championship standings.

Castroneves put his Penske-Dallara-Honda on the pole at Richmond two weeks later, but it was Sam Hornish out front at the end of the day. Helio ran with his teammate for much of the race until a tire problem dropped him to a disappointing 10th-place finish. Hornish then made it three-in-a-row for Team Penske with a win at Kansas, where Castroneves was fortunate to recover for a 6th-place finish after backing into the wall early in the race, necessitating a rear wing replacement. This left Sam Hornish with a 20-point lead over his teammate after 8 of 14 races.

Nashville produced the first disappointment for Team Penske since Watkins Glen. Neither of the Captain's drivers was particularly strong on the 1.333-mile superspeedway. Hornish ended his day bouncing off the second turn concrete, while Castroneves labored to an unremarkable fifth-place finish. With Ganassi's Scott Dixon and Dan Wheldon taking the top two spots, Sam Hornish saw his once-comfortable championship lead shrink to only five points over Dixon, while Helio dropped to third place, one more point back. With 9 races complete in the shortened 14-event season, no driver outside of the Penske and Ganassi teams had yet to see the winner's circle.

That two-team domination was finally broken at Milwaukee, as Tony Kanaan put Andretti-Green Racing on the board for the first time this season. Sam Hornish

With their new Honda engines, former Toyota teams Marlboro-Penske and Target-Ganassi won 12 of the 14 IRL races in 2006 and finished 1-2-3-4 in the championship. All the effort put into chassis refinements when they were handicapped with the weaker engines finally paid off after a Honda motor was bolted in. *Alan Hummel*

never led a lap, but hung on for a second-place finish, rebuilding his lead to 25 points over Scott Dixon. Helio Castroneves started from the pole at Milwaukee and led early, but was taken out of contention after contact with Ed Carpenter midway through the race.

Castroneves rebounded with a strong showing on the high banks of Michigan International Speedway, winning the pole and then leading 61 laps en route to his fourth victory of the season. Sam Hornish had a much less rewarding experience at MIS, dropping out early and finishing dead last. Heading into the final three races of the 2006 season, the championship was a four-

way battle between the two Penske drivers, defending champion Dan Wheldon and his Target-Ganassi teammate Scott Dixon.

These four drivers took the top four spots two weeks later on the 1.5-mile Kentucky tri-oval, with Hornish winning, followed by Dixon, Castroneves and Wheldon. Fortunately for Hornish, Wheldon botched a pit stop late in the race, knocking himself out of contention for the win after leading a race-high 66 laps. With two to go, Sam Hornish led his teammate by just seven points, with Wheldon and Dixon 17 and 26 points further back and still in the hunt.

The pentultimate race in this closely contested championship was on the Infineon road course in Sonoma, California. For Sam Hornish, the only one of the four championship contenders without any significant road racing experience, the mission here was not necessarily to win, but to get out without losing too much ground. For Helio Castroneves, Sonoma presented an opportunity to close the gap on his teammate, or maybe even jump into the lead. As it turned out, however, this weekend wasn't about the Penske drivers or their Target-Ganassi challengers. This weekend was all about Marco Andretti who, at the age of 19 years, five months and 14 days, became the youngest Indy-car winner in history, giving his dad's team its second win of the 2006 season. Scott Dixon, Helio Castroneves and Dan Wheldon finished fourth, fifth and sixth respectively, while Sam Hornish hung on for ninth. This moved Castroneves into the championship lead by a single point over his Penske teammate, with Wheldon and Dixon 19 and 21 points back, still well within range as the IRL headed for the season finale in Chicago.

In 2003, the IRL title chase came down to a five-man battle—Penske drivers Helio Castroneves and Gil de Ferran among them, at the wild Texas Motor Speedway. De Ferran won the battle but lost the war on that day, claiming victory in the final race of his driving career, but falling just short of Scott Dixon in the final points tally. In 2006, the Captain's drivers enjoyed much more control over their own destinies. The strategy for Sam and Helio going into the Chicagoland race was to avoid trouble, stay within 20 points of the Ganassi teammates and race each other for the championship when the time was right.

For Scott Dixon and Dan Wheldon, the gameplan was quite different. They had to charge from the drop of the green flag, both attempting to pick up the valuable three bonus points paid for leading the most laps. As Dixon and Wheldon traded the lead, banging wheels at least twice during the first several laps, Hornish and Castroneves laid back and followed their gameplan. On the first round of pit stops, Helio suffered a devastating blow to his championship hopes, picking up a pit lane speeding penalty that sent him to the back of the field.

As it would turn out, he'd fight his way back up as high as third position late in the race, but a long battle with the lapped car of Tony Kaanan ultimately cost him any shot of getting to the front. Sam Hornish, meanwhile, drove a flawless race, leading only eight laps and finishing third behind Wheldon and Dixon.

With bonus points for most laps led, Dan Wheldon ended the day holding 475 championship points, exactly the same total Sam Hornish owned after his third-place finish. Hornish may well have been able to challenge the Ganassi drivers, but there was no need to take that risk. Because he'd won more races than Wheldon over the course of the season, Roger Penske knew that his driver would be crowned champion in a tie situation. Over the radio, the Captain calmly reminded Hornish that the goal on this day was not necessarily to win the battle, but rather to prevail in the war. And that is exactly what they did. Sam Hornish Jr. patiently settled for third in the race, claiming his record-extending third IRL title. Roger Penske, after five years of trying, finally got his first, making it an even dozen Indy-car championships including his USAC and CART titles.

During the course of the 2006 season, there finally appeared to be real movement toward a reunification of American open-wheel racing. Unlike prior forced efforts, this situation evolved out of a chance meeting between IRL founder Tony George and Champ Car co-owner Kevin Kalkhoven. The two men reportedly had several informal discussions and by mid-season there were media claims that a settlement was imminent, possibly in time to plan for a common 2007 schedule. Although both George and Kalkhoven were understandably guarded in their comments, the rhetoric was unilaterally upbeat and optimistic, giving credibility to the speculation that something was about to happen. But as the second half of the season passed, there was a conspicuous lack of any further discussion on the subject. At the final Champ Car race in October, Kalkhoven suggested that the whole thing was blown out of proportion. "Tony and I talked," he said, "but there was nothing specific." Clearly, something had changed. Indy-car racing was going to remain divided for the foreseeable future.

EPILOGUE

"You want to be recognized as a great competitor and one that has built the sport in terms of bringing drivers along… No matter what people think of me, I can go home and feel like I've done a good job and put everything into it."
—Roger Penske, 2004

The numbers are staggering. Through the end of the 2006 season, the Penske Racing Team had won 260 major auto races around the world. They have captured 20 national championships, including 12 Indy-car titles. Roger Penske's drivers have won the Indianapolis 500 fourteen times, nearly triple the number of victories attributed to any other owner in history. The Captain's team has had success in all types of racing—Indy-cars, sports cars, Formula-1, endurance racing and NASCAR. Penske Racing is, by any credible definition

of the word, a dynasty; and Roger Penske is universally recognized as the preeminent personality in American motorsport. Gary Graves of *USA TODAY* wrote: "Penske sees a greater honor as he walks through Gasoline Alley. Spectators look at him as if he's racing royalty, and competitors view him with a mix of awe at his success and a resolve to beat him. He politely acknowledges both, and that respect seems to be all he needs."

As Penske Racing completed its 40th season of competition in 2006, this team remained the standard of excellence against which all challengers are judged. Heading into their fifth decade of competition, Team Penske will be defending it's hard-earned Indy Racing League title with returning champion Sam Hornish Jr. and two-time Indianapolis winner Helio Castroneves. Penske Racing South will be back with two teams in the NASCAR Nextel Cup series, with Ryan Newman and Kurt Busch working to secure the team's long overdue first championship in that series

Roger Penske is 70 years old now. When he's not busy directing his Indy-car and NASCAR teams on race weekends, he oversees a business empire that he has built over the past four decades, an enterprise that generates annual sales revenues in excess of $11 billion and employs 34,000 people at 1700 locations around the world. Penske Corporation is described as a closely-held diversified transportation services company. It is comprised of Penske Truck Leasing, United Auto Group, Transportation Resource Partners, Penske Automotive Group, and Penske Performance. The common thread in all these businesses is the automobile, making auto racing the ideal promotional vehicle for the entire enterprise. Roger Penske has managed to combine his two lifelong passions—business and auto racing—into an extraordinarily successful, exciting and hugely profitable endeavor; and by all accounts, he has enjoyed almost every minute of it.

When asked about his retirement plans—a reasonable question at this stage in his life—Penske is quick to insist that no such plans exist. But when asked specifically about future plans for his racing team, he is more evasive. Before the IRL Grand Prix of St. Petersburg in 2005, when questioned about what he'd still like to accomplish in the sport, Penske offered a strangely insipid response, saying that he'd like to win both the Indianapolis 500 and the NASCAR World 600 on the same day. While that might be a very ambitious goal for any other team owner, for the Captain it would be little more than a simple matter of luck. After all, his drivers have, for years, been among the favorites in both of these events, so this hardly seemed like a typical Roger Penske stretch goal.

The real question that was being posed to the most successful man in U.S. auto racing history was this: "is there anything else in Penske Racing's future—anything other than Indy-cars and NASCAR?" Although he didn't reveal it at the time, the Penske organization would soon announce plans for a return to sports car racing, fielding a new factory-supported Porsche prototype in the American Le Mans Series. This "return to its roots" marked the first really new initiative for the Penske team since its NASCAR homecoming 15 years earlier, and it was certainly welcomed by longtime Penske Racing fans who fondly remembered the glory days of the old Trans-Am and Can-Am.

But the even more specific question that many fans would like the Captain to answer is this one: "will Penske Racing ever compete in Formula-1 again?" After all, that is the undisputed pinnacle of the sport of auto racing. That is where the world championship is decided. That is where Roger Penske's team challenged Jackie Stewart, Niki Lauda, James Hunt, Emerson Fittipaldi, Denny Hulme, Jody Scheckter and other racing legends thirty years ago; and that is where Roger Penske's close friend and partner, Mark Donohue, paid the ultimate price on an unfamiliar racecourse in Zeltweg, Austria.

Penske Racing ultimately scored one victory in its two full years on the Formula-1 circuit in the mid-1970s. That may not sound overly impressive to the typical American racing fan today, but at this elite level of the sport, it was truly a remarkable achievement. Consider that Jaguar Motors, with the company's high-performance reputation on the line and nearly unlimited resources at their disposal, fielded an F-1 team for five years between 2000 and 2004 without ever winning a single race. Formula-1 is, and always has been, a seg-

Penske Racing president Tim Cindric debriefs Sam Hornish Jr. after the 2007 St. Petersburg Grand Prix. Cindric joined the team in the 2000 reorganization and has been a major contributor to the success of both the Indy car and American Le Mans programs.

ment of the sport where the price of admission is simply astronomical—not just monetarily and technically, but also in terms of the undivided focus and commitment required to survive, let alone succeed. Although Roger Penske's team beat the seemingly insurmountable odds, building a competitive program and taking it to the top step of the podium in only two years, the Captain ultimately concluded that they couldn't sustain the level of commitment and focus that would be required to see the effort through to a championship. And if they couldn't do that, there was really no point in being there. So to everyone's surprise and disappointment, Penske Racing left Formula-1 at the end of the 1976 season and has never returned.

Roger Penske's legacy as the most successful Indy-Car team owner in history is secure and untouchable. And while his team's NASCAR achievements may never quite reach the same celestial levels, Penske has nonetheless established himself as an influential leader and key contender in that series as well. Still, it's hard to believe that this international entrepreneur, who has built a business empire that spans the globe, could really be content to restrict the scope of his racing legacy to the North American continent. Mario Andretti once compared Roger Penske to Enzo Ferrari

After being away from sports car racing for more than three decades, Roger Penske entered into an agreement with Porsche to develop and race their new RS Spyder P2 prototype in the American Le Mans Series. Following minor teething problems, the pair of Penske Porsches combined to score seven P2 class wins in 10 outings, including one outright race victory en route to claiming the 2006 ALMS P2 Championship. Despite rampant interest and speculation, the Captain has consistently maintained that there are no plans to return to the 24-Hours-of-Le Mans anytime soon. *LAT*

and Colin Chapman. But if he does not take his team back to Formula-1, Penske can never hope to attain the same level of worldwide respect earned by Ferrari, Chapman, Ken Tyrrell, Frank Williams and other legendary F1 team owners. To most of the world, Formula-1 is the only form of racing that commands this universal esteem. Outside of the United States, unfortunately, NASCAR is viewed as a technically primitive mutation of the sport. And even the Indy-car series, despite all the worldwide fame and fanfare associated with the Indianapolis 500, is considered unworthy of any serious comparison to Formula-1. To ultimately be judged against the greatest teams in the history of motorsport, Roger Penske would have to return to that battleground that he abandoned 30 years ago.

The primary issues that led Penske to withdraw from Formula-1 in 1976 would seem to be less significant factors today. At that time, he had a new wife and a young family to consider. He was also in the early stages of shaping a flourishing business empire, which demanded

his undivided attention. These commitments made it impossible for him to spend an endless amount of time bouncing around Europe and everywhere else that the Formula-1 circuit traveled. Today, however, Roger Penske's children are grown and have families of their own. And today, Roger Penske's legacy as one of the greatest business leaders of all time is secure. Today, it seems, Roger Penske would have the flexibility to adjust his priorities—if he really wanted to make a full assault on the world championship.

This would, of course, still be a formidable challenge. Formula-1 is bigger, more complex technically, more political, and much more expensive than ever before. Starting from scratch, as Roger Penske and Mark Donohue did back in 1974, is probably not an option for any team today. It would require a different approach, most likely partnering with or acquiring the assets of an existing team that already had a foundation established in today's complicated Formula-1 world. There have been rumors over the past several years that Penske was planning to do just that. Speculation about a possible Penske Racing buyout or partnership with the Minardi, Toyota, or Jordon Formula-1 programs has found its way into print, though nothing has ever materialized. With major rule changes planned for 2008 that could help level the playing field, there was more conjecture that Penske Racing might be contemplating a return, but the Captain killed that rumor saying, "It would be a great opportunity to be in that sport, but right now we just don't see it as an option. We've got the Indy cars, the long-distance racing with Porsche and our two NASCAR cars. Our plate is pretty full. If I can't be involved in it directly myself, it really doesn't give me the returns, both personally and from a business perspective."

Even a public figure of Roger Penske's stature has the right to determine what is important to him and how he spends his own time and resources. However, the simple reality that speculation and questions about this continue to surface in the first place is testimony to the fact that many people want to see Penske Racing return to Formula-1. If that happens, then there will be another chapter in the already incomparable Penske Racing story.

APPENDIX I: PENSKE TEAM RACE VICTORIES

United States Road Racing Championship

1	1966	SCCA	Kent, Washington	Mark Donohue	Lola-Chevrolet
2	1967	SCCA	Las Vegas	Mark Donohue	Lola-Chevrolet
3	1967	SCCA	Riverside	Mark Donohue	Lola-Chevrolet
4	1967	SCCA	Bridgehampton	Mark Donohue	Lola-Chevrolet
5	1967	SCCA	Watkins Glen	Mark Donohue	Lola-Chevrolet
6	1967	SCCA	Kent, Washington	Mark Donohue	Lola-Chevrolet
7	1967	SCCA	Mid-Ohio	Mark Donohue	Lola-Chevrolet
8	1968	SCCA	Riverside	Mark Donohue	McLaren-Chevrolet
9	1968	SCCA	Laguna Seca	Mark Donohue	McLaren-Chevrolet
10	1968	SCCA	St. Jovite	Mark Donohue	McLaren-Chevrolet
11	1968	SCCA	Watkins Glen	Mark Donohue	McLaren-Chevrolet
12	1968	SCCA	Mid-Ohio	Mark Donohue	McLaren-Chevrolet

Can-Am

1	1966	CASC/SCCA	Mosport	Mark Donohue	Lola-Chevrolet
2	1968	CASC/SCCA	Bridgehampton	Mark Donohue	McLaren-Chevrolet
3	1972	CASC/SCCA	Road Atlanta	George Follmer	Porsche 917/10K
4	1972	CASC/SCCA	Mid-Ohio	George Follmer	Porsche 917/10K
5	1972	CASC/SCCA	Elkhart Lake	George Follmer	Porsche 917/10K
6	1972	CASC/SCCA	Edmonton	Mark Donohue	Porsche 917/10K
7	1972	CASC/SCCA	Laguna Seca	George Follmer	Porsche 917/10K
8	1972	CASC/SCCA	Riverside	George Follmer	Porsche 917/10K
9	1973	CASC/SCCA	Watkins Glen	Mark Donohue	Porsche 917/30K
10	1973	CASC/SCCA	Mid-Ohio	Mark Donohue	Porsche 917/30K
11	1973	CASC/SCCA	Elkhart Lake	Mark Donohue	Porsche 917/30K
12	1973	CASC/SCCA	Edmonton	Mark Donohue	Porsche 917/30K
13	1973	CASC/SCCA	Laguna Seca	Mark Donohue	Porsche 917/30K
14	1973	CASC/SCCA	Riverside	Mark Donohue	Porsche 917/30K

World Endurance Sports Cars

1	1969	FIA	24 Hours of Daytona	M. Donohue/Charlie Parsons	Lola-Chevrolet

Trans-Am

1	1967	SCCA	Marlboro	Mark Donohue	Chevrolet Camaro
2	1967	SCCA	Las Vegas	Mark Donohue	Chevrolet Camaro
3	1967	SCCA	Kent, Washington	Mark Donohue	Chevrolet Camaro
4	1968	SCCA	Sebring	Mark Donohue/Craig Fisher	Chevrolet Camaro
5	1968	SCCA	War Bonnett	Mark Donohue	Chevrolet Camaro
6	1968	SCCA	Lime Rock	Mark Donohue	Chevrolet Camaro
7	1968	SCCA	Mid-Ohio	Mark Donohue	Chevrolet Camaro
8	1968	SCCA	Bridgehampton	Mark Donohue	Chevrolet Camaro
9	1968	SCCA	Meadowdale	Mark Donohue	Chevrolet Camaro
10	1968	SCCA	St. Jovite	Mark Donohue	Chevrolet Camaro
11	1968	SCCA	Bryar	Mark Donohue	Chevrolet Camaro
12	1968	SCCA	Castle Rock	Mark Donohue	Chevrolet Camaro
13	1968	SCCA	Kent, Washington	Mark Donohue	Chevrolet Camaro
14	1969	SCCA	Mid-Ohio	Ron Bucknum	Chevrolet Camaro
15	1969	SCCA	Bryar	Mark Donohue	Chevrolet Camaro
16	1969	SCCA	St. Jovite	Mark Donohue	Chevrolet Camaro
17	1969	SCCA	Watkins Glen	Mark Donohue	Chevrolet Camaro
18	1969	SCCA	Laguna Seca	Mark Donohue	Chevrolet Camaro
19	1969	SCCA	Kent, Washington	Ron Bucknum	Chevrolet Camaro
20	1969	SCCA	Sears Point	Mark Donohue	Chevrolet Camaro
21	1969	SCCA	Riverside	Mark Donohue	Chevrolet Camaro
22	1970	SCCA	Bridgehampton	Mark Donohue	American Motors Javelin
23	1970	SCCA	Elkhart Lake	Mark Donohue	American Motors Javelin
24	1970	SCCA	St. Jovite	Mark Donohue	American Motors Javelin
25	1971	SCCA	Lime Rock	Mark Donohue	American Motors Javelin
26	1971	SCCA	Edmonton	Mark Donohue	American Motors Javelin
27	1971	SCCA	Donnybrook	Mark Donohue	American Motors Javelin
28	1971	SCCA	Elkhart Lake	Mark Donohue	American Motors Javelin
29	1971	SCCA	St. Jovite	Mark Donohue	American Motors Javelin
30	1971	SCCA	Watkins Glen	Mark Donohue	American Motors Javelin
31	1971	SCCA	Michigan	Mark Donohue	American Motors Javelin

Formula-A

1	1970	SCCA	Mosport	Mark Donohue	Lola-Chevrolet
2	1970	SCCA	Sebring	Mark Donohue	Lola-Chevrolet

Formula-1

1	1976	FIA	Austria	John Watson	Penske-Cosworth

Indy-Cars

1	1971	USAC	Pocono 500	Mark Donohue	McLaren-Offenhauser
2	1971	USAC	Michigan 200	Mark Donohue	McLaren-Offenhauser
3	1972	USAC	Trenton 200	Gary Bettenhausen	McLaren-Offenhauser
4	**1972**	**USAC**	**Indianapolis 500**	**Mark Donohue**	McLaren-Offenhauser
5	1973	USAC	Texas 200	Gary Bettenhausen	McLaren-Offenhauser
6	1975	USAC	Michigan 150	Tom Sneva	McLaren-Offenhauser
7	1977	USAC	Texas 200	Tom Sneva	McLaren-Cosworth
8	1977	USAC	Pocono 500	Tom Sneva	McLaren-Cosworth
9	1978	USAC	Milwaukee 150	Rick Mears	Penske-Cosworth
10	1978	USAC	Atlanta 150	Rick Mears	Penske-Cosworth
11	1978	USAC	Trenton 150	Mario Andretti	Penske-Cosworth
12	1978	USAC	Brands Hatch	Rick Mears	Penske-Cosworth
13	**1979**	**USAC**	**Indianapolis 500**	**Rick Mears**	Penske-Cosworth
14	1979	CART	Trenton 150	Bobby Unser	Penske-Cosworth
15	1979	CART	Trenton 150	Bobby Unser	Penske-Cosworth
16	1979	CART	Michigan 126	Bobby Unser	Penske-Cosworth
17	1979	CART	Watkins Glen	Bobby Unser	Penske-Cosworth
18	1979	CART	Trenton 150	Rick Mears	Penske-Cosworth
19	1979	CART	Ontario 500	Bobby Unser	Penske-Cosworth
20	1979	CART	Michigan 150	Bobby Unser	Penske-Cosworth
21	1979	CART	Atlanta 150	Rick Mears	Penske-Cosworth
22	1980	CART	Milwaukee 150	Bobby Unser	Penske-Cosworth
23	1980	CART	Pocono 500	Bobby Unser	Penske-Cosworth
24	1980	CART	Watkins Glen	Bobby Unser	Penske-Cosworth
25	1980	CART	Ontario 500	Bobby Unser	Penske-Cosworth
26	1980	CART	Michigan 150	Mario Andretti	Penske-Cosworth
27	1980	CART	Mexico City	Rick Mears	Penske-Cosworth
28	**1981**	**USAC**	**Indianapolis 500**	**Bobby Unser**	Penske-Cosworth
29	1981	CART	Atlanta 126.32	Rick Mears	Penske-Cosworth
30	1981	CART	Atlanta 126.32	Rick Mears	Penske-Cosworth
31	1981	CART	Riverside 313.5	Rick Mears	Penske-Cosworth
32	1981	CART	Michigan 148	Rick Mears	Penske-Cosworth
33	1981	CART	Watkins Glen	Rick Mears	Penske-Cosworth
34	1981	CART	Mexico City	Rick Mears	Penske-Cosworth
35	1982	CART	Phoenix 150	Rick Mears	Penske-Cosworth
36	1982	CART	Atlanta 200	Rick Mears	Penske-Cosworth
37	1982	CART	Pocono 500	Rick Mears	Penske-Cosworth
38	1982	CART	Riverside	Rick Mears	Penske-Cosworth
39	1983	CART	Cleveland 310	Al Unser	Penske-Cosworth
40	1983	CART	Michigan 200	Rick Mears	Penske-Cosworth
41	**1984**	**USAC**	**Indianapolis 500**	**Rick Mears**	March-Cosworth
42	**1985**	**USAC**	**Indianapolis 500**	**Danny Sullivan**	March-Cosworth

43	1985	CART	Pocono 500	Rick Mears	March-Cosworth
44	1985	CART	Phoenix 150	Al Unser	March-Cosworth
45	1985	CART	Miami	Danny Sullivan	March-Cosworth
46	1986	CART	Meadowlands	Danny Sullivan	March-Cosworth
47	1986	CART	Cleveland	Danny Sullivan	March-Cosworth
48	**1987**	**USAC**	**Indianapolis 500**	**Al Unser**	March-Cosworth
49	1987	CART	Pocono 500	Rick Mears	March-Ilmor Chevrolet
50	**1988**	**USAC**	**Indianapolis 500**	**Rick Mears**	Penske-Ilmor Chevrolet
51	1988	CART	Milwaukee 200	Rick Mears	Penske-Ilmor Chevrolet
52	1988	CART	Portland 200	Danny Sullivan	Penske-Ilmor Chevrolet
53	1988	CART	Michigan 500	Danny Sullivan	Penske-Ilmor Chevrolet
54	1988	CART	Nazareth 200	Danny Sullivan	Penske-Ilmor Chevrolet
55	1988	CART	Laguna Seca	Danny Sullivan	Penske-Ilmor Chevrolet
56	1989	CART	Phoenix 200	Rick Mears	Penske-Ilmor Chevrolet
57	1989	CART	Milwaukee 200	Rick Mears	Penske-Ilmor Chevrolet
58	1989	CART	Pocono 500	Danny Sullivan	Penske-Ilmor Chevrolet
59	1989	CART	Elkhart Lake 200	Danny Sullivan	Penske-Ilmor Chevrolet
60	1989	CART	Laguna Seca	Rick Mears	Penske-Ilmor Chevrolet
61	1990	CART	Phoenix 200	Rick Mears	Penske-Ilmor Chevrolet
62	1990	CART	Cleveland 200	Danny Sullivan	Penske-Ilmor Chevrolet
63	1990	CART	Nazareth 200	Emerson Fittipaldi	Penske-Ilmor Chevrolet
64	1990	CART	Laguna Seca	Danny Sullivan	Penske-Ilmor Chevrolet
65	**1991**	**USAC**	**Indianapolis 500**	**Rick Mears**	Penske-Ilmor Chevrolet
66	1991	CART	Detroit	Emerson Fittipaldi	Penske-Ilmor Chevrolet
67	1991	CART	Michigan 500	Rick Mears	Penske-Ilmor Chevrolet
68	1992	CART	Australia	Emerson Fittipaldi	Penske-Ilmor Chevrolet
69	1992	CART	Cleveland	Emerson Fittipaldi	Penske-Ilmor Chevrolet
70	1992	CART	Elkhart Lake	Emerson Fittipaldi	Penske-Ilmor Chevrolet
71	1992	CART	Mid-Ohio	Emerson Fittipaldi	Penske-Ilmor Chevrolet
72	1993	CART	Long Beach	Paul Tracy	Penske-Ilmor Chevrolet
73	**1993**	**USAC**	**Indianapolis 500**	**Emerson Fittipaldi**	Penske-Ilmor Chevrolet
74	1993	CART	Portland	Emerson Fittipaldi	Penske-Ilmor Chevrolet
75	1993	CART	Cleveland	Paul Tracy	Penske-Ilmor Chevrolet
76	1993	CART	Toronto	Paul Tracy	Penske-Ilmor Chevrolet
77	1993	CART	Elkhart Lake	Paul Tracy	Penske-Ilmor Chevrolet
78	1993	CART	Mid-Ohio	Emerson Fittipaldi	Penske-Ilmor Chevrolet
79	1993	CART	Laguna Seca	Paul Tracy	Penske-Ilmor Chevrolet
80	1994	CART	Phoenix 200	Emerson Fittipaldi	Penske-Ilmor
81	1994	CART	Long Beach	Al Unser Jr.	Penske-Ilmor
82	**1994**	**USAC**	**Indianapolis 500**	**Al Unser Jr.**	Penske-Mercedes
83	1994	CART	Milwaukee 200	Al Unser Jr.	Penske-Ilmor
84	1994	CART	Detroit	Paul Tracy	Penske-Ilmor
85	1994	CART	Portland	Al Unser Jr.	Penske-Ilmor
86	1994	CART	Cleveland	Al Unser Jr.	Penske-Ilmor
87	1994	CART	Mid-Ohio	Al Unser Jr.	Penske-Ilmor

88	1994	CART	Loudon 200	Al Unser Jr.	Penske-Ilmor
89	1994	CART	Vancouver	Al Unser Jr.	Penske-Ilmor
90	1994	CART	Nazareth 200	Paul Tracy	Penske-Ilmor
91	1994	CART	Laguna Seca	Paul Tracy	Penske-Ilmor
92	1995	CART	Long Beach	Al Unser Jr.	Penske-Ilmor Mercedes
93	1995	CART	Nazareth 200	Emerson Fittipaldi	Penske-Ilmor Mercedes
94	1995	CART	Portland	Al Unser Jr.	Penske-Ilmor Mercedes
95	1995	CART	Mid-Ohio	Al Unser Jr.	Penske-Ilmor Mercedes
96	1995	CART	Vancouver	Al Unser Jr.	Penske-Ilmor Mercedes
97	1997	CART	Nazareth 225	Paul Tracy	Penske-Ilmor Mercedes
98	1997	CART	Rio	Paul Tracy	Penske-Ilmor Mercedes
99	1997	CART	St. Louis 300	Paul Tracy	Penske-Ilmor Mercedes
100	2000	CART	Nazareth	Gil de Ferran	Reynard-Honda
101	2000	CART	Detroit	Helio Castroneves	Reynard-Honda
102	2000	CART	Portland	Gil de Ferran	Reynard-Honda
103	2000	CART	Mid-Ohio	Helio Castroneves	Reynard-Honda
104	2000	CART	Laguna Seca	Helio Castroneves	Reynard-Honda
105	2001	CART	Long Beach	Helio Castroneves	Reynard-Honda
106	**2001**	**IRL**	**Indianapolis 500**	**Helio Castroneves**	Dallara-Oldsmobile
107	2001	CART	Detroit	Helio Castroneves	Reynard-Honda
108	2001	CART	Mid-Ohio	Helio Castroneves	Reynard-Honda
109	2001	CART	Rockingham	Gil de Ferran	Reynard-Honda
110	2001	CART	Houston	Gil de Ferran	Reynard-Honda
111	2002	IRL	Phoenix 200	Helio Castroneves	Dallara-Chevrolet
112	**2002**	**IRL**	**Indianapolis 500**	**Helio Castroneves**	Dallara-Chevrolet
113	2002	IRL	Pikes Peak 225	Gil de Ferran	Dallara-Chevrolet
114	2002	IRL	Gateway 200	Gil de Ferran	Dallara-Chevrolet
115	2003	**IRL**	**Indianapolis 500**	Gil de Ferran	Panoz-Toyota
116	2003	IRL	Nashville	Gil de Ferran	Panoz-Toyota
117	2003	IRL	Gateway	Helio Castroneves	Dallara-Toyota
118	2003	IRL	Nazareth	Helio Castroneves	Dallara-Toyota
119	2003	IRL	Texas	Gil de Ferran	Panoz-Toyota
120	2004	IRL	Homestead	Sam Hornish, Jr.	Dallara-Toyota
121	2004	IRL	Texas	Helio Castroneves	Dallara-Toyota
122	2005	IRL	Phoenix	Sam Hornish, Jr.	Dallara-Toyota
123	2005	IRL	Richmond	Helio Castroneves	Dallara-Toyota
124	2005	IRL	Milwaukee	Sam Hornish, Jr.	Dallara-Toyota
125	2006	IRL	St. Petersburg	Helio Castroneves	Dallara-Honda
126	2006	IRL	Twin Ring Motegi Japan	Helio Castroneves	Dallara-Honda
127	**2006**	**IRL**	**Indianapolis 500**	**Sam Hornish Jr.**	**Dallara-Honda**
128	2006	IRL	Texas	Helio Castroneves	Dallara-Honda
129	2006	IRL	Richmond	Sam Hornish, Jr.	Dallara-Honda
130	2006	IRL	Kansas	Sam Hornish, Jr.	Dallara-Honda
131	2006	IRL	Michigan	Helio Castroneves	Dallara-Honda
132	2006	IRL	Kentucky	Sam Hornish, Jr.	Dallara-Honda

Winston/Nextel Cup

1	1973	NASCAR	Riverside	Mark Donohue	AMC Matador
2	1974	NASCAR	Ontario	Bobby Allison	AMC Matador
3	1975	NASCAR	Riverside	Bobby Allison	AMC Matador
4	1975	NASCAR	Daytona 125	Bobby Allison	AMC Matador
5	1975	NASCAR	Darlington	Bobby Allison	AMC Matador
6	1975	NASCAR	Darlington	Bobby Allison	AMC Matador
7	1991	NASCAR	Bristol	Rusty Wallace	Pontiac
8	1991	NASCAR	Pocono	Rusty Wallace	Pontiac
9	1992	NASCAR	Richmond	Rusty Wallace	Pontiac
10	1993	NASCAR	N. Carolina	Rusty Wallace	Pontiac
11	1993	NASCAR	Bristol	Rusty Wallace	Pontiac
12	1993	NASCAR	N. Wilkesboro	Rusty Wallace	Pontiac
13	1993	NASCAR	Martinsville	Rusty Wallace	Pontiac
14	1993	NASCAR	New Hampshire	Rusty Wallace	Pontiac
15	1993	NASCAR	Richmond	Rusty Wallace	Pontiac
16	1993	NASCAR	Dover	Rusty Wallace	Pontiac
17	1993	NASCAR	N. Wilkesboro	Rusty Wallace	Pontiac
18	1993	NASCAR	N. Carolina	Rusty Wallace	Pontiac
19	1993	NASCAR	Atlanta	Rusty Wallace	Pontaic
20	1994	NASCAR	N. Carolina	Rusty Wallace	Ford
21	1994	NASCAR	Martinsville	Rusty Wallace	Ford
22	1994	NASCAR	Dover	Rusty Wallace	Ford
23	1994	NASCAR	Pocono	Rusty Wallace	Ford
24	1994	NASCAR	Michigan	Rusty Wallace	Ford
25	1994	NASCAR	Bristol	Rusty Wallace	Ford
26	1994	NASCAR	Dover	Rusty Wallace	Ford
27	1994	NASCAR	Martinsville	Rusty Wallace	Ford
28	1995	NASCAR	Martinsville	Rusty Wallace	Ford
29	1995	NASCAR	Richmond	Rusty Wallace	Ford
30	1996	NASCAR	Martinsville	Rusty Wallace	Ford
31	1996	NASCAR	Sears Point	Rusty Wallace	Ford
32	1996	NASCAR	Michigan	Rusty Wallace	Ford
33	1996	NASCAR	Pocono	Rusty Wallace	Ford
34	1996	NASCAR	Bristol	Rusty Wallace	Ford
35	1997	NASCAR	Richmond	Rusty Wallace	Ford
36	1998	NASCAR	Pocono	Jeremy Mayfield	Ford
37	1998	NASCAR	Phoenix	Rusty Wallace	Ford
38	1999	NASCAR	Bristol	Rusty Wallace	Ford
39	2000	NASCAR	Bristol	Rusty Wallace	Ford
40	2000	NASCAR	California	Jeremy Mayfield	Ford
41	2000	NASCAR	Pocono	Jeremy Mayfield	Ford
42	2000	NASCAR	Pocono	Rusty Wallace	Ford

43	2000	NASCAR	Michigan	Rusty Wallace	Ford
44	2000	NASCAR	Bristol	Rusty Wallace	Ford
45	2001	NASCAR	California	Rusty Wallace	Ford
46	2002	NASCAR	New Hampshire	Ryan Newman	Ford
47	2003	NASCAR	Texas	Ryan Newman	Dodge
48	2003	NASCAR	Dover	Ryan Newman	Dodge
49	2003	NASCAR	Chicago	Ryan Newman	Dodge
50	2003	NASCAR	Pocono	Ryan Newman	Dodge
51	2003	NASCAR	Michigan	Ryan Newman	Dodge
52	2003	NASCAR	Richmond	Ryan Newman	Dodge
53	2003	NASCAR	Dover	Ryan Newman	Dodge
54	2003	NASCAR	Kansas	Ryan Newman	Dodge
55	2004	NASCAR	Martinsville	Rusty Wallace	Dodge
56	2004	NASCAR	Michigan	Ryan Newman	Dodge
57	2004	NASCAR	Dover	Ryan Newman	Dodge
58	2005	NASCAR	New Hampshire	Ryan Newman	Dodge
59	2006	NASCAR	Bristol	Kurt Busch	Dodge

Busch Series

1	2001	NASCAR	Michigan	Ryan Newman	Ford
2	2005	NASCAR	Watkins Glen	Ryan Newman	Dodge
3	2005	NASCAR	Michigan	Ryan Newman	Dodge
4	2005	NASCAR	Bristol	Ryan Newman	Dodge
5	2005	NASCAR	Dover	Ryan Newman	Dodge
6	2005	NASCAR	Charlotte	Ryan Newman	Dodge
7	2005	NASCAR	Homestead	Ryan Newman	Dodge
8	2006	NASCAR	Texas	Kurt Busch	Dodge
9	2006	NASCAR	Watkins Glen	Kurt Busch	Dodge

American Le Mans Series

1	2006	IMSA	Mid-Ohio	T. Bernhard/R. Dumas	Porsche RS Spyder

APPENDIX 2: PENSKE RACING SERIES CHAMPIONSHIPS

1	1967	SCCA	United States Road Racing (USRRC)	Mark Donohue	Lola-Chevrolet
2	1968	SCCA	United States Road Racing (USRRC)	Mark Donohue	Lola-Chevrolet
3	1968	SCCA	Trans-Am	Mark Donohue	Chevrolet-Camaro
4	1969	SCCA	Trans-Am	Mark Donohue	Chevrolet-Camaro
5	1971	SCCA	Trans-Am	Mark Donohue	AMC Javelin
6	1972	CASC/SCCA	Can-Am	George Follmer	Porsche 917/10K
7	1973	CASC/SCCA	Can-Am	Mark Donohue	Porsche 917/30K
8	1977	USAC	Indy-Car National Championship	Tom Sneva	McLaren-Cosworth Penske-Cosworth
9	1978	USAC	Indy-Car National Championship	Tom Sneva	Penske-Cosworth
10	1979	CART	Indy-Car National Championship	Rick Mears	Penske-Cosworth
11	1981	CART	Indy-Car National Championship	Rick Mears	Penske-Cosworth
12	1982	CART	Indy-Car National Championship	Rick Mears	Penske-Cosworth
13	1983	CART	Indy-Car National Championship	Al Unser, Sr.	Penske-Cosworth
14	1985	CART	Indy-Car National Championship	Al Unser, Sr.	March-Cosworth
15	1988	CART	Indy-Car National Championship	Danny Sullivan	Penske-Ilmor Chevrolet
16	1994	CART	Indy-Car National Championship	Al Unser, Jr.	Penske-Ilmor
17	2000	CART	Indy-Car National Championship	Gil de Ferran	Reynard-Honda
18	2001	CART	Indy-Car National Championship	Gil de Ferran	Reynard-Honda
19	2006	IRL	Indy-Car National Championship	Sam Hornish Jr.	Dallara-Honda
20	2006	IMSA	American Le Mans Series LMP2	S. Maassen / L. Luhr	Porsche RS Spyder

ABOUT THE AUTHOR

Alan Hummel grew up near Media, Pennsylvania, within a few miles of Penske Racing's original shop in the Philadelphia suburb of Newtown Square. His father had a 42-year career with the Sun Oil Company, Roger Penske's primary financial backer during the team's formative years of the late 1960s and early '70s. Because of these associations, Alan and his father became devoted fans just after the Penske team was launched. They attended their first race in 1969, and within a couple of years were traveling up and down the east coast to six or eight events each season as Penske and Mark Donohue competed in the Trans-Am, Can-Am, Indy-Cars, NASCAR, endurance racing and Formula-1. They were there for Penske Racing's very first Indy-Car victory, the 1971 Pocono 500, and attended 31 Indianapolis 500s, including all but the first of the team's record 14 wins at the Brickyard.

Although Alan entertained some teenage dreams of a career in racing, those plans never evolved beyond a week at racing school. In 1980, he received a B.S. degree in Engineering from Drexel University in Philadelphia. For the next 21 years he worked in the chemical industry in engineering, supervisory, and business project management roles, before leaving to start his own business in 2001. Since then, he has owned and operated a family sports/entertainment complex near Pensacola Florida, where he lives with his wife Diana and children Mark and Michelle. He now spends his free time acting as team manager and crew chief for Michelle's budding kart racing career (see photo).

REFERENCES

The Unfair Advantage, 2nd Ed. by Mark Donohue with Paul Van Valkenburg, Bentley Publishers, 2000.
Rusty Wallace.... The Decision to Win by Bob Zeller with Rusty Wallace, David Bull Publishing, 1999.
Can-Am by Pete Lyons, MBI Publishing, 1995.
Trans-Am .... The Pony Car Wars 1966-1972 by Dave Friedman, MBI Publishing, 2001.
CART—the First 20 Years by Rick Shaffer, Hazelton Publishing, 1999.

Competition Press & AutoWeek / AutoWeek, various issues: 1973-2006.
Sports Illustrated, various issues: 1971-1973, 1976-1980, 1982-1984.
Car and Driver, September 1971, April 1977, August 1984.
Vintage Motorsport, July/August 1973.

Stock Car Racing, May 1974.
Sports Car, April 1974.
RACER, September 1994.
Road & Track, May 1962, October, 1972, August 1974, January 1975.
Indycar Racing, February, 1990.
The Indianapolis Star, various issues: 1972-1985, 1991, 2004, 2006.
The Delaware County Daily Times, August 20, 1975, May 28, 1999.
The Sentinel Star, February 16, 1974.
The Pensacola News Journal, May 28, 2001.
The Philadelphia Bulletin, May 28, 1972, August 20, 1975.
The Philadelphia Inquirer, May 28, 1972, August 18, 1975, August 21, 1975.
The St. Petersburg Times, April 3, 2005.
The Wilmington Delaware Morning News, August 18, 1975, August 20, 1975.
Miller-Team Penske Media Guide 1996.
NASCAR Winston Cup Series Media Guide, 1993.
Our Sun Magazine, Summer 1968, Summer 1972.
Sun News (Sun Oil Company), 1975-1977.
Tom Sneva Fan Club Newsletter, 1977-1979.
Sunoco Racing Program, 1972.
Sunoco Racing Program, 1973.
Sears DieHard Racing News, 1973.
The Norton Spirit—1978 Racing with the Champion, 1978.
SCCA Sports Car, April 1974
Watkins Glen Official Program, July 21-22 1972
Indianapolis 500 Official Programs, 1971-2006

Internet Resources:

www.amx-perience.com
www.autonews.com
www.autoweek.com
www.espn.com
www.f1cartvideos.com
www.grandprix.com
www.autoracingsport.com
www.motorsports.com
www.oreopolis.com
www.penskeracing.com
www.sportingnews.com
www.spokesmanreview.com
www.usatoday.com

www.nascar.com
www.indycar.com/stats/
www.classiccars.com
www.oldracingcars.com
www.motorsportshalloffame.com
www.chicanef1.com
www.usacracing.net
www.indy500.com
www.indystar.com
www.unfairadvantageracing.com
www.racing-reference.info
www.ajnascarracing.com
www.thatsracin.com

RACING

AUTOMOTIVE

RECREATIONAL VEHICLES & OTHER

TRUCKS

More Great Titles From **Iconografix**

All Iconografix books are available from direct mail specialty book dealers and bookstores worldwide, or can be ordered from the publisher. For book trade and distribution information or to add your name to our mailing list and receive a **FREE CATALOG** contact:

Iconografix, Inc.
PO Box 446, Dept BK
Hudson, WI, 54016
Telephone: (715) 381-9755, (800) 289-3504 (USA), Fax: (715) 381-9756
info@iconografixinc.com
www.iconografixinc.com

More great books from **Iconografix**

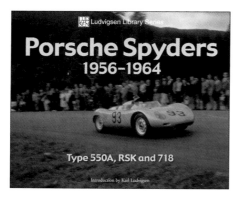
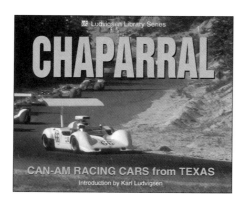
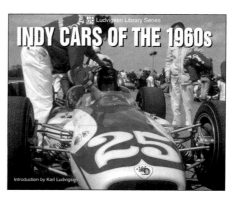
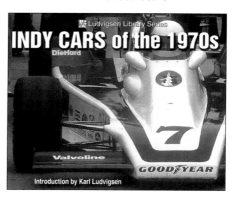
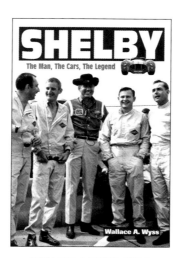
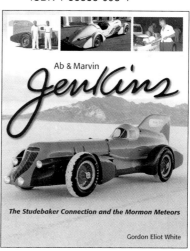